Compliance with International Human Rights Law in Africa

Compliance with International Human Rights Law in Africa

Essays in Honour of Frans Viljoen

Edited by
ADEROMOLA ADEOLA

OXFORD
UNIVERSITY PRESS

OXFORD
UNIVERSITY PRESS

Great Clarendon Street, Oxford, OX2 6DP,
United Kingdom

Oxford University Press is a department of the University of Oxford.
It furthers the University's objective of excellence in research, scholarship,
and education by publishing worldwide. Oxford is a registered trade mark of
Oxford University Press in the UK and in certain other countries

First Edition published in 2022

Impression: 1

Published in the United States of America by Oxford University Press
198 Madison Avenue, New York, NY 10016, United States of America

British Library Cataloguing in Publication Data

Data available

Library of Congress Control Number: 2021945530

ISBN 978–0–19–285699–9

DOI: 10.1093/oso/9780192856999.001.0001

Printed and bound by
CPI Group (UK) Ltd, Croydon, CR0 4YY

Soli Deo (JESUS CHRIST) Gloria!
This book truly would not have been possible but for HIS love for Frans Viljoen!
(John 3:16).

Acknowledgements

All Glory to JESUS CHRIST for the possibility of having this book.

A while back, five of Frans Viljoen's former doctoral students thought it would be a great idea to do a book in honour of Frans Viljoen. Significant among these were: Ramadi Bonolo Dinokopila, Busingye Kabumba, Japhet Biegon, John Ambani and Remember Miamingi.

When I was contacted to take the lead on this initiative, I was thrilled. And for two reasons. First, it was a book for Frans Viljoen who I first knew in 2008 near my penultimate completion year as an undergraduate law student. I'd later know Frans for more than a decade and in this period, I must say that not very many erudite scholars are invested both in the personal and academic growth of their students as the man Frans Viljoen. I was also very thrilled because it finally gave me the opportunity to do something in return for Frans Viljoen who never likes to take the spotlight. So, to Frans, I sincerely apologize, in arrears, for 'plotting this coup'. But as with the Orient Express, I am not the only one with a hand in this!

Very special thanks go to Magnus Killander for his kind encouragements and Carole Viljoen who gave us an immense support through providing us with the list of doctoral students that Frans has had over the years. I am also very grateful to Christof Heyns who was so thrilled by this initiative and gave us a very personal and inspiring foreword for this book. It is often said that an apple does not fall too far from the tree. And in an academic setting, Christof and Frans have portrayed this.

I'd also like to thank Merel Alstein at the Oxford University Press for agreeing to publish this book. Merel's steadfast commitment towards seeing this book get to its end is remarkable. Her kind patience and enthusiasm towards the development of this book is very much appreciated. And also special thanks to Jack McNichol, John Smallman, Charlotte Holloway and Ashirvad Moses for the lovely editorial work.

Short background story on the Tribute to Christof Heyns written by Frans Viljoen

I went to meet Christof on the 31st of May 2019 telling him of a very top secret to honour Frans Viljoen with this book, now published. Christof was pleased with this idea. He was elated. Sincerely, you could tell that this was a man who was truly committed to seeing Frans honored in every way. But also, just seeing Frans smile.

I thought he would take some time to write this foreword seeing how busy he was at the time. He was a member of the Human Rights Committee and the Director of the Institute for International and Comparative Law in Africa, even meeting him in the office at the time was almost a miracle given his strong passion and commitment towards work and really touching the lives of people, be it his students, his family, friends and colleagues.

But then on Sunday, 2 June 2019, at 22:28 (South African time), a mail dropped in my mailbox. It was Christof. He had taken out time to write the foreword so quickly, literally pouring his heart in the lovely piece for Frans and then saying over email that "I had some thoughts on this and wrote them down while they were still fresh in my mind. Please find attached."

Little did anyone know what will happen on 28 March 2021. On that day, Christof departed.

And suddenly, there was a serious conflict on how to proceed with the final outcome of the book. This book was very well near publication at the time. There was a conflict because knowing Frans very well, he would have wanted this book to be in Christof's name. However, as this book was highly classified, Frans could not be told a single word about this book. He might very nicely try to talk those involved out of this initiative not wanting to be in the spotlight.

But again, Christof would have wanted to see Frans celebrated. And reading his foreword, one is quickly drawn to the fact that Frans had really made him proud. But knowing the great relationship between both men, Frans would also have wanted to give a response to a foreword by Christof, but then the cat would have had to be let out of the bag which was not an option at the time.

And so, to get here, I just had to ask Frans one simple question, hoping that he would not become too curious.

The question was: what did Christof mean to you?

And in that question, Frans himself wrote a brilliant tribute for Christof Heyns. In his email response of 8 June 2021, Frans also said something significant about Christof:

> "He was an inspiring mentor to me, personally, and personal cheerleader, a voice of considerable and considered reason, a wise soundboard, an enduring friend and a second brother ..."

ADEOLA ADEROMOLA

Foreword

Frans Viljoen was a student in his final year of LLB in my comparative law course when I started teaching at the University of Pretoria in 1987. He wrote a paper on a topic we had touched upon during a discussion in class. It was during the time of the state of emergency, and Nelson Mandela and others were still languishing in jail. He wrote about the distinction between the legality and the legitimacy of legal systems, and the role of martyrs.

His paper was in Afrikaans, with the heading: 'Om te lewe en te sterwe' (To live and to die). There was a spelling mistake in the word 'sterwe' (do die), which had been written as 'strewe', (strive), which in fact make just as much sense. The paper took what we had talked about in class to an entirely next level. It brought together law and society, and engaged in a refreshing and creative way with the realities of our country, and it was very well crafted. I kept the paper in my top drawer for many years to come, as an inspiration about the joys that we as teachers get when we work with young talent.

I was delighted when, after his return from his masters' studies at Cambridge, Frans approached me to serve as his doctoral supervisor. He was my first doctoral student. His thesis was on the African regional human rights system, seen in the context of the other regional systems, at a time when very little had been done in this area. It was a tour de force, and the standard by which I would come to judge all later doctoral dissertations. It became the basis of his *magnum opus*, *The International Protection of Human Rights in Africa* (OUP), now in its third edition, and widely regarded as the leading text in this field.

Some years later, Frans and I, now colleagues, were sitting next to each other when a first year LLB student was trying out to be in the Faculty's team for the Jessup International Law Moot Court Competition. As the student started to speak, Frans leaned over to me and said 'Isn't it remarkable how you can spot brilliance in a few seconds?' The student ended up winning the award as the best oralist in the Jessup international rounds in Washington, DC. Frans's remark reminded me of how I felt when I had read his student essay.

Three decades later, it is a singular pleasure to see the impact that Frans has had on so many doctoral students from the continent. This book is a living testimony to the role that he has played at the most advanced level of providing guidance to students, namely the doctoral level. This is not the place to focus on all the other contributions that he has made, for example through the 'master's programme', the moots courts and the many other endeavours in which he has been involved so far. It is clear that even if guiding the students whose work is reflected in this book to graduation was the only thing he ever did, it would have been a remarkable achievement in itself. Not many academics whom I know have delivered more than 30 doctoral students, from over 15 countries, many of whom are today leaders in their respective fields across the African continent. In many respects he has founded an entire new field of research at the highest level on the continent.

I have always been intrigued by the story of Professor Irenrius, who taught at Bologna, Italy, in the eleventh century. He was the leader of the school of glossators, who developed a new way of dealing with the Roman law texts. Students from what is today known as the various countries of Europe crossed the Alps (hence they were referred to as the *ultramontani*) to study under his guidance, before returning to where they had come from, and shaping the law in accordance with what they had learned. Before the Europe we know today was formed, these young people were exposed by Professor Irnerius to what would later become the basic tenets of the common commercial law, the common legal framework that made the emergence of Europe as a coherent entity possible.

In my view Frans has played a similar role, in a very different context. Yet, I very much doubt that he would make such a claim himself. That was commercial law in Europe, then, while Frans' commitment lies here, in Africa, to human rights. And Frans is not prone to trumpet his own achievements—he would rather spend his energy on making a further contribution.

So how should we then think of him as a doctoral supervisor? Frans has at some point described himself essentially as a teacher. A much more modest take, therefore. Yet it also seems to me a fitting description, if the term 'teacher' is understood to refer to those who help others to acquire knowledge, competence or virtue, whether they are his students, his teachers or anyone less. I am very happy to be among those who have learned from him.

CHRISTOF HEYNS (PROF)
Director, Institute for International and
Comparative Law in Africa & UN Special Rapporteur
on Extrajudicial, Summary or Arbitrary Executions

Tribute to Christof Heyns by Frans Viljoen

(10 January 1959–28 March 2021)

To call Christof a colleague does not feel right. For me, as for most of his other "colleagues", engaging with him quickly broke down boundaries between mere collegiality and friendship. This is so, I think, because he never saw anyone as a holder of a position, as an instrument, but as a person. His instinctive warmth and genuine kindness stem from an abundant generosity and sense of humanity. The outpourings of grief and appreciation from so many in the last weeks speak not only to the high esteem in which Christof was held across the world, but also to the depth of his inter-personal connections and bonds.

I was privileged to be taught by Christof as an undergraduate student, to be supervised by him for doctoral studies, and to be mentored by him within the Centre for Human Rights. To me, personally, he was so many things, among them: a constant confidence-booster; a wise sounding board; an inspirational role model; and a dear friend.

Thinking about Christof as a colleague, more broadly, three aspects stand out.

1 Christof as teacher-mentor

Many colleagues – and students -- in the Centre mentioned his influential role as teacher and mentor. Generations of students benefited from his sharp intellect and boundless enthusiasm in front of a classroom. Christof was doctoral supervisor to a number of South African academics: Bernard Bekink, Henk Botha, Willem Gravett, Magnus Killander, Wessel Le Roux. Christof was generous with his time and influential in his advice.

As a teacher, Christof's ardent efforts to systematize, to create a holistic view, was often on display. I have on numerous occasions seen him, at the start of the lecture, draw on the board a diagram depicting what looked like wiring of electric circuits. But during his lecture, he "connected the dots", brought to life the diagram, and set off a light bulb in his listeners' minds. Few were as earnest in their efforts to simplify, to be clearly understood, to help students see "the bigger picture". Christof was a big picture person. This was possible for him to give that picture because he was so fully and effortlessly a master of his subject fields. As a teacher and academic mentor, he exemplifies to me the "truth" that it takes a very smart person to simplify things, to be understood by the proverbial "six year old".

2 Christof as founder-initiator and visionary

Christof was a visionary, mixing imagination, daring, and fearlessness. In the Centre, I call him "initiator-in-chief". If something can be conceived, Christof reckoned, it can be achieved. And many things were (conceived and achieved). His visions are with us. And will remain here for very long.

Let me name but a few examples.

Centre for Human Rights

Christof was part – with people like with Johann van der Westhuizen, Duard Kleyn and Niek Grov -of the founding fathers of the Centre for Human Rights. Starting the Centre was quite unthinkable in those dark days of states of emergency in apartheid South Africa. With Christof's constant support and his commanding presence, the Centre became a reality and prospered. It is through Christof's insight and singular insistence that the Centre was established as an "academic department". This year, the Centre celebrates 35 years of existence.

In 1992, he dreamed up the idea that students from all African universities would, in a simulated exercise, argue a human rights case before the African Human Rights Court. Remember, this was even before the advent of the democratic South Africa, and before there even was such a Court in existence. And these were the days before the internet and when getting a fax through to a let's say Ethiopia was a cause of considerable celebration. The African Human Rights Moot Court Competition was born. This year, we mark 30 years of African Moot taking place without interruption, across the length and breadth of the continent.

The Nelson Mandela World Human Rights Moot Court Competition followed in 2009, and the first national schools moot competition was held in 2010. Both of these still prosper.

Christof in 2000 initiated the Master's in Human Rights and Democratisation in Africa. Christof was resourceful. He famously used the air sickness bag on board SAA flying back from a meeting in Venice to conceptualise the Human Rights Master's.

Today, 22 years later, there are close to 600 graduates across the continent, and in the wider world, acting as agents of positive social change. In 2003, in collaboration with colleagues at the University of the Western Cape, he initiated the Master's in International Trade and Investment Law in Africa. This programme is even more relevant today, with economic integration in Africa accelerating.

He was a wordsmith at heart. He deeply appreciated the value of sharing information, and cultivating African scholarship was an abiding passion. He was a co-founder and editor of the African Human Rights Law Journal, in 2001. Together with colleagues Danie Brand and Lizette Hermann, later joined by Charles Fombad, he was the mastermind behind the Pretoria University Law Press (PULP). PULP has since then published more than 200 books and is publishing 5 regularly appearing journals.

As Dean, Christof insisted on a greater focus on post-graduate studies, and in particular doctoral studies at the Faculty. He secured funding for full-time doctoral students and made the Faculty a magnet for talented prospective students from across the African continent.

After his Deanship, Christof thought up and brought into being the Institute for Comparative and International Law in Africa.

At a broader University level, he left his mark in numerous ways. One of these is his vision of a hub for postgraduate researchers and visitors which is now concretised as "Future Africa".

3 Leader/ nurturer/ cultivator

Beyond envisioning, Christof also was uniquely able to make things happen. His optimism and idealism came with strong doses of realism and perseverance. He was a hard worker, and made the hours count.

But his success and accomplishment always came by working with others. Leading and nurturing others. He found great joy in everyone's success. Because he fitted so comfortably into his own skin, inhabited his life so completely, he was able to be at ease – and set at ease – whoever he met. He was warm in congratulations and acknowledgement, and always careful, caring, and constructive in criticism.

His personal ethic is captured in the phrase he often used at the Centre: "excellence with Ubuntu".

A life interrupted and an ongoing legacy

I had the privilege to work with Christof on a study (and book) on the impact of the United Nations human rights treaties on the lives of people in countries around the world. Part of our theoretical ponderings was the question: How does one measure 'impact'?

Looking at the impact of Christof's life and work, I am reminded that the Centre's logo – Africa as a colourful butterfly – was his brainchild. This choice is based on the 'butterfly theory', the notion that a seemingly insignificant change or action in one part of the world can have momentous or consequential outcomes in other places far away. Whether it was developing new norms on the world stage, a discussion with a doctoral student, or ensuring that someone who worked as a cleaner be appointed as PULP's assistant, Christof touched and changed lives.

Now, Christof's is a life interrupted.

But his **unfinished business** is only positive and makes him imminently and continuously present. As colleagues paid tribute to his life, I was deeply struck by the extent and immediacy of Christof's ongoing projects and activities. From these tributes, we know that he was going to miss having breakfast on Sunday in the Stellenbosch Botanical Gardens; lecturing the HRDA student on Tuesday; discussing implementation with the human rights clinic students in Buenos Aires on

Thursday; and working on a comprehensive edited volume of essays on peaceful assemblies through the week. The list continues …

Christof's life is a work-in-progress, and we are fortunate to still be able to play a part in its continuation. His unfinished works invite us to be part of his ongoing and evolving legacy.

May we find great comfort in this opportunity, and in the unique and untold ways in which Christof's moral, inspiring, and consequential life left its mark on each of ours.

Table of Contents

List of Contributors

DR ADEM K ABEBE is the Editor of the ConstitutionNet, International Idea, Hague, The Netherlands. He was formerly a Senior Research Fellow, Max Planck Foundation for International Peace and the Rule of Law and a research fellow at the Centre for Good Governance and Human Rights, University of Cambridge, United Kingdom. His authored works include *Amicus Curiae Participation before regional human rights bodies in Africa* (Journal of African Law 2014). He is co-author of the *Annual Review of Constitution-Building* (International IDEA 2018).

DR ADEROMOLA ADEOLA is an Associate Professor of Law at the Faculty of Law, Kabarak University, Kenya. She is the lead editor of *Arts of Human Rights, Commingling Art, Human Rights and the Law in Africa* (Springer 2019), and among others, she is the author of the *Internally Displaced Person in International Law* (Edward Elgar 2020) and *Development-induced displacement and human rights protection in Africa: the Kampala Convention* (Routledge 2021).

DR VICTOR AYENI is the Head of Postgraduate Programmes in Law and Senior Lecturer at the Adekunle Ajasin University, Nigeria. He is a Barrister and Solicitor of the Supreme Court of Nigeria and member of the Nigerian Association of Law Teachers. He is the editor of *The impact of the African Charter and the Maputo Protocol in selected African states* (Pretoria University Law Press 2016).

DR JAPHET BIEGON is an Extraordinary Lecturer at the Centre for Human Rights, Faculty of Law, University of Pretoria. He is also Amnesty International's Africa Regional Advocacy Coordinator. He leads and coordinates the organization's advocacy initiatives targeting the African Union. He previously sat on the advisory board of the ESCR Human Rights Law Implementation Project, a collaborative project between four academic human rights centres (Bristol, Essex, Middlesex and Pretoria) and the Open Society Justice Initiative. He holds a Doctor of Laws Degree from the University of Pretoria, South of Africa. He has published extensively on a wide range of issues relating to the African human rights system.

PROF LILIAN CHENWI is Professor of Law at the University of Witwatersrand in South Africa. She is co-editor of *The Protection of Economic, Social and Cultural Rights in Africa: International Regional and National Perspectives* (Cambridge University Press 2016) and co-editor of the book *Extraterritorial Human Rights Obligations from an African Perspective* (Intersentia 2018).

DR LIRETTE LOUW is the Legal Adviser to the Speaker of the National Assembly in the South African Parliament. She has published on human rights issues in Africa including in the American Journal of International Law and the Journal of African Law. She is the co-author of the seminal piece on 'State Compliance with the Recommendations of the African Commission on Human and Peoples' Rights', co-authored with Frans Viljoen in 2007 in the *American Journal of International Law.*

DR REMEMBER MIAMINGI is the African Union Peace and Security's Child Advisor. He is a South Sudanese human rights and governance expert. He has extensive experience in Pan-African advocacy and human rights-related issues. He has been a Promoter for the Pan-African Centre for the Study and Support of Family (PACSSF) since October 2014. The PACSSF is an African research and policy platform committed to putting family wellbeing at the heart of sustainability development policies in Africa. PACSSF's theory of change: 'Through research, PACSSF will foster sustainable democracy and development in Africa through improving family wellbeing by filling gaps in knowledge that currently constraint the way policy makers in Africa see and treat family wellbeing in policies.' His authored works include *The Republic of South Sudan: Introductory Note* (Edited by the Institute for Comparative and International Law in Africa and published by the Oxford University Press 2015); State Reporting and the realisation of children's rights in Africa (Pretoria University Law Press 2020).

DR TARISAI MUTANGI is Head of Legal Postgraduate Programmes and lectures international human rights law at the University of Zimbabwe. He has published widely primarily in the areas of domestic implementation of international law standards as well as on international judicial and quasi-judicial institutions such as the African Union human rights bodies. He conducts litigation before these international institutions where he is also admitted as counsel. He is a Senior Consultant with Utafiti Afrika Consuting, focusing primarily on the African human rights system.

List of Abbreviations

ABDP	l' Association Burundaise pour la Defense des Droits des Prisonniers
ACERWC	African Committee of Experts on the Rights and Welfare of the Child
ACHPR	African Commission on Human and Peoples' Rights
ACRWC	African Charter on the Rights and Welfare of the Child
ACtHPR	African Court on Human and Peoples' Rights
AGA	African Governance Architecture
AHSG	Assembly of Heads of State and Government
AIPPA	Access to Information and Protection of Privacy Act
ANPPCAN	African Network for the Prevention and Protection of Children against Abuse and Neglect
APRM	African Peer Review Mechanism
AU	African Union
CEDAW	Convention on the Elimination of All Forms of Discrimination against Women
CEJIL	Centre for Justice and International Law
CEN-SAD	Community of Sahel Sub-Saharan Africa
CoE	Council of Europe
CoM	Committee of Ministers
COMESA	Common Market on Eastern and Central Africa
CRC	Convention on the Rights of the Child
CRP	Constitutional Rights Project
CUP	Cambridge University Press
DRC	Democratic Republic of Congo
EAC	East African Community
EACJ	East African Court of Justice
EALA	East African Legislative Assembly
ECCAS	Economic Community of Central African States
ECCJ	ECOWAS Community of West African States
ECJ	European Court of Justice
ECOWAS	Economic Community Court of Justice
ECtHR	European Court of Human Rights
GAOAS	General Assembly of the Organization of American States
HRC	Human Rights Committee
HRJI	Human Rights Judgment Impact
HRTs	Human Rights Tribunals
HYPREP	Hydrocarbon Pollution Restoration Project
ICCPR	International Covenant on Civil and Political Rights
ICJ	International Court of Justice
ICRC	International Committee of the Red Cross

ICTY	International Criminal Tribunal for the former Yugoslavia
IDP	Internally Displaced Persons
IGAD	Inter-Governmental Authority on Development
IHRDA	Institute for Human Rights and Development in Africa
ILC	International Legal Compliance
IOM	International Organization for Migration
LDA	Lunatics Detention Act
MHLAP	Mental Health Leadership and Advocacy Programme
MNCs	Multinational oil companies
MOU	Memorandum of Understanding
MRA	Media Right Agenda
NEPAD	New Partnership for Africa's Development
NGO	Non-governmental Organizations
NHRI	National Human Rights Institutions
OAS	Organization of American States
OAU	Organisation of African Unity
OSJI	Open Society Justice Initiative
OUP	Oxford University Press
PALU	Pan African Lawyers Union
PJP	Pilot Judgment Procedure
PSC	Peace and Security Council
RECs	Regional Economic Communities
RSISTF	Rivers State Internal Securities Task Force
SADC	Southern African Development Community
SAHRC	South African Human Rights Commission
UDHR	Universal Declaration of Human Rights
UK	United Kingdom
UMA	Arab Maghreb Union
UN	United Nations
UNCRC	United Nations Convention on the Rights of the Child
UNEP	United Nations Environment Programme
UNICEF	United Nations Children's Emergency Fund
US	United States
VMCZ	Voluntary Media Council of Zimbabwe
WHO	World Health Organization

1
Introduction
Essays in Honour of Frans Viljoen

Aderomola Adeola

1 Introduction

There is a fundamental question as to what human rights norms require compliance within the African human rights system. In answering this question, Frans Viljoen's seminal work on International Human Rights Law in Africa is a classic reference document for everyone seeking an explanation.[1] Given the existence of this scholarly pièce de résistance by Frans Viljoen, this book will not engage this question. As such, authors seeking to critically understand the corpus of international human rights law in Africa need to first read the scholarly monograph by Frans Viljoen published by the Oxford University Press.

In this book, the authors critically examine the question of compliance with international human rights law, building on the pertinent body of existing scholarship.[2] However, it is useful to briefly reflect on the evolution of the human rights

[1] Frans Viljoen, *International Human Rights Law in Africa* (OUP 2012).

[2] Authors also draw on notable scholarship in the field, including: Issa G Shivji, 'The Concept of Human Rights in Africa' (Council for the Development of Economic and Social Research 1989); Oji U Umozurike, *The African Charter on Human and Peoples' Rights* (Martinus Nijhoff Publishers 1997); Vincent OO Nmehielle, *The African Human Rights System: Its Laws, Practice and Institutions* (Martinus Nijhoff Publishers 2001); Christof Heyns (ed), *Human Rights in Africa 1999* (Martinus Nijhoff Publishers 2002); Fatsah Ouguergouz, *The African Charter on Human and People's Rights: A Comprehensive Agenda for Human Dignity and Sustainable Democracy in Africa* (Martinus Nijhoff Publishers 2003); Chidi A Odinkalu, 'Back to the Future: The Imperative of Prioritizing for the Protection of Human Rights in Africa' (2003) 47(1) Journal of African Law 1–37; Nsongurua J Udombana, *Human Rights and Contemporary Issues in Africa* (Malthouse Press 2003); Obiora C Okafor, *The African Human Rights System, Activist Forces and International Institutions* (CUP 2007); Malcolm Evans and Rachel Murray (eds), *The African Charter on Human and Peoples' Rights: the System in Practice, 1986-2006* (CUP 2008); Kofi O Kufuor, *The African Human Rights System: Origin and Evolution* (Palgrave Macmillan 2010); Manisuli Ssenyonjo (ed), *The African Regional Human Rights System: 30 Years After the African Charter on Human and Peoples' Rights* (Martinus Nijhoff Publishers 2011); Makau Mutua, *Human Rights: A Political and Cultural Critique* (University of Pennsylvania Press 2002); George W Mugwanya, *Human Rights in Africa: Enhancing Human Rights Through the African Regional Human Rights System* (2003); Kiwinda M Mbondenyi, *International Human Rights and their Enforcement in Africa* (LawAfrica Publishers 2011); Dinah Shelton and Paolo G Carozza, *Regional Protection of Human Rights* (OUP 2013); Rachel Murray and Debra Long, *The Implementation of the Finding of the African Commission on Human and Peoples' Rights* (CUP 2015); Bonny Ibhawoh, *Human Rights in Africa* (CUP 2018); Eunice N Sahle, *Human Rights in Africa: Contemporary Debates and Struggles* (Palgrave Macmillan 2019);

Aderomola Adeola, *Introduction* In: *Compliance with International Human Rights Law in Africa.* Edited by: Aderomola Adeola, Oxford University Press. © Aderomola Adeola 2022. DOI: 10.1093/oso/9780192856999.003.0001

corpus in Africa to provide a concise reflection for the context of the book. Over the last decades, the African human rights system has emerged as one of the robust human rights systems. Comprising of a rich panoply of norms—both soft and hard—the African human rights system has emerged as a significant regime making notable contributions to international law in a plethora of ways. While its visible emergence started with the adoption of the African Charter on Human and Peoples' Rights (African Charter), the crooning emerged in the late 1960s with the development of the Organization of African Unity (OAU) Convention Governing Specific Aspects of Refugee Problems in Africa (OAU Refugee Convention).[3]

Before the adoption of the OAU Refugee Convention in 1969, the idea of developing a regional text on human rights emerged during the First Congress of African Jurists in Lagos, Nigeria, from 3 to 7 January 1961.[4] From this continental meeting of jurists emerged a resolution, famously called 'Laws of Lagos'. Paragraph 4 of the Laws of Lagos reinforced the need for 'African Governments to study the possibility of adopting an African Convention on Human Rights'.[5] Drawing on the significant stride from the Law of Lagos, the UN (United Nations) Commission of Human Rights held at least six conferences between 1966 and 1979 to foster regional political will towards developing a human rights regime.[6]

However, the continental language on human rights reflected in normative frameworks of the 1960s leaned towards humanitarianism, specifically the pertinence of addressing the welfare of populations that fled their states of origin due to conflict situations, particularly in the East African region in the mid-1960s. Earlier in 1963, when the OAU was formed, regional cooperation towards achieving 'a better life for the peoples of Africa' was expressed in the OAU Charter,[7] however, the fundamental premise on which the OAU emerged was cast against the vestiges of colonialism and the urgency of consolidating the hard-won victories of independence. As such, the ideology of regional cooperation on which political freedom at the level of the nation-state could be consolidated. Though there were differing political persuasions on the nature of regionalization, evidenced from the Monrovia and Casablanca blocs, there was a consensus that promoting a unified regional vision built on the values of pan-Africanism was integral to redefining the course of the future and breaking free from the colonial past.

Rachel Murray, *The African Charter on Human and Peoples' Rights: A Commentary* (OUP 2019); Ilias Bantekas and Lutz Oette, *International Human Rights Law and Practice* (CUP 2020).

[3] OAU Convention Governing Specific Aspects of Refugee Problems in Africa (1969); African Charter on Human and Peoples' Rights (1981).

[4] Ouguergouz, *The African Charter on Human and People's Rights: A Comprehensive Agenda for Human Dignity and Sustainable Democracy in Africa* (n 2), 20.

[5] ibid.

[6] See also Githu Muigai, 'From the African Court on Human and Peoples' Rights to the African Court of Justice and Human Rights' in Ssenyonjo (ed), *The African Regional Human Rights System: 30 Years After the African Charter on Human and Peoples' Rights* (n 2), 265, 267.

[7] OAU Charter (1963), art 2(1)(b).

But shortly after countries gained independence, the regional cooperation was tested—not by external aggression—but by internal crisis across the newly independent states due to ethnic pluralities and socio-political differences from the legacy of arbitrary colonial borders. This was the reality in 1961 when Rwandese refugees fled into Tanzania, the Democratic Republic of Congo and Uganda, prompting the OAU, in part, to initiate a regional response towards refugee protection.[8] While there was an existing global framework on refugee protection (the 1951 Refugee Convention),[9] the regime was not suited to the refugee problem in Africa. It had a dateline limitation given its evident focus on events occurring prior to January 1951 and was limited in geographical location to Europe. Neither of these realities captured the regional dimension of the problem in Africa.[10] Consequently, the OAU Refugee Convention was adopted, however, as a regional supplement to the 1951 Refugee Convention, whose limitations were subsequently addressed with the adoption of a 1967 Protocol.

As with the OAU Charter, the OAU Refugee Convention accentuates the 1948 Universal Declaration on Human Rights,[11] but does not incorporate the language of rights in the context of refugee protection. Perhaps, it may be argued that as an effective complement to the 1951 UN Refugee Convention and its 1967 Protocol, human rights are implicit and may be drawn from the global refugee regime. However, what it lacks in an explicit rights-based provision, it makes up for in its humanitarian approach to refugee protection. This may be seen through several provisions, including (a) the expanded definition of refugees to accommodate the realities of peoples across the African continent, (b) the principle of non-discrimination, which mandate states to ensure that the Convention is applied 'to all refugees without discrimination as to race, religion, nationality, membership of a particular social group or political opinions' and (c) an expansion of the principle of non-refoulement in prohibiting 'rejection at the frontier'[12] of the state of asylum.

However, the landscape on human rights was coming to life at the global level with the adoption of two sets of human rights covenant in 1966.[13] Also, this gave a significant impetus to the regional process and became a premise for canvassing regional processes. Murray observes that the '[e]ncouragement at the UN level for regional human rights mechanisms, NGO lobbying and a recognition by some

[8] See Emmanuel O Awuku, 'Refugee Movements in Africa and the OAU Convention on Refugees' (1995) 39(1) JAL 79–80: Viljoen, (n 1) 241.

[9] UN Convention Relating to the Status of Refugees (1951); UN Protocol Relating to the Status of Refugees (1967).

[10] In 1967, the UN subsequently adopted a protocol to address these limitations in the 1951 Refugee Convention. However, prior to this time, countries within the African region had begun to develop a regional framework subsequently adopted in 1969 as a regional complement to the global framework.

[11] See OAU Charter (n 7), art 2(1)(e).

[12] OAU Refugee Convention (n 3) art 2(3).

[13] International Covenant on Civil and Political Rights (1966); International Covenant on Economic, Social and Cultural Rights (1966).

African leaders themselves that human rights in another state were also their concern fed into the adoption by the OAU of the African Charter'.[14] In 1981, the African Charter was adopted in Nairobi, Kenya.

With the adoption of the African Charter, the regional landscape on human rights was defined. Several frameworks have emerged over the past four decades giving significant impetus to the continental human rights landscape both from a normative and institutional landscape. These instruments include the African Charter on the Rights and Welfare of the Child (1990),[15] Protocol to the African Charter on Human and Peoples' Rights on the Rights of Women in Africa (2003),[16] African Youth Charter (2006), African Union Convention for the Protection and

[14] Rachel Murray, *Human Rights in Africa: From the OAU to the African Union* (CUP 2004) 22.

[15] For discussion on this framework, please see Bankole Thompson, 'Africa's Charter on Children's Rights: A Normative Break with Cultural Traditionalism' (1992) 41(2) ICLQ 432–444; Karin CJM, Arts 'The International Protection of Children's Rights in Africa: the 1990 OAU Charter on the Rights and Welfare of the Child' (1993) 5(1) Afr J Int Comp Law 139–162; Frans Viljoen, 'Supra-National Human Rights Instruments for the Protection of Children in Africa: the Convention on the Rights of the Child and the African Charter on the Rights and Welfare of the Child' (1998) 31(2) Comp & Int'l L J S Afr 199–212; Amanda Lloyd, 'A Theoretical Analysis of the Reality of Children's Rights in Africa: An Introduction to the African Charter on the Rights and Welfare of the Child' (2002) 2 AHRLJ 11; Danwood M Chirwa, 'The Merits and Demerits of the African Charter on the Rights and Welfare of the Child' (2002) 10(2) Int'l J Child Rights 157; Dejo Olowu, 'Protecting Children's Rights in Africa: A Critique of the African Charter on the Rights and Welfare of the Child' (2002) 10 Int'l J Child Rights 127; Julia Sloth-Nielsen and Benyam D Mezmur, 'Surveying the Research Landscape to Promote Children's Legal Rights in an African Context' (2007) 7(2) AHRLJ 330; Michael Gose, 'The African Charter on the Rights and Welfare of the Child' (Community Law Centre 2002); Thoko Kaime, *The African Charter on the Rights and Welfare of the Child: A Socio-Legal Perspective* (Pretoria University Law Press 2009); Chris M Peter and Ummy A Mwalimu, 'The African Charter on the Rights and Welfare of the Child' in Abdulqawi A Yusuf and Fatsah Ouguergouz (eds), *The African Union: Legal and Institutional framework* (Martinus Nijhoff Publishers 2012) 477–493; Jones Adu-Gyamfi and Frank Keating, 'Convergence and Divergence between the UN Convention on the Rights of the Child, and the African Charter on the Rights and Welfare of the Child' (2013) 3(1) SJHR 47–58; Amana T Mbise, 'The Diffusion of the United Nations Convention on the Rights of the Child (UNCRC) More Than the African Charter on the Rights and Welfare of the Child (ACRWC) in Africa: the Influence of Coercion and Emulation' (2016) 60(5) Int Soc Work 1233–1243; Virginia P Lalli, *The African Charter on the Rights and Welfare of the Child* (Author House 2018).

[16] For discussion on this framework, please see Martin S Nsibirwa, 'A Brief Analysis of the Draft Protocol to the African charter on Human and Peoples' Rights on the Rights of Women' (2001) 1(1) AHRLJ 40–63; Dejo Olowu, 'A Critique of the Rhetoric, Ambivalence, and Promise in the Protocol of the African Charter on Human and Peoples' Rights on the Rights of Women in Africa' (2006) 8(1) Hum Rights Review 78–101; Kaniye SA Ebeku, 'Considering the Protocol on the Rights of Women in Africa' (2006) 36(1) Africa Insight 24–34; Fareda Banda, 'Blazing a Trail: The African Protocol on Women's Rights Comes into Force' (2006) 50(1) JAL 72–84; Emezat Mengesha, 'Reconciling the Need for Advancing Women's Rights in Africa and the Dictates of International Trade Norms: the Position of the Protocol on the Rights of Women in Africa' (2006) 6(1) AHRLJ 208–224; Christine Ocran, 'The Protocol to the African Charter on Human and Peoples' Rights on the Rights of Women in Africa' (2007) 15(1) Afr J Int Comp Law 147–152; Japhet Biegon, 'Towards the Adoption of a Guidelines for State Reporting Under the African Union Protocol on Women's Rights: A Review of the Pretoria Gender Expert Meeting, 6–7 August 2009' (2009) 9(2) AHRLJ 615–643; Frans Viljoen, 'An Introduction to the Protocol to the African Charter on Human and Peoples' Rights on the Rights of Women in Africa' (2009) 16 JCRSJ 11–46; Mizanie A Tadesse, 'The African Women Protocol as Supplemental to the African Charter and Other Human Rights Instruments: A Brief Analysis' (2014) 5(1) BDU Journal of Law 1–35; Faiz J Mohamed, "11 years of the African Women's Rights Protocol: Progress and Challenges" (2014) 57 Development 71–76.

Assistance of Internally Displaced Persons in Africa (2009),[17] Protocol to the African Charter on Human and Peoples' Rights on the Rights of Older Persons (2016),[18] Protocol to the African Charter on Human and Peoples' Rights on the Rights of Persons with Disabilities in Africa (2018).[19] From an institutional perspective, the establishment of the African Commission on Human and Peoples' Rights,[20] the African Committee of Experts on the Rights and Welfare of the Child[21] and the African Court on Human and Peoples' Rights,[22] are notable. And evidently, the landscape continues to evolve with the emergence of human rights-related norms (such as those on governance, peace and security, migration

[17] Chaloka Beyani, 'The Elaboration of a Legal Framework for the Protection of Internally Displaced Persons in Africa' (2006) 50(2) JAL 187, 195; Stephanie Ojeda 'The Kampala Convention on Internally Displaced Persons: Some International Humanitarian Law Aspects' (2010) 29(3) RSQ 58; Lauren Groth, 'Engendering Protection: An Analysis of the 2009 Kampala Convention and Its Provision for Internally Displaced Women' (2011) 23(2) Int'l J Refug Law 221; Won Kidane, 'Managing forced. Displacement by Law in Africa: The Role of the New African Union IDPs Convention' (2011) 44(1) VJTL 1–85; Flavia Z Guistiniani, 'New Hopes and Challenges for the Protection of IDPs in Africa: the Kampala Convention for the Protection and Assistance of Internally Displaced Persons in Africa' (2011) 39(2) DJILP 347; Katinka Ridderbos, 'The Kampala Convention and Obligations of Armed Groups' (2011) 37 Forced Migration Review 36; Mehari T Maru, *The Kampala Convention and its Contribution to International Law: Legal Analyses and Interpretations of the African Union Convention for the Protection and Assistance of Internally Displaced Persons* (Eleven Publishing 2014); Allehone M Abebe, *The Emerging Law on Forced Migration in Africa: Development and Implementation of the Kampala Convention on Internal Displacement* (Routledge 2016); Aderomola Adeola, *Development-Induced Displacement and Human Rights in Africa: the Kampala Convention* (Routledge 2020).

[18] For discussion on this framework, please see Danwood M Chirwa and Chipo I Rushwaya, 'Guarding the Guardians: A Critical Appraisal of the African Charter on the Rights of Older Persons in Africa' (2019) 19(1) HRLR 53–82.

[19] Serges AD Kamga, 'A Call for a Protocol to the African Charter on Human and Peoples' Rights on the Rights of Persons with Disabilities in Africa' (2013) 21(1) Afr J Int'l Comp Law 219–249.

[20] See Ibrahim B El-Sheikh, 'The African Commission on Human and Peoples: Prospects and Problems' (1989) 7(3) NQHR 272–283; Wolfgang Benedek, 'The African Charter and Commission on Human and Peoples' Rights; How to Make it More Effective' (1993) 11(1) NQHR 25–40; Laurie S Wiseberg, 'The African Commission on Human and Peoples' Rights' (1994) 22(2) A Journal of Opinion 34–41; Rachel Murray, *The African Commission on Human and Peoples' Rights and International Law* (Hart Publishing 2000); Udeme Essien, 'The African Commission on Human and Peoples' Rights: Eleven Years Later' (2000) 6 Buff Hum Rts L Rev 93–112.

[21] For discussion on this framework, please see Amanda Lloyd, 'How to Guarantee Credence: Recommendations and Proposals for the African Committee of Experts on the Rights and Welfare of the Child' (2004) 12(1) Int'l J Child Rights 21–40; Benyam D Mezmur, 'The African Committee of Experts on the Rights and Welfare of the Child: an update' (2006) 6 AHRLJ 549–571; Julia Sloth-Nielsen, 'Regional Frameworks for Safeguarding Children: the Role of the African Committee of Experts on the Rights and Welfare of the Child' (2014) 3(4) Social Sciences 948–961.

[22] For discussion on this framework, please see Makau Mutua, 'The African Human Rights Court: A Two-Legged Stool?' (1999) 21(2) HRQ 342–363; Nsongurua N Udombana, '"Towards the African Court on Human and Peoples' Rights: Better Late than Never' (2000) 3 Yale Hum Rts & Dev L J 45–111; Kithure Kindiki, 'The Proposed Integration of the African Court of Justice and the African Court of Human and Peoples' Rights: Legal Difficulties and Merits' (2007) 15(1) Afr J Int Comp Law 138–46; Frans Viljoen, 'Understanding and Overcoming Challenges in Accessing the African Court of Human and Peoples' Rights' (2018) 67(1) ICLQ 63–98; Getahun K Antigegn, 'The Role of African Court on Human and Peoples' Rights for Human Rights Protection: the Case of Libyan Crises' (2020) 7(1) AJSS 38–43; Josephine J Dawuni, 'Vive la Diversité or Aluta Continua? Achieving Gender Equality on the African Court on Human and Peoples' Rights' (2019) 34(3) CJIL 384.

and technology)[23] and the formation of institutions with human rights-related mandates.[24]

Aside from the regional normative landscape, there are also evident developments at the level of the regional economic communities (RECs), which are the sub-regional substratum of the regional AU system.[25] Significantly, these developments have taken evident form in the context of the ECOWAS and EAC region.[26] But this is not to suggest that there are no evident progressions in other regions, such as in IGAD.[27] Many of these progressions in these regions have mostly formed in the context of migration and mobilities.[28] However, there is work required in other sub-regions such as SADC, ECCAS and UMA. It is useful to emphasize that the presence of human rights principles in these sub-regional economic groupings, albeit to varying degrees, demonstrates a significant level of acceptance of

[23] Protocol Relating to the Establishment of the Peace and Security Council of the African Union (2002); African Charter on Democracy, Elections and Governance (2007); African Union Convention on Cyber Security and Personal Data Protection (2014); Protocol to the Treaty Establishing the African Economic Community Relating to Free Movement of Persons, Right of Residence and Right of Establishment (2018).

[24] Frans Viljoen and Evarist Baimu, 'Courts for Africa: Considering the Co-existence of the African Court on Human and Peoples' Rights and the African Court of Justice' (2004) 22(2) NQHR 241–267; Jeremy Sarkin, 'The African Commission on Human and Peoples' Rights and the Future African Court of Justice and Human Rights: Comparative Lessons from the European Court of Human Rights' (2011) 18(3) S Afr J Int Aff 281–293; Rachel Murray, 'The Human Rights Jurisdiction of the African Court of Justice and Human and Peoples' Rights' in Charles C Jalloh, Kamari M Clarke and Vincent O Nmehielle, *The African Court of Justice and Human and Peoples' Rights in Context: Development and Challenges* (CUP 2019) 965–988.

[25] These RECs are Economic Community of West African States (ECOWAS); East African Community (EAC); Common Market on Eastern and Central Africa (COMESA); Southern African Development Community (SADC); Economic Community of Central African States (ECCAS), Arab Maghreb Union (UMA); Community of Sahel Sub-Saharan Africa (CEN-SAD); and the Inter-Governmental Authority on Development (IGAD). For discussion on human rights within some of these RECs, please see: Lucyline N Murungi and Jacqui Gallinetti, 'The Role of Sub-Regional courts in the African Human Rights System' (2010) 7(13) SUR International Journal of Human Rights 119–143; Solomon T Ebobrah, 'Human Rights Realisation in the African Sub-Regional Institutions' in Ssenyonjo (n 2) 283–300.

[26] See Solomon T Ebobrah, 'Critical Issues in the Human Rights Mandate of the ECOWAS Court of Justice' (2010) 54(1) JAL 1–25; Karen J Alter, Laurence R Helfer and Jacqueline R McAllister, 'A New International Human Rights Court for West Africa: the ECOWAS Community Court of Justice' (2013) 107(4) AJIL 737–779; Enyinna S Nwauche, 'The ECOWAS Community Court of Justice and the Horizontal Application of Human Rights' (2013) 13(1) AHRLJ 30–54; Ally Possi, 'The East African Court of Justice: Towards Effective Protection of Human Rights in the East African Community' (2013) 17(1) Max Planck Yearbook of United Nations Law Online 173–195; James Gathii, 'Mission Creep or a Search for Relevance: the East African Court of Justice's Human Rights Strategy' (2013) 24(2) DJCIL 249–296; Mihreteab T Taye, 'The Role of the East African Court of Justice in the Advancement of Human Rights: Reflections on the Creation and Practice of the Court' (2019) 27(3) Afr J Int Comp Law 359–377.

[27] See 'IGAD sensitizes experts from human rights institutions of member states on the African human rights system' Intergovernmental Authority on Development 25 September 2019 https://igad.int/divisions/peace-and-security/2240-igad-sensitizes-experts-from-human-rights-institutions-of-member-states-on-the-african-human-rights-system.

[28] See Aderomola Adeola, 'The African Union Protocol on Free Movement of Persons in Africa: development, provisions and implementation challenges' (2019) 3 AHRY 260–275.

human rights norms across the continent. Moreover, in the constitutions of all AU Member States, human rights norms are embedded to varying degrees.

But a fundamental question that has become imperative to answer is to what extent is there compliance with human rights norms. This question has become vital to interrogate in view of the pertinence of understanding the impact of human rights treaties at the level where they matter the most—the domestic level. As Frans Viljoen emphasized, the 'ultimate test of international human rights law is the extent to which it takes root in national soil'.[29] This book interrogates the question of compliance with the African human rights system.

Scholarship in this book is drawn from regional experts in the field of discourse. It is imperative to emphasize at the onset that all the authors in this book were former doctoral supervisees of Frans Viljoen that have gone on to significantly work in the field of human rights from various perspectives—both within the academic and activist spheres. And it is imperative to underscore the fact that these experts have greatly benefited from the scholarship of the man—Frans Viljoen.

2 Structure of the Book

There are nine chapters in this book that significantly interrogate the question of compliance with international human rights law in Africa. The first chapter introduces the discussion in this book, providing a brief insight into the African human rights system.

In Chapter 2, titled 'Compliance Studies in the African Human Rights System: Reflections on the State of the Field', Japhet Biegon sets the scene through a brilliant rendition on compliance studies within the African human rights system and engaging the subject from a critical reflection on the state of the field while also providing potential future research agenda. He observes that while scholarship in this area is emerging, there is a need for further deliberate engagement, also from interdisciplinary perspectives.

In Chapter 3, titled 'Beyond Compliance: Do Decisions of Regional Human Rights Tribunals in Africa Make a Difference?' Victor Ayeni provides a significant scholarly engagement on the decisions of human rights tribunals in Africa and the extent of compliance with the decisions of these tribunals. Reflecting on six regional and sub-regional contexts in five selected countries (Nigeria, Tanzania, The Gambia, Uganda and Zimbabwe), this chapter argues that there has been progress in the contribution of relevant decisions of selected HRTs to an eventual outcome at the domestic level; however, there is much to be done in ensuring that the decisions of human rights tribunals have a significant domestic effect. He argues that,

[29] Viljoen (n 1) 517.

'domestic activist forces and transnational compliance actors must take more seriously the national process of implementation'.

In Chapter 4, titled 'Compliance with the Prohibition of the Death Penalty in Africa', Lilian Chenwi critically examines the issue of the death penalty in Africa. The application of the death penalty on the African continent continues to be an issue of debate and concern. Over the years, there has been a growing trend towards the abolition of the death penalty, emphasizing the need to enhance and protect human rights. Arguably, this trend emanates from recognizing the death's penalty inconsistency with international human rights law. Although there is no explicit general prohibition of the death penalty in international law, existing human rights instruments have become significant in orchestrating a continent-wide shift. This chapter examines the extent of compliance with these instruments in the prohibition of the death penalty in Africa.

In Chapter 5, titled 'Compliance beyond anniversaries: the African Union Convention for the Protection and Assistance of Internally Displaced Persons (Kampala Convention) in Domestic Laws and Policies', Aderomola Adeola discusses the issue of compliance with the regional law on internal displacement in Africa (Kampala Convention). Over the last decade, this chapter examines the extent to which the Kampala Convention has led to laws and policies at the domestic level. While there has been some evident progress in domestic compliance from a law and policy dimension, this is low in comparative terms with the extent of ratification and support given to the normative framework at the continental level. This chapter discusses some key variables for realising compliance at the domestic level: norm influencers, international support, external spotlight, post-conflict reconstruction and peer-to-peer learning.

In Chapter 6, titled Legitimacy as a Challenge to Compliance with the Norms on the Protection of Children in Africa', Remember Miamingi fundamentally critiques the normative framework on children's rights in Africa. He argues that the 'continued inability of human rights norms and standards to effectively end impunity is forcing international and national policy makers to shift the policy battlefront to issues of compliance with human rights'. Through a reflection on the African Children's Charter, he underscores the need to give attention to issues of legitimacy, particularly cultural legitimacy within the regional context, in view of existing philosophies and cultural heritage on childhood in Africa. Overall, this chapter interrogates legitimacy, critiquing the process and formulation of the African Children's Charter and how these affect compliance.

In Chapter 7, titled 'Member States' Compliance with the Recommendations of the African Commission on Human and Peoples' Rights, Lirette Louw notably considers the compliance of AU Member States with the recommendations of the African Commission under the individual complaints system provided in the Charter. This chapter argues that there are factors, both permanent and variable to the system, which, if focused on, could harvest positive results, in as far as securing improved state compliance to the African Commission's recommendations and thereby contributing to the realization of human and peoples' rights on the continent.

In Chapter 8, titled 'Horizontal' Compliance With the Decisions of the African Court on Human and Peoples' Rights', Adem Kassie Abebe develops an innovative approach to the furtherance of compliance with decisions of supranational human rights tribunals beyond the vertical context of decisions of these tribunals applying only to the respondent states. Through a reflection on the African Court, he introduces the idea of 'horizontal' compliance where the Court can seek to ensure compliance with its decisions involving the validity of laws vis-à-vis states with comparable legal provisions to the respondent state.

In Chapter 9, titled 'Enforcing Compliance With the Judgments of the African Court on Human and Peoples' Rights: Prospects and Challenges', Tarisai Mutangi crucially reflects on how compliance can be bridged with the decisions of the African Court at the domestic level. He identifies a two-tier enforcement mechanism: at the international and national levels. At the international level, he discusses the role of the AU Assembly and the African Court. Drawing on comparative reflections, specifically, from Europe and the Inter-American human rights systems, this chapter argues that the African Court may utilize a range of initiatives in advancing compliance. He, however, emphasizes the need for an activist judiciary. On the second tier, he argues that various arms of government (executive, legislative and judiciary) have important roles to perform. Moreover, he emphasizes the need for national human rights institutions to take centre stage. In the end, he makes a crucial point in that 'monitoring compliance is a process of pooling efforts as opposed to observing a hierarchy of mechanisms'.

2

Compliance Studies and the African Human Rights System

Reflections on the State of the Field

Japhet Biegon

1 Introduction

In the mid-2000s, a teacher and student combined efforts to tackle what had become an issue of growing concern in the African human rights system: the paucity of research on State implementation and compliance with the recommendations of the African Commission on Human and Peoples' Rights (ACHPR). The pair, Frans Viljoen and Lirette Louw collected data through desk research and interviews on steps taken by States to implement 44 decisions in which the ACHPR had found a violation in the ten-year period between 1994 and mid-2003. They then used this data to identify the factors that most influence compliance and implementation. They published the results of their findings in the first issue of the 2007 edition of the *American Journal of International Law*.[1] This article blazed a trail. It marked the first-ever attempt to analyse comprehensively and systematically what becomes of decisions of an African human rights treaty body after they have been delivered or published.

More than ten years have passed since the publication of Viljoen and Louw's seminal article. In that intervening period, so much has happened in the African human rights system. The caseload of the ACHPR has gradually but steadily increased to stand at more than 600 since its inception.[2] Two more regional bodies,

[1] Frans Viljoen and Lirette Louw, 'State Compliance with the Recommendations of the African Commission on Human and Peoples' Rights' (2007) 101 AJIL 1 (Viljoen and Louw, *State Compliance*). This article drew upon Lirette Louw's doctoral thesis, 'An Analysis of State Compliance with the Recommendations of the African Commission on Human and Peoples' Rights' (Unpublished LLD Dissertation, University of Pretoria 2005).

[2] The ACHPR does not publish comprehensive statistics regarding the cases in its docket. In November 2017, when the ACHPR celebrated its 30th anniversary, it indicated that it had received 663 communications since inception and concluded more than 400. See Opening Statement on the Celebration of the African Commission on Human and Peoples' Rights by Honourable Commissioner Lawrence Murugu Mute, Vice Chairperson of the African Commission on Human and Peoples' Rights, 2 November 2017, Banjul, The Gambia, available at https://www.achpr.org/public/Document/file/English/opening_statement_on_30th_anniversary_celebrations___vc.pdf

Japhet Biegon, *Compliance Studies and the African Human Rights System* In: *Compliance with International Human Rights Law in Africa*. Edited by: Aderomola Adeola, Oxford University Press.
DOI: 10.1093/oso/9780192856999.003.0002

the African Court on Human and Peoples' Rights (ACtHPR) and the African Committee of Experts on the Rights and Welfare of the Child (ACERWC), have become operational. The ACtHPR received a total of 281 cases from its inauguration in July 2006 to mid-June 2020[3] and issued a final judgment in 92 cases. The ACERWC has been the least utilized body of the three,[4] but even so, it is slowly building its stature through the quality and reach of the few decisions it has issued.[5]

With the growth and maturity of the regional human rights bodies, the question of compliance and implementation has become even more important and urgent. In parallel, researchers are increasingly interested in the subject. The result is a burgeoning and rich body of 'compliance/implementation studies'. This literature has mostly drawn upon Viljoen and Louw's article of more than a decade ago and subsequent works and teachings of Viljoen on the subject.[6] The latter's contribution has been far more profound and inspiring than what literature itself can reveal. For one, if there is a growing cadre of compliance/implementation scholars and practitioners in the field of human rights in Africa, a group that we may call an 'epistemic community',[7] then it is precisely because Viljoen has grown and mentored most of them as his doctoral supervisees.[8]

As a practitioner and activist, Viljoen has engaged with the three regional bodies at critical junctures, nudging and helping them assess, design or reform their working methods, including those relating to following-up and monitoring State

[3] For statistics on the cases received and determined by the ACtHPR, see https://www.african-court.org/en/index.php/cases/2016-10-17-16-18-21

[4] The ACERWC has received less than 20 cases since its inception in 2002. See https://www.acerwc.africa/table-of-communications/

[5] See eg Mezmur Benyam, 'Happy 18th Birthday to the African Children's Charter: Not Counting its Days But Making the Days Count' [2017] *AHRY* 125.

[6] Frans Viljoen, 'The African Human Rights System and Domestic Enforcement' in Malcolm Langford and others (eds), *Social Rights Judgments and the Politics of Compliance: Making it Stick* (CUP 2017) 351 (Viljoen, *Domestic Enforcement*); Frans Viljoen, 'State Compliance with the Recommendations of the African Commission on Human and Peoples' Rights', in Mashood Baderin and Manisuli Senyonjo (eds), *International Human Rights Law: Six Decades After the UDHR and Beyond* (Ashgate 2010) 411.

[7] Haas defines an 'epistemic community' as 'a network of professionals with recognized expertise and competence in a particular domain and an authoritative claim to policy-relevant knowledge within that domain or issue area'. Peter Haas, 'Introduction: Epistemic Communities and International Policy Coordination' (1992) 46 Intl Org 1, 3.

[8] Most doctoral theses supervised by Professor Frans Viljoen at the University of Pretoria have interrogated the question of implementation/compliance or some other sister concept such as impact, influence, reception, effect, enforcement and incorporation. They include the following: Tarisai Mutangi, 'Examining Compliance by States with Judgments of the African Court on Human and Peoples' Rights: Prospects and Challenges' (Unpublished LLD Thesis, University of Pretoria 2010) (Mutangi, *Examining Compliance*); Solomon Ebobrah, 'Legitimacy and Feasibility of Human Rights Realization Through Regional Economic Communities in Africa: The Case of the Economic Community of West African States' (Unpublished LLD Thesis, University of Pretoria 2010); Japhet Biegon, 'The Impact of the Resolutions of the African Commission on Human and Peoples' Rights' (Unpublished LLD Dissertation, University of Pretoria 2016); Victor Ayeni, 'State Compliance with and Influence of Reparation Orders by Regional and Sub-Regional Human Rights Tribunals in Five African States' (Unpublished LLD Dissertation, University of Pretoria 2018) (Ayeni, *State Compliance*).

implementation and compliance.[9] Under his leadership, the Centre for Human Rights at the University of Pretoria has established a Litigation and Implementation Unit. A key objective of the Unit is to 'follow-up on implementation of decisions of international and regional human rights bodies'.[10] It has thus far been involved in an implementation research project involving four universities and covering countries in Africa, the Americas and Europe.[11] This project reflects the recent surge in scholarship about compliance with the decisions of regional human rights bodies not only in Africa but also in the Americas and Europe.[12]

In tribute to Viljoen's central and unparalleled contribution to the subject, this chapter takes stock of the compliance/implementation studies in the African human rights system. Rather than draw an inventory, it filters out the main trends and issues in the literature and charts its potential future trajectory. In exploring a field as expansive as the one at hand, it is not possible with the limited available space to delve into the essential details or offer an exhaustive analysis. It suffices to highlight the broad contours and features of the field. Confronted with a similar task, Viljoen opted to adopt 'the expansive – and eclectic – gaze of the land surveyor rather than the microscopic search of the prospector in his quest for that one elusive diamond or golden nugget'.[13] Like teacher, like student, I consciously adopt a similar frame here.

This chapter is located within the broader literature that concerns itself with the difference, if any, that international human rights law makes in reality.[14] Here again, Viljoen has carved a niche and led from the front. Building on a

[9] See eg Report of the Regional Seminar on the Implementation of Decisions of the African Commission on Human and Peoples' Rights, 12–15 August 2017, Dakar, Senegal (African Commission on Human and Peoples' Rights, 2017) < https://www.achpr.org/public/Document/file/English/report_regional_seminar_eng.pdf; Ending Violence and Other Human Rights Violations Based on Sexual Orientation and Gender Identity: A Joint Dialogue of the African Commission on Human and Peoples' Rights, Inter-American Commission on Human Rights and United Nations (Pretoria University Law Press 2016).

[10] Centre for Human Rights, 'About the Litigation and Implementation Unit' https://www.chr.up.ac.za/units/about-liu

[11] Centre for Human Rights, 'Human Rights Law Implementation Project', https://www.chr.up.ac.za/projects/30-units/litigation/268-implementation-litigation-unit

[12] Examples of the most recent academic analyses of implementation and compliance beyond the African regional human rights systems include the following: Oyvind Stiansen, 'Delayed But Not Derailed: Legislative Compliance with European Court of Human Rights judgments' (2019) 23 IJHR 1221; Constanza Danceanu, 'Systematic Review of the Causes of Latin American States' Compliance With International Human Rights Law' (2019) 41 HRQ 553; Jeanice Koorndijk, 'Judgments of the Inter-American Court of Human Rights Concerning Indigenous and Tribal Land Rights in Suriname: New Approaches to Stimulating Full Compliance' (2019) 23 IJHR 1615.

[13] Frans Viljoen, 'Contemporary Challenges to International Human Rights Law and the Role Human Rights Education' (2011) De Jure 207, 209 (Viljoen, *Contemporary Challenges*).

[14] See eg Oona Hathaway, 'Do Human Rights Treaties Make a Difference?' (2001) 101 YLJ 1935 (Hathaway, *Human Rights Treaties*); Douglas Cassel, 'Does International Human Rights Law Make a Difference?' (2001) 2 CJIL 121; Beth Simmons, *Mobilizing for Human Rights: International Law in Domestic Politics* (CUP 2009) (Simmons, *Mobilizing for Human Rights*); Linda Keith, 'The United Nations International Covenant on Civil and Political Rights: Does it Make a Difference in Human Rights Behaviour?' (1999) 36 J Peace Res 95.

2001 pioneering study on the impact of the United Nations (UN) human rights treaties that he undertook and authored with Christof Heyns,[15] an expanding list of Viljoen's writings interrogate the impact of the African human rights system at the domestic level.[16] His interest in this area has cascaded to many of his students who have been collectively involved in two major academic studies that have documented the impact of the African Charter on Human and Peoples' Rights and its Protocol on the Rights of Women in Africa (Maputo Protocol) in selected African countries.[17] Others like the present author have concentrated on the impact of the system's soft law.[18]

The terms 'compliance' and 'implementation' are used interchangeably in this chapter. However, it must be acknowledged that although they are closely associated, they have different meanings. Compliance is the alignment between the factual situation at the domestic level and a decision of a regional body. It connotes conformity with a regional decision. Implementation is the action of putting in place measures to give effect to a regional decision. In this context, compliance is a *status* or an *outcome,* while implementation is a *process*. Implementation may result in either partial or full compliance. However, compliance may also be attained independently of implementation because of sheer coincidence or some other neutral factor.

2 African System's Evolving Focus and Priorities

Before exploring trends and issues in compliance studies, it is important to contextualize the discussion. This section accordingly looks at the evolution of the African human rights system, for it tells its own story about compliance and serves

[15] Christof Heyns and Frans Viljoen, 'The Impact of the United Nations Human Rights Treaties on the Domestic Level' (2001) 23 HRQ 483. As at the time of this writing, Christof and Viljoen have launched a new research project for the second edition of the 2001 study. The new study will have an expanded geographical and thematic scope. See Christof Heyns and Frans Viljoen, 'What Difference Does the UN Human Rights Treaty System Make and Why? A New Global Academic Study to Answer this Question Launched in Collaboration with the UN High Commissioner for Human Rights' (OpenGlobalRights, 11 February 2020) < https://www.openglobalrights.org/what-difference-does-un-human-rights-treaty-system-make/

[16] Frans Viljoen, 'The Impact and Influence of the African Regional Human Rights System on Domestic Law' in Scott Sheeran and Nigel Rodley (eds), *Routledge Handbook of International Human Rights Law* (Routledge 2013) 445; Frans Viljoen, 'Exploring the Theory and Practice of the Relationship Between International Human Rights Law and Domestic Actors (2009) 22 LJIL 177; Frans Viljoen, 'Application of the African Charter on Human and Peoples' Rights by Domestic Courts in Africa' (1999) 43 JAL 1.

[17] Victor Ayeni (ed), *The Impact of the African Charter and the Maputo Protocol in Selected African States* (Pretoria University Law Press 2016); Centre for Human Rights *The Impact of the African Charter and the Women's Protocol in Selected African States* (Pretoria University Law Press 2012).

[18] Japhet Biegon, 'The Incorporation of the Thematic Resolutions of the African Commission into the Domestic Laws of African Countries' in Shyllon Ololade (ed), *The Model Law on Access to Information for Africa and Other Regional Instruments: Soft Law and Human Rights in Africa* (Pretoria University Law Press 2018) 190.

as a fitting historical backdrop to understanding the existing corpus of studies on the subject.

There is a consensus among scholars and practitioners that international human rights law and practice has evolved in two overlapping phases. In particular, international human rights normative and institutional architecture has over time transitioned from an 'era of legislation' to an 'era of implementation'.[19] The history and development of the African human rights system in the last four decades largely mirrors this evolution. The main emphasis during the first phase was standard setting and institution building. This phase saw the elaboration of a large body of international and regional instruments accompanied by relatively complex institutional frameworks. As standards and institutions proliferated, the question of their impact on the lived realities of people became a growing concern. Therefore, during the last two decades or so, attention has largely shifted to State practice relating to compliance. During this second phase, talk of 'compliance deficit', 'implementation challenge' or 'enforcement crisis' has become common. This phase has also coincided with the steady rise of compliance studies as scholars interrogate when, how, where and under what conditions does compliance take place.

The African system's foundation stone was laid in 1981 with the adoption of the African Charter on Human and Peoples' Rights (African Charter).[20] Its monitoring body, the ACHPR, started its operations in 1987 and functioned as the sole regional human rights treaty body for about a decade and a half. By the time the ACHPR celebrated its twentieth anniversary in 2006, the ACtHPR and the ACERWC had joined the system. The ACERWC monitors the implementation of the African Charter on the Rights and Welfare of the Child (African Children's Charter),[21] the regional pendant to the UN Convention on the Rights of the Child.[22] The ACtHPR complements the protective mandate of the ACHPR.[23] It provides judicial supervision of State compliance with the African Charter and 'any other relevant human rights instrument ratified by the states concerned'.[24] The three bodies operate under the auspices of the African Union (AU), the successor to the Organization of African Unity (OAU). They are the key institutional pillars of the African system. Over the years, the system's normative framework has also expanded to include a range of other regional human rights treaties as well as soft law instruments.[25]

[19] In Larger Freedom: Towards Development, Security and Human Rights for All: Report of the Secretary-General, A/59/2005, 21 March 2005, para 132.

[20] Adopted 27 June 1981, entered into force 21 October 1986, OAU Doc CAB/LEG/67/3 rev 5.

[21] Adopted 11 July 1990, entered into force 29 November 1999, OAU Doc CAB/LEG/24.9/49(1990).

[22] Adopted 20 November 1989, entered into force 2 September 1990.

[23] Art 2, Protocol to the African Charter on Human and Peoples' Rights on the Establishment of an African Court on Human and Peoples' Rights, adopted 10 June 1998, entered into force 25 January 2004, OAU/LEG/MIN/AFCHPR/PROT(I) rev 2 (African Court Protocol).

[24] African Court Protocol, art 3.

[25] The other key AU human rights treaties are as follows: Protocol to the African Charter on the Rights of Women in Africa, adopted 11 July 2003, entered into force 25 November 2005; Protocol to the African Charter on the Rights of Persons with Disabilities, adopted 29 January 2018, not yet in force; Protocol to the African Charter on the Rights of Older Persons, adopted 31 January 2016, not yet

2.1 The ACHPR

The ACHPR started its work from the wrong footing and in a context in which commentators had pointed out many design and normative flaws in the African Charter.[26] It adopted an opaque and restrictive working procedure that saw it lock the public out of its first eight sessions. It also did not publish its decisions on communications until 1994, more than five years into operations. The veil of secrecy with which it had clothed itself fuelled criticism for the ACHPR. Perhaps the harshest denunciation came from Mutua, who, in 1993, predicted a bleak future for the ACHPR and famously described it as 'a façade, a yoke that African leaders have put around our necks'.[27] However, as the years passed, the ACHPR fine-tuned its procedures and cured most of the flaws in the African Charter through a purposive and flexible interpretation. As the ACHPR published more of its decisions during the 1990s, it became apparent that there was little State compliance with these decisions.

During its twenty-second ordinary session held in November 1997, the ACHPR's chairperson observed that none of its decisions had been implemented.[28] The following year, the ACHPR investigated the issue more deeply when discussing a document prepared by the secretariat that showed that only one decision had been implemented.[29] This poor rate of implementation did not escape the attention of scholars. Writing in 1998, Odinkalu and Christensen observed as follows, 'in those few cases that have been decided on their merits there remains, as yet, no evidence that the states complied either habitually or at all with the views of the Commission'.[30] Other scholars blamed this state of affairs partly on the failure of the ACHPR to institute a follow-up mechanism for tracking the implementation of its decisions.[31] The problem of non-compliance would gain prominence in the years to come, especially after the transformation of the OAU to the AU in 2002.

in force; AU Convention for the Protection and Assistance of Internally Displaced Persons (Kampala Convention), adopted 23 October 2009, entered into force 6 December 2012.

[26] Ebow Bondzie-Simpson, 'A Critique of Human Rights in Africa and the African Charter on Human and Peoples' Rights (1988) 31 HLJ 643.

[27] Makau Mutua, 'The African Human Rights System in Comparative Perspective' (1993) 3 Rev Afr Commission on Hum & Peo Rts 5, 11.

[28] Rachel Murray, 'Report of the 1997 Sessions of the African Commission on Human and Peoples' Rights – 21st and 22nd Sessions: 15-25 April and 2-11 November 1997' (1998) 19 Hum Rts L J 169, 170.

[29] Non-Compliance of State Parties to Adopted Recommendations of the African Commission: A Legal Approach, Twenty Fourth Ordinary Session, Banjul, 22 to 31 October 1998, Doc/OS/50b (XXIV), reprinted in Rachel Murray and Malcolm Evans (eds), *Documents of the African Commission on Human and Peoples' Rights* (Bloomsbury Publishing 2001) 758.

[30] Chidi Odinkalu and Camilla Christensen, 'The African Commission on Human and Peoples' Rights: The Development of its Non-State Communications Procedure' (1998) 20 HRQ 235, 279–280.

[31] Nsongurua Udombana, 'Toward the African Court on Human and Peoples' Rights: Better Late Than Never' (2000) 3 Yale Hum Rts & Dev L J 45 (Udombana, *Toward the African Court*); Joe Oloka-Onyango, 'Human Rights and Sustainable Development in Contemporary Africa: A New Dawn, or Retreating Horizons' (2000) 6 Buff Hum Rts L Rev 39.

Several significant developments took place between 2002 and 2006. First, the ACHPR held a retreat in September 2003 in Addis Ababa, Ethiopia, where the need for a follow-up mechanism was reiterated.[32] Second, the ACHPR established the Working Group on Specific Issues Relevant to its Work in May 2005 and gave it the mandate to institute the follow-up mechanism envisaged in the 2003 retreat.[33] Third, the ACHPR held a brainstorming meeting with the AU Commission in May 2006 in Banjul, The Gambia, where the problem of non-compliance was noted once again. A suggestion was made that the AU Peace and Security Council (PSC) should perhaps take the responsibility of enforcing the decisions of the ACHPR.[34] It was also recommended that the ACHPR 'develop and execute an implementation plan for the follow up of their decisions, resolutions and recommendations'.[35] Little came out of these three developments, but they helped build the momentum for what would come next.

The fourth development was a game-changer, even if on a theoretic level. In November 2006, during its fortieth ordinary session convened to coincide with its twentieth anniversary, the ACHPR took its very first concrete step in engaging states on the matter of non-compliance. It adopted a resolution calling on all State Parties to the African Charter to respect its existing decisions 'without further delay', and for any future decisions, to report on steps taken to comply within 90 days of being notified.[36] The ACHPR also decided that it would henceforth submit a report on the status of compliance with its decisions to every session of the AU Executive Council. In its 2010 Rules of Procedure adopted, the ACHPR codified a more elaborate follow-up and monitoring procedure. Under Rule 112(2), a respondent state must inform the ACHPR of the measures taken to implement a decision of the ACHPR within 180 days of the issuance of the decision. Rule 112(4) further provides for the designation of a rapporteur to monitor implementation by such a respondent state. Under Rule 112(7), the ACHPR may refer cases of persistent non-compliance to the relevant policy organs of the AU.

[32] Report of the Retreat of Members of the African Commission on Human and Peoples' Rights (ACHPR), Addis Ababa, Ethiopia, 24 to 26 September 2003, available at <https://nhri.ohchr.org/EN/Regional/Africa/AfricanDocumentsPage/ACHPR-Retreat-Report-Final.pdf> accessed 7 July 2020.

[33] Resolution on the Creation of a Working Group on Specific Issues Relevant to the Work of the African Commission on Human and Peoples' Rights, adopted at the 37th ordinary Session, ACHPR/Res 77(XXXVII)05.

[34] Report of the Brainstorming Meeting on the African Commission on Human and Peoples' Rights: 9 to 10 May 2006, Banjul, The Gambia, 20th Activity Report, Annex II (Brainstorming Report). For an academic reflection on this proposal and the role of the AU more generally in enforcing the decisions of the ACHPR, see George Mukundi and Abiola Ayinla, 'Twenty Years of Elusive Enforcement of the Recommendations of the African Commission on Human and Peoples' Rights: A Possible Remedy' (2006) 6 AHRLJ 465.

[35] Brainstorming Report (n 34).

[36] Resolution on the Importance of the Implementation of the Recommendations of the African Commission on Human and Peoples' Rights by State Parties (adopted during the 40th Ordinary Session, Banjul, The Gambia, 29 November 2006) ACHPR/Res 97(XXXX)06.

In July 2020, the ACHPR published a new set of Rules of Procedure.[37] In the new Rules of Procedure, the follow-up and monitoring procedure is spelt out in Rule 125. It largely mirrors the provisions of Rule 112 of the 2010 Rules, albeit with two major additions. First, it provides that whenever a State submits information on the status of implementation, the ACHPR is duty-bound to submit this information to the complainant for their review and comments. Second, it provides that the ACHPR may request a national human rights institution to inform it of any action taken to monitor or facilitate the implementation of its decisions.

Since adopting the 2010 Rules of Procedure, the ACHPR has paid much more attention to compliance. Its engagement with States in the post-decision phase has also significantly improved. It has convened seminars and workshops to discuss compliance,[38] placed the subject on the agenda of its ordinary sessions,[39] held at least a single implementation hearing,[40] and referred cases of noncompliance to the relevant AU political organs.[41] It has also followed-up on or inquired about the status of implementation using its mainstream working methods, such as country visits,[42] adoption of resolutions[43] and review of state party reports.[44] Since January 2017, it regularly includes information about the implementation of its decisions

[37] See Rules of Procedure of the African Commission on Human and Peoples' Rights, 2020 (adopted during the 27th Extraordinary Session, Banjul, The Gambia, 19 February to 4 March 2020) available at https://www.achpr.org/public/Document/file/English/Rules%20of%20Procedure%202020_ENG.pdf (accessed 11 July 2020).

[38] Report of the Second Regional Seminar on the Implementation of Decisions of the African Commission on Human and Peoples' Rights, Zanzibar, Tanzania, 4 to 6 September 2018 available at https://www.achpr.org/news/viewdetail?id=3 (accessed 9 July 2020); Report of the Regional Seminar on the Implementation of Decisions of the African Commission on Human and Peoples' Rights, Dakar, Senegal, 12 to 15 August 2017, available https://www.achpr.org/public/Document/file/English/report_regional_seminar_eng.pdf (accessed 11 July 2020).

[39] See eg Final Communiqué of the 63rd Ordinary Session of the African Commission on Human and Peoples' Rights, Banjul, The Gambia, 24 October to 13 November 2018, para 23(ii); Final Communiqué of the 57th Ordinary Session of the African Commission on Human and Peoples' Rights, Banjul, The Gambia, 4 to 18 November 2015, para 18(xiii).

[40] See eg 34th Activity Report of the African Commission on Human and Peoples' Rights (adopted during the 23rd Ordinary Session of the AU Executive Council, Addis Ababa, Ethiopia, 19 to 23 May 2013) EX.CL/796 (XXIII) para 16.

[41] Combined 32nd and 33rd Activity Report of the African Commission on Human and Peoples' Rights (adopted during the 22nd Ordinary Session of the AU Executive Council, Addis Ababa, Ethiopia, 21 to 25 January 2013) EX.CL/782(XXII) rev 2, para 24, noting as follows, 'The Commission would like to bring to the attention of the Executive Council the refusal of the Republic of Botswana to implement the Commission's decision in Communication 313/05 – *Kenneth Good v Botswana* ... The Commission is bringing this refusal to the attention of the Council for appropriate action'.

[42] Report of the Joint Promotion Mission to the Kingdom of Swaziland by Commissioner Pansy Tlakula and Commissioner Solomon Dersso, 7 to 11 March 2016 (adopted during the 60th Ordinary Session, Niamey, Niger, 8 to 22 May 2017) para 5(ix).

[43] See eg Resolution Calling on the Republic of Kenya to Implement the Endorois Decision (adopted during the 54th Ordinary Session, Banjul, The Gambia, 22 October to 5 November 2013), ACHPR/Res 257(LIV) 2013; Resolution on the Human Rights Situation in the Kingdom of Swaziland (adopted during the 51st Ordinary Session, Banjul, The Gambia, 18 April to 2 May 2012) ACHPR/Res 216(LI) 2012.

[44] ACHPR Concluding Observations and Recommendations – Kenya: Combined 8th to11th periodic report, 2008–2014 (adopted during the 19th Extra-ordinary Session, Banjul, The Gambia, 16 to 25 February 2016).

in its activity reports. But as discussed in the next section on trends and issues, notwithstanding the existence of its own clear rules on follow-up, the ACHPR's practice has been inconsistent and *ad hoc* at best. With only one case of full compliance recorded in the last three years,[45] the rate of compliance with the ACtHPR's decisions remains relatively low.

2.2 The ACERWC

The ACERWC was inaugurated in May 2002, just about two months before the AU was launched. It thus commenced operations in a broader context of much optimism in Africa; the creation of the AU signalled a shift towards greater supranational supervision of domestic respect for human rights. However, the ACERWC was extremely slow in seizing the moment and picking up momentum. Although it received its first case in 2005 and the second in 2009, it was not until 2011 that it issued its first decision. This sluggish start is partly because the ACERWC lacked a permanent secretariat for the first five years, a problem exacerbated by the little institutional support it received from the AU. However, the inaugural members are also to blame for what Viljoen described as the 'lackadaisical attitude' and 'lacklustre performance' of the ACERWC in those early years.[46] They lacked the requisite competence to effectively discharge their mandate and spent most of their time addressing matters of form rather than substance.[47]

In the last few years, the ACERWC has largely redeemed itself, prompting writers such as Viljoen to soften their stance and criticism.[48] Its docket of cases remains very small, but the few decisions it has issued contain 'well articulated, progressive, and innovative finding[s]'.[49] Learning from the experience of the ACHPR, the ACERWC has paid keen attention to compliance issues from the outset. In its initial Guidelines for Communications adopted in 2007, the ACERWC provided for the procedure of monitoring implementation of its decisions. It was a basic procedure, simply requiring it to designate a member responsible for monitoring its decisions.[50] In its first decision, though, it went further than the Rules of Procedure required. It indicated that it would appoint a member to monitor implementation

[45] In June 2019, Cameroon informed the ACHPR that it had fully complied with the decision in *Mbiankeu Genevieve v Cameroon,* Communication 389/10. See 47th Activity Report of the African Commission on Human and Peoples' Rights (adopted during the 36th Ordinary Session of the AU Executive Council, Addis Ababa, Ethiopia, 6 to 7 February 2020) EX.CL/1205(XXXVI) para 33.

[46] Frans Viljoen, *International Human Rights Law in Africa* (1st edn, OUP 2007) 221.

[47] ibid.

[48] Frans Viljoen, *International Human Rights Law in Africa* (2nd edn, OUP 2012) 408 (Viljoen, *Human Rights Law in Africa*).

[49] ibid.

[50] Guidelines for the Consideration of Communications Provided for in art 44 of the African Charter on the Rights and Welfare of the Child, art 4.

and gave the respondent state a deadline within which to report on the measures taken to implement the decision.[51]

In October 2014, the ACERWC adopted a new set of guidelines on communications.[52] The new guidelines clarify that a rapporteur shall be appointed for each decision to follow-up on implementation. The rapporteur is required to report at each ordinary session of the ACERWC on the progress made by the State concerned to implement a decision issued against it. Where incidents of non-compliance are persistent, the ACERWC may notify the relevant AU policy organs. To supplement the 2014 Guidelines, the ACERWC has in place a dedicated set of guidelines on implementation.[53] These guidelines, adopted in May 2018, provide instructions on the content of a state's report on the implementation and procedure of initiating and holding an implementation hearing. The purpose of an implementation hearing is to assess progress, identify challenges and nudge the State concerned towards full implementation. After holding an implementation hearing, the ACERWC may issue recommendations on how to achieve full implementation, or if it has concluded that the State concerned has failed to take any measures towards implementation, refer it to the AU Assembly. The ACERWC has enjoyed a relative if rare cordial relationship with State Parties, with those found in violation of the African Children's Charter cooperating with it to address the infringement and implement the Committee's decision.

2.3 The ACtHPR

The ACtHPR was established to principally address the design and structural weaknesses of the ACHPR, particularly its quasi-judicial character and the perceived non-binding nature of its decisions. The inability of the ACHPR to cajole compliance with its decisions led many to describe it as a 'toothless bulldog',[54] fortifying the numerous calls in the 1990s for the establishment of a regional human rights court. After a drafting process spanning four years, the treaty establishing the ACtHPR was adopted by the OAU in 1998. It came into force in 2004, and the inaugural judges of the ACtHPR were sworn into office in July 2006. The first case arrived at the ACtHPR in 2009. There was then a brief hiatus before a steady stream of cases flowed into the ACtHPR from 2011 onwards. However, most early cases were against non-State Parties and thus thrown out at the admissibility stage. The

[51] *Institute for Human Rights and Development in Africa (IHRDA) & Open Society Justice Initiative on behalf of Children of Nubian Descent in Kenya v Kenya* Dec 2/Com/002/2009, 22 March 2011, (2011) *AHRLR* 181 (ACERWC 2011) para 69(5).

[52] Revised Guidelines for the Consideration of Communications (adopted during the 1st Extraordinary Session, Addis Ababa, Ethiopia, 7 to 11 October 2014).

[53] Guidelines for Implementation of Decisions on Communications (adopted during the 31st Ordinary Session, Bamako, Mali, 24 April to 4 May 2018).

[54] See eg Udombana, *Toward the African Court* (n 31) 64.

ACtHPR issued its first merit judgment in June 2013, and since then, its body of case law has expanded quite rapidly, notwithstanding the restricted access to the Court for individuals and Non-governmental Organizations (NGOs).[55]

Given the history that led to its establishment, the issue of compliance has been prominent in the evolution of the ACtHPR. At a normative level, States Parties to the African Court Protocol have an explicit obligation to 'comply with the judgment in any case to which they are parties within the time stipulated by the Court and to guarantee its execution'.[56] The ACtHPR is required to report cases of non-compliance to the AU Executive Council.[57] The latter has the ultimate mandate of monitoring the execution of the judgments.[58] The ACtHPR first reported a State Party (Libya) to the Executive Council for non-compliance in January 2014 and prepared a dedicated report on non-compliance describing how the Libyan government had ignored its orders and correspondence.[59] Since then, however, the ACtHPR simply lists in a table the cases in which the States concerned have not taken action to comply with the judgment. Where some measures of implementation have been taken, it very briefly describes these in the table.

In January 2014, when the ACtHPR reported its first case of non-compliance, the Executive Council simply noted the report and the reservations of Libya.[60] Instead of taking action against the State, it asked the ACtHPR to propose a 'concrete reporting mechanism' that would enable the ACtHPR to notify it of cases of non-compliance 'at any time, when the interest of justice so requires'.[61] The ACtHPR acted on this instruction, and in February 2019, submitted to the Executive Council a draft policy framework for reporting and monitoring execution of its decisions.[62] As at the time of writing, the draft framework had not been formally adopted. In the meantime, the ACtHPR has continued to compile information about the implementation of its decisions. In September 2020, the ACtHPR adopted a new set of Rules of Court, which introduces a formal procedure for monitoring compliance with its judgments. Rule 81 not only requires states to report on measures

[55] African Court Protocol, arts 5(3) and 34(6). See also Frans Viljoen, 'Understanding and Overcoming Challenges in Accessing the African Court on Human and Peoples' Rights' (2018) 67 ICQL 63.

[56] African Court Protocol, art 30.

[57] African Court Protocol, art 31.

[58] African Court Protocol, art 29(2).

[59] Interim Report of the African Court on Human and Peoples' Rights Notifying the Executive Council of Non-compliance by a State, in accordance with art 31 of the Protocol https://en.african-court.org/images/Other%20Reports/AFCHPR_Interim_Report__Non_compliance_by_a_State__-_Libya.pdf (accessed 11 July 2020).

[60] Decision on the 2013 Activity Report of the African Court on Human and Peoples' Rights (adopted during the 24th Ordinary Session of the AU Executive Council, Addis Ababa, Ethiopia, 21 to 28 January 2014) EX.CL/Dec.806(XXIV) para 1.

[61] ibid, para 9.

[62] Draft Framework for Reporting and Monitoring Execution of Judgments and other Decisions of the African Court on Human and Peoples' Rights, annexed to the Activity Report of the African Court on Human and Peoples' Rights, 1 January to 31 December 2018 (adopted during the 34th Ordinary Session of the AU Executive Council, Addis Ababa, Ethiopia, 8 to 9 February 2019) EX.CL/1126(XXIV).

taken to implement decisions of the Court but also allows the Court to proactively gather information on compliance, hold implementation hearings and refer cases of non-compliance to the relevant AU policy organs.

The ACtHPR's record shows that non-compliance has become a persistent problem. In its 2019 Activity Report, the ACtHPR observed as follows, 'One of the greatest challenges that the Court is facing, and which, if not addressed immediately, may undermine the effective discharge of its mandate, is the non-compliance with the decisions of the Court'.[63] As of the end of 2019, the ACtHPR had issued remedial orders in 35 judgments in which it had found violations. Yet, only two judgments against Burkina Faso had been fully complied with. Tanzania, against which most of the judgments had been issued, had complied with only certain aspects of some judgments. Côte d'Ivoire had filed its report on the status of compliance. The rest of the States Parties against which judgments have been issued (eg Libya, Rwanda and Kenya) had not complied at all. Some of them had openly indicated that they would not comply.

3 Trends and Issues in Compliance/Implementation Studies

In 2005, William Bradford compiled and published an annotated bibliography of major academic works on 'international legal compliance' (ILC).[64] His list covered more than 40 pages and about 140 entries. Perhaps reflecting the general neglect of African scholarship on international law,[65] Bradford's list did not have a single entry with a special focus on Africa. It could also be that nothing existed or the little that did exist only 'tangentially connected to ILC or are largely descriptive, rather than analytical'.[66] But if Bradford were to compile a second edition of his bibliography now, he will or should include some African works, not least Viljoen and Louw's 2007 article. This was the first systematic study on State compliance with the decisions of an African regional human rights body. It has inspired more research on this subject with the attendant result that a burgeoning body of compliance literature focusing on the African human rights system now exists.

This section identifies the major trends and issues in this body of literature. It problematizes these by looking at both the method and the scope of inquiry. Five specific trends are discussed: the increasing usage of empirical research; the

[63] Activity Report of the African Court on Human and Peoples' Rights, 1 January to 31 December 2019 (adopted during the 36th Ordinary Session of the Executive Council, Addis Ababa, Ethiopia, 6 to 7 February 2020) EX.CL/1204(XXXVI) para 56.

[64] William Bradford, 'International Legal Compliance: Surveying the Field' (2005) 36 GJIL 495 (Bradford, *International Legal Compliance*).

[65] Christof Heyns and Magnus Killander, 'Africa in International Human Rights Textbooks' (2008) 15 RADIC 130; Frans Viljoen, 'Africa's contribution to the Development of International Human Rights and Humanitarian Law' (2001) 1 AHRLJ 18.

[66] Bradford, *International Legal Compliance* (n 64) 496.

seeming preference for in-depth case studies of cases or countries; the interrogation of unexamined truisms or assumptions; the redirecting of the analytical lens to sub-regional courts and tribunals; and the evaluation of the mechanisms of the regional bodies for monitoring compliance.

3.1 Increasing Usage of Empirical Research

Empirical research is an evidence-based approach to studying a phenomenon; it is concerned with the reality of a situation and the concreteness, accuracy and reliability of information and data. Along this line of understanding, Simmons and Breidenbach have defined 'empirical research' as the 'systematic examination of observable phenomena from which the researcher explicitly seeks to draw broader conclusions about the way the world – or some part of it – works'.[67] Empirical studies are usually divided into those that use either quantitative or qualitative research methods, although many scholars increasingly adopt a combination of the two methods. The arguably most common quantitative method is the large-N statistical analysis with the associated coding and control variables. On the other hand, qualitative approaches include targeted interviews, participant or ethnographic observation, questionnaires and surveys.

Viljoen and Louw's 2007 study is a piece of empirical research par excellence. It proceeded from the premise that commentators who were lamenting about the lack of compliance with the decisions of the ACHPR were doing so on the basis of speculation. It, therefore, sought to draw a more accurate picture based on 'empirical findings'. The authors gathered data about compliance over a three-year period using a series of interviews with ACHPR commissioners and secretariat staff, State representatives, national human rights institutions and NGOs. They also undertook a content analysis of the primary documents of the ACHPR as well as verified media reports. Using the collected data, they developed a coding system in which they categorized the degree of compliance to range from 'non-compliance' to 'full compliance'. 'Partial compliance' and 'situational compliance' also fell somewhere along the continuum. To test what factors are more or less predictive of compliance, they turned to statistical analysis and used the Fisher Exact Test.

In employing qualitative and quantitative approaches to assessing compliance, Viljoen and Louw's study neatly dovetailed into what scholars have called the 'empirical turn' in international legal scholarship generally,[68] and in international

[67] Beth Simmons and Andrew Breidenbach, 'The Empirical Turn in International Economic Law' (2011) 20 Minn J Int'l L 198 (Simmons and Breidenbach, *Empirical Turn*).

[68] Gregory Shaffer and Tom Ginsburg, 'The Empirical Turn in International Legal Scholarship' (2012) 106 AJIL 1 (Shaffer and Ginsburg, *Empirical Turn*); Simmons and Breidenbach, *Empirical Turn* (n 67).

human rights law specifically.[69] Compliance scholars in the African human rights system have followed in their footsteps, systematically and empirically tracking what States do in the post-decision phase or how the mechanisms developed to monitor this phase work in practice.[70] Most writers have adopted desk research combined with qualitative methods of data collection, mainly semi-structured interviews, questionnaires and participant observation. It follows that studies that incorporate statistical or quantitative analysis are particularly few. One that stands out is Ayeni's doctoral thesis that borrows insights from scholars in the European and Inter-American systems to develop a mathematical formula for calculating a new category of compliance called 'aggregate compliance'.[71]

The obvious bias for qualitative approaches to studying compliance in the African system (and indeed elsewhere) is not without reasonable justification. For one, it is a validation of the claim that qualitative approaches are more appropriate for studying state behaviour, such as compliance with decisions of regional or international human rights bodies. As Shaffer and Ginsburg have noted, qualitative approaches allow for a deeper understanding of how legal rules or decisions affect states and non-state actors alike.[72] The preference for qualitative approaches is also a pragmatic choice, or more accurately, a natural adaptation to circumstances. As a general trend across the continent, recorded or official information and data on what governments are doing or have done to implement decisions of regional human rights bodies are unavailable or inaccessible. The regional bodies are also not consistent and proactive in their collection of this data, and whatever is submitted to them by States is usually scant at best or not subsequently released to the public. In other words, neither the States nor the regional bodies have made available a sufficient amount of compliance data that would allow for a rigorous quantitative analysis. In the absence of a repository of data accumulated over time and space, researchers must go out to the field and actively look for information from various sources and actors.

A predictable drawback of qualitative approaches is that since they are context-specific, they are not a very solid and reliable basis for drawing general conclusions that can be extrapolated or applied to other different settings. However, this problem does not necessarily diminish the utility of studies that rely on qualitative

[69] Oona Hathaway, 'The New Empiricism in Human Rights: Insights and Implications' (2004) 98 ASIL Proceedings 206.

[70] The increasing usage of empirical research has not necessarily supplanted theoretical or doctrinal analyses. See eg Chairman Okoloise, 'Circumventing Obstacles to the Implementation of Recommendations by the African Commission on Human and Peoples' Rights' (2018) 18 AHRLJ 27; Rowland Cole, 'The African Court on Human and Peoples' Rights: Will Political Stereotypes Form an Obstacle to the Enforcement of its Decisions' (2010) 43 Comp & Int'l LJ S Afr 23; Roger-Claude Liwanga, 'From Commitment to Compliance: Enforceability of Remedial Orders of Africa Human Rights Bodies' (2015) 41 Brook J Int'l L 99; Katrin Nyman-Metcalf and Ioannis Papageorgiou, 'Why Should We Obey You? Enhancing Implementation of Rulings by Regional Courts' (2017) 1 AHRY 167.

[71] Ayeni, *State Compliance* (n 8).

[72] Shaffer and Ginsburg, *Empirical Turn* (n 68) 5.

approaches. By combining qualitative and quantitative approaches, thus leveraging the relative strengths and advantages of both approaches, researchers have been able to convincingly show that some factors or actors are more relevant than others in inducing or impeding State compliance across geographical boundaries. Still, empirical studies are often fraught with other methodological challenges.[73] The most stubborn of these is the difficulty associated with determining the causal linkages between a decision of an international human rights body and State behaviour. It should not be surprising, therefore, that scholars have always pointed out and scrutinized methodological flaws in each other's work.

The exchange between compliance scholars has occasionally led to intense but insightful debate, such as the one in the 2003 edition of the *European Journal of International Law* between Goodman and Jinks, on the one hand, and Hathaway, on the other.[74] Or the 2011 debate between Posner and Simmons in the *New York University Journal of International Law and Politics*.[75] This level of debate is yet to take place amongst compliance scholars in the African system. However, there is some scrutiny of Viljoen and Louw's categorization of compliance. Their study identified three types of compliance with the decisions of the ACHPR: 'full compliance', denoting the implementation of all the recommendations in a decision or the expression of unequivocal political will to comply; 'partial compliance', describing instances of implementation of only some of the recommendations and 'non-compliance', referring to complete lack of implementation of any of the recommendations. They also coined the term 'situational compliance' to refer to cases of implementation caused by changes in circumstances rather than a positive and deliberate action of the State concerned.

Abebe faults Viljoen and Louw's definition of full compliance because it relies on the notion of political will, which is difficult to measure and may lead to an exaggeration of a State's compliance rate.[76] He also argues that their definition of partial compliance is even more problematic because it 'necessarily expands the concept of compliance, potentially converting instances of functional noncompliance into partial compliance'.[77] After the publication of Viljoen and Louw's study, more nuanced approaches to categorizing compliance have emerged. Focusing on European and Inter-American courts of human rights, Hawkins and Jacoby have disaggregated partial compliance into several discrete forms, including 'split

[73] Harold Jacobson, 'Conceptual, Methodological and Substantive Issues Entwined in Studying Compliance' (1998) 19 MJIL 569.

[74] Ryan Goodman and Derek Jinks, 'Measuring the Effect of Human Rights Treaties' (2003) 14 EJIL 171; Oona Hathaway, 'Testing Conventional Wisdom' (2003) 14 EJIL 185.

[75] Eric Posner, 'Some Skeptical Comments on Beth Simmon's Mobilizing for Human Rights' (2011–2012) 44 NYU J Int'l & Pol 819; Beth Simmons, 'Reflections on Mobilizing for Human Rights' (2011–2012) 44 NYU J Int'l J & Pol 729.

[76] Daniel Abebe, 'Does International Human Rights Law in African Courts Make a Difference?' (2016) 56 Va J Intl L 527, 550.

[77] ibid.

decision', 'state substitution' and 'slow motion compliance'.[78] Others like Hillebrecht and Ayeni have introduced the concept of 'aggregate compliance', which they, separately, use as a proxy for measuring and comparing the compliance records of two or more states or human rights bodies.[79] In its basic understanding, a State or a human rights body's aggregate compliance record is the aggregate of the different categories of compliance, including full, partial and non-compliance, arrived at using a mathematical formula.

3.2 Preference for In-Depth Case Studies

As a baseline study in the African system, Viljoen and Louw's 2007 analysis covered a fairly large number of decisions issued over a relatively long period and concerned a reasonably long list of countries. It tracked the implementation of all 44 decisions in which the ACHPR found violations between 1994 (when the ACHPR first published its decisions) and mid-2003 (the cut-off point for the study). These decisions concerned 17 States Parties to the African Charter. Viljoen and Louw's study remains the most comprehensive in terms of material scope. Subsequent compliance studies have adopted a limited scope, carefully cherry-picking and concentrating on substantially fewer numbers of cases and countries. Indeed, some analyses narrow down to only one or two decisions or countries.[80] A case-study approach thus seems to be emerging as the staple of compliance scholarship in the African system.

The basis for a case or country selection expectedly varies from study to study. A 2017 work by Viljoen takes a thematic approach and explores compliance with four ACHPR decisions that dealt predominantly with socio-economic rights.[81] Comparing the findings of this study with those of the 2007 baseline analysis, he finds an overlap in the factors predictive of compliance in respect of civil and political rights and socio-economic rights. Ayeni focused on decisions issued against five countries: The Gambia, Nigeria, Tanzania, Uganda and Zambia. He further delineated his focus using a time-based criterion that saw the temporal scope run from 1 January 2000 to 31 December 2015. But insofar as it examines a total of 75

[78] Darren Hawkins and Wade Jacoby, 'Partial Compliance: Comparison of the European and Inter-American Courts of Human Rights' (2010) 6 J Int'l L & Int'l Rel 35.

[79] Courtney Hillebrecht, 'Rethinking Compliance: The Challenge and Prospects of Measuring Compliance with International Human Rights Tribunals' (2009) 1 JHRP 362; Ayeni, *State Compliance* (n 8).

[80] Derek Inman and others, 'The (un)willingness to Implement the Recommendations of the African Commission on Human and Peoples' Rights: Revisiting the Endorois and the Mamboleo Decisions' (2018) 2 AHRY 400; Renee Morhe and Richard Mensah, 'State Compliance with Decisions of the African Court: The Case of Alfred Agbesi Woyeme v Ghana' (2019) 3 AHRY 435; Japhet Biegon (ed), *Silver Granules in Stretches of Sand: Implementation of Decisions of Regional Human Rights Treaty Bodies in East Africa* (Kenyan Section of the International Commission of Jurists 2020) forthcoming.

[81] Viljoen, *Domestic Enforcement* (n 6).

remedial orders issued over a 15-year period, Ayeni's doctoral thesis may at first glance seem to be comparatively broad in material scope. However, a closer look, with a disaggregation lens, reveals that it covers orders issued in only 13 decisions of the three AU regional human rights bodies. The rest of the orders he examines are contained in decisions issued by courts operating at the sub-regional level.[82]

The narrow focus of more recent studies allows for closer scrutiny of the political, social and economic contexts in which compliance takes place. The limited scope is also a function of the general inclination towards qualitative research approaches. These approaches almost always go together with in-depth studies of particular cases or countries. In any event, without the availability of accumulated compliance data as discussed above, it would be arduous to conduct studies involving large numbers of cases or countries unless significant resources are channelled towards the involvement of multiple country-based researchers.

3.3 Interrogating and Challenging Assumptions

Compliance scholars across the world have long been in the business of testing the plausibility of assumptions around international law and international relations and how these affect compliance and implementation. One prominent example is the seminal study by Hathaway[83] probing the assumption that a country's ratification of a human rights treaty necessarily leads to improvements of the human rights situation on the ground. She tested this assumption and found that the opposite is more probable. Treaty ratification may have the unexpected effect of relieving pressure off a country and creating room for the human rights situation to worsen.

In the African system, one assumption that has preoccupied the mind and time of scholars concerns the legal status of the decisions of the two regional quasi-judicial bodies – the ACHPR and the ACERWC. The assumption comes in two interrelated parts (1) the decisions of the two bodies are not binding on States because they are 'soft law', and (2) compliance with the decisions is generally low because of their non-binding nature. These assumptions have fuelled the derision that the ACHPR has historically experienced as well as the associated process leading to the establishment of the ACtHPR.

In 2004, Viljoen and Louw challenged the first part of the assumption.[84] They argued that the decisions were legally binding on account of a proper textual and holistic reading of the African Charter and the practice of the ACHPR and the

[82] Infra, s 3.3.

[83] Hathaway, *Human Rights Treaties* (n 14).

[84] Frans Viljoen and Lirette Louw, 'The Status of the Findings of the African Commission: From Moral Persuasion to Legal Obligations' (2004) 48 JAL 1.

AU. Article 1 of the African Charter imposes an obligation on States to recognize and take legislative and other measures to give effect to the rights enshrined in the Charter. The reference to 'other measures' certainly includes the obligation to abide by the decisions of the ACHPR, the body charged with interpreting the Charter. In relation to practice, the AU's action of adopting the ACHPR's activity reports containing these decisions accords them a binding status, 'the act of stating "your findings become ours", is an act of adoption that "converts" the Commission's findings into legal decisions, had they lacked that status previously'.[85]

If Viljoen and Louw challenged the first part of the assumption with strong doctrinal arguments, recent empirical studies have shattered the second with compelling empirical evidence. The two had already prepared the ground back in 2007 when they suggested that the binding nature of the judgments of the ACtHPR would not in itself guarantee improved compliance.[86] They have been proven right by subsequent empirical studies. In a study that adopted interviews and other field activities in order to identify the factors that influence State implementation of the 'findings' of the ACHPR, Murray and Long established that the legal status of the findings is not a decisive factor.[87] Another study reached a similar conclusion. It stated, 'the concern that States may not be implementing the decisions of the African Commission because they are not binding has not so far been borne out in the research we have conducted: in the majority of situations that we have been examining the State has not at all questioned the legal status of the African Commission's decision'.[88]

Perhaps more importantly, by comparing the aggregate rate of compliance with the decisions of the ACHPR vis-à-vis those of sub-regional courts, Ayeni struck at the heart of the assumption. He finds that decisions of the ACHPR have produced more compliance in The Gambia, Nigeria and Zimbabwe compared to the decisions of the relevant sub-regional courts in the same countries.[89] Of course, the sample used in Ayeni's study is significantly small, but he confirms the key finding in Viljoen and Louw's 2007 article that the factors most likely to influence compliance are non-legal (and include a democratic system of government and the involvement of NGOs in submitting cases to regional bodies and subsequently following them up in the post-decision phase).

[85] ibid, 10.

[86] Viljoen and Lirette, *State Compliance* (n 1) 33.

[87] Rachel Murray and Debra Long, *The Implementation of the Findings of the African Commission on Human and Peoples' Rights* (CUP 2015) 24–25.

[88] Rachel Murray and others, 'Monitoring Implementation of the Decisions and Judgments of the African Commission and Court on Human and Peoples' Rights' (2017) 1 *AHRY* 150, 164 (Murray and others, *Monitoring Implementation*).

[89] Ayeni, *State Compliance* (n 8) 120–121.

3.4 Redirecting the Analytical Lens to Sub-Regional Courts

The AU regional human rights bodies co-exist and operate alongside the courts or tribunals of RECs such as the EAC, ECOWAS and SADC. The RECs have been primarily created to foster regional integration and trade, but they have also incorporated some elements of human rights protection in their broader mandates.[90] In the same vein, while the core function of the judicial arms of the RECs is to address disputes arising from issues of regional integration and trade, they increasingly exercise jurisdiction over human rights-related cases. The EAC and ECOWAS courts are the most active in this regard. The East African Court of Justice (EACJ) does not have an express human rights mandate but has used the EAC Treaty as the legal basis for determining human rights cases. The ECOWAS Community Court of Justice (ECCJ) has an explicit human rights jurisdiction. It determines human rights cases on the basis of the African Charter. Before it became defunct in 2012, the SADC Tribunal considered human rights-related cases based on the SADC Treaty. As at the time of writing, there was some movement towards reviving the SADC Tribunal but most likely without the mandate to receive human rights-related cases from individuals.

Scholarship on the sub-regional courts has evolved in three intersecting phases. The first phase was predominated by doctrinal analyses of the human rights mandates of the courts.[91] Then as the courts faced mounting political backlash for issuing far-reaching, if not controversial human rights judgments, scholars naturally turned to examine this issue during the second phase.[92] Scholarship on the courts is now in its third phase. The primary focus is compliance with the judgments of the courts. Two doctoral theses completed at the University of Pretoria in 2013 and 2017 provide comprehensive assessments of State compliance with the judgments of the ECCJ and the EACJ, respectively.[93] Particular sections of the two theses that focus on the 'broader impact' of the judgments have been subsequently converted

[90] See generally Frans Viljoen, 'The Realization of Human Rights in Africa Through Sub-Regional Institutions' [1999] AYBIL 186.

[91] See James Gathii, 'Mission Creep or a Search for Relevance: The East African Court of Justice's Human Rights Strategy' (2013) 24 Duke J Comp & Int'l L 249; Solomon Ebobrah, 'Critical Issues in the Human Rights Mandate of the ECOWAS Court of Justice' (2010) 54 JAL 1; Karen Alter and others, 'A New International Human Rights Court for West Africa: The ECOWAS Community Court of Justice' (2013) 107 AJIL 737; Solomon Ebobrah, A Rights-Protection Goldmine or a Waiting Volcanic Eruption? Competence of, and Access to, the Human Rights Jurisdiction of the ECOWAS Community Court of Justice' (2007) 7 AHRLJ 328.

[92] Karen Alter and others, 'Backlash Against International Courts in West, East and Southern Africa: Causes and Consequences' (2016) 27 EJIL 293; Laurie Nathan, 'The Disbanding of the SADC Tribunal: A Cautionary Tale' (2013) 35 HRQ 870; Erika de Wet, 'The Rise and Fall of the Tribunal of the Southern Africa Development Community: Implications for Dispute Settlement in Southern Africa' (2013) 28 ICSID Rev 45.

[93] Horace Adjolohoun, 'Giving Effect to the Human Rights Jurisprudence of the Court of Justice of the Economic Community for West African States: Compliance and Influence' (Unpublished LLD Thesis, University of Pretoria 2013); Victor Lando, 'The Domestic Effect of the East African Community's Human Rights Practice' (Unpublished LLD Thesis, University of Pretoria 2017).

to journal articles.[94] Ayeni's thesis also covers compliance with selected judgments of the two sub-regional courts.

The studies on compliance with and impact of the judgments of the sub-regional courts show that the judgments have had numerous catalytic effects within the States concerned as well as in neighbouring countries. For example, Horace argues that the *Koraou Judgment*[95] concerning the practice of slavery in Niger has impacted human rights systems and mechanisms beyond ECOWAS, including in Mauritania, where slavery is prevalent.[96] Lando similarly finds that the judgment of the EACJ in the *Anyang' Nyong'o Case*[97] not only spurred legal reform in Kenya but it also had the spill-over effect of precipitating similar suits in relation to Tanzania and Uganda, which subsequently prompted changes in law and policy in the two countries.[98] These findings lend credence to the argument that international human rights law, in its many forms and guise, is an impactful tool in socializing and mobilizing state and non-state domestic actors.[99]

3.5 Evaluating Mechanisms for Monitoring Compliance

A new strand of empirical research evaluates the mechanisms established by the regional bodies to monitor and follow-up compliance. In their 2007 study, Viljoen and Louw examined whether follow-up by the ACHPR was predictive of compliance. They found that it was indeed a relevant factor and that the *ad hoc* nature of the follow-up activities had inhibited State compliance.[100] Scholars have interrogated this issue further, mainly in reaction to the efforts of the regional bodies to institutionalize follow-up mechanisms and regularize their practice in that regard. In collaboration with others, Murray has led the research on this front.[101] A major finding in the literature is that while there is now a flurry of follow-up activities being undertaken by the ACHPR and the ACtHPR, a coherent or strategic approach is yet to be adopted. It is also evident that the two regional bodies have

94 Horace Adjolohoun, 'The ECOWAS Court as a Human Rights Promoter? Assessing Five Years' Impact of the Koraou Slavery Judgment' (2013) 31 NQHR 342 (Adjolohoun, *Koraou Judgment*); Victor Lando, 'The Domestic Impact of the Decisions of the East African Court of Justice' (2018) 18 AHRLJ 463 (Lando, *Domestic Impact of EACJ*).

95 (2008) AHRLR 182 (ECOWAS 2008).

96 Adjolohoun, *Koraou Judgment* (n 94) 367.

97 [2006] EACJ 3 (27 November 2006).

98 Lando, *Domestic Impact of EACJ* (n 94) 469–471.

99 See generally Simmons, *Mobilizing for Human Rights* (n 14).

100 Viljoen and Louw, *State Compliance* (n 1) 17.

101 Rachel Murray and others, *Monitoring Implementation* (n 88); Rachel Murray and Elizabeth Mottershaw, 'Mechanisms for the Implementation of Decisions of the African Commission on Human and Peoples' Rights' (2014) 26 HRQ 349; Rachel Murray, 'Confidentiality and the Implementation of the Decisions of the African Commission on Human and Peoples' Rights' (2019) 19 AHRLJ 1 (Murray, *Confidentiality and Implementation*).

no specific yardsticks for measuring compliance or verifying the information submitted to them by States.

The ACERWC is a notable exception in terms of some consistency in undertaking follow-up activities. In relation to its decisions concerning Kenya and Senegal, it has conducted country visits to follow-up on implementation and held public hearings to assess the actual extent of compliance.[102] It has also closely monitored the implementation of the amicable settlement that Malawi entered with the complainants in a case concerning the definition of a child under the laws of the country.[103]

One previously unexamined issue is the potential impact of the confidentiality clause in Article 59 of the African Charter on the implementation of ACHPR decisions. Article 59(1) provides that 'all measures taken within the provisions of the present chapter shall remain confidential until the Assembly of Heads of State and Government shall otherwise decide'. This provision has long been seen largely as an impediment in the realization of access to information insofar as it shrouds in secrecy the communications procedure of the ACHPR.[104] However, the new empirical analysis shows that although the provision is inapplicable to the post-decision phase, the ACHPR has extended it to this phase, thereby adversely affecting efforts by other relevant actors to monitor implementation.[105] In a sense, the ACHPR wrongly applies the provision resulting in the concealment of a range of critical information, including the measures taken by States to implement decisions, the evidence presented to it by complainants and its own assessment of compliance.

4 Future Research Agenda and Trajectory

The corpus of compliance studies in the African system is growing, but it is still relatively modest in breadth and depth. Much remains to be written, and many questions are still unanswered. Several relevant doctoral theses are yet to be converted into publications. New lines of inquiry still need to be opened. There is also the necessity to diversify the methodological approaches to include greater use of quantitative and statistical methods. The implementation of many cases and the compliance rate of many countries remain unexamined. The small sample of cases and countries that most existing studies cover has meant that authors are keen to

[102] Benyam Mezmur and Mbuton Kahbila, 'Follow-up as a "Choice-less Choice": Towards Improving the Implementation of Decisions on Communications of the African Children's Committee' (2018) 2 AHRY 200, 215–218.

[103] ibid, 218–219. See also Benyam Mezmur, 'No Second Chance for First Impressions: The First Amicable Settlement Under the African Children's Charter' (2019) 19 AHRLJ 62, 83–84.

[104] Magnus Killander, 'Confidentiality Versus Publicity: Interpreting Article 59 of the African Charter on Human and Peoples' Rights' (2006) 6 AHRLJ 574.

[105] Murray, *Confidentiality and Implementation* (n 101).

advise that the findings and conclusions therein should not be quickly generalized or extrapolated.

I do not intend to catalogue here all the areas and corners to which literature may expand and stretch. Instead, I suggest two potential routes that compliance scholars should perhaps pursue to build a more robust body of knowledge. First, I argue for more energy to be channelled towards generating interdisciplinary research, a task that calls for greater involvement of non-lawyers in the enterprise of studying compliance and implementation in the African system. Second, I suggest that much more attention should be directed at understanding the broader impact of the decisions of regional bodies, that is, the indirect effects of the decisions at the domestic level, such as changes in societal attitudes and public discourse.

4.1 Interdisciplinary Research and Collaborations

Compliance studies in the African system are predominantly legal because it is mostly international human rights lawyers who churn them out. The studies are primarily conducted in law faculties and published in legal journals. Yet, these very studies show that implementation and compliance primarily hinge on non-legal factors such as politics, history, relations and social-cultural contexts. Lawyers, trained to be textual analysts of mainly laws and procedures, are admittedly constrained in untangling State behaviour concerning compliance and implementation.[106] They must seek to understand these other disciplines and incorporate insights from them in their study of compliance and/or join hands with other experts in producing such studies.[107] On this, there is a great lesson to be borrowed from Viljoen.

In his pivotal book, *International Human Rights Law in Africa*, Viljoen admits that he writes as someone trained in international law and not in other disciplines.[108] He adds, 'my writing joins the dominant "legal" discourse, but it does so self-consciously, while making modest efforts to broaden and supplement that approach'.[109] It is not surprising that Viljoen subsequently created a forum and space for a discourse on the nexus between human rights law and a range of other disciplines.[110] He also consistently calls on international human rights lawyers to

[106] On the nature and limits of legal research methods in studying human rights, see generally Fons Coomans and others (eds), *Methods of Human Rights Research* (Intersentia 2009).

[107] This kind of collaboration would not be new. International lawyers have long collaborated, for instance, with international relations experts. See Anne-Marie Slaughter and others, 'International Law and International Relations Theory: A New Generation of Interdisciplinary Scholarship' (1998) 92 AJIL 367. Examples of compliance studies in the Africa system authored through interdisciplinary collaborations include Nyman-Metcalf and Papageorgiou (n 70).

[108] Viljoen, *Human Rights Law in Africa* (n 48) 41.

[109] ibid.

[110] Frans Viljoen (ed), *Beyond the Multi-disciplinary Perspectives on Human Rights* (Pretoria University Law Press 2012). Viljoen has also been the singular force behind the expansion of the academic post-graduate programme on human rights and democratization in Africa offered at the Centre

broaden their frame of analysis to include perceptions from other disciplines and collaborate with political scientists, anthropologists, sociologists, historians and international relations scholars.[111]

Social scientists in Africa must also take the initiative and engage in compliance scholarship. Existing studies discussed above already show lawyers' impressive incorporation of social science research methodologies. In some of these, social scientists have played a role, albeit as advisors or expert assistants. Time is ripe for them to originate the studies themselves. Beyond the continent, social scientists have been active in generating human rights scholarship more generally.[112] They are also active in studying State behaviour in respect of international law.[113] The greater involvement of social scientists in studying compliance in the African human rights system will no doubt bring important and much-needed new insights and approaches.[114]

4.2 Broader Impact of Decisions

The core objective of compliance studies in the African system is to assess the extent to which States implement the specific orders or recommendations contained in cases issued by the regional bodies. This constitutes the 'direct impact' of the decisions. Direct impact may be *de jure*, such as the legal reform that Lando describes in his analysis of the impact of EACJ cases.[115] Direct impact may also be de facto, such as Niger's payment of compensation to the complainant in the *Koraou*

for Human Rights, Faculty of Law, University of Pretoria, to include non-lawyers who graduate with an MPhil degree upon completion. Under his leadership, the Centre for Human Rights has, in the last decade, adopted a more multidisciplinary approach in all its programmes and activities.

[111] See eg Viljoen, *Contemporary Challenges* (n 13) 217 (making the following appeal: 'International human rights lawyers have to work with relevant experts or acquire the skills required to engage with the real effects of human rights [whether provided for at the international or domestic level] in the lives of real people. The effect of these insights on norm creators and operators may, in turn, be both sobering and inspiring)'.

[112] A 2009 review of major political science journals shows that while before 1980 they carried just over 30 human rights-related articles, the number rose steadily each decade since the 1980s. To be exact, 85% more human rights-related articles were published in major political science journals in the 2000s than in the 1990s. See Sonia Cardenas, 'Mainstreaming Human Rights: Publishing Trends in Political Science' (2009) 42 PS Polit Sci & Polit 161.

[113] Emilie Hafner-Burton and others, 'Political Science Research on International Law: The State of the Field' (2012) 106 AJIL 47.

[114] A good recent example of the intellectual benefits that may accrue from an interdisciplinary approach to studying cases in the African system is Brenda Kombo's analysis of the African Court's case in *APDF and IHRDA v Mali* 2018 2 *RJCA* 393. Both a lawyer and an anthropologist, Kombo analyses the case using an interdisciplinary approach combining doctrinal legal research methodology and legal anthropology to situate the case in a broader socio-cultural and historical context. See Brenda Kombo, 'Silences that Speak Volumes: The Significance of the African Court Decision in *APDF and IHRDA v Mali* for Women's Human Rights on the Continent' (2019) 3 AHRY 389.

[115] Lando, *Domestic Impact of EACJ* (n 94).

Judgment.[116] Focus on direct impact necessarily leads to the adoption of a frame of analysis that is both compliance and state centric.[117] This frame is not sufficient if one intends, as it should be the case, to also understand the 'broader' or 'indirect' impact of decisions. In this context, indirect impact refers to 'the manifold ways in which international human rights law may influence prevailing discourses, in changing attitudes and thinking, in raising awareness and the like'.[118]

Existing studies already acknowledge and attempt to assess the indirect impact of the decisions of regional bodies. A leading study in this regard is Okafor's analysis of how civil society actors in Nigeria and South Africa have integrated the African Charter and the decisions of the ACHPR in their programmes, action and thinking.[119] Although criticized for lapses in methodology,[120] the study is a good starting point for in-depth studies on the indirect impact of the decisions of all three regional bodies. Indeed, Okafor invites readers to consider his conclusions as 'tentative guides for ongoing future thought and action in this area'.[121] A few scholars have already taken the challenge from him and scrutinized, for instance, the extent to which and how decisions of regional bodies are cited and used in domestic constitutional litigation.[122] But more analysis is still required. There is a particular need to expand the assessment of indirect impact to go beyond the legal sphere and to cover other relevant spaces and discourses.

Two studies concerning the indirect impact of the ACHPR decision in *CEMIRIDE and MRG on behalf of Endorois Welfare Council v Kenya* (*Endorois Decision*)[123] may point us to a potential future direction of travel for research. The first is a 2011 academic piece by a scholar of comparative politics.[124] She examines the potential of the decision to trigger discourses of identity, indigeneity and belonging both within and outside the Endorois community. Within the community, as soon as the decision was delivered, a debate ensued on who is and is not an Endorois and thus who should and should not benefit from the ACHPR decision. Indeed, the legitimacy of the Endorois Welfare Council as the community's representative organization was put into question.[125] The second is a policy study

[116] Adjolohoun, *Koraou Judgment* (n 94) 346.
[117] Chinedu Okafor, *The African Human Rights System: Activist Forces and International Institutions* (CUP 2007) 30–31, 33–35.
[118] Viljoen, *Exploring Theory and Practice* (n 16) 180.
[119] Okafor, *Activist Forces* (n 117).
[120] Viljoen, *Exploring Theory and* Practice (n 16) 181.
[121] Okafor, *Activist Forces* (n 117) 301.
[122] Bonolo Dinokopila, 'The Impact of Regional and Sub-regional Courts and Tribunals on Constitutional Adjudication in Africa' in Charles Fombad (ed) *Constitutional Adjudication in Africa* (OUP 2017) 225.
[123] (2009) AHRLR 75 (ACHPR 2009).
[124] Gabrielle Lynch, 'Becoming Indigenous in the Pursuit of Justice:
The African Commission on Human and Peoples' Rights and the Endorois' (2011) 111/142 African Affairs 24.
[125] ibid, 41.

by the NGO (ESCR-Net).[126] It explores how the involvement of Endorois women in advocacy and campaigning activities calling for State implementation of the *Endorois Decision* has affected gender norms within the community. Although the key recommendations of the ACHPR have not been implemented, the study finds that the *Endorois Decision* has provided the impetus to advance substantive gender equality in the community.

5 Conclusion

As a tribute to Viljoen, this chapter examines some of the human rights themes and issues that he is most passionate about and in which he has a proven record of thought leadership. Yet, it only scratches the surface in terms of highlighting his immense contribution to the growth and maturity of the African regional human rights system and the academic scholarship around it. For compliance scholars and indeed many human rights researchers, the study of how international human rights law percolates from the international arena to the domestic setting is an intellectually stimulating and fulfilling endeavour. It may thus be too easy to forget that at the heart of compliance studies is the fate and plight of real people – women, men and children hailing from diverse backgrounds, histories and geographies – and that the purpose of scholarship is to contribute to (re)imagining and (re)creating a better world. It is this broader vision that has inspired and continues to inspire Viljoen's writings, teachings and activism. It is indeed this vision that drew him to the study of international human rights law in the first place. I should end by letting him tell us in his own words how that happened:[127]

> My interest in international human rights law dates from the time when, as a law student at the University of Pretoria in the mid-1980s, I came to appreciate its importance to the struggle against apartheid, and its role in discrediting apartheid locally and abroad. Not only was it pivotal in the birth and growth of the African National Congress, but human rights law provided the window through which I, a white South African, could critically assess myself and the society in which I was living. International human rights served as the basis for the 'shame' that was mobilized around the world, and which impacted nationally in South Africa.

[126] ESCR-Net, *The Emerging Leadership of Endorois Women: An Indirect Impact of the Endorois Case* (ESCR-Net, 2019).

[127] Viljoen, *Human Rights Law in Africa* (n 48) xi.

3

Beyond Compliance

Do Decisions of Regional Human Rights Tribunals in Africa Make a Difference?

Victor Ayeni

1 Introduction

Analysis of human rights judgment compliance is one of the fastest growing subfields of international legal scholarship.[1] Some scholars have claimed that compliance is a primary test of the adequacy of international law.[2] Oette, for example, argues that compliance and enforcement constitute 'a litmus test for the effectiveness of the international human rights system'.[3] Using compliance as a test of the effectiveness of human rights bodies, described in this chapter as human rights tribunals (HRTs), implies that without a theory of state compliance, it is impossible to assess the effectiveness of HRTs. Effectiveness, for this purpose, is defined as the extent or degree to which the decision of an HRT induces the desired change at the

[1] Robert Howse and Ruti Teitel, 'Beyond Compliance: Rethinking Why International Law Really Matters' (2010) 174 New York University Public Law and Legal Theory Working Papers 1, 2; Oona A Hathaway, 'Do Human Rights Treaties Make a Difference?' (2002) 111 YLJ 1935, 1935–2042. Some of the recent works on human rights judgment compliance include Darren Hawkins and Wade Jacoby, 'Partial Compliance: Comparison of the European and Inter-American Courts of Human Rights' (2010–2011) 6 JILIR 35, 35–85; James L Cavallaro and Stephanie E Brewer, 'Reevaluating Regional Human Rights Litigation in the Twenty-First Century: The Case of the Inter-American Court' (2008) 102 AJIL 768, 768–827; Courtney Hillebrecht, 'The Effect of International Human Rights Tribunals on Domestic Practice and Policy' (Unpublished PhD thesis, University of Wisconsin-Madison, 2010); Diana Kapiszewski and Matthew M Taylor, 'Compliance: Conceptualizing, Measuring, and Explaining Adherence to Judicial Rulings' (2013) 38 LSI 803, 803–835. For an annotated bibliography of the major works on compliance with international law, see William C Bradford, 'International Legal Compliance: An Annotated Bibliography' (2004) 30 NCJ Int' Law 379, 379–423.

[2] See, for instance, Andrew T Guzman, 'A Compliance-Based Theory of International Law' (2002) 90 CLR 1823, 1826; Oona A Hathaway, 'Between Power and Principle: An Integrated Theory of International Law' (2005) UCLR 469, 473; Beth A Simmons, 'Compliance with International Agreements' (1998) 1 Ann Rev Polit Sci 75, 75; Jana V Stein, 'Do Treaties Constrain or Screen? Selection Bias and Treaty Compliance' (2005) 99 APSR 611, 611; Shima Baradaran and others, 'Does International Law Matter?' (2013) 97 MLR 743, 743.

[3] Lutz Oette, 'Bringing the Enforcement Gap: Compliance of States Parties with Decisions of Human Rights Treaty Body' (2010) 16 Interights Bulletin 51, 51.

Victor Ayeni, *Beyond Compliance* In: *Compliance with International Human Rights Law in Africa*. Edited by: Aderomola Adeola, Oxford University Press. © Victor Ayeni 2022. DOI: 10.1093/oso/9780192856999.003.0003

domestic level.[4] Far too many observers of HRTs evaluate the effectiveness of international human rights regimes from equivalent understandings of domestic legal systems.[5] HRTs that operate much like domestic courts are considered strong and effective, while those that function differently are considered 'weak' or 'ineffective'.[6] For these scholars, the future of HRTs' decisions lies in their similarity to the judicial processes at the domestic level; the closer HRTs are to their domestic equivalent, the more effective they are likely to be.[7]

However, Howse and Teitel have challenged this emerging orthodoxy based on an analogy between international HRTs and domestics courts, and argue that to be effective, HRTs do not have to operate and generate compliance exactly like domestic courts. Too much focus on compliance 'obfuscates the character of international legal normativity', and the concept of compliance, especially viewed as rule observance, is inadequate for understanding how international law has normative effects.[8] The need to reach beyond the compliance optic, without abandoning it, has been articulated by many scholars.[9] Okafor, for instance, argues that the compliance-focused frame of reference is inadequate as a way of understanding the worth or value of international HRTs fully and that state compliance does not exhaust the totality of ways decisions of HRTs can matter fundamentally or have significant effects at the domestic level.[10] Compliance-centric narratives result in a near-exclusive focus on states, state actors and state actions.[11] While the compliance narrative should admittedly be the starting point of the analysis of the impact and overall effectiveness of HRTs, it should not be the ultimate measure of the efficacy of HRTs' decisions.[12]

[4] See Rachel Murray and Debra Long, *The Implementation of the Findings of the African Commission on Human and Peoples' Rights* (CUP 2015) 29; Kal Raustiala, 'Compliance and Effectiveness in International Regulatory Cooperation' (2000) 32 Case W Res J Int'l L 387, 393–394.

[5] See, for instance, Martti Koskenniemi's arguments in Martti Koskenniemi, 'The Pull of the Mainstream' (1990) 88 Mich L R 1946, 1954–1955.

[6] See Richard Gittleman, 'The African Charter on Human and Peoples' Rights' (1981–1982) 22 VJIL 667, 694; Henry J Steiner and Philip Alston, *International Human Rights in Context: Law, Politics and Morals* (OUP 2000) 920; Joseph Oloka-Onyango, 'Human Rights and Sustainable Development in Contemporary Africa: A New Dawn, or Retreating Horizons?' (2000) 6 Buff Hum Rts L R 72, 72.

[7] See, for instance, Obiora C Okafor, *The African Human Rights System: Activist Forces and International Institutions* (CUP 2007) 276.

[8] Howse and Teitel (n 1) 2.

[9] See César Rodríguez-Garavito, 'Beyond Enforcement: Assessing and Enhancing Judicial Impact' in Malcolm Langford, César Rodríguez-Garavito and Julieta Rossi (eds), *Social Rights Judgments and the Politics of Compliance: Making It Stick* (CUP 2017) 79–108; Howse and Teitel (n 1) 2; Okafor (n 7) 273; Murray and Long (n 4) 69–86; Victor O Ayeni (ed), *The Impact of the African Charter and the Maputo Protocol in Selected African States* (2016) 1–331; Horace S Adjolohoun, 'Giving Effect to the Human Rights Jurisprudence of the Court of Justice of the Economic Community of West African States: Compliance and Influence' (Unpublished LLD thesis, University of Pretoria 2013), 264–317; Faith N Kabata, 'Impact of International Human Rights Monitoring Mechanisms in Kenya' (Unpublished LLD thesis, University of Pretoria 2015).

[10] Okafor (n 7) 33, 285.

[11] Okafor (n 7) 31; Murray and Long (n 4) 69; Dia Anagnostou and Alina Mungiu-Pippidi, *Why Do States Implement Differently the European Court of Human Rights Judgment? The Case on Civil Liberties and the Rights of Minorities* (JURISTRAS Project, 2009).

[12] ibid.

The primary shortcoming of the compliance frame is its narrowness. The most important aspect of a decision that matters for compliance analysis is the reparation order. Even though the communication procedure of HRTs was established primarily to provide tangible remedies to victims of human rights violations, it also serves the purpose of interpreting provisions of human rights treaties to guide future actions of states.[13] The compliance-focused narrative is ill-designed to evaluate the 'vertical' and 'horizontal' influences of the interpretive enterprise in which HRTs are engaged. Reparation orders constitute only a small, although important, part of the jurisprudence of HRTs. Every part of a tribunal's decision serves a purpose; so is every stage of a tribunal's complaint procedure. Why then should one component of the process be used as the sole determinant of the effectiveness of HRTs' regimes? Why should the effectiveness of an HRT be determined solely by cases won by the complainants? In fact, why does a case have to be decided on the merits before it can contribute to HRTs' goal of domestic human rights change? Drawing from these questions, this chapter argues that the compliance optic, though important, is too narrow to evaluate the contributions of HRTs' decisions to domestic human rights change in the selected African states.

Another shortcoming of a compliance-focused narrative is 'state-centrism'.[14] Compliance analysis usually focuses almost exclusively on states and state institutions.[15] It has been argued that the focus on states and state institutions as primary actors in international law compliance downplays the transnational processes leading to domestic human rights change and the roles of non-state actors, subnational entities, civil society organizations and social movements in creating the necessary impetus and momentum that produce human rights change.[16] Since compliance analysis is mostly concerned with the correspondence between specific reparation orders and actions of state actors, it usually fails to account for indirect and other unintended contributions of HRTs' decisions to the promotion of human rights at the domestic level. Any contribution of an HRT's decision, no matter how important, that is not directly linked to a reparation order, is statistically insignificant in a compliance analysis.

Like most theories of compliance with international law, human rights judgment compliance theories tend to undertheorize the criticality of 'interpretation, interaction and internationalization' to how decisions and reparation orders of HRTs obtain their meaning.[17] It is generally assumed that reparation orders of HRTs have an agreed meaning. One of the important questions often taken for granted in human rights judgment compliance literature is the nature of international legal

[13] See, for instance, African Charter, art 45(3); African Children's Rights Charter, art 42(c); African Court Protocol, art 3.
[14] Okafor (n 7) 43, 49.
[15] Baradaran and others (n 2) 747.
[16] ibid.
[17] See a similar argument in Howse and Teitel (n 1) 3.

obligation and the defining moment when it comes into being. International legal obligations are quite fluid and evolve. The adoption of a treaty or the delivery of a decision by an HRT is the beginning of a broad process of norm internalization and adherence.[18] Many legal experts advocated alternative lenses of looking at the law, and in this case, a decision as a process rather than a finished product.[19] The only way to fully understand international law, whether treaty provisions or reparation orders of HRTs, is to 'situate it within a broader social context'.[20] Koh has articulated the view that international law is complied with through a three-part process of *interaction, interpretation* and *internalization.*[21] Building on Koh's transnational legal process theory, Alkoby argues that 'even after binding commitments are made, their clarification, interpretation and implementation is constantly renegotiated and reflected upon in light of changing circumstances, new information, or a deepening consensus among the key actors'.[22] The domestic effects of HRTs' decisions may only be understood fully in the light of these transnational processes.

Accounts of the rates of compliance with decisions of HRTs are mostly simplistic and reductionist and do not provide an accurate picture of the manifold ways in which decisions and communication procedures of HRTs are effective at the domestic level. Often, compliance is the result of coincidence, inadvertence or reasons extrinsic to decisions of HRTs.[23] One of the primary shortcomings of existing scholarship and approaches to human rights judgment compliance is that they fail to consider the time taken to achieve compliance so long as eventual compliance is recorded.[24] In some cases, the time taken to respond to a decision can be a matter of life and death for the victims. Thus, a decision that has a high compliance rate may have a low positive impact value and the other way around.

In many cases, African regional and sub-regional HRTs do not issue reparation orders for states to implement. Even in cases where some reparation orders are issued, these orders are clearly inadequate. In landmark decisions, such as the *Jawara v The Gambia* (*Jawara* case)[25] and the *Katabazi* case,[26] only one reparation order

[18] See Asher Alkoby, 'Theories of Compliance with International Law and the Challenge of Cultural Difference' (2008) 4 JILIR 151, 152.

[19] See Harold H Koh, 'The 1994 Roscoe Pound Lecture: Transnational Legal Process' (1996) 75 Neb Law Rev 181, 181–207 (Koh, *Transnational Legal Process*); Alkoby (n 18); Martha Finnemore and Stephen J Toope, 'Alternatives to 'Legalization': Richer Views of Law and Politics' (2001) 55 IO 743, 750.

[20] Alkoby (n 18).

[21] Koh 'Transnational Legal Process' (n 19) 203–205; Harold H Koh, 'The 1998 Frankel Lecture: Bringing International Law Home' (1998) 35 Hous Law Rev 623, 626 (Koh 'Bringing International Law Home').

[22] Alkoby (n 18).

[23] See Ayeni (n 9) 9; Raustiala (n 4) 391.

[24] Courtney Hillebrecht, *Domestic Politics and International Human Rights Tribunals: The Problem of Compliance* (CUP 2014) 375–376.

[25] *Jawara v The Gambia* (2000) AHRLR 107 (ACHPR 2000).

[26] *Katabazi and Others v Secretary-General of the EAC and Attorney General of Uganda* (2007) AHRLR 119 (EAC 2007) decided by the EACJ on 1 December 2007.

was issued by the relevant HRTs. A compliance frame of analysis is, no doubt, inadequate to evaluate the contributions of the above-listed cases to domestic human rights change in Africa. The point is that the notion of compliance is much too narrow an angle of vision to capture the domestic legal effects and influence of the decisions of regional and sub-regional HRTs in Africa.[27]

The impact of the decisions of the selected HRTs obviously can go beyond the five African states selected for analysis in this chapter. This is because judgments of some of the selected HRTs, such as the African Court, ECCJ, EACJ and SADC Tribunal, arguably have *erga omnes* effects. The International Court of Justice (ICJ), for instance, in the *Barcelona Traction* case, distinguished between the obligations of states towards other individual states and obligations towards the international community as a whole.[28] The latter obligation is referred to as *erga omnes*, and all states have a legal interest in its protection. According to Abebe, 'scholars working from this perspective are concerned not only with the ex post behavior of the parties in a given case but also with the behavior of all states' subject to the jurisdiction of the HRTs'.[29] The impact of the decisions of the selected HRTs may also go beyond the five states chosen on the basis of the *res interpretata* theory. The interpretive content of decisions given by the selected HRTs binds all state parties to the relevant human rights treaty interpreted by the tribunal.[30]

Drawing from the above arguments, this chapter examines the various forms of legal effects and impact of selected decisions of six regional and sub-regional HRTs in the five selected states, namely Nigeria, Tanzania, The Gambia, Uganda and Zimbabwe. The HRTs chosen for the study are: The African Commission on Human and Peoples' Rights (African Commission), African Court on Human and Peoples' Rights (African Court), African Committee of Experts on the Rights and Welfare of the Child (African Children's Rights Committee), ECCJ, EACJ and the Tribunal of the Southern African Development Community (SADC Tribunal). The cases selected are those decided by the respective tribunals between 1 January 2000 and 31 December 2015 (the two cut-off dates for the study).[31] Throughout

[27] Howse and Teitel (n 1) 4.

[28] See *Barcelona Traction, Light and Power Company Ltd* (Second Phase) [1970] ICJ Rep 32; *Legality of the Threat or Use of Nuclear Weapons* (Advisory Opinion) 1996 ICJ Rep 226; *Legal Consequences of the Construction of a Wall in the Occupied Palestinian Territory* (Advisory Opinion) 2004 ICJ Rep 15. See also Erika de Wet, 'Invoking Obligations *Erga Omnes* in the Twenty-First Century: Progressive Developments Since Barcelona Traction' (2013) 38 SAYIL 1, 2; Karl Zemanec, 'New Trends in the Enforcement of *Erga Omnes* Obligations' (2000) 4 Max Planck Yearbook of United Nations Law 1–52.

[29] Daniel Abebe, 'Does International Human Rights Law in African Courts Make a Difference?' (2017) 56 VGIL 527, 533–534.

[30] See generally Adam Bodnar, '*Res Interpretata*: Legal Effect of the European Court of Human Rights' Judgments for Other States than Those Which were Party to the Proceedings' in Yves Haeck and Eva Brems (eds), *Human and Civil Liberties in the 21st Century* (2014) 223–262; Armin von Bogdandy and others (eds), *Transformative Constitutionalism in Latin America: The Emergence of a New Ius Commune* (OUP 2017) 401.

[31] The full list of the 32 selected cases is as follows: **African Commission:** Communication 205/97 *Kazeem Aminu v Nigeria*; Communication 224/98 *Media Rights Agenda v Nigeria*; Communication 218/98 *Civil Liberties Organisation and Others v Nigeria*; Communication 155/96 *Social and Economic*

the article, the terms 'impact', 'effects' and 'influence' are used interchangeably. The conceptualization of 'impact' draws from various studies, including Heyns and Viljoen,[32] Okafor[33] and Kabata.[34] The chapter is divided into four sections, namely, introduction, what constitutes the impact of HRTs' decisions, examples of the impact of HRTs' decisions and conclusion.

The argument made throughout this chapter is not that HRTs' decisions alone have caused domestic human rights change but that the relevant decisions of the selected HRTs contributed in a valuable way to the eventual outcome. In other words, the claims made in this chapter with respect to the impact of HRTs' decisions are not one of attribution but contribution. Because correlation does not necessarily mean causation, this chapter does not attempt to draw causal links but only to establish correlations and contributions. The focus is also not only on the reparation orders but the entire decision, and in a few cases, the communication procedure of the selected HRTs from submission of the communication to the issuance of findings.

2 What Constitutes the Impact of a Human Rights Decision?

The impact of an HRT's decision is the totality of effects or influences of the decision in the promotion and protection of human rights at the national, regional and global levels.[35] Other scholars, such as Swart, define the impact of HRTs' decisions as the influence exerted by the existence and work of international human

Rights Action Centre (SERAC) v Nigeria; Communication 147/95 and 149/96 *Jawara v The Gambia*; Communication 241/2001 *Purohit v The Gambia*; Communication 245/2002 *Zimbabwe Human Rights NGO Forum v Zimbabwe*; Communication 284/2003 *ZLHR v Zimbabwe*; Communication 294/2004 *ZLHR & IHRD v Zimbabwe*; Communication 297/2005 *Scanlen & Holderness v Zimbabwe*; Communication 288/2004 *Shumba v Zimbabwe*; Communication 295/04 *Noah Kazingachire and others v Zimbabwe*. **African Court:** Application 009 and 011/2011 *Mtikila and Others v Tanzania*; Application No 005/2013 *Alex Thomas v Tanzania*. **African Children's Rights Committee:** Communication 2/2009 *Hansungule and Others (on behalf of children in Northern Uganda) v Uganda*. ECCJ: ECW/CCJ/JUD/01/09 *Djot Bayi v Nigeria*; ECW/CCJ/JUD/07/10 *SERAP v Nigeria (Education)*; ECW/CCJ/JUD/18/12 *SERAP v Nigeria (Environment)*; ECW/CCJ/JUD/01/14 *Alimu Akeem v Nigeria*; ECW/CCJ/JUD/15/14 *Modupe Dorcas Afolalu v Nigeria*; ECW/CCJ/APP/10/10 *SERAP v Nigeria (Bundu Waterfront* case); ECW/CCJ/JUD/03/08 *Manneh v The Gambia*; ECW/CCJ/JUD/08/10 *Saidykhan v The Gambia*; ECW/CCJ/PP/30/11 *Deyda Hydara v The Gambia*. **EACJ:** Ref 1 of 2007 *Katabazi v Uganda & Others*; Ref No 1 of 2010 *Sibalu v Uganda*; Ref No 5 of 2011 *Mohochi v Uganda*; Ref No 2 of 2012 *Among Anita v Uganda*; Ref No 9 of 2010 *African Network for Animal Welfare v Tanzania*. **SADC Tribunal**: SADCT 07/2008 *Tembani v Zimbabwe*; SADCT 02/2007 *Campbell v Zimbabwe*; SADCT 05/2008 *Dongo v Zimbabwe*.

[32] Christof Heyns and Frans Viljoen (eds), *The Impact of the United Nations Human Rights Treaties on the Domestic Level* (Kluwer International Law 2002) 1.
[33] Okafor (n 7).
[34] Kabata (n 9).
[35] See Heyns and Viljoen (n 32) 1. See also Murray and Long (n 4) 70.

rights bodies.[36] This influence may be direct or indirect.[37] While the direct effect of a human rights decision is immediate and anticipated, the indirect effect is less immediate, incidental and incremental.[38] Although the decision of an HRT may undoubtedly have consequences beyond the domestic arena, the primary focus of the analysis in this chapter is the domestic level effects of human rights decisions. HRTs' decisions may have effects at the domestic level in a variety of ways. Four distinctions, at least, can be made: positive and negative impact, intended and unintended impact, direct and indirect impact, ex ante and ex post impact.[39]

The impact of an HRT's decision may be positive or negative; it is positive if the decision leads to an improvement in human rights condition at the domestic level; and negative if human rights condition in a state deteriorates because of the decision.[40] Negative impact includes cases where a decision receives violent resistance, opposition or political backlash. The impact of an HRT's decision is intended if it is anticipated by the tribunal and unintended if the impact is merely accidental.[41] A direct impact of a human rights decision is the immediate consequence of the decision, whereas the indirect impact is the secondary and other remote, though equally important, effects.[42] The direct and indirect impacts of human rights decisions are sometimes used interchangeably with the intended and unintended impact of the decisions. There is, however, a fine distinction between them. A direct impact of a human rights decision is not necessarily intended, while an indirect impact may be intended; in other words, an unintended effect could result directly from a human rights decision. In the context of decisions of HRTs, intended impact entails the specific instances of state compliance that are in response to particular reparation orders of HRTs.[43] The indirect impact of a human rights decision may sometimes be obvious and discernible, such as domestic political reforms and judicial reference, or subtle and unobtrusive effects such as attitudinal changes and change in perception.[44] Finally, human rights judgment impact (HRJI) may be ex ante or ex post. An ex ante impact relates to the potential or probable effects of a human rights decision, while ex post impact relates to the actual and real-world effects of the decision.[45]

[36] Mia Swart, 'Can Regional and Sub-Regional African Courts Strengthen the Rule of Law in Africa? Questions of Impact and Enforcement' in Charles C Jalloh and Olufemi Elias (eds), *Shielding Humanity: Essays in International Law in Honour of Judge Abdul G Koroma* (Brill Nijhoff 2015) 706.

[37] Heyns and Viljoen (n 32).

[38] ibid.

[39] Gauthier D Beco, 'Human Rights Impact Assessments' (2009) 27 NQHR 139, 143.

[40] ibid.

[41] Beco (n 39) 144.

[42] ibid. See Paul Hunt and Gillian MacNaughton, 'Impact Assessments, Poverty and Human Rights: A Case Study Using the Rights to the Highest Attainable Standard of Health' (2006) 6 Health and Human Rights Working Paper Series 1, 11.

[43] Frans Viljoen, 'The Impact and Influence of the African Regional Human Rights System on Domestic Law' in Scott Sheeran and Nigel Rodley (eds), *Routledge Handbook of International Human Rights Law* (Routledge 2016) 447.

[44] ibid.

[45] Beco (n 39) 143–144.

There are two main approaches to judicial impact studies: the neorealist and constructivist approaches.[46] On the one hand, neorealist scholars such as Rosenberg, the author of *The Hollow Hope: Can Courts Bring About Social Change?*, focus on the direct or tangible effects of court decisions.[47] The constructivist perspective, on the other hand, focuses on change in attitudes, alteration of social actors' perceptions and the legitimation of litigants' worldview.[48] One of the earliest scholars to use the constructivist frame to assess the impact of judicial decisions, McCann, states that 'although judicial victories often do not translate automatically into desired social change, they can help to redefine the terms of both immediate and long term struggles among social groups'.[49] In terms of methodology, the neorealist approach insists on quantitative evidence of direct material effects, whereas the constructivist approach encourages qualitative techniques that allow the analysis of indirect non-material effects of judicial decisions.[50]

As expected, the traditional neorealist perspectives on the impact of the African human rights system, which focused on material effects, described the African Charter and its implementing mechanisms as 'ineffectual and dysfunctional'.[51] The traditional approach, arguably, misses out on the less obvious, subtle and more nuanced effects of the African Commission's decisions and African human rights norms in general, such as changes in attitudes as well as legal and political empowerment of the litigating community. The non-material effects of HRTs' decisions also include the totality of political, organizational, informational and jurisprudential effects and influences of the decision to promote and protect human rights at the domestic level and in other human rights protection systems.

The political effects of a decision may relate to the political empowerment of the litigating community, especially in public interest litigation (PIL), by giving the community a voice and platform on issue areas that they have previously neglected. The decision of an HRT, if properly deployed, can alter the power relations of subnational entities and frame political discourses in a limited yet significant way. The organizational impact of an HRT's decision entails the provision of the

46 Rodríguez-Garavito (n 9) 83.

47 See Gerald N Rosenberg, *The Hollow Hope: Can Courts Bring About Social Change?* (1981) cited in Rodríguez-Garavito (n 9) 83–84. On the effects of the United States (US) Supreme Court decision in *Brown v Board of Education*, generally believed to be a major tipping point in the history of racial segregation in the US, Rosenberg's empirical study found that *Brown* had little effect, thus attributing the revolution in race relations in the US to the political mobilization of the 1960s and the anti-discrimination legislation resulting from the mobilization. The crux of Rosenberg's controversial arguments is that courts alone cannot bring about significant social change.

48 Rodríguez-Garavito (n 9) 84–85.

49 Michael W McCann *Rights to Work: Pay Equity Reform and the Politics of Legal Mobilisation* (Chicago University Press 1994) 285. See also Rodríguez-Garavito (n 9) 84–85.

50 ibid.

51 See, for instance, Claude E Welch, 'The African Commission on Human and Peoples' Rights: A Five Year Report and Assessment' (1992) 14 HRQ 1, 4; Gittleman (n 6) 694; Emmanuel Bello, 'The Mandate of the African Commission on Human and Peoples' Rights' (1988) 1 AJIL 31, 55.

impetus for new social movement groupings to be formed.[52] A human rights decision can empower an existing social movement or trigger a new one.[53] Human rights decisions create an informational impact by releasing large amounts of important information to the public about the relevant issue, thereby contributing to transparency and accountability.

As easy as it may sound, establishing any direct causality between a human rights decision and a state of affairs or an observable behaviour of domestic actors is very complex.[54] One major challenge identified in previous studies is that 'unobserved factors limit the ability to establish causality'.[55] Numerous unobservable factors contribute to domestic human rights change. This implies that HRTs cannot take sole credit for the change, even if it conforms to a reparation order issued for the state to implement. For instance, the ongoing clean-up of Ogoniland and the building of a new Tanka Tanka Hospital in The Gambia, although related to various decisions of the African Commission, have not been caused solely or even primarily by the Commission's decisions.[56] Human rights decisions do not operate in isolation; they are a part of a complex web of legal normativity. Hardly any domestic level human rights change has been caused solely by the decision of an HRT; success in every case depends on a multiplicity of factors.[57]

The legal basis for assessing the impact of decisions of regional HRTs in Africa derives mainly from article 1 of the African Charter, which obliges states to 'give effect' to the rights contained in the Charter.[58] This obligation is open-ended, thus allowing states not only legislative but also administrative and other measures to give effect to their obligations under the Charter. As such, the provisions of article 1 of the African Charter imply that states have some leeway with regard to the specific measures to take unless explicit measures have been prescribed by the relevant HRTs.[59] In some resolutions, the African Commission has urged domestic courts to incorporate provisions of the African Charter and decisions of the Commission

[52] See, for instance, Malcolm Langford, César Rodríguez-Garavito and Julieta Rossi, 'Introduction: From Jurisprudence to Compliance' in Langford, Rodríguez-Garavito and Rossi (eds), *Social Rights Judgments and the Politics of Compliance: Making It Stick* (n 9) 24–25; Cathy Albisa and Amanda Shanor, 'United States: Education Rights and the Parameters of the Possible' in Langford, Rodríguez-Garavito and Rossi (eds), *Social Rights Judgments and the Politics of Compliance: Making It Stick* (n 9) 280–281; Malcolm Langford and Steven Kahanovitz, 'South Africa: Rethinking Enforcement Narrative' in Langford, Rodríguez-Garavito and Rossi (eds), *Social Rights Judgments and the Politics of Compliance: Making It Stick* (n 9) 332–346.

[53] ibid.

[54] Ayeni (n 9) 1.

[55] See Richard A Berk, 'An Introduction to Sample Selection Bias in Sociological Data' (1983) 48 Am Sociol Rev 386, 386–388; Baradaran and others (n 2) 767.

[56] The 2011 UNEP report played a key role in the Ogoni clean-up while the series of workshops organized by the World Bank in partnership with local NGOs helped push the situation of persons living with mental disabilities on the national agenda in the Gambia.

[57] See Okafor (n 7) 1–336.

[58] Viljoen (n 43) 446.

[59] ibid.

into their judgments.[60] The African Commission has also stated that the duty to give effect to the African Charter is not limited to the three arms of government but also extends to non-state actors, civil society organizations, legal practitioners, legal academics, law societies and judicial associations.[61]

Arguably, the state obligation in article 1 of the African Charter applies to decisions of the regional and sub-regional HRTs selected for this study.[62] Besides the fact that all the 55 member states of the African Union, except Morocco, are state parties to the African Charter,[63] all the selected regional and sub-regional HRTs have established clearly in their jurisprudence that they have the competence to interpret provisions of the African Charter.[64] In terms of article 1 of the African Charter, states have an obligation, which goes beyond complying with reparation orders, to guarantee the full impact of HRTs' decisions. It is against this background that this chapter examines the domestic level impact of decisions of African regional and sub-regional HRTs in the selected states.

There have been limited studies of the broader impact of decisions of African regional and sub-regional HRTs in Africa.[65] The few available studies have focused on the direct and intended impact, viewed from the lens of state compliance.[66] These studies mostly conclude that decisions of African HRTs are rarely complied with.[67] In addition to analysing compliance, Adjolohoun studied the impact of nine decisions of the ECCJ and concluded that human rights judgment impact has been clearer in 'compliant than in noncompliant states'.[68] The study also found that domestic courts have been the 'most productive channels of influence' for decisions

[60] See African Commission 'Resolution on the role of lawyers and judges in the integration of the Charter and the enhancement of the Commission's work in national and sub-regional systems', adopted during the 19th ordinary session of the African Commission, 26 March to 4 April 1996, Ouagadougou, Burkina Faso.

[61] Viljoen (n 43).

[62] Both the African Commission and the African Court interpret the African Charter. The African Charter is also the primary general human rights treaty of the African Children's Rights Committee. The ECCJ relies mainly on the African Charter for its catalogue of human rights. The recent decision of the Appellate Division EACJ in the *Democratic Party v Uganda* also has clarified the jurisdiction of the EACJ to interpret provisions of the African Charter.

[63] African Union 'List of countries which have signed, ratified/acceded to the African Charter' https://au.int/sites/default/files/treaties/7770-sl-african_charter_on_human_and_peoples_rights_2.pdf (access 31 August 2017).

[64] See (n 62).

[65] See, for instance, Adjolohoun (n 9); Viljoen (n 43) 446.

[66] See Frans Viljoen and Lirette Louw, 'State Compliance with the Recommendations of the African Commission on Human and People's Rights, 1994–2004' (2007) 101 AJIL 1, 1–34; Lirette Louw, 'An Analysis of State Compliance with the Recommendations of the African Commission on Human and Peoples' Rights' (Unpublished LLD thesis, University of Pretoria, 2005); Murray and Long (n 4); Tarisai Mutangi, 'An Examination of Compliance by States with the Judgments of the African Court on Human and Peoples' Rights: Prospects and Challenges'(Unpublished LLD thesis, University of Pretoria, 2009); Adjolohoun (n 9).

[67] See Viljoen and Louw (n 66); Louw (n 66); Murray and Long (n 4); George M Wachira and Abiola Ayinla, 'Twenty Years of Elusive Enforcement of the Recommendations of the African Commission on Human and Peoples' Rights: A Possible Remedy' (2006) 6 AHRLJ 465, 488.

[68] Adjolohoun (n 9) 315.

of the ECCJ, whereas the Executive has been the 'poorest driver of influence'.[69] The influence of the decisions of the ECCJ has been made possible through an active civil society and regional Bar association.[70] Aside from the above examples, the available scholarship has focused on the impact of human rights treaties at the domestic level,[71] or the impact of the decisions of domestic courts.[72]

For decades, the default position among international law experts was that human rights treaties had a constraining effect on state behaviour.[73] Empirical evidence of recent years, however, demonstrates that the real domestic effect of treaties is almost negligible.[74] In fact, some studies found a negative relationship between human rights treaty ratification and domestic level human rights practice; human rights practice at the domestic level tend to worsen following treaty ratification.[75] Thankfully, qualitative studies—and more recent quantitative research—have given some cause for optimism, suggesting that human rights treaties do give rise to positive consequences.[76] Most, if not all, of the studies on the domestic effects of human rights treaties agree that treaty effects are conditional on a multiplicity of factors which includes state-level characteristics, the nature of the treaty as well as the extent of interaction, persuasion and pressure applied on national actors by domestic and international compliance networks.[77]

3 Examples of the Impact of the Decisions of Human Rights Tribunals in Five Selected States

This section discusses six significant ways in which decisions of the relevant regional and sub-regional HRTs have made a difference in the five selected states.

[69] ibid.

[70] Adjolohoun (n 9) 316.

[71] Hathaway (n 1) 1935–2042.

[72] See Langford, Rodríguez-Garavito and Rossi (n 52) 109–350. See, eg Kabata (n 9).

[73] Beth A Simmons and Daniel J Hopkins, 'The Constraining Power of International Treaties: Theory and Methods' (2005) 99 Am Political Sci Rev 623, 623; Brett A Leeds, 'Alliance Reliability in Times of War: Explaining State Decisions to Violate Treaties' (2003) 57 IO 801, 801; Beth A Simmons, 'International Law and State Behaviour: Commitment and Compliance in International Monetary Affairs' (2000) 94 Am Political Sci Rev 819, 819.

[74] Emilie M Hafner-Burton and Kiyoteru Tsutsui, 'Human Rights in a Globalizing World: The Paradox of Empty Promises' (2005) 110 AJS 1373, 1373–1411; Hathaway (n 1); Linda C Keith, 'The United Nations International Covenant on Civil and Political Rights: Does it Make a Difference in Human Rights Behavior?' (1999) 36 J Peace Res 95, 95–118.

[75] ibid.

[76] Beth A Simmons, 'From Ratification to Compliance: Quantitative Evidence on a Spiral Model' in Thomas Risse, Stephen C Ropp and Kathryn Sikkink (eds), *The Persistent Power of Human Rights: From Commitment to Compliance* (2013); Eric Neumayer, 'Do International Human Rights Agreements Improve Respect for Human Rights?' (2005) 49 JCR 925, 925; Beth A Simmons, *Mobilizing for Human Rights* (2009); Hillebrecht (n 24).

[77] See Ayeni (n 9) 3; Daniel W Hill, 'Estimating the Effects of Human rights Treaties on State Behavior' (2010) 72 JOP 1161, 1161; George W Downs, David M Rocke and Peter N Barsoom, 'Is the Good News About Compliance Good News About Cooperation?' (1996) 50 IO 379, 379–406.

These instances include amicable settlement of other disputes and proactive remediation of violations even before a regional or sub-regional HRT gets a chance to decide on the merits; positive material and non-material benefits for successful applicants in the form of compensation, restitution and overall sense of pride and empowerment (not forming part of the relevant reparations orders); legislative and policy reforms (not forming part of the relevant reparations orders) resulting directly or indirectly from HRTs' decisions; the use of HRTs' decisions as tools for social mobilization, advocacy and research; and, finally, the judicial impact of HRTs' decisions. Of course, other less observable consequences, such as the possible deterrence effects of HRTs' decisions, are also captured in an omnibus section on other impacts of HRTs' decisions. While the impact of HRTs' decisions may be negative, the narrative below focuses on examples of the positive impact of HRTs' decisions. The important aspect of the analysis in this chapter is that a significant part of the positive domestic effects of HRTs' decisions may not have been captured in a compliance-focused narrative.

3.1 Amicable Settlement and Proactive Remediation of Violations

The communication procedure of HRTs in a few cases has served as a catalyst for amicable settlement of disputes and self-initiated redress of human rights violations. International human rights litigation has the potential of exposing states to undesirable negative publicity. This type of publicity could affect the standing of some states before their donors and development partners. In a bid to avoid the 'naming and shaming' and negative publicity associated with defending a potentially 'scandalous human rights violations' case, in many cases analysed in this study, states have been found to exhibit two patterns of behaviour (a) submitting to an amicable settlement of the disputes; and (b) taking proactive measures to redress the violations before the communication is declared admissible or before a decision is made on the merits.

This chapter finds clear instances where governments adopted significant proactive measures to remedy alleged violations prior to a finding of violation by HRTs. These measures are significant because most of them were adopted after the complaints that led to the decisions had been submitted to the relevant HRTs. The proactive 'public relations type' remediation is a common trend observed in some of the cases selected for the study. However, it is noteworthy that none of the cases selected for this study has been settled amicably. This is due to what is regarded in empirical legal studies as 'selection bias or selection effects', in the sense that all cases involving amicable settlement have been excluded from the analysis at the start of the research. It is significant, however, that a few cases involving the studied countries have been resolved by the African Commission and other HRTs through amicable settlement.[78]

While instances of amicable settlement in the African Commission are undeniably few and far between, the few examples demonstrate that amicable resolution of complaints is a crucial channel through which the communication procedure of HRTs makes a difference at the domestic level. Although the legal instruments establishing the African Court provide for the possibility of amicable settlement of disputes,[79] the Court has achieved little success in this regard. Despite the low record of achievement on amicable resolution of disputes, a former Judge of the Court, Ouguergouz J, has pointed out that the Court may be in a better position to persuade a state to 'soften its position' in anticipation of an 'unfavorable judicial decision'.[80] Like the African Court, none of the sub-regional HRTs selected for the study has achieved notable amicable resolution of its cases.

In the context of the complaint procedure of HRTs, proactive remediation is a process whereby states engage in 'damage control' after complaints have been lodged with a relevant HRT. It may be borne out of a genuine concern for the victims or merely a 'publicity stunt', depending on the nature of the state implementing the remediation. Proactive remediation is slightly different from an amicable settlement. Unlike amicable settlement, which is a mutual process that involves both parties to the case, with or without the supervision of the HRT, proactive remediation is mostly a one-sided process controlled by government officials.

One case that clearly demonstrates proactive remediation is the *Ogoniland* case.[81] The case was submitted to the African Commission in 1996, challenging

[78] The first communication submitted against The Gambia to the African Commission, Communication 44/90 *Peoples' Democratic Organisation for Independence and Socialism v Gambia*, was struck out by the Commission on 31 October 1996 following amicable resolution of the issues raised in the communication. Other cases resolved by the African Commission through amicable settlement include: *Modise v Botswana* (2000) AHRLR 30 (ACHPR 2000); *Kalenga v Zambia* (2000) AHRLR 321 (ACHPR 1994); communication 71/92 *Rencontre Africaine pour la Defence des Droits de l'Homme v Zambia*; *Association pour la Défense des Droits de l'Homme et des Libertés v Djibouti* (2000) AHRLR 80 (ACHPR 2000); *Open Society Justice Initiative (on behalf of Njawe Noumeni) v Cameroon* (2006) AHRLR 75 (ACHPR 2006). Quite recently, on 27 October 2016, the African Children's Rights Committee resolved through amicable settlement the fourth communication submitted to it: Communication No 004/Com/001/2014 *Institute for Human Right and Development in Africa v Malawi*. See African Children's Rights Committee 'Amicable Settlement on Communication No 004' http://www.acerwc.org/amicable-settlement-on-communication-no-004/ (accessed 18 May 2017).

[79] African Court Protocol, art 9 (stating that the Court may try to reach an amicable settlement in a case pending before it in accordance with the provisions of the Charter). This provision also derives from art 52 of the African Charter, which empowers the African Commission, whose protective mandate the Court complements, to 'try all appropriate means to reach an amicable solution based on the respect of human and peoples' rights'. This provision, however, relates only to inter-state communications.

[80] See Fatsah Ouguergouz, 'The Establishment of an African Court of Human and Peoples' Rights: A Judicial Premiere for the African Union' (2005) 11 Afr YIL 79, 130; Frans Viljoen, *International Human rights Law in Africa* (OUP 2012) 440.

[81] *Social and Economic Rights Action Centre (SERAC) and Another v Nigeria*(*Ogoniland* case) (2001) AHRLR 60 (ACHPR 2001).

the environmental degradation of Ogoniland, which continues to have a severe impact on the means of livelihood and health of the Ogoni people. Before the Commission's decision in October 2001, the civilian administration that took over power in May 1999 had taken some 'remedial actions' as an act of acknowledgement of the inappropriate actions of the previous regimes.[82] In a *Note Verbale* submitted to the African Commission in October 2000, the government admitted 'the gravamen of the complaints' and outlined the 'remedial measures' to redress the violations.[83] The remedial measures stated in the *Note Verbale* include establishing a number of national institutions such as the Federal Ministry of Environment, the Niger Delta Development Commission and a Judicial Commission of Enquiry to investigate allegations of human rights violations. In acknowledging the significance of these 'proactive remedial measures', the African Commission urges the government to keep it informed of the 'outcome' of the 'work' of the institutions.[84]

In another communication decided by the African Commission, *Media Rights Agenda v Nigeria*,[85] Niran Malaolu and three other journalists were arrested and detained without trial. The other journalists were released, but Malaolu was denied access to his lawyer, doctor and family. Following a secret trial conducted under the Treason and Other Offences (Special Military Tribunals) Decree of 1986, he was convicted and sentenced to life imprisonment. While the communication was pending before the African Commission, on 4 March 1999, the Nigerian government granted clemency to Malaolu alongside 95 others. The law under which he was tried, the Treason and Other Offences (Special Military Tribunals) Decree of 1986, was also repealed in preparation for a return to civil rule in May 1999.[86] This remediation happened before the African Commission's decision which was formally adopted on 6 November 2000.

In 2005, some Zimbabwean NGOs submitted a communication to the African Commission, *Scanlen & Holderness v Zimbabwe*,[87] alleging that a 2002 law of Zimbabwe, the Access to Information and Protection of Privacy Act (AIPPA), contravened various provisions of the African Charter. In its decision adopted on 3 April 2009, the Commission recommended, among other things, the repeal of sections 79 and 80 of the AIPPA and the decriminalization of offences relating to accreditation and practice of journalism. However, earlier in 2007, while the communication was still pending before the African Commission, the

[82] Frans Viljoen, 'The African Human rights System and Domestic Enforcement' in Langford, Rodríguez-Garavito and Rossi (eds), *Social Rights Judgments and the Politics of Compliance: Making It Stick* (n 9) 372.

[83] *Ogoniland* case, para 30.

[84] *Ogoniland* case.

[85] Communication 224/98 *Media Rights Agenda and Others v Nigeria* (2000) AHRLR 200 (ACHPR 1998).

[86] See Constitution of the Federal Republic of Nigeria (Certain Consequential Repeals) Decree No 63 of 1999, Laws of the Federation of Nigeria. This law repealed not only the Treason and Other Offences (Special Military Tribunals) Decree 1986 but also the Treason and Treasonable Offences Decree 1993.

[87] Communication 297/2005 *Scanlen & Holderness v Zimbabwe*.

government of Zimbabwe adopted the Access to Information and Protection of Privacy (Amendment) Act which repealed sections 79 and 80 of the 2002 Act.[88] The Amendment Act also repealed section 83 of the AIPPA, which criminalized activities relating to accreditation and the practice of journalism. Thus, at the time of the African Commission's decision, a few of the violations alleged had been redressed. Despite these legislative changes, press freedom in Zimbabwe has not improved significantly, as Zimbabwe has been rated 'not free' or 'partly free' by the Freedom House from 2002 until 2020.

In the ECCJ case of *Djotbayi Talbia and Others v Nigeria*,[89] ten applicants, who were aboard a foreign vessel rendering assistance to another vessel in distress 16 nautical miles off the coast of Nigeria, were arrested and detained by the officials of the Nigerian Navy on the allegation that the applicants were taking crude oil on board. They were paraded before the national press as crude oil thieves. On 27 July 2004, a Federal High Court in Nigeria ordered their release as the subsequent investigation revealed the cargo being loaded on to their vessel was fuel oil, not crude oil.[90] The Nigerian government initially refused to release the applicants immediately; however, they were released soon after a complaint was submitted to the ECCJ.[91]

The earliest impact of the communication procedure of an HRT is either proactive remediation or amicable resolution. As demonstrated in these cases, both processes constitute an important channel through which decisions or communication procedures of HRTs make a difference or have a significant impact at the domestic level. If given sufficient publicity, the process of submitting a communication can trigger the government into acquiescing to amicable resolution or taking some proactive actions to remedy the violations; and these measures are often missed out in compliance-focused analysis, since the measures are not taken to 'give effect' to any reparation orders of HRTs.

3.2 Provision of Tangible Benefits for Victims

As earlier argued, the traditional approach to the domestic effects of the African human rights system focused on the material benefits for the applicants and tangible changes in laws and policies.[92] This approach overlooked other subtle and unquantifiable non-material benefits where successful applicants benefit from

[88] Email from B Chinowawa, Zimbabwe Lawyers for Human Rights, on 4 April 2017. See also Access to Information and Protection of Privacy (Amendment) Act of 2007. The Amendment Act was gazetted and entered into force on 11 January 2008.

[89] ECW/CCJ/APP/10/06 *Djotbayi Talbia & 14 Others v Nigeria & 4 Others.*

[90] ibid.

[91] The government of Nigeria later released the applicants after this complaint had been filed. See ECW/CCJ/APP/10/06 *Djotbayi Talbia & 14 Others v Nigeria & 4 Others.*

[92] See Welch (n 52 above); Gittleman (n 6). See generally n 52 above.

an HRT's decisions. Decisions of regional and sub-regional HRTs in the studied countries have resulted in positive changes in the lives of litigants in a few cases.[93] The benefits for the applicants have manifested in various forms, including release from prison,[94] obtaining full presidential pardon,[95] payment of compensation,[96] apology from government or a formal acknowledgement of the 'gravamen' of the violation,[97] provision of new public facilities or infrastructure for the benefit of the complainants,[98] reopening of businesses and return of confiscated equipment,[99] payment of costs awarded in favour of complainants[100] and the protection of wildlife.[101] Some examples of the cases where state actions to implement an HRT's decision resulted in direct material and non-material benefits for the complainants are discussed below. It is noteworthy that in a few of the cases discussed below, the impact analysis coincides with the compliance narrative. However, the focus here is not the status of compliance with each reparation order but rather to highlight instances where the five selected states provided tangible benefits for the victims of human rights violations due to the selected HRTs' decisions. In some cases, the benefits provided are not specified in the reparation orders.

Following the judgment of the ECCJ in *Alimu Akeem v Nigeria*,[102] where the ECCJ ordered the government of Nigeria to release the applicant and pay him the sum of five million Naira, the government released the complainant and paid him the money as ordered by the ECCJ.[103] In another case, *Modupe Dorcas Afolalu v Nigeria*,[104] the applicant's husband died due to the post-election violence in Zaria in Kaduna on 18 April 2011. The applicant alleged discrimination in the process of payment of compensation to victims of post-election violence. The ECCJ ordered

[93] See Open Society Justice Initiative (OSJI) 'Conference Report: The Impacts of Strategic Litigation on Indigenous Peoples' Land Rights' (2016) 3 https://www.opensocietyfoundations.org/sites/default/files/slip-landrights-nairobi-20161014.pdf (accessed 30 May 2017).

[94] See the following cases in Appendix I & II of the thesis: *Media Rights Agenda and Others v* Nigeria (2000) AHRLR 200 (ACHPR 1998); *Djotbayi Talbia & 14 Others v Nigeria & 4 Others* ECW/CCJ/APP/10/06; *Alimu Akeem v Nigeria* ECW/CCJ/JUD/01/14.

[95] See *Civil Liberties Organisation, Legal Defence Centre, Legal Defence and Assistance Project v Nigeria* (2001) AHRLR 75 (ACHPR 2001) in Appendix I.

[96] See generally in Appendix I: *Ogoniland* case; *Alimu Akeem case*; *Modupe Dorcas Afolalu* case; ECW/CCJ/APP/10/10 *SERAP v Nigeria* (*Bundu Waterfront* case).

[97] See *Ogoniland* case in App I.

[98] See generally in App I: *Gambian Mental Health* case; *Ogoniland* case.

[99] See also in App I: Communication 284/2003 *Zimbabwe Lawyers for Human Rights & Associated Newspapers of Zimbabwe v Zimbabwe.*

[100] See generally Appendix II: *Katabazi and Others v S-G EAC & A-G Uganda*, Ref No 1 of 2010, decided by the EACJ on 1 December 2007; *Sitenda Sibalu v S-G EAC, A-G Uganda & others*, Judgment of 30 June 2011.

[101] See in App II *African Network for Animal Welfare v AG Tanzania*, Ref No 9 of 2010, decided by the First Instance Division on 20 June 2014, and the Appellate Division on 29 July 2015.

[102] *Alimu Akeem* case.

[103] Interview with Sola Egbeyinka (Legal Practitioner, Falana & Falana Chambers, Abuja, Nigeria) on 20 May 2016.

[104] *Modupe Dorcas Afolalu* case.

the government of Nigeria to pay the applicant 10 million Naira for all the harm caused. This money was paid to the applicant soon after the judgment.[105]

In *Constitutional Rights Project v President Ibrahim Babangida,*[106] a Lagos High Court relied on the African Charter and a decision of the African Commission in *Constitutional Rights Project (in respect of Zamani Lakwot and 6 Others) v Nigeria* to restrain the government of Nigeria from executing Zamani Lakwot and others sentenced to death.[107] The convicts were not executed and eventually released from prison.[108] In *Constitutional Rights Project v Nigeria* (*Nigerian Detention* case),[109] five persons accused of armed robbery and kidnapping were arrested and detained for two years without trial by the government of Nigeria. The Constitutional Rights Project (CRP) submitted the communication to the African Commission on behalf of the detainees. The African Commission held the detention as a violation of the African Charter and recommended that government should charge or release the detainees. Soon after the Commission's decision, the complainants were charged.[110] In another communication, *Centre for Free Speech v Nigeria,*[111] four Nigerian journalists were tried and convicted secretly by a military tribunal. A communication was submitted to the African Commission on their behalf and the Commission recommended the release of the journalists. Following this decision, the journalists were released.[112]

In *Constitutional Rights Project (in respect of Wahab Akanmu and Others) v Nigeria,*[113] 100 detainees were tried, convicted and sentenced to death for armed robbery. The Decree under which they were convicted made no provision for appeal. The CRP, on behalf of the detainees, submitted a communication to the African Commission that found that the Decree violated several provisions of the African Charter and recommended compensation for the applicants. At first, the death sentence imposed on the detainees was commuted to terms of imprisonment.[114] The CRP used the decision of the African Commission to pressure the government and eventually secured the release of all the detainees.[115] While the release was not a direct act of compliance with reparation orders of the Commission,

[105] Egbeyinka (n 103).

[106] *Constitutional Rights Project v President Ibrahim Babangida and two Others,* Suit M/102/93, Lagos State High Court, per Onalaja J (unreported). See Okafor (n 7) 98, 124.

[107] Okafor (n 7) 278.

[108] ibid.

[109] (2000) AHRLR 248 (ACHPR 1999).

[110] Viljoen and Louw (n 66) 10; Victor O Ayeni, 'Domestic Impact of the African Charter on Human and Peoples' Rights and the Protocol on the Rights of Women in Africa: A Case Study of Nigeria' (Unpublished LLM dissertation, University of Pretoria, 2011) 25.

[111] *Centre for Free Speech v Nigeria* (2000) AHRLR 250 (ACHPR1999).

[112] Viljoen and Louw (n 66) 10; Ayeni (n 110).

[113] Communication 60/91 *Constitutional Rights Project (in respect of Wahab Akanmu and Others) v Nigeria.*

[114] Ayeni (n 110).

[115] Okafor (n 7) 125.

the African Commission's decision nonetheless played the role of a legitimizing force.[116]

Political prisoners whose complaints were determined by the African Commission in *Media Rights Agenda v Nigeria*[117] *and Civil Liberties Organisation & 2 Others v Nigeria*[118] were granted clemency and released.[119] In relation to the *Ogoniland* case, the infamous Rivers State Internal Securities Task Force (RSISTF) was disbanded. The government subsequently invited the United Nations Environment Programme (UNEP) to undertake an independent scientific assessment of Ogoniland, culminating in the UNEP report on the *Environmental Assessment of Ogoniland*.[120] The Nigerian government also set up the Hydrocarbon Pollution Restoration Project (HYPREP) to lead and coordinate the clean-up of Ogoniland.[121] While all these developments are not directly attributable to the *Ogoniland* case, there is no doubt the case made some valuable contributions to the processes resulting in the ongoing reclamation of Ogoniland. Due to The *Gambian Mental Health* case, the government of The Gambia has taken limited yet significant steps to formulate a mental health law and policy for The Gambia.[122] In 2009, nearly six years after The *Gambian Mental Health* case, a new mental health facility, called the Tanka Tanka Psychiatric Hospital, was built. According to information from the Mental Health Leadership and Advocacy Programme (MHLAP), an NGO based in The Gambia, the facility at the new hospital is much better than the Psychiatric Unit of the Royal Victoria Hospital, which was the only facility available when The *Gambian Mental Health* case was decided.[123]

Following the decision of the EACJ in the *Katabazi* case in November 2007, the 22 applicants detained since 16 November 2016 were released without further charges even though the reparation order of the EACJ, in this case, did not expressly require the release of the applicants.[124] Another case that demonstrates how a decision of sub-regional HRTs may result in real-time protection of the rights of applicants is *Hon Dr Jerry Ugwoke v Nigeria*.[125] In this case, the applicant, Jerry Ugokwe, in April 2003 was declared the winner of a seat in Nigeria's

[116] Okafor (n 7) 125.

[117] *Media Rights Agenda and Others v Nigeria (2000) AHRLR 200 (ACHPR 1998).*

[118] *Civil Liberties Organisation, Legal Defence Centre, Legal Defence and Assistance Project v Nigeria* (2001) AHRLR 75 (ACHPR 2001).

[119] See App I.

[120] UNEP *Environmental Assessment of Ogoniland* (2011) http://web.unep.org/disastersandconflicts/where-we-work/nigeria/what-we-do/environmental-assessment-ogoniland-report; See Langford, Rodriguez-Garavito and Rossi, (n 52) 4.

[121] US Chamber of Commerce Foundation 'Hydrocarbon Pollution Restoration Project by Shell Oil Company' https://www.uschamberfoundation.org/hydrocarbon-pollution-restoration-project.

[122] See analysis in App I.

[123] Interview with Dawda Samba (Executive Director, MHLAP, Online, via Skype) on 20 March 2017; Viljoen (n 80) 378–379.

[124] Ally Possi, 'The East African Court of Justice: Towards Effective Protection of Human Rights in the East African Community' (Unpublished LLD thesis, University of Pretoria, 2014) 181.

[125] ECW/CCJ/JUD/03/05 *Ugwoke v Nigeria*.

lower legislative house (the House of Representatives). His opponent contested the victory before an Election Tribunal and had his election overturned in November 2004. Dissatisfied, Ugokwe approached the Nigerian Court of Appeal, which affirmed the Electoral Tribunal's decision. In May 2009, Ugokwe submitted his application to the ECCJ, arguing that his right to a fair hearing had been infringed by the Electoral Commission and the Election Tribunal. The ECCJ, relying on Ugokwe's application, granted a special interim order restraining Nigerian authorities from swearing-in another candidate in place of the applicant. On receiving the special interim order of the ECCJ, Nigeria's Attorney-General, addressed a letter to the Speaker of the House of Representatives stating that no one should be sworn in to replace the applicant until the ECCJ decided the case on the merits.[126] Indeed, the Speaker complied with the directive, and no one was sworn in until the case was finalized by the ECCJ.[127]

The most extensive of the non-material impact of HRTs' decisions on successful applicants are observed in cases litigated by or on behalf of local communities such as the Ogoni people.[128] The decision of the African Commission in the *Ogoniland* case, for instance, has been praised for framing the environmental degradation of Ogoniland as a human rights issue.[129] The case legitimated the agitations of the Ogoni people and drew international attention to their plights and the condition of Ogoniland. Various Ogoni groups and movements have been formed around the issues articulated in the decision.[130] The case also helped to build domestic socio-economic rights jurisprudence in Nigeria and bolstered the courage of Nigerian judges on social justice issues.[131] The case has also been credited for setting in motion a train of litigation before domestic courts against the Nigerian government and transnational oil companies operating in Nigeria.[132]

Multinational companies responsible for human rights violations in the *Ogoniland* case have paid various sums as compensation to Ogoni communities.[133] In addition, the government has attempted indirectly to compensate Ogoni communities by providing alternate housing, creating jobs and providing special financial support for indigent students of Niger Delta origin.[134] However, these jobs, in

[126] *Ugokwe v Nigeria*, para 10.
[127] Adjolohoun (n 9) 165.
[128] See *Ogoniland* case. See also Communication 276/03 *Centre for Minority Rights Development (Kenya) and Another v Kenya* (*Endorois Case*).
[129] Viljoen (n 80) 375.
[130] Viljoen (n 80) 375.
[131] Viljoen (n 80) 375.
[132] See, for instance, *Jonah Gbemre v Shell Petroleum Development Company and Others* (Suit no FHC/B/CS/53/05, Nigerian Federal High Court, Benin City, 14 November 2005 (*Nigerian Gas Flaring* case). In the case, the court restrained SPDC and the Nigerian-owned oil corporation from flaring gas and ordered the Attorney-General to set in motion legislation to end gas flaring in Nigeria. Although the Court referred extensively to provisions of the African Charter, no reference was made to the African Commission's decision in the *Ogoniland* case.
[133] See App I.
[134] ibid.

many cases, are 'inappropriate to their lifestyle, poorly paid, menial and not commensurate with their previous income level'.[135] It is arguable that the outcome of the *Ogoniland* case may have influenced domestic courts and policymakers to have more consideration and sympathy towards other oil-producing communities in the Niger Delta area who have suffered similar environmental degradation because of oil pollution.[136]

In a general sense, cases brought on behalf of local communities have been found to have the effect of empowering local women.[137] Successful human rights litigation has also been linked to complainants' psychological health and sense of identity.[138] A sense of pride and solidarity is common among a winning community, while feelings of loss, neglect and exasperation are not uncommon when states delay in complying with decisions of HRTs. Non-compliance could also make successful litigants feel a sense of resentment over lost time and resources.[139]

A good example of the capacity of human rights decisions to empower litigants into social mobilization is *Scanlen & Holderness v Zimbabwe*.[140] In this case, the African Commission recommended that the government of Zimbabwe should adopt legislation providing a framework for self-regulation by journalists. Using this decision, various civil society organizations under the aegis of the Voluntary Media Council of Zimbabwe (VMCZ) are pushing for the adoption of a Media Practitioners Bill, which would result in self-regulation.[141] A zero draft of the Bill has been prepared. At the time of this assessment, VMCZ has been holding consultative meetings in various locations in Zimbabwe to gather the views of journalists on the Bill.[142] The argument, thus far, is that decisions of regional and sub-regional HRTs in Africa, in some instances, have led to the provision of material and non-material benefits and empowerment to the litigating individual or community.

3.3 Legislative and Policy Reforms

In a limited number of cases, decisions of the selected regional and sub-regional HRTs have contributed to legislative processes culminating in the adoption of new laws and policies or the reform of old laws. Legislative reform is one of the clearest indications of the indirect impact of the decisions of regional and sub-regional

[135] See OSJI conference report (n 93) 4.
[136] See, for instance, *Jonah Gbemre* case.
[137] OSJI conference report (n 93) 6.
[138] OSJI conference report (n 93) 6.
[139] OSJI conference report (n 93) 6.
[140] Communication 297/2005 *Scanlen & Holderness v Zimbabwe*.
[141] Email from B Chinowawa (Zimbabwe Lawyers for Human Rights) on 4 April 2017.
[142] See B Matendere, 'VMCZ Drafts Bill on Media Self-Regulation' *The Zimbabwean* 21 July 2016 http://thezimbabwean.co/2016/07/vmcz-drafts-bill-on-media-self-regulation/.

HRTs. In most cases studied, legislative processes usually result indirectly from HRTs' decisions, either after an intervening decision by a domestic court or an intense campaign by activist forces at the domestic level, using decisions of HRTs. Some instances where decisions of African regional and sub-regional HRTs have led to domestic legislative reforms include the repeal of draconian military Decrees in Nigeria, amendment of parliamentary Rules of Procedure in Kenya and Uganda consequent upon various decisions of the EACJ, legislative debates and ongoing amendment of a controversial press law in Burundi and the repeal of certain offending provisions of AIPPA in Zimbabwe. The legislative impact analysis below is limited mainly to the studied countries, with only a few notable exceptions.

Upon transition from military to civilian rule in 1999, the African Commission's recommendations in at least ten cases involving Nigeria were implemented to some extent.[143] Many of the military decrees previously declared by the African Commission as violating the African Charter were repealed.[144] These include the Treason and Other Offences (Special Military Tribunals) Decree of 1986 declared by the African Commission as violating the African Charter in *Media Rights Agenda v Nigeria*[145] *and Civil Liberties Organisation & 2 Others v Nigeria.*[146]

Another legislative reform influenced directly or indirectly by decisions of the African Commission relates to the Nigerian *Civil Disturbances (Special Tribunal) Decree No 2 of 1987.* This legislation, enacted by the military administration of General Babangida, established a special tribunal for the trial of persons alleged to have engaged in acts of civil disturbance. The composition of the five-member tribunal included a serving member of the military.[147] Persons convicted by the tribunal had no right of appeal to any superior court, and the Decree abrogated the supervisory jurisdiction of the High Court over proceedings of the tribunal.[148] These features of the tribunal were challenged in several communications before the African Commission, such as the *Zamani Lakwot case*[149] *and Civil Liberties Organisation v Nigeria.*[150] In these cases, the African Commission found that the Decree violated provisions of the African Charter. Activist forces comprising human rights NGOs, the media and courageous judges relied on the African Commission's decisions to 'mount a loud and intense campaign' against the Decree.[151] On 5 June 1996, a new Decree, the Civil Disturbances (Special

[143] Ayeni (110) 26.

[144] See Constitution of the Federal Republic of Nigeria (Certain Consequential Repeals) Decree 63 of 1999.

[145] *Media Rights Agenda and Others v Nigeria* (2000) AHRLR 200 (ACHPR 1998).

[146] *Civil Liberties Organisation, Legal Defence Centre, Legal Defence and Assistance Project v Nigeria* (2001) AHRLR 75 (ACHPR 2001).

[147] See Civil Disturbances (Special Tribunal) Decree No 2 of 1987, s 2.

[148] See Civil Disturbances (Special Tribunal) Decree No 2 of 1987, s 8.

[149] Communication 87/93 *Constitutional Rights Project (in respect of Zamani Lakwot and 6 Others) v Nigeria.*

[150] Communication 129/94 *Civil Liberties Organisation v Nigeria.*

[151] Okafor (n 7) 129.

Tribunal) (Amendment) Decree, was promulgated, thus effectively repealing the 1987 Decree. The new Decree removed the member of the armed forces from the tribunal and provided for a right of appeal for persons convicted by the tribunal.[152]

In another instance, the *Newspapers Registration Decree 43 of 1993* case,[153] the government of Nigeria promulgated the infamous Decree 43 of 1993, which set out stringent conditions for the operation of media business in Nigeria. Two Nigerian NGOs, CRP and Media Right Agenda (MRA), approached the African Commission to have the Decree set aside. The African Commission held that the Decree violated several provisions of the African Charter. Relying on the African Commission's decision, some human rights NGOs in Nigeria approached a Lagos High Court requesting the Court to declare the Decree null and void. The Court, per Humponu-Wusu J, held that any national legislation (including Decree 43 of 1993) that conflicts with the African Charter is void to the extent of such conflict.[154] Decree 43 was subsequently repealed.[155]

Activist forces in Nigeria also deployed the African Commission's decision to secure an amendment to section 2A of the *State Security (Detention of Persons) Decree* of 1994. The provision precluded any court from issuing a *writ of habeas corpus* for the release of any person detained under the Decree. In *Constitutional Rights Project and Civil Liberties Organisation (on behalf of Ken Saro-Wiwa) v Nigeria*, the African Commission declared the provisions of the Decree to be 'Charter illegal'.[156] This Decree was also condemned by the African Commission in the *Zamani Lakwot* case. The incessant criticisms from the African Commission, together with campaigns mounted by activist forces at the domestic level, led to an amendment of the Decree on 7 June 1996.[157] The new Decree, the State Security (Detention of Persons) (Amendment) (No 2) (Repeal) Decree No 18 of 1996, restored the legal capacity of courts to issue the writ of *habeas corpus* or other writs for the release of any person detained under the Decree. In addition, the military also ordered a comprehensive review of the cases of all persons previously detained under the 1994 Decree.[158] Sequel to this review, about 12 detainees regained their freedom.[159]

The decision of the African Court in *Mtikila & Others v Tanzania*[160] has prompted the inclusion in the Draft Constitution of Tanzania 2014 of a

[152] Okafor (n 7) 129.

[153] Communications 105/93, 128/94, 130/94 and 152/96 *Media Rights Agenda and Constitutional Rights Project v Nigeria.*

[154] See *Richard Akinola v General Ibrahim Babangida and three others*, Suit M/462/93; *Media Rights Agenda and Another v A-G of the Federation*, Suit FHC/L/CS/908/99 (unreported). Both cases are cited in Okafor (n 7) 101.

[155] Okafor (n 7) 102.

[156] See Communications 137/94, 154/96 and 161/97 *Constitutional Rights Project and Civil Liberties Organisation (on behalf of Ken Saro-Wiwa) v Nigeria.*

[157] Okafor (n 7) 131.

[158] ibid.

[159] Okafor (n 7) 131.

[160] *Mtikila* case.

proposal for independent candidacy. Section 216 of the Final Draft of the Proposed Constitution as approved by Parliament in October 2014 provides for the right of independent candidates to contest any election in Tanzania.[161] The Minister of Justice and Constitutional Affairs of Tanzania, Dr Harrison Mwakyembe, stated on 21 November 2016, during the tenth-anniversary symposium of the African Court, that the government was aware of the *Mtikila* decision and the obligations it imposed on the state.[162] The Minister stated that the independent presidential candidate issue has not been 'ditched' and was included in the Proposed Constitution, which awaits a referendum for its adoption.[163] In compliance with the reparation order of the Court, the full judgment of the Court in the *Mtikila* case has been published on the official website of the government of Tanzania since 18 January 2016.[164] The case has also had an unintended impact. The decision has popularized the African Court and led to a floodgate of litigations submitted against Tanzania at the African Court.[165] According to the Pan African Lawyers Union (PALU), the *Mtikila* case gave applicants from the states that have made the article 34(6) declaration 'more gut' to approach the Court. Tanzania, which ratified the Court Protocol in 2006 and made the article 34(6) Declaration in 2010, formally withdrew its declaration in 2019, thus becoming the second country, after Rwanda, to withdraw its special declaration, which enables individual and NGO access to the Court.[166]

Of the six HRTs selected for this study, the decisions of the EACJ have had the most extensive legislative impact at the domestic level in recent years.[167] Some of the cases in which decisions of the EACJ have directly influenced legislative debates and reforms at the state level are discussed below. Even though not studied here, developments in Kenya in relation to the EACJ had a spill-over effect in Uganda, one of the countries selected for the study. For the election of Kenya's representatives in the East African Legislative Assembly (EALA), the Kenyan Parliament in 2001 enacted the East African Community (Election of Members of the Assembly) Rules 2001. In *Peter Anyang' Nyong'o and 10 others v the Attorney General of the*

[161] Proposed Constitution of the United Republic of Tanzania, approved by Parliament in October 2014 http://www.humanrights.or.tz/downloads/proposed%20constitution%20-%20english%20version.docx (accessed 21 April 2017).

[162] AllAfrica 'Independent Candidacy Not Ditched – Govt' http://allafrica.com/stories/201611230534.html.

[163] ibid. The referendum, earlier stated for 30 April 2015, failed to hold due to protests from opposition political parties.

[164] 'Rev. Mtikila TLS & LHRC vs URT (Application No 009& 011/2011' 18 January 2016 http://sheria.go.tz/index.php?option=com_docman&task=cat_view&gid=44&Itemid=68.

[165] Skype communication with E Chijarira (PALU) on 5 May 2015.

[166] Chijarira (n 165). See also Centre for Human Rights, 'Press Statement: Centre for Human Rights Expresses Concern about Tanzania's Withdrawal of Access to the African Court by Individuals and NGOs' 05 December 2019, available at https://www.chr.up.ac.za/press-statements/1916-press-statement-centre-for-human-rights-expresses-concern-about-tanzania-s-withdrawal-of-access-to-the-african-court-by-individuals-and-ngos.

[167] See generally Victor Lando, 'The Domestic Effect of the East African Community's Human Rights Practice' (Unpublished LLD thesis, University of Pretoria, 2017).

Republic of Kenya and 5 others,[168] the EACJ found the 2001 Rules of Procedure to be in violation of article 50 of the EAC Treaty since the Rules did not require Parliament to conduct an election as required by the EAC Treaty. Following the decision of the EACJ in the *Anyang' Nyongo'* case, the Kenyan Parliament on 23 May 2007 passed new nomination Rules, the Treaty for the Establishment of the East African Community (Election of Members of the Assembly) Rules 2007, which set out an elaborate procedure for the election of Kenya representatives for the EALA.[169]

Influenced by the decision of the EACJ in the *Peter Anyang' Nyongo'* case,[170] domestic actors in Uganda sought similar ruling against the government of Uganda. In *Democratic Party* and *Mukasa Mbidde v S-G EAC & A-G Uganda,*[171] the applicants argued that the Rules of Procedure of the Parliament of Uganda did not give equal opportunity and full participation rights to some interest groups in the election of Uganda's representatives to the EALA as required by the EAC Treaty. According to article 50 of the EAC Treaty, members of the EALA are to be elected by national assemblies of each state, provided all political parties, shades of opinions, gender and other special interests are well represented. Consequently, the EACJ ordered the government of Uganda to amend the Rules of Procedure of the Parliament of Uganda to bring it in line with article 50 of the EAC Treaty. On 18 May 2012, the Parliament of Uganda amended its Rules of Procedure, purportedly to comply with the decision of the EACJ.[172]

Not satisfied with how the Rules of Procedure were amended, Anita Among approached the EACJ to set aside the 2012 Parliamentary Rules of Procedure. The EACJ in *Among Anita v A-G Uganda and Another,*[173] a case decided in 2013, ordered the Parliament of Uganda to amend the 2012 Rules of Procedure further to bring it fully in conformity with article 50 of the EAC Treaty. On 9 August 2016, the Parliament of Uganda formally constituted a Standing Committee to review the Rules of Procedure of the Uganda Parliament. One of the four objectives of the Committee is to 'align the Rules to the observations and decisions of the EACJ with respect to the election petition of Uganda's representatives to the EALA'.[174] The report of the Committee, which expressly referenced the *Anita Among* case, has been submitted to Parliament since January 2017.[175]

[168] *Anyang' Nyongo and 10 others v A-G Kenya & 2 others,* Ref No 1 of 2006.

[169] See Kenya National Assembly Official Records (Hansard) 23 May 2007, 1583–1602.

[170] *Anyang' Nyongo* case.

[171] *Democratic Party and Mukasa Mbidde v S-G EAC and A-G Uganda*, Ref No 6 of 2011, decided 10 May 2012.

[172] *Among Anita v A-G Uganda and S-G EAC and A-G Uganda*, Ref No 2 of 2012, decided by the EACJ on 29 November 2013.

[173] *Among Anita case.*

[174] See Report of the Standing Committee on Rules, Privileges and Discipline on the Amendment of the Rules of Procedure of the Parliament of Uganda (January 2017) 3 https://www.scribd.com/document/337292458/Report-on-the-Amendment-of-the-Rules-of-Procedure-of-the-Parliament-of-Uganda#download&from_embed.

[175] See Report of the Standing Committee on Rules, Privileges and Discipline (n 174 above) 26.

There has been limited impact of HRTs' decisions on legislative processes in The Gambia and Zimbabwe. In *The Gambian Mental Health* case,[176] the African Commission requested the government of The Gambia to repeal the Lunatics Detention Act (LDA). Although this legislation has not been repealed as of July 2017, The Gambia's Ministry of Health and some civil society organizations supported by the World Health Organization (WHO) had a series of workshops to enact new mental health legislation for The Gambia.[177] A zero draft of the proposed mental health legislation has been produced, but the draft Bill is yet to be presented to either cabinet or parliament.[178] In Zimbabwe, the communication procedure of the African Commission in *Scanlen & Holderness v Zimbabwe*[179] facilitated the repeal in 2007 of sections 79, 80 and 83 of AIPPA.[180]

3.4 Judicial Impact of HRTs' Decisions

Despite the criticisms and widespread characterization of regional and sub-regional human rights regimes in Africa as weak and ineffective,[181] it is undeniable that HRTs' decisions in Africa have had a considerable judicial or jurisprudential impact. The 'jurisprudential effect' is perhaps the biggest and most wide-ranging impact of decisions of regional and sub-regional HRTs in Africa. Their decisions have served as a *medium of communication* amongst various tribunals, a *trigger of independent claims* before domestic courts, and an *authoritative source of legal norms*. Construed as a medium of 'transnational judicial communication', there is a plethora of cases where HRTs in Africa have referenced one another to strengthen their arguments and legitimize their decisions. As a trigger of independent claims, decisions of HRTs have been relied upon as a basis for making independent claims in a series of litigations before domestic and international HRTs. Finally, decisions of HRTs serve as a channel for the creation and elaboration of legal norms through authoritative interpretation of treaty provisions.

3.4.1 Transnational Judicial Communication

There has been extensive jurisprudential correspondence among the various regional, sub-regional and domestic tribunals in Africa.[182] Slaughter describes the process by which courts from different countries talk to one another as 'transjudicial

[176] *Gambian Mental Health* Case.
[177] Samba (n 123).
[178] Samba (n 123).
[179] Communication 297/2005 *Scanlen & Holderness v Zimbabwe*.
[180] See Appendix I.
[181] See Okafor (n 7) 41.
[182] See Hélène Lambert, 'Transnational Judicial Dialogue Harmonization and the Common European Asylum System' (2009) 58 ICLQ 519, 520; James C Hathaway, *The Rights of Refugees Under International Law* (CUP 2005) 1–2.

communication'.[183] Other scholars have described it as 'transnational judicial dialogue',[184] 'transnational legal communication',[185] or simply transjudicialism.[186] Transnational judicial communication generally takes three forms: horizontal, vertical and mixed vertical-horizontal.[187] Horizontal communication occurs between courts of coordinate status, whether national or supranational.[188] This is the type of communication that takes place where the African Court, in its judgments and other rulings, refers to the jurisprudence of the African Commission. Vertical communication occurs between national and international courts, such as where a domestic court refers to the jurisprudence of a regional HRT or where a regional HRT relies on the decision of a domestic court.[189] The mixed vertical-horizontal communication occurs where supranational courts serve as an avenue for horizontal communication and vice versa.[190] In other words, best practices in national legal systems are incorporated into judgments of supranational tribunals, in turn assimilated by other states.

The various forms of transjudicial communication enhance the effectiveness of HRTs, promote the acceptance of reciprocal obligations and enhance the persuasiveness and legitimacy of decisions of HRTs.[191] Because of its capacity to promote cross-fertilization among national and international legal systems, transnational judicial communication is becoming a common practice among judiciaries globally.[192] Some instances of vertical and horizontal transnational judicial communication involving the selected sub-regional and regional HRTs in Africa are discussed below.

Even though no systematic searches were carried out, the evidence based on the data gathered during the study demonstrates that there has been more horizontal than vertical transnational judicial communication in Africa. In other words, the number of times regional and sub-regional HRTs in Africa cite each other is relatively higher than the number of times domestic courts cited their decisions. The limited use of international legal jurisprudence in domestic courts has been attributed to the lack of knowledge and mistrust of international human rights

[183] Anne-Marie Slaughter, 'A Typology of Transjudicial Communication' (1994) 29 U of Rich L R 99, 99–137.

[184] Lambert (n 181) 519; Olga Frishman, 'Transnational Judicial Dialogue as an Organisational Field' (2013) 19 Eur Law J 739, 739; MA Waters, 'Meeting Norms and Identity: The Role of Transnational Judicial Dialogue in Creating and Enforcing International Law' (2005) 93 GLJ 487, 487.

[185] Markus Wagner, 'Transnational Legal Communication: A Partial Legacy of Supreme Court President Aharon Barak' (2011) 47 TLR 437, 437.

[186] See Elaine Mark, 'General Principles of Law and Transnational Judicial communication' in Laura Pineschi (ed), *General principles of law - The Role of the Judiciary, Ius Gentium: Comparative Perspectives on Law and Justice* (Springer 2015) 46.

[187] Slaughter (n 183) 103.

[188] Slaughter (n 183) 103.

[189] Slaughter (n 183) 106.

[190] Slaughter (n 183) 111.

[191] Slaughter (n 183) 112–124.

[192] See Mary A Glenton, *Rights Talk: The Improvement of Political Discourse* (1988) 158.

jurisprudence as 'foreign law'.[193] In the *Campbell* cases, for instance, the SADC Tribunal cited the jurisprudence of the African Commission copiously.[194] The Tribunal referred to the African Commission's *Constitutional Rights Project and Others v Nigeria*,[195] and *Zimbabwe Human Rights NGO Forum v Zimbabwe*.[196] In the *Katabazi* case, the EACJ referred to the decision of the African Commission in *Constitutional Rights Project v Nigeria*[197] to enrich its own jurisprudence.[198] In the Reparation Ruling in the *Mtikila* case, the African Court referred to the jurisprudence of the African Commission on the right to and effective remedy as set out in *Jawara v The Gambia* and *Gabriel Shumba v Zimbabwe*.[199] In the *Children in Northern Uganda* case, the African Children's Rights Committee referenced several decisions of the African Commission, including the *Ogoniland* case and The *Gambian Mental Health* case.[200] In the *Talibe* case, the Committee also cited the jurisprudence of the African Commission on admissibility and effective remedy copiously as set out in the *Jawara* case.[201]

Of the six selected HRTs, the only tribunal that rarely cites decisions of other regional and sub-regional HRTs is the ECCJ.[202] In *SERAP v Nigeria* (the *Niger Delta Environmental Pollution* case), a case whose factual circumstances largely overlap with the African Commission's decision in the *Ogoniland* case, the ECCJ failed to reference the *Ogoniland* case, even though the applicant made explicit reference to it in their written submission.[203] The ECCJ tends to mostly rely on the jurisprudence of the ICJ, European Court of Human Rights (ECtHR) and domestic courts of ECOWAS states, especially Nigeria.[204] The African Commission has, however, incorporated jurisprudence of the ECCJ in many of its decisions. For instance, in 2008, the African Commission issued a resolution requesting the government of The Gambia to comply with ECCJ's judgment in the *Manneh* case.[205] In clarifying the rights to work, particularly the right to equal pay for equal work, the African

[193] Magnus Killander and Horace Adjolohoun, 'International Law and Domestic Human Rights Litigation in Africa: An Introduction' in Magnus Killander (ed), *International Law and Domestic Human Rights Litigation in Africa* (Pretoria University Law Press 2010) 3; Murray and Long (4) 75.

[194] See Swart (n 36) 711.

[195] *Constitutional Rights Project and Others v Nigeria*(2000) AHRLR 227 cited in the *Campbell* case, para 41.

[196] *Zimbabwe Human Rights NGO Forum v Zimbabwe*(2006) AHRLR 128 (ACHPR 2006) cited in the *Campbell* case, para 43.

[197] *Constitutional Rights Project and Another v Nigeria*(2000) AHRLR 235 (ACHPR 1999).

[198] *Katabazi*case, paras 48–50. See also Adjolohoun (n 9) 118.

[199] See *Mtikila v Tanzania* (Reparation ruling) paras 22, 24, 25.

[200] *Children in Northern Uganda* case, paras 38, 73.

[201] See *Centre for Human Rights and la Rencontre Africaine pour la Defense des Droits de l'Homme (on behalf of Senegales Talibés) v Senegal* (*Talibe* case), ACERWC, Communication/001/2012, 15 April 2014.

[202] See Adjolohoun (n 9) 209; Viljoen (n 80) 496.

[203] See Viljoen (80) 374.

[204] Viljoen (n 80) 496.

[205] ACHPR/Res 134 (XXXXIIII) 08: Resolution on the Human Rights Situation in the Republic of The Gambia. See also Viljoen (n 80) 496–497; Adjolohoun (n 9) 209–210.

Commission in *Dabalorivhuwa Patriotic Front v South Africa*[206] borrowed from the ECCJ's judgment in *Etim Moses Essein v The Gambia*.[207] In *Interights and Others v DRC*,[208] the African Commission also referred to the decisions of the ECCJ in *Ebrimah Manneh v The Gambia* and *Koraou v Niger (Niger Slavery* case).[209] Despite not citing the decisions of other HRTs, the ECCJ is good at citing itself. For instance, the ECCJ's decision in the *Federal Republic of Nigeria and Others v Djot Bayi Talbia* (Application for review)[210] was cited in *Dr Rose Mbatomon Ako v The West African Monetary Agency and Others*.[211] The jurisprudence of the ECCJ in the case of *Musa Saidykhan v The Gambia (Application for review)*[212] was also quoted extensively in a subsequent case of *Mbatomon Ako v The West African Monetary Agency and 5 Others*.[213]

Horizontal judicial communication is prevalent not only amongst regional and sub-regional HRTs, but it is also in the form of communication common to domestic courts. There are, however, a couple of occasions relevant to this study when domestic courts engaged in vertical correspondence with regional and sub-regional HRTs in Africa. For instance, the Uganda High Court in *Birungi and 2 Others v A-G of Uganda and Another* referred to the decision of the EACJ in the *Katabazi* case to clarify the responsibility of the Secretary-General of the EAC.[214] In *Constitutional Rights Project v President Ibrahim Babangida*,[215] a Lagos High Court relied on the African Charter and the decision of the African Commission in *Constitutional Rights Project (in respect of Zamani Lakwot and 6 Others) v Nigeria* to restrain the government of Nigeria from executing Zamani Lakwot and others who were sentenced to death.[216] The convicts were not executed and eventually released from prison.[217]

The *Democratic Party and Mukasa Mbidde* case provides an example of a mixed vertical-horizontal transnational judicial communication. The case was submitted to the EACJ following a decision of the Constitutional Court of Uganda in *Jacob Oulanyah v Attorney General*,[218] which was decided based on an earlier decision

[206] Communication 335/07 *Dabalorivhuma Patriotic Front v South African Communication*, para 133.

[207] ECW/CCJ/APP/05/07 *Etim Moses Essein v The Gambia*.

[208] Communication 274/03 and 282/03 *Interights and Others v DRC*.

[209] ECW/CCJ/JJD/06/08 *Koraou v Niger* (*Niger Slavery* case) (2008) AHRLR 182 (ECOWAS 2008). See *Interights and Others v DRC*, para 70.

[210] ECW/CCJ/APP/10/06 (ECW/CCJ/RUL/04/10) *Federal Republic of Nigeria v Djot Bayi Talbia*.

[211] ECW/CCJ/JUD/28/15 *Mbatomon Ako v WAMA and Others*.

[212] ECW/CCJ/APP/11/07, Ruling No. ECW/CCJ/APP/RUL/03/12, *Musa Saidykhan v The Gambia* (Application for review case), judgment delivered on 7 February 2012.

[213] ECW/CCJ/JUD/28/15 *Mbatomon Ako v WAMA and Others*.

[214] *Kamurali Jeremiah Birungi and 2 Others v A-G Uganda and S-G EAC*, National Assembly Election Petition No 002 of 2012 (Unreported).

[215] *Constitutional Rights Project v President Ibrahim Babangida and two Others*, Suit M/102/93, Lagos State High Court, Onalaja J (unreported). See also Okafor (n 7) 98.

[216] Okafor (n 7) 278.

[217] ibid.

[218] *Jacob Oulanyah v Attorney General*, Constitutional Petition No 28 of 2006.

of the EACJ in the *Anyang' Nyong'o* case.[219] The impact of the *Anyang' Nyong'o* case is not limited to Kenya only; the case triggered two complaints submitted against Uganda in the *Democratic Party and Mukasa Mbidde* case and the *Anita Among* case, both of which are part of the cases selected for this study. The vertical transnational judicial communication in the *Jacob Oulanyah* case is significant because it is the first time an apex court of any state, in this case, Uganda, referenced the jurisprudence of the EACJ. The Uganda High Court has subsequently referred to the *Anyang' Nyong'o* case in cases such as *Akidi Margaret v Adong Lilly and the Electoral Commission*[220] and *Toolit Simon Akesha v Oulanyah Jacob L'Okori and Electoral Commission.*[221]

3.4.2 The 'Knock-On or Spill-Over effect'

When an event or a situation has a knock-on effect, it creates a 'ripple effect'. In other words, it causes other events or situations.[222] In addition to transnational judicial communication between domestic and supranational judicial bodies, decisions of regional or sub-regional HRTs have had limited 'knock-on' effects on the work of national and other international tribunals. In other words, the decisions have indirectly, in most cases without any explicit reference, influenced the legal reasoning of other courts or formed the basis of independents claims before domestic courts and other HRTs. This type of 'spill-over' effect is clearly different from instances where courts directly cite each other's jurisprudence to strengthen and legitimize their arguments. The 'knock-on effect' usually happens where human rights NGOs use domestic courts and other supranational tribunals as a vehicle for the execution of the reparation orders of regional and sub-regional HRTs.

In 1993, seven Nigerians of the Kataf ethnic minority were arrested, detained, tried and subsequently sentenced to death by a Civil Disturbances Special Tribunal. The CRP, a Nigerian NGO based in Lagos, submitted a communication to the African Commission in the *Zamani Lakwot* case,[223] seeking to halt the execution of the convicts. The African Commission issued an interim measure urging the government of Nigeria to suspend the proposed execution pending the determination of CRP's communication. Armed with this decision, the CRP approached a Lagos High Court requesting an order directing the Nigerian government to respect the interim measure of the African Commission. The Court, per Onalaja J, granted the application.[224] The Court held that the injunction was necessary to prevent the

[219] *Anyang' Nyongo* case.

[220] *Akidi Margaret v Adong Lilly and the Electoral Commission*, Election Petition No 0004 of 2011 (unreported).

[221] *Toolit Simon Akesha v Oulanyah Jacob L'Okori and Electoral Commission*, High Court Election Petition No 001 of 2011 (unreported).

[222] See the Cambridge English Dictionary http://dictionary.cambridge.org/dictionary/english/knock-on-effect.

[223] See *Zamani Lakwot* case (n 149).

[224] See Constitutional Rights Project v President Ibrahim Babangida and two Others (n 215). See also Evelyn A Ankumah, *The African Commission on Human and Peoples' Rights* (1996) (Martinus Nijhoff

government from executing the applicants, thereby rendering nugatory any anticipated decision of the African Commission.[225]

In *SERAP v Nigeria* (*SERAP Right to Education* case), the ECCJ held that every child of school age in Nigeria has a right to education. Many scholars have postulated that this decision could influence the approach of Nigerian judges to the justiciability of the right to education.[226] On 2 March 2017, a Federal High Court in Abuja in the case of *LEDAP v Federal Ministry of Education and Another* (*LEDAP Right to Education* case) held that the right to primary and junior secondary education is justiciable in Nigeria.[227] This is the first time the socio-economic right to education of children has been sanctioned as justiciable by a domestic court in Nigeria. Although the *SERAP v Nigeria (SERAP Right to Education* case) was not specifically referenced in the decision, the reasoning in the case may have been one factor that emboldened the judge and the legal counsels in the *LEDAP Right to Education* case.

The 'knock-on effects' of HRTs' decisions have not been positive in all cases. For instance, on 2 February 2016, a High Court in Ghana in the case of *Chude Mba v Ghana*[228] denied an application seeking to enforce a judgment of the ECCJ.[229] According to the Court, judgments of the ECCJ cannot be enforced by domestic courts since Ghana was yet to domesticate the Protocol establishing the ECCJ.[230] In *Gramara and Another v Zimbabwe,*[231] two of the 77 applicants in the *Mike Campbell* case[232] filed a case at the High Court of Zimbabwe seeking an order for the registration and enforcement of the SADC Tribunal's decision in the *Campbell* case. The Zimbabwean High Court on 26 January 2010 held that the decision could not be registered nor enforced in Zimbabwe as doing so would undermine the authority of the Supreme Court of Zimbabwe and contravene section 16B of Zimbabwe's Constitution.[233] Another 'knock-on effect' of the *Campbell* case is *Fick and Another v Republic of Zimbabwe.*[234] In that case, six of the original applicants

Publishers, The Hague, Boston) 72–73; Imram O Smith, 'Enforcement of Human Rights Treaties in a Military Regime: Effects of Ouster Clauses on the Application of the African Charter on Human and Peoples' Rights in Nigeria' (2000) 9 Review of the ACHPR 192, 194; Okafor (n 7) 98.

[225] See Okafor (n 7) 98–99.

[226] See, for instance, Enyinna S Nwauche, 'Enforcing ECOWAS Law in West African National Courts' (2011) 55 J Afr Law 181, 197.

[227] See 'Nigerian Court Declares Free Primary, Junior Secondary Education an Enforceable Right' *Premium Times* 2 March 2017 http://www.premiumtimesng.com/news/headlines/225057-nigerian-court-declares-free-primary-junior-secondary-education-enforceable-right.html.

[228] *Chude Mba v Ghana*, Suit No HRCM/376/15, decided by the Accra High Court on 2 February 2016.

[229] *Chude Mba v Ghana*, ECW/CCJ/APP/01/13, decided by the ECCJ on 6 November 2013.

[230] ibid.

[231] *Gramara and Another v Zimbabwe* Suit No HC 5483/09, decided on 26 January 2010.

[232] *Mike Campbell (Pvt) Ltd & Others v The Republic of Zimbabwe* Case No SADC(T) 2/2007.

[233] *Gramara* case.

[234] See *Fick and Another v Republic of Zimbabwe* (SADC (T) 01/2010) [2010] SADCT 8 (16 July 2010).

in the *Campbell* case applied to the SADC Tribunal in order that the Tribunal may report the failure of Zimbabwe to comply with the *Campbell* case to the SADC Summit. On 16 July 2010, the Tribunal agreed to report the non-compliance to the Summit and granted costs in favour of the applicants.[235] These processes led to the eventual suspension of the SADC Tribunal.[236]

The SADC Tribunal decision in the *Tembani* case[237] has equally had a limited 'knock-on effect' on the communication procedure of the African Commission. In 2012, a communication, *Luke Tembani and Another v Angola and 13 Others (Luke Tembani* case), was submitted to the African Commission by Norman Tjombe on behalf of Luke Tembani and Benjamin John Freeth.[238] The complainants allege that the decisions of the SADC Summit on 16–17 August 2010 and 20 May 2011 to suspend the SADC Tribunal violates the African Charter. The African Commission on 5 November 2013 held that the African Charter does not impose on member states of SADC an obligation to ensure access to the SADC Tribunal. The *Luke Tembani* case is the first time in Africa that an HRT established under a regional treaty was asked to pronounce on the obligations of member states of a sub-regional treaty.

Still determined to make the government of Zimbabwe comply with the decisions of the SADC Tribunal, some of the applicants in the *Mike Campbell* case approached a South African High Court in Pretoria to have the orders of the SADC Tribunal enforced in South Africa.[239] The South African High Court held that the decision of the SADC Tribunal in the *Campbell* case could be registered, recognized and enforced in South Africa.[240] This decision was affirmed by the Supreme Court of Appeal and the Constitutional Court of South Africa.[241] On 21 September 2015, a property in Cape Town belonging to the government of Zimbabwe was auctioned off for ZAR 3.76 million to cover the costs order in the *Fick* case (CC).[242] This is the first time, at least in Africa, that the asset of a foreign government was subject to execution for the sole purpose of implementing the judgment of an international HRT.

235 ibid.

236 See Gerhard Erasmus, 'The New Protocol for the SADC Tribunal: Jurisdictional Changes and Implications for SADC Community Law' https://www.tralac.org/images/docs/6900/us15wp012015-erasmus-new-protocol-sadc-tribunal-20150123-fin.pdf. See decision of the High Court of Botswana made after the suspension of the SADC Tribunal in *Maria Ferreira Swart v SADC*, delivered on 11 October 2011 where a Botswana High Court claimed it had jurisdiction in a dispute between SADC and its employees.

237 *Tembani v Zimbabwe* Case No 7/2008 SADC (T), 5 June 2009.

238 Communication 409/12 *Luke Tembani and Benjamin John Freeth v Angola and 13 Others*, decided by the African Commission on 5 November 2013.

239 See *Government of the Republic of Zimbabwe v Fick and Others* (2011) ZAGPPHC 76.

240 *Government of the Republic of Zimbabwe v Fick and Others*(2011) ZAGPPHC 76 ('Fick High Court').

241 See *Government of the Republic of Zimbabwe v Fick and Others* (2012) ZASCA 122 ('Fick SCA'); *Government of the Republic of Zimbabwe v Fick and Others* (2013) ZACC 22, 2013 (5) SA 325 (CC).

242 Jenni Evans 'Zim Govt Property in Cape Town Sold for R3.7m' *News24* 21 September 2015 http://www.news24.com/SouthAfrica/News/Zim-govt-property-in-Cape-Town-sold-for-R37m-20150921.

3.4.3 Norm-Setting and Creation of Authoritative Jurisprudence

Another significant impact of HRTs' decisions is norm creation through authoritative interpretation of treaty provisions. Provisions of treaties are not exhaustive; luckily, the lacuna in the various human rights treaties are continuously filled through the interpretive jurisprudence of HRTs. Norms set by HRTs may never be used in subsequent proceedings of any HRT, yet they represent authoritative interpretations of those norms for all actors. The usefulness of HRTs' interpretive jurisprudence goes beyond the courtroom, thus making it fall outside the scope of 'transnational judicial communication'. Researchers, policymakers, legislators and civil society have derived inspiration from the authoritative interpretations of HRTs.

The African Commission, for instance, elaborated on the right to an effective remedy in the *Jawara* case.[243] In the *Mtikila* case (Ruling on reparation),[244] the African Court set out the legal framework governing the right to reparation under the African human rights system. In the *Djot Bayi Talbia* case,[245] the ECCJ noted that articles 9 and 10 of the ECCJ Protocol do not specifically provide for 'a right to reparation'.[246] The ECCJ used the opportunity presented in the case to expound on the principles of 'just and equitable reparation' under international law.[247] It has been suggested that this decision could influence subsequent cases before the ECCJ where no other relief would be appropriate other than just and equitable reparation.[248] In *Musa Saidykhan v The Gambia (Application for review)*, the ECCJ elaborated on the general principles guiding application for review.[249] Judicial and non-judicial actors have cited the jurisprudence of the tribunals in the above cases.[250] The norms are also relied upon by legal counsels and litigants in subsequent cases. In exceptional cases, the jurisprudence may be cited by the tribunal or by other similar HRTs.

The case of *James Katabazi and 21 others v The S-G of EAC and AG Uganda*[251] has been instrumental to developing the limited human rights jurisdiction of the EACJ. The question of whether the EACJ has jurisdiction to entertain cases involving human rights violations was first raised in this case.[252] The reasoning of the EACJ in the *Katabazi* case has remained a recurring feature in subsequent

[243] *Jawara* case.
[244] *Mtikila*case (Ruling on reparation).
[245] *Djob Bayi Talbia* case.
[246] See J Ukaigwe *ECOWAS law* (2016) 194.
[247] ibid.
[248] Ukaigwe (n 246).
[249] ECW/CCJ/APP/11/07, Ruling No ECW/CCJ/APP/RUL/03/12, *Musa Saidykhan v The Gambia* (Application for review case), judgment delivered on 7 February 2012.
[250] Few examples of these types of references have been highlighted under 'transnational judicial communication'.
[251] *Katabazi* case.
[252] *Katabazi* case.

cases that involve an allegation of human rights violations.[253] Although all the important jurisprudential contributions of African regional and sub-regional HRTs' decisions cannot be highlighted here, the argument is that decisions of HRTs create legal norms that affect general understanding and application of legal principles by judicial and non-judicial actors.

3.5 Tool for Research, Advocacy and Social Mobilization

In many cases, decisions of African regional and sub-regional HRTs have served as an important tool for social mobilization, advocacy and research. There is already a growing body of literature on the case law of regional and sub-regional HRTs in Africa.[254] While all the instances related to this theme cannot be cited here, one clear example of the use of an HRT's decision for social mobilization is the *Olajide Afolabi* case, which was instrumental to the human rights jurisdiction of the ECCJ.[255] In that case, a Nigerian businessman who had concluded a business arrangement with his customers in Benin suffered huge losses in his business when the Nigerian government, without any prior notice, closed the *Seme* border; thus, failing to gain entry to Benin to complete his business transactions. Afolabi approached the ECCJ to enforce his right to freedom of movement, free movement of goods and services, as well as the right of ingress and egress as guaranteed in the 1993 revised ECOWAS Treaty and article 12 of the African Charter. Painfully, the ECCJ held that only a state party to the ECOWAS Treaty might approach the ECCJ on behalf of its nationals.[256]

After the judgment was delivered in the *Afolabi* case, the judges issued a joint press release lamenting the unfairness of their decision and calling on all ECOWAS member states to allow private litigants access to the ECCJ.[257] To demonstrate their commitment to this campaign, the ECCJ published a booklet to elaborate on why the ECOWAS laws that produced the *Afolabi* decision must change.[258] This booklet was widely disseminated by the ECCJ. Ultimately, the vibrant advocacy

[253] See *Mohochi v A-G Uganda* (*Mohochi* case) Ref No 5 of 2011; *Independent Medical Legal Unit v Attorney General of Kenya* (*Independent Medical Legal Unit* case) Ref No 3 of 2010; *Sitenda Sebalu v Secretary General of EAC* (*Sebalu* case) Ref No 1 of 2010 (First Instance Division).

[254] See, for instance, M G Nyarko and H M Ekefre, 'Recent Advances Children's Rights in the African Human Rights System: A Review of the Decision of the African Committee of Experts on the Rights and Welfare of the Child in the Talibe Case' (2016) 15 LPICT 385–395; O Windridge, 'A Watershed Moment for African Human Rights: *Mtikila & Others v Tanzania* at the African Court on Human and Peoples' Rights' (2015) 15 AHRLJ 299–328.

[255] ECW/CCJ/JUD/01/04 *Afolabi Oladjide v Nigeria*.

[256] See *Olajide Afolabi* case, para 62.

[257] Lillian Okenwa, 'ECOWAS Court' *This Day (Nigeria)* (28 April 2004), referred to in Karen J Alter, Laurence R Helfer and Jacqueline R McAllister, 'A New International Human Rights Court for West Africa: The ECOWAS Community Court of Justice' (2013) 107 AJIL 737, 750.

[258] ibid.

by the ECCJ and other stakeholders together with indirect coalition building by the ECOWAS Commission and the West African Bar Association, following the *Afolabi* case, gave rise to the adoption of the 2005 Supplementary Protocol, which confers on the ECCJ express human rights jurisdiction.

The *Mtikila* case has also prompted social mobilization around issues of independent candidacy in the electoral process of Tanzania.[259] The *Ogoniland* case has been an important tool for human rights NGOs advocating for the socio-economic rights of local communities in Nigeria. The *Gambian Mental Health* case has contributed to advocacy on mental health issues in The Gambia. The decisions of HRTs to release substantial information to the public, which provides incentives for social mobilization, advocacy and research. The various cases involving The Gambia and Zimbabwe, for instance, released substantial information about human rights violations in the two countries. Some of the human rights violations that the two countries are usually criticized for come from the information released through the decisions of HRTs.

3.6 Other Forms of Impact of HRTs' Decisions

HRTs' decisions have resulted in limited yet significant attempts to hold multinational oil companies (MNCs) and other similar non-state actors accountable for human rights violations in their host communities. In response to the ECCJ judgment in *SERAP v Nigeria* (*Niger Delta Environmental Degradation* case), SERAP stated that the judgment was 'an important step towards accountability for government and oil companies that continue to prioritize profit-making above the well-being of the people of the region'.[260] It further stated that the judgment 'laid down minimum standards of operations for government and oil companies involved in the exploitation of oil and gas in the region'.[261] The *Ogoniland* case has also contributed to the limited accountability for human rights violations by non-state actors, especially MNCs operating in Ogoniland.

The decision of an HRT provides a permanent record of human rights violations in specific contexts, and it usually does so in considerable detail. It is a permanent record of those violations for future references. HRTs' decisions invest in those allegations the status of proven facts. Unlike news reports which summarized versions of the violations and trends only for a relatively short period, the information contained in judicial decisions is perpetually in the domain of public discourse. The cases are studied in various law schools, year after year and referred

[259] *Mtikila* case.
[260] Amnesty International 'Ground-Breaking ECOWAS Court Judgment Orders Government to Punish Oil Companies Over Pollution' 16 December 2012 https://www.amnesty.org/en/press-releases/2012/12/ground-breaking-ecowas-court-judgment-orders-government-punish-oil-companie/.
[261] ibid.

to by courts from time to time. Decisions of HRTs also increase the level of awareness about the human rights and activities of HRTs. The *Mtikila* case, for example, was singled out by respondents interviewed during this study as a major case that popularized the African Court.[262] The same is true of the *Ogoniland* case of the African Commission, the *Katabazi* case in the EACJ and the *Mike Campbell* case in the SADC Tribunal. One of the most important yet subtle effects of HRTs' decisions is deterrence. Decisions of HRTs generally have a limited constraining effect on the future behaviour of state and non-state actors.[263] This effect is, however, largely unobtrusive and very difficult, if not impossible, to verify. While the full extent of the domestic effects of African regional and sub-regional HRTs' decisions is too broad for an all-encompassing discussion in a single piece, the analysis in this chapter highlights some of the most important contributions of regional and sub-regional HRTs' decisions in Africa.

4 Conclusion

Despite the low level of compliance across the six regional and sub-regional HRTs discussed in scholarly literature, the various cases and themes discussed in this chapter suggest that decisions and individual communication procedures of African regional and sub-regional HRTs have had a modest yet significant impact in each of the five states selected for the study. Some domestic legislation has been repealed, reparation measures have been implemented, resources have been allocated and some institutions were created in the studied countries as a direct consequence of decisions and communication procedures of African regional and sub-regional HRTs. While the domestic effects of HRTs' decisions are too numerous to itemize or interrogate in great depth in a single analytical piece, this chapter identifies five major ways in which the decisions of African regional and sub-regional HRTs made a difference in the selected states.

The examples of the state-level impact of HRTs' decisions include amicable settlement of disputes and proactive remediation of violations; provision of positive material and non-material benefits for successful applicants; legislative and policy reforms; the use of HRTs' decisions as tools for social mobilization, advocacy and research; the judicial impact of HRTs' decisions which may take the form of 'authoritative norm-setting', 'transnational judicial communication' and other 'knock-on effects'; holding MNCs and other similar non-state actors accountable for human rights violations; providing a permanent record of human rights violations; increasing the level of awareness about human rights and activities of HRTs; and creating limited deterrence effects on state actions.

262 Skype communication with E Chijarira (PALU) on 5 May 2015.
263 See Simmons and Hopkins (n 73); Stein (n 2) 611–622.

For instance, birth registration for children has greatly improved in Uganda since the African Children's Rights Committee's decision in the *Children in Northern Uganda* case. The government of Nigeria has committed resources to the clean-up of Ogoniland. Mental health patients now live under better conditions in The Gambia, thanks to the advocacy following The *Gambian Mental Health* case. While more certainly needs to be done, even the most critical pessimist can only imagine what the African continent would be like without these communication procedures and decisions.

The evidence and discussions in this chapter demonstrate that the compliance ratings of states may sometimes provide a false reflection of the effectiveness and impact of HRTs' decisions. Tribunals whose decisions have the highest compliance ratings do not necessarily have the most impact in the studied countries. The analysis also shows that human rights decisions do not operate in isolation; they are a part of a complex web of legal normativity. Ascertaining the actual effects of human rights decisions thus requires reaching beyond the state compliance narrative.[264] there is seldom a reference by states to the decisions of the relevant HRTs when state actors take measures to 'comply' with HRTs' decisions. In many cases, state officials are completely oblivious of the HRT's decision with which they are 'complying', as other domestic mechanisms or circumstances have induced compliance. This disconnection between state behaviour and human rights decisions, as earlier argued, highlights how peripheral these decisions are in the way African governments approach human rights issues at the domestic level. While the state compliance narrative obviously remains one of the most important ways to measure the effectiveness of HRTs, it is not the only measure of the effectiveness of an HRT.

One lesson gained from interacting with various domestic actors during this study is that the implementation of HRTs' decisions is not as straightforward as human rights experts generally tend to assume. Even without an HRT's decision involved, the review of a national constitution may take decades to complete due to various competing interests. Although the government of Tanzania has yet to adopt a new constitution in accordance with the orders of the African Court, the *Mtikila* decision has provoked a national conversation. It has pushed national actors from a state of denial to gradual acceptance of the judgment, and that is significant.[265] While there is no systematic way to gather the evidence, the *Mtikila* decision has influenced the perception of state actors across Africa on the issue of independent candidacy. Decisions of HRTs are no more than tools of transnational legal processes.[266] They are not finished products that translate automatically into reality at the domestic level; they are tools that can be used to negotiate certain outcomes. In his rational choice analysis of international tribunals, Andrew Guzman

264 Okafor (n 7) 284.
265 See AllAfrica (n 162).
266 See Koh 'Transnational Legal Process' (n 19); Koh 'Bringing International Law Home' (n 21).

argues that international tribunals are simply 'tools to produce a particular kind of information.' Guzman explained how the type of information produced by an international tribunal might influence a state's behaviour towards compliance.[267]

If HRTs' decisions are to have more effects at the domestic level, domestic activist forces and transnational compliance actors must take the national process of implementation more seriously. The evidence in this chapter seems to suggest that HRTs' decisions do not translate automatically into tangible outcomes without significant social mobilization around the case. Thus, the most important factor predictive of human rights judgment impact is the extent of social mobilization built around a case because social mobilization increases the political cost of non-compliance. It should, however, be noted that the success of social mobilization depends on other factors such as 'media response, public receptivity and pre-existing understanding of the issues.'[268] It has also been suggested that human rights decisions would have greater impact if HRTs engage in 'dialogical activism'. This approach entails the use of 'reflexive remedies' such as 'broad-brush remedies'. These types of remedies may be given content through consent orders and settlement, delayed declaration of invalidity and the involvement of state representatives and other relevant stakeholders in the formulation of remedies. Reflexive remedies encourage state actors sometimes to come up with more efficient and lower-cost ways to achieve the goal of the litigation. It also addresses issues of democratic legitimacy and institutional competence of HRTs to adjudicate, especially in ESCRs cases. Overall, reflexive remedies tend to deepen democratic participation, promote social mobilization and improve human rights judgment impact.[269]

[267] Andrew T Guzman, 'International Tribunals: A Rational Choice Analysis' (2008) 157 Uni PA Law Rev 171, 180.

[268] Langford, Rodríguez-Garavito and Rossi (n 52) 30.

[269] See generally Langford, Rodríguez-Garavito and Rossi (n 52) 26–32.

4

Compliance with Prohibition of the Death Penalty in Africa

Lilian Chenwi

1 Introduction

Over the years, there has been a growing worldwide trend for the abolition of the death penalty.[1] Over the past two decades, for instance, more and more countries have abolished the death penalty, as evidenced by global statistics at the time of writing. The statistics indicate a continuous increase in the number of countries that have abolished the death penalty and a significant decrease in executions globally.[2] In addition, a significant number of states (121) supported a 2018 United Nations (UN) resolution for a moratorium on the use of the death penalty with a view to abolishing it.[3] This reaffirms a global consensus towards the abolition of the death penalty.

The application of the death penalty can be traced as far back as pre-colonial times for some African societies, and for others, its institutionalization was introduced by the colonial powers.[4] For more than a decade now, its abolition in the continent has been sought. The African Commission on Human Rights (African

[1] Roger Hood and Carolyn Hoyle, *The Death Penalty: A Worldwide Perspective* (5th edn, OUP 2015) ch 1.

[2] By the end of 2018, 106 countries had abolished the death penalty *in law* for all crimes, an increase compared to 60 in 1996, 64 in 1997, 70 in 1998, 102 in 2015 and 104 in 2016. Twenty-eight countries had abolished the death penalty *in practice* and eight for ordinary crimes only. In total, 142 countries had abolished the death penalty *in law or practice*. On the number of executions, by the end of 2018, it decreased by over 30% to at least 690 in 20 countries (lowest figure in the past decade), compared to at least 993 in 23 countries in 2017, at least 1,032 in 23 countries in 2016 and the number of death sentences imposed dropped by 17% to at least 2,591 in 53 countries, compared to the 'record-high' of 3,117 in 55 countries in 2016. See Amnesty International, 'Global Report: Death Sentences and Executions 2018' AI Index: ACT 50/9870/2019 (2019) 8–9 and 48; Amnesty International, 'Global Report: Death Sentences and Executions 2017' AI Index: ACT 50/7955/2018 (2018) 5–7 and 40; Amnesty International, 'Global Report: Death Sentences and Executions 2016' AI Index: ACT 50/5740/2017 (2017) 4–5 and 42; Amnesty International 'Global Report: Death Sentences and Executions 2015' AI Index: ACT 50/3487/2016 (2016) 4.

[3] UN General Assembly, Resolution 73/175: Moratorium on the Use of the Death Penalty (17 December 2018), UN Doc A/RES/73/175 (2019).

[4] Lilian Chenwi, *Towards Abolition of the Death Penalty in Africa: A Human Rights Perspective* (PULP 2007) 18 and 20. Also see, generally, Andrew Novak, 'Capital Punishment in Precolonial Africa: The Authenticity Challenge' (2018) 50(1) J Leg Plur Unoff Law 71–93.

Lilian Chenwi, *Compliance with Prohibition of the Death Penalty in Africa* In: *Compliance with International Human Rights Law in Africa.* Edited by: Aderomola Adeola, Oxford University Press. © Lilian Chenwi 2022.
DOI: 10.1093/oso/9780192856999.003.0004

Commission) and its Working Group on Death Penalty and Extra-Judicial, Summary or Arbitrary Killings in Africa (Working Group on Death Penalty)[5] have repeatedly urged African states to abolish the death penalty or introduce a moratorium on its application.[6] The Commission's 2019 resolution on the death penalty, while acknowledging the existence of a 'continental and worldwide trend towards the abolition of the death penalty', urges states 'that still retain the death penalty to observe a moratorium on the death penalty' and on executions, with a view to abolishing it.[7] Abolition of the death penalty, as emphasized by the Commission, is in line with international law requiring states that have not yet abolished it to take steps towards its abolition to safeguard human rights, including the right to life, dignity and freedom from torture, and cruel, inhuman or degrading treatment or punishment.[8] African regional and national jurisprudence have emphasized the prohibition or abolition of the death penalty so as to enhance and protect human rights.[9] A transnational judicial dialogue on prohibiting or restricting the use of the death penalty has also been established.[10] With the prohibition of the death penalty increasingly viewed as a human rights norm, more and more African states, as seen in section 2 below, are abandoning the practice of the death penalty.

With evidence of a decline in the use of the death penalty in the African region, this chapter considers Africa's compliance with the prohibition of the death penalty. In this regard, it considers four aspects: the question of its general prohibition, specifically the desirability of its abolition; prohibition of the mandatory death penalty; prohibition of the death penalty for certain offenders; and prohibition of the death penalty for certain offences. Though the chapter does not consider the prohibition of its application where relevant safeguards are not adhered to, such as procedural guarantees relevant to a fair trial, among others, this should not diminish the importance of this prohibition. In fact, as emphasized by the African

[5] On its establishment, see Res 79: Resolution on the Composition and the Operationalization of the Working Group on the Death Penalty (5 December 2005), ACHPR/Res 79 (XXXVIII) 05.

[6] See, eg African Commission on Human and Peoples' Rights, Resolution 42: Resolution Urging States to Envisage a Moratorium on Death Penalty (15 November 1999), ACHPR/Res.42(XXVI)9; African Commission on Human and Peoples' Rights, Resolution 136: Resolution Calling on State Parties to Observe a Moratorium on the Death Penalty (24th November 2008), ACHPR/Res 136(XXXXIIII).08; African Union, '59th Ordinary Session of the African Commission on Human and Peoples' Rights: Inter-Session Activity Report (May – October 2016)' (2016) para 12.

[7] African Commission on Human and Peoples' Rights, Resolution 416: Abolition of the Death Penalty in Africa (14 May 2019), ACHPR/Res 416 (LXIV) 2019.

[8] African Commission on Human and Peoples' Rights, General Comment 3 on the African Charter on Human and Peoples' Rights: The Right to Life (art 4) (2015) para 22.

[9] For a discussion of relevant African regional and national jurisprudence, see Carlson Anyangwe, 'Emerging African Jurisprudence Suggesting the Desirability of the Abolition of Capital Punishment' (2015) 23/1 Afr J Int Comp Law 1–28. Also, see generally, Chenwi, *Towards Abolition* (note 4 above) chs 3–5.

[10] On the transnational judicial dialogue in death penalty challenges, and specifically in the context of mandatory death penalty', see generally Andrew Novak, 'The "Judicial Dialogue" in Transnational Human Rights Litigation: *Muruatetu & Anor v Republic* and the Abolition of the Mandatory Death Penalty in Kenya' (2018) 18 Human Rights Law Review 1–20.

Commission, proceedings must 'stringently' meet 'the highest standards of fairness'; otherwise, the death penalty should not be applied, as its application will amount to a violation of, inter alia, the right to life and applicable fair trial rights.[11]

In dealing with each of the focused aspects, the chapter considers the position of the death penalty in international human rights law with reference to key UN human rights treaties (which African states are parties to[12]) and their subsequent interpretation, with the view of establishing the prohibitions relating to the death penalty contained in them and its basis.[13] Also, a consideration of the death penalty in relevant African human rights instruments and their subsequent interpretation is undertaken, to establish the existence of a prohibition and its extent and the regional treaties' compliance with international norms on the death penalty.[14] Statistics on the death penalty in Africa and/or other recent developments relating to its abolition/prohibition are considered, applicable to a specific prohibition, to further establish African states' compliance or not with the respective prohibitions. This chapter does not seek to provide comprehensive information on individual African states' compliance in theory and practice with the identified prohibitions. Rather, it provides an overview while citing some illustrative examples.

2 Desirability of Abolition of the Death Penalty

There is no explicit *general* prohibition of the death penalty under international law, as some instruments merely place restrictions on its use (banning its application in certain circumstances) while others are silent on it. Also, customary international law does not prohibit the death penalty, but state practice and *opinio juris* on the death penalty are increasingly changing towards favouring its abolition. Though international human rights treaties do not contain an explicit general prohibition

[11] African Commission, General Comment 3 (n 8) paras 24 and 26. Subsequent exoneration of people sentenced to death (thus confirming their innocence 'in the eyes of the law') is illustrative of unfair trials and the existent risk of executing the innocent. In Africa, eg, exonerations of prisoners under sentence of death have been recorded: 42 in 2015, 43 in 2016, 49 in 2017 and at least three in 2018. See: Amnesty International, 'Death Sentences and Executions 2015' (n 2) 7; Amnesty International, 'Death Sentences and Executions 2016' (n 2) 6, 32, 38–39; Amnesty International, 'Death Sentences and Executions 2017' (n 2) 9, 31 and 37; Amnesty International, 'Death Sentences and Executions 2018' (n 2) 11; Human Rights Committee, Concluding Observations on the Fifth Periodic Report of Cameroon, UN Doc CCPR/C/CMR/CO/5 (2017) paras 23–24.

[12] The ratification status of treaties stated in this chapter is updated as of the end of February 2019 and excludes Western Sahara with respect to UN treaties, as it is not recognized as a state by the UN, hence not able to ratify UN treaties.

[13] Though this chapter focuses on international human rights treaties, it should be noted that treaties in other fields of international law (eg, international humanitarian law treaties) have addressed the question of the death penalty.

[14] It should also be emphasized that though treaties from other regional systems—the Inter-American and European system—are not discussed, this does not imply a dismissal of their importance to the abolition course in Africa, as they serve as persuasive authority from which African states can draw inspiration.

of the death penalty, they emphasize the desirability of its general abolition, among other specific prohibitions. Accordingly, a move towards its prohibition in international law is increasingly evident from recent international standards in support of its abolition and subsequent interpretation of existing international standards that view its application as a violation of human rights.

2.1 UN Standards

The Universal Declaration of Human Rights[15] (UDHR) makes no mention of the death penalty. It, however, guarantees, inter alia, the right to life in article 3. It has been recognized that 'a firm step' towards upholding article 3 is [a]bolition of the death penalty in a state's legislation.[16] Since several UN resolutions on the abolition of the death penalty refer to article 3, it has been argued that the provision favours abolition.[17]

The pro-abolitionist principle is reinforced in the International Covenant on Civil and Political Rights[18] (ICCPR). Though the ICCPR does not explicitly abolish the death penalty, it refers to it. Article 6 prohibits arbitrary deprivation of life[19] and prohibits states parties from invoking provisions in article 6 'to delay or to prevent the abolition of capital punishment'.[20] In elaborating on article 6, the Human Rights Committee has held that '[t]he prohibition on arbitrary deprivation of life contained in article 6, paragraph 1 further limits the ability of States parties to apply the death penalty' and that article 6(6) ICCPR is reflective of the 'pro-abolitionist spirit of the Covenant'.[21] Article 6(6) 'reaffirms the position that States parties that are not yet totally abolitionist should be on an *irrevocable path towards complete eradication of the death penalty, de facto and de jure*, in the foreseeable future', as it 'cannot be reconciled with full respect for the right to life, and *abolition of the death penalty is both desirable and necessary* for the enhancement of human dignity and progressive development of human rights'.[22] It is thus 'contrary to the object and purpose of article 6 for States parties to take steps to increase de facto the rate and extent in which they resort to the death penalty, or to reduce the number of pardons and commutations'.[23] The Committee further held that though article 6(2)

[15] Adopted 10 December 1948, GA Resolution 217A (III), UN Doc A/810 at 71 (1948).

[16] UN Office of the High Commissioner for Human Rights, *Moving Away from the Death Penalty: Lessons in South-East Asia* (UN 2012) 6, https://www.ohchr.org/Lists/MeetingsNY/Attachments/27/moving_away_from_death_penalty_web.pdf (accessed 12 March 2019).

[17] William Schabas, *The Abolition of the Death Penalty in International Law* (3rd edn, CUP 2002) 42–43; Chenwi, *Towards Abolition* (n 4) 61–62.

[18] Adopted 16 December 1966, entered into force 23 March 1976, UN Doc A/6316 (1966).

[19] ICCPR, art 6(1).

[20] ibid, art 6(6).

[21] Human Rights Committee, General Comment 36 on art 6 of the International Covenant on Civil and Political Rights, on the Right to Life, UN Doc CCPR/C/GC/36 (2018) paras 5 and 51.

[22] ibid, para 50. Emphasis added.

[23] ibid.

ICCPR does not explicitly prohibit the death penalty on the grounds of it being 'cruel, inhuman or degrading punishment per se', it has been established in 'subsequent agreements by the States parties or subsequent practice establishing such agreements … that the death penalty is contrary to article 7 of the Covenant under all circumstances'.[24] In order to fully uphold and promote progressive development of human rights, states parties to the ICCPR (which includes 52 African states that have ratified it), therefore, have an obligation to, inter alia, progressively move towards its abolition and refrain from actions aimed at preventing it.

The reference to abolition in article 6 ICCPR has been viewed by states parties to the Second Optional Protocol to the International Covenant on Civil and Political Rights, aiming at the abolition of the death penalty[25] (ICCPR-OP2), as a strong suggestion that abolition of the death penalty is desirable.[26] ICCPR-OP2's adoption was based on states' desire to 'undertake … an international commitment to abolish the death penalty'.[27] The Protocol prohibits executions and requires states parties to 'take all necessary measures to abolish the death penalty within [their] jurisdiction'.[28] However, it does not provide for the complete abolition of the death penalty as states parties are allowed to enter reservations regarding its use during wartime at the time of ratification or accession.[29] There is, however, a limit to such reservations. As held by the Human Rights Committee, 'no reservation to the prohibition against arbitrary deprivation of life of persons and to the strict limits provided in Article 6 with respect to the application of the death penalty is permitted'.[30] Though ICCPR-OP2 does not provide for the complete abolition of the death penalty, it strongly emphasizes the desirability of its abolition at the international level. Furthermore, 'adherence' to ICCPR-OP2 as held by the Human Rights Committee requires that states parties 'become an abolitionist country in practice as well as in law'.[31] It is also worth noting that there is no termination provision in ICCPR-OP2 and as held by the Human Rights Committee, 'States parties cannot denounce it' and their '[a]bolition of the death penalty is therefore legally irrevocable'.[32] Moreover, as held by the Committee, 'the abolition of the death penalty should apply retroactively to individuals charged or convicted of a capital offence'.[33] This understanding is justified by the principle of 'retroactive leniency (*lex*

[24] ibid, para 51.
[25] Adopted 15 December 1989, entered into force 11 July 1991, UN Doc A/44/49(1989).
[26] ICCPR-OP2, preamble.
[27] ibid.
[28] ICCPR-OP2, arts 1(1) and (2).
[29] ibid, art 2.
[30] Human Rights Committee, General Comment 36 (n 21) para 68.
[31] Human Rights Committee, Concluding Observations on the Initial Report of Liberia, UN Doc CCPR/C/LBR/CO/1 (2018) para 29.
[32] Human Rights Committee, General Comment 36 (n 21) para 34.
[33] ibid, para 38.

motior)', expressed in article 15(1) ICCPR, and 'the fact that the need for applying the death penalty cannot be justified once it had been abolished'.[34]

Sixteen African states are party to ICCPR-OP2 and are thus bound by its obligations—which in a nutshell, as seen above, are obligations to not resort to executions, abolish the death penalty within their jurisdictions and abstain from reintroducing it. Notwithstanding, the limited ratification of the Protocol by African states (comprising just over a third of African states) raises questions about the commitment of African states to human rights standards and the abolition of the death penalty, in some cases, their de facto abolitionist status. Also, the fact that some African states that have abolished the death penalty have not ratified ICCPR-OP2 is a concern. Mauritius and Côte d'Ivoire, for example, abolished the death penalty in 1995 and 2015, respectively, but, at the time of writing, had not acceded to ICCPR-OP2 despite a recommendation from the Human Rights Committee to this effect.[35] On the other hand, however, it is plausible that all African states parties to ICCPR-OP2 are, at the time of writing, either abolitionist for all crimes or abolitionist in practice, with the exception of The Gambia that is classified as retentionist but is taking steps towards abolition.[36]

2.2 African Regional Standards

The commitment of African states to dealing with the question of abolition in a legally binding treaty is questionable. The African Union (AU) is yet to adopt a regional treaty with the explicit provision on the abolition of the death penalty. As part of its efforts in working towards abolition, the African Commission adopted, in 2015, a draft Protocol to the African Charter on Human and Peoples' Rights on the Abolition of the Death Penalty and forwarded it to the AU for formal adoption.[37] Sadly though, the AU Specialized Technical Committee on Legal Affairs declined to consider the draft Protocol, citing the lack of a legal basis for its adoption.[38] Notwithstanding, the Working Group on Death Penalty has continued with recommendations, sensitization and lobbying for states to support the draft Protocol.[39] The Working Group is of the view, and rightly so that the draft

[34] ibid.

[35] Human Rights Committee, Concluding Observations on the Fifth Periodic Report of Mauritius, UN Doc CCPR/C/MUS/CO/5 (2017) paras 17–18; Human Rights Committee, Concluding Observations on the Initial Report of Côte d'Ivoire, UN Doc CCPR/C/CIV/CO/1 (2015) para 14.

[36] Amnesty International, 'Death Sentences and Executions 2018' (n 2) 48–49.

[37] Adopted at its 56th session, 21 April – 7 May 2015. See African Union, 'Final communiqué of the 56th Ordinary Session of the African Commission on Human and Peoples' Rights (21 April – 7 May 2015)' 9.

[38] Amnesty International, 'Death Sentences and Executions 2015' (2) 12.

[39] African Union, '60th Ordinary Session of the African Commission on Human and Peoples' Rights: Intersession Activity Report (November 2016 – April 2017)' (2017) para 11; African Union, '61st Ordinary Session of the African Commission on Human and Peoples' Rights: Inter-Session Activity Report (June – November 2017)' (2017) para 39; African Union, '64th Ordinary Session of

Protocol is 'a great step toward the abolition of the death penalty in the continent'.[40] Accordingly, the 2019 resolution on the death penalty adopted by the African Commission reiterated the call for states to support the AU's adoption of the draft Protocol.[41]

Furthermore, the African Charter on Human and Peoples' Rights[42] (African Charter), like the UDHR, is silent on the death penalty. However, the African Commission, in elaborating on the right to life in the Charter, has interpreted its silence on the death penalty to imply its non-recognition, 'even in limited circumstances'.[43] The Commission, in its general comment on the right to life, strongly emphasized the desirability of abolition or establishment of a moratorium on the death penalty, in line with African and global trends.[44] It held that 'States that have not yet abolished the death penalty' are required by international law 'to take steps towards its abolition' so as to secure the rights to life, dignity, freedom from torture, and cruel, inhuman or degrading treatment, among other rights.[45] For states that have already abolished the death penalty in law, they 'shall not reintroduce it, nor facilitate executions in retentionist States through *refoulement*, extradition, deportation, or other means including the provision of support or assistance that could lead to a death sentence'.[46] For states that have put in place a moratorium on the death penalty, they 'must take steps to formalise abolition in law, allowing no further executions'.[47] The Commission further clarified what a comprehensive moratorium on execution entails: 'the cessation of executions' and prosecutors to 'refrain from seeking the death penalty' and judges to 'choose not to impose it' during sentencing.[48] This is a welcomed elucidation considering that African states with a de facto moratorium in place have continued to pass death sentences and have significant numbers of people on death row, instead of cessation of death sentences, reduction of numbers of death row and commutation of death sentences. Burkina Faso, the Democratic Republic of Congo (DRC) and Ghana are examples,

the African Commission on Human and Peoples' Rights: Intersession Activity Report (November 2018 – April 2019)' (2019) para 24, African Union, '65th Ordinary Session of the African Commission on Human and Peoples' Rights: Intersession Activity Report (May – October 2019)' (2019) para 29.

40 African Union, '57th Ordinary Session of the African Commission on Human and Peoples' Rights: Inter-Session Activity Report of the Chairperson, ACHPR (May-November 2015)' (2015) para 50; African Union, '56th Ordinary Session of the African Commission on Human and Peoples' Rights: Inter-Session Activity Report of the Working Group on Death Penalty and Extrajudicial, Summary or Arbitrary Killings in Africa (April 2014 – April 2015)' (2015) para 54.

41 African Commission, Res 416 (n 7) para 7.

42 Adopted 27 June 1981, entered into force 21 October 1986, OAU Doc CAB/LEG/67/3 rev 5, 21 ILM 58 (1982).

43 African Commission, General Comment 3 (n 8) para 22.

44 ibid.

45 ibid.

46 ibid, para 23.

47 ibid.

48 ibid.

where the Human Rights Committee, while praising them for observing a de facto moratorium on the death penalty, was concerned about the continuous imposition of death sentences and, in DRC and Ghana, the large number of persons on death row (in case of Ghana, 'for a long period').[49] It thus called on the states to consider/pursue efforts towards abolition and ratification of ICCPR-OP2 and for DRC to commute the sentences of those on death row, and Ghana to 'revise its criminal code so as to eliminate mandatory death sentence'.[50]

Following its general comment, in 2017, the African Commission adopted a resolution on the right to life, urging states parties to the African Charter 'that have established a moratorium on executions to undertake further practical steps towards the abolition of the death penalty, in accordance with their regional and international legal obligations, by reinforcing their moratorium and by encouraging judicial authorities to refrain from imposing the death penalty'.[51] The Commission further urged those 'that have not already abolished the death penalty to immediately establish a moratorium on executions and to adopt measures aimed at the full abolition of the death penalty'.[52] Previous resolutions of the African Commission have also advocated states to establish a moratorium on the death penalty and consider its abolition.[53] This call was reiterated in its 2019 resolution on the death penalty, in which it urged states parties to the African Charter 'to observe a moratorium on the death penalty with a view to abolishing it', take 'practical steps towards the full abolition of the death penalty in law' and ratify ICCPR-OP2.[54] By virtue of being a party to the Charter, all African states (except for Morocco that has neither signed nor acceded to the Charter) are thus obliged to work towards the general prohibition of the death penalty. They are also required to include in their periodic reports to the Commission 'information on the steps they are taking to move towards the abolition of the death penalty in their countries'.[55]

The pro-abolitionist position under the African Charter has been fortified in the Protocol on Amendments to the Protocol on the Statute of the African Court of Justice and Human Rights.[56] As stated in article 43A of the Protocol, the death

[49] Human Rights Committee, Concluding Observations on the Initial Report of Burkina Faso, UN Doc CCPR/C/BFA/CO/1 (2016) para 21; Human Rights Committee, Concluding Observations on the Fourth Periodic Report of the Democratic Republic of the Congo, UN Doc CCPR/C/COD/CO/4 (2017) para 23; Human Rights Committee, Concluding Observations on the Initial Reports of Ghana, UN Doc CCPR/C/GHA/CO/1 (2016) para 19.

[50] Human Rights Committee, CO: Burkina Faso, CCPR/C/BFA/CO/1 (n 49) para 22; Human Rights Committee, CO: DRC, CCPR/C/COD/CO/4 (n 49) para 24; Human Rights Committee, CO: Ghana, CCPR/C/GHA/CO/1 (n 49) para 20.

[51] African Commission on Human and Peoples' Rights, Resolution 375: Resolution on the Right to Life in Africa – ACHPR/Res.375 (LX) 2017 (22 May 2017) para 4.

[52] ibid, para 5.

[53] See, eg African Commission, Res 42 (n 6) para 2; African Commission on Human and Peoples' Rights, Res 136: Resolution Calling on State Parties to Observe a Moratorium on the Death Penalty (24 November 2008) paras 2–4.

[54] African Commission, Res 416 (n 7) paras 2, 3 and 5.

[55] ibid, para 6.

[56] Adopted 27 June 2014, not yet in force (with 15 signatories only and no ratifications).

penalty is excluded as a sentence that the Court can impose for persons convicted of international crimes.

2.3 Compliance in Practice

It is clear from section 2.2 above that the formal regional position on abolition is in line with that at the UN level (explained in section 2.1), both requiring states to, inter alia, take irrevocable efforts towards abolition. However, to understand whether the desirability of abolition (in line with international standards) has translated into practice, consideration of the status of the death penalty in Africa and other relevant developments is crucial.[57]

Statistics from Amnesty International and the Working Group on Death Penalty[58] reveal that a significant majority of African states have abolished the death penalty in law or practice. Amnesty International's statistics[59] show that by the end of 2018: 20 African states[60] have abolished the death penalty for all crimes (compared to one in 1981); one African state has abolished the death penalty for ordinary crimes only;[61] 18 African states,[62] though retaining the death penalty for ordinary crimes such as murder, have not carried out executions in the past ten years and are thought to have established a practice or policy of not carrying out executions (thus considered abolitionist in practice), and 16 African states[63] retain the death penalty for ordinary crimes (thus considered retentionist). The end of 2018 also saw an overall decrease in executions, but the gain is blemished by a spike in death sentences and/or an increase in executions in some African countries (eg, Egypt and South Sudan).[64]

[57] The discussion in this regard draws on parts from Lilian Chenwi, 'The Downfall of the Mandatory Death Penalty in Kenya' (2019) 63(1) Journal of African Law 25–51.

[58] The Working Group on Death Penalty is also tasked with collecting information and monitoring the use of the death penalty in Africa and reports on the status of the death penalty. See African Commission, Res 79 (n 5).

[59] Amnesty International, 'Death Sentences and Executions 2018' (n 2) 48–49.

[60] Angola, Benin, Burundi, Cape Verde, Congo, Côte d'Ivoire, Djibouti, Gabon, Guinea, Guinea-Bissau, Madagascar, Mauritius, Mozambique, Namibia, Rwanda, São Tomé and Príncipe, Senegal, Seychelles, South Africa and Togo.

[61] Burkina Faso. The country is classified as such on the basis that, though its Penal Code excludes the death penalty, it can still be imposed for military crimes under the country's Code of Military Justice. See Amnesty International, 'Death Sentences and Executions 2018' (n 2) 42.

[62] Algeria, Cameroon, Central African Republic, Eritrea, Eswatini (former Swaziland), Ghana, Kenya, Liberia, Malawi, Mali, Mauritania, Morocco, Niger, Sierra Leone, Tanzania, Tunisia, Western Sahara and Zambia.

[63] Botswana, Chad, Comoros, DRC, Egypt, Equatorial Guinea, Ethiopia, Gambia, Lesotho, Libya, Nigeria, Somalia, South Sudan, Sudan, Uganda and Zimbabwe.

[64] Amnesty International, 'Death Sentences and Executions 2018' (n 2) 31–45. Amnesty International's report focuses on north and sub-Saharan Africa; therefore, executions and death sentences could have been imposed in other parts of Africa and not recorded in the report. Hence, see also, African Union, '62nd Ordinary Session of the African Commission on Human and Peoples' Rights: Inter-Session Activity Report (December 2017 – April 2018)' (2018) para 22.

Statistics from the Working Group on Death Penalty[65] indicate that by October 2019, 44 African states 'have abolished the death penalty in law or in practice', comprising 21 who 'have abolished the practice by way of enacting national legislation'[66] and 23 who 'have not carried out an execution for ten years.[67] The Working Group differs in its approach from Amnesty International in relation to typology used in classifying states. The difference in typology has resulted in some states classified by Amnesty International as retentionists for retaining the death penalty for ordinary crimes—Comoros, DRC, Lesotho and Zimbabwe—being classified by the Working Group under states that 'have not carried out an execution for ten years'. However, this difference in classification is corroborated by available reports at the time of writing which indicate that the last known executions took place in these states as follows: Comoros in 1997, DRC in 2003, Lesotho in 1995 and Zimbabwe in 2005.[68]

Despite noting 'with satisfaction some of the positive developments in Africa regarding the abolition of the death penalty', the Working Group has expressed concern over its use in some African states, particularly South Sudan, Somalia, Egypt, Botswana and Sudan.[69] It has thus urged Botswana, Egypt, Sudan and South Sudan to put in place a moratorium on the death penalty in line with Resolution 136 of the African Commission, suspend execution of those on death row and commute their death sentences to life imprisonment.[70] The Human Rights Committee has also raised concern regarding Sudan's use of the death penalty and requested that the state should 'consider imposing a moratorium on the death penalty and ratifying [ICCPR-OP2]' and report by 2 November 2020 on the implementation of this recommendation.[71]

The establishment of the Working Group on Death Penalty, it should be emphasized, is a positive African regional development towards the abolition of the death penalty, considering its mandate, which includes developing 'a strategic plan(s) including a practical and legal framework on the abolition of the Death Penalty' in the continent.[72] Other key positive developments include the holding in 2009,

[65] African Union, '65th Ordinary Session of African Commission (n 39) para 22.

[66] 'Angola, Benin, Burkina Faso, Burundi, Cape Verde, Congo (Republic of), Côte d'Ivoire, Djibouti, Gabon, Guinea, Guinea-Bissau, Madagascar, Mauritius, Mozambique, Namibia, Rwanda, Sao Tome and Principe, Senegal, Seychelles, South Africa, and Togo.'

[67] 'Algeria, Cameroon, Central African Republic, Comoros, Democratic Republic of Congo, Eritrea, Eswatini, Ethiopia, Ghana, Kenya, Lesotho, Liberia, Malawi, Mali, Mauritania, Niger, Saharawi Arab Democratic Republic, Sierra Leone, Tanzania, Tunisia, Uganda, Zambia, and Zimbabwe.'

[68] See World Coalition against the Death Penalty, 'Worldwide Database', http://www.worldcoalition.org/worldwide-database.html (accessed 13 March 2019); Cornell Center on the Death Penalty Worldwide, 'Death Penalty Database: Lesotho', https://www.deathpenaltyworldwide.org/ (accessed 13 March 2019).

[69] African Union, '62nd Ordinary Session of African Commission (n 64) para 23; African Union, '64th Ordinary Session of African Commission (n 39) para 17.

[70] African Union, '62nd Ordinary Session of African Commission (n 64) para 23, paras 13 and 32.

[71] Human Rights Committee, Concluding Observations on the Fifth Periodic Report of the Sudan, UN Doc CCPR/C/SDN/CO/5 (2018) paras 29–30 and 56.

[72] African Commission, Res 79 (n 5).

2010 and 2018 of three African regional conferences on the death penalty, which all ended with declarations on the need to take steps, including combined efforts, towards its abolition on the continent.[73] Also, some African states have recently taken steps towards abolishing the death penalty through constitutional challenges or legislative amendments, imposition of a moratorium on the death penalty, or commitments to abolish it. In January 2016, Benin, for example, abolished the death penalty as a result of a landmark decision by its Constitutional Court finding laws providing for the death penalty to be void in light of the country's international human rights obligations.[74] In 2017, Guinea abolished it due to the adoption and entry into force of a new Code of Military Justice that did not mention the death penalty.[75] In 2017 still, The Gambia signed ICCPR-OP2 and ratified it in 2018. The following year (in February 2018), The Gambia declared 'a moratorium on the application of the death penalty' in the country, which the Working Group on Death Penalty and Human Rights Committee welcomed and urged the state to accelerate efforts towards its abolition in law.[76] In 2018, Burkina Faso adopted a new Penal Code that abolished the death penalty.[77] On abolition commitments, the Ministry of Justice of Niger reportedly stated in 2017 'that a plan to abolish the death penalty had been submitted to the government'.[78] It is important for such commitments to include a timeline to ensure accountability.

Furthermore, the willingness of the African Court on Human ad Peoples' Rights (African Human Rights Court), while acting *proprio motu* for most of the applications, to issue provisional measures in cases before it relating to the death penalty is also noteworthy. The Court based its provisional measures decision on human rights grounds: in 19 cases against Tanzania that being on death row creates a situation of extreme gravity and risk of irreparable harm to the rights of the applicants if the death penalty is carried out.[79] In one case against Ghana, it held that

[73] The Kigali Framework Document on the Abolition of the Death Penalty in Africa, adopted by the First Sub-Regional Conference for Central, Eastern and Southern Africa on the Question of the Death Penalty in Africa in Kigali, Rwanda (2009); The Cotonou Framework Document Towards the Abolition of the Death Penalty in Africa, adopted by the Second Regional Conference for North and West Africa on the Question of the Death Penalty in Africa, adopted in Cotonou, Benin (2010); Final declaration of the African Congress, adopted by the Third Regional Congress against the Death Penalty, Abidjan, Côte d'Ivoire (2018).

[74] African Union, '61st Ordinary Session of the African Commission' (n 39) para 21.

[75] African Union, '59th Ordinary Session of African Commission' (n 6) para 13; Amnesty International 'Death Sentences and Executions in 2017' (n 2) 10.

[76] African Union, '62nd Ordinary Session of African Commission (n 64) paras 14 and 18–19; Human Rights Committee, Concluding Observations on The Gambia in the Absence of Its Second Periodic Report, UN Doc CCPR/C/GMB/CO/2 (2018) paras 27–28; Amnesty International 'Death Sentences and Executions 2017' (n 2) 11, 35.

[77] Amnesty International, 'Death Sentences and Executions 2018' (n 2) 42.

[78] Amnesty International, 'Death Sentences and Executions in 2017' (n 2) 36.

[79] *Guehi v Tanzania*, Application 001/2015, Order for Provisional Measures (18 March 2016); *Rajabu and Others v Tanzania*, Application 007/2015, Order for Provisional Measures (18 March 2016); *Lazaro v Tanzania*, Application 003/2016, Order for Provisional Measures (18 March 2016); *Rutechura v Tanzania*, Application 004/2016, Order for Provisional Measures (18 March 2016); *Augustino and Another v Tanzania*, Application 015/2016, Order for Provisional Measures (3 June 2016); *Jeshi v Tanzania*, Application 017/2016, Order for Provisional Measures (3 June 2016); *Faustine v. Tanzania*,

the risk of executing the death penalty would endanger the enjoyment of rights in the African Charter.[80] State compliance with such provisional measures is crucial, as the death penalty is a matter of life or death. Sadly though, Tanzania indicated a willingness to comply only with some provisional measure orders and not others.[81] Subsequently, the Chief Justice of Tanzania, during his swearing-in ceremony in September 2017, 'stated that he cannot assent to the execution of prisoners sentenced to death', which the Working Group on Death penalty views as 'a very strong signal to the effect that there is a need for Tanzania to consider abolishing the death penalty'.[82] The African Human Rights Court subsequently found the case against Ghana to be inadmissible because the UN Human Rights Committee had already ruled on the case, addressing the same issues before the Court.[83] It should be noted, however, that Ghana had failed to comply with the Committee's decision, hence the case before the African Human Rights Court; thus, a missed opportunity for the Court to address the issue. As regards Tanzania, the Court has subsequently ordered it to abolish the mandatory death penalty, as explained below.[84]

Lastly, the commutation of death sentences is also noteworthy. In 2015, at least 501 commutations were recorded in Africa: DRC (one), Egypt (three), Ghana (14), Malawi (at least five), Mali (16), Nigeria (121), Swaziland (two), Zambia (332) and Zimbabwe (seven).[85] The number increased to at least 2874 in 2016: Ghana (four), Kenya (2747), Mauritania (15), Nigeria (105),[86] Sudan (one)[87] and Zimbabwe

Application 018/2016, Order for Provisional Measures (3 June 2016); *Mukwano v Tanzania*, Application 021/2016, Order for Provisional Measures (3 June 2016); *Juma v Tanzania*, Application No. 024/2016, Order for Provisional Measures (3 June 2016); *Damian v Tanzania*, Application 048/2016, Order for Provisional Measures (18 November 2016); *John v Tanzania*, Application 049/2016, Order for Provisional Measures (18 November 2016); *Gabriel and Another v. Tanzania*, Application 050/2016, Order for Provisional Measures (18 November 2016); *Zabron v Tanzania*, Application 051/2016, Order for Provisional Measures (18 November 2016); *Msuguri v Tanzania*, Application 052/2016, Order for Provisional Measures (18 November 2016); *Josiah v Tanzania*, Application 053/2016, Order for Provisional Measures (18 November 2016); *Henerico v Tanzania*, Application 056/2016, Order for Provisional Measures 6–20 (18 November 2016); *Anatori v Tanzania*, Application No. 057/2016, Order for Provisional Measures (18 November 2016); *Hussein v. Tanzania*, Application 001/2018, Order for Provisional Measures (11 February 2019); *Chalula v Tanzania*, Application 003/2018, Order of Provisional Measures (19 May 2019).

[80] *Johnson v Ghana*, Application 016/2017, Order for Provisional Measures (28 September 2017).

[81] African Court on Human and Peoples' Rights, 'Report on the Activities of the African Court on Human and Peoples Rights: 1 January 31–December 2016', Doc EX.CL/999(XXX) (2017) paras 21(ii) and 57.

[82] African Union, '61st Ordinary Session of African Commission' (n 39) para 20.

[83] *Johnson v Ghana*, Application 016/2017, Ruling (Jurisdiction and Admissibility), (28 March 2019) paras 46–57). See s 3.1 below on the Human Rights Committee's decision.

[84] See s 3.2 below.

[85] Amnesty International, 'Death Sentences and Executions in 2015' (n 2) 7, 58–60, 61–62. Liberia was also listed but unclear if commutation or pardon and with no figures indicated.

[86] An additional 33 pardons were granted.

[87] An additional 17 pardons were granted.

(two).[88] In 2017, there was a decrease in commutations recorded to at least 237: Egypt (162), Mauritania (one), Morocco/Western Sahara (one), Nigeria (68)[89] and Zimbabwe (two).[90] The number increased in 2018 to at least 352, including Benin (14), Egypt (at least 289), Nigeria (at least 32), Sudan (one) and Zimbabwe (at least 16).[91]

Generally, while there are trends towards compliance with the call for the general abolition of the death penalty, there is still a long way to go in terms of its general abolition in law than in practice, as only 20 African states have totally abolished it. The progress made thus far, especially in sub-Saharan Africa, has been seen 'as a beacon of hope for abolition'.[92] Notwithstanding, a crucial issue to note in terms of compliance are some post-abolition concerns that have been raised.

The first relates to compliance with the understanding stated above that 'the abolition of the death penalty should apply retroactively to individuals charged or convicted of a capital offence'. This concern is based on delays in commuting the death sentences of those sentenced to death before abolition. Guinea is an example in this regard. In 2016, it adopted a revised Criminal Code,[93] abolishing the death penalty for ordinary crimes; and in 2017, its National Assembly adopted a new Code of Military Justice,[94] abolishing the death penalty for all crimes.[95] Despite this positive development, by October 2018, the death sentences imposed before the legislative changes had still not been commuted, which the Human Rights Committee found regretful and contrary to article 6 ICCPR.[96] Therefore, it requested that Guinea takes all necessary measures to ensure that the sentences of those still under death sentence are commuted as soon as possible and initiate a process of accession to ICCPR-OP2.[97] The second concern relates to ensuring post-abolition that all domestic laws that allowed for the death penalty are accordingly, and within a reasonable time, amended to exclude reference to it. This has

[88] African Union, '61st Ordinary Session of African Commission' (n 39) para 21; Amnesty International 'Death Sentences and Executions 2016' (n 2) 6, 38–39. Egypt, Morocco/Western Sahara and Niger were also listed but unclear if commutation or pardon and with no figures indicated.

[89] An additional 17 people were pardoned.

[90] Amnesty International, 'Death Sentences and Executions 2017' (n 2) 8, 31, 32, 36–37. Cameroon and Tunisia were also listed but unclear if commutation or pardon and with no figures indicated.

[91] In addition, pardons were granted in Egypt/Western Sahara (five), Nigeria (16), Sudan (five). Malawi, South Sudan and Tanzania were also listed but unclear if commutation or pardon and with no figures indicated. See Amnesty International, 'Death Sentences and Executions 2018' (n 2) 33, 37, 41, 43–44.

[92] Nii Akrofi Smart-Abbey, 'Amnesty International Lauds Strides by Africa to Scrap Death Penalty' Africanews (2018), http://www.africanews.com/2018/04/13/amnesty-international-lauds-strides-by-africa-to-scrap-death-penalty (accessed 15 March 2020).

[93] Adopted 4 July 2016, entered into force 26 October 2016.

[94] Adopted 31 May 2017, entered into force 28 December 2017.

[95] Amnesty International, 'Death Sentences and Executions in 2016' (n 2) 9, 35, 36, 38; Amnesty International, 'Death Sentences and Executions in 2017' (n 2) 5,10.

[96] Human Rights Committee, Observations Finales Concernant le Troisième Rapport Périodique de la Guinée, UN Doc CCPR/C/GIN/CO/3 (2018) para 27.

[97] ibid, para 28. By the end of 2018, 'at least eight people remained under the sentence of death' in the country (see Amnesty International, 'Death Sentences and Executions 2018' (n 2) 42).

not always been the case. Seychelles, for example, abolished the death penalty in 1993, article 15(2) of its Constitution provides that no domestic law should make provision for the death penalty and its Extradition Act prohibits the extradition of persons to countries where they would face the death penalty for the offence committed. However, other national legislation makes reference to 'the sentence of death' in contravention of the constitutional prohibition.[98] The Human Rights Committee expressed concern over this in August 2018 and called on Seychelles 'to remove the discrepancy between the Constitution and other national legislation that contains mention of "the sentence of death" in order to streamline all national laws and ensure compliance with the constitutional prohibition of the death penalty'.[99] Also, Benin abolished the death penalty in January 2016, but by the end of 2017 (almost two years later), domestic laws allowing for the death penalty had not been amended.[100] Also, the remaining death sentences in Benin were only commuted in February 2018.[101]

A third concern relates to reinstatement of the death penalty post-abolition, which is contrary to international standards prohibiting reinstatement of the death penalty once abolished, as seen in the case of The Gambia and Liberia. The Gambia had initially abolished the death penalty in 1993 but reinstated it in 1995, contrary to international standards prohibiting reinstatement once abolished. Hence, the Human Rights Committee has urged The Gambia to 'abolish the death penalty in its laws and remove it from the Constitution'.[102] Liberia ratified ICCPR-OP2 in 2005 but reintroduced the death penalty in 2008 in the country's Penal Code, and judges continue to pass death sentences, which the Human Rights Committee has found to be 'contrary to its obligations' under ICCPR-OP2.[103] The Committee was 'also concerned that the death penalty is mandatory for certain crimes' despite mandatory death penalty being contrary to article 6 ICCPR, to which Liberia is a state party. It thus called upon Liberia to 'remove any provisions in its legislation that provide for the death penalty, commute all existing death sentences and refrain from carrying out any executions'.[104] During its dialogue with the Committee, Liberia confirmed 'its commitment to respect its international obligations as a State party to [ICCPR-OP2]'.[105] In 2018, no death sentences or executions were recorded for Liberia.[106]

[98] Committee against Torture, Concluding Observations on the Initial Report of Seychelles, UN Doc CAT/C/SYC/CO/1 (2018) para 10.
[99] ibid, paras 10 and 11.
[100] Amnesty International, 'Death Sentences and Executions 2017' (n 2) 35.
[101] Amnesty International, 'Death Sentences and Executions 2018' (n 2) 41.
[102] Human Rights Committee, CO: Gambia, CCPR/C/GMB/CO/2 (n 76) paras 27–28.
[103] Human Rights Committee, CO: Liberia, CCPR/C/LBR/CO/1 (n 31) para 28.
[104] ibid, para 29.
[105] ibid, para 28.
[106] Amnesty International, 'Death Sentences and Executions 2018' (n 2) 39.

3 Prohibition of the Mandatory Death Penalty[107]

The mandatory death penalty is the automatic imposition of the death sentence upon conviction for a capital offence, with a court having no discretion in sentencing and thus obliged to impose the death penalty once an offender is found guilty of a capital offence irrespective of any extenuating circumstances. International human rights law, as seen below, prohibits the mandatory death penalty on human rights grounds.

3.1 UN Treaties

In elucidating article 6 of the ICCPR, the Human Rights Committee has held that the mandatory death penalty is 'arbitrary and thus inconsistent with article 6'.[108] This is because it does not allow for a court to exercise discretion in sentencing, as the court is not allowed to consider 'the personal circumstances of the offender and the particular circumstances of the offence, including its specific attenuating elements'.[109] The Committee held further that even if the 'right to seek pardon or commutation on the basis of the special circumstances of the case or the accused' is guaranteed, it is however 'not an adequate substitute for the need for judicial discretion in the application of the death penalty'.[110]

The Committee has further found it 'incompatible with the [ICCPR] that the death penalty is mandatory for the crimes of murder, aggravated robbery, treason and terrorism resulting in the death of a person', and called for the abolition of mandatory death sentences.[111] The Committee has thus expressed concern over the retention of the mandatory death penalty for certain crimes in Liberia, reiterating 'its position that the mandatory death sentence is contrary to' article 6 of the ICCPR.[112]

The question of the mandatory death penalty has also been addressed in cases before the Human Rights Committee. In *Thompson v St. Vincent and the Grenadines* and *Rolando v Philippines*, for example, the Committee found that the mandatory death penalty was contrary to the right to life, thus in breach of article 6(1) ICCPR, as it does not allow for the consideration of whether the death penalty is appropriate in the circumstances of the convicted person's case.[113] Also, in

[107] This section draws on parts from Chenwi, 'Downfall of Mandatory Death Penalty' (n 57).
[108] Human Rights Committee, General Comment 36 (n 21) para 37.
[109] ibid.
[110] ibid.
[111] Human Rights Committee, Concluding Observations on the Initial Report of Uganda, UN Doc CCPR/CO/80/UGA (2004) para 13.
[112] Human Rights Committee, CO: Liberia, CCPR/C/LBR/CO/1 (n 31) para 28.
[113] *Thompson v St. Vincent and the Grenadines*, Communication 806/1998, UN Doc CCPR/C/70/D/806/1998 (2000) para 8.2; *Rolando v Philippines*, Communication 1110/2002, UN Doc CCPR/C/82/D/1110/2002 (2004) para 5.2.

Lubuto v Zambia, in dealing with the question of the compatibility of the mandatory death penalty for aggravated robbery with article 6(2) ICCPR, which prohibits the death penalty for crimes not considered 'the most serious',[114] the Committee found the mandatory death penalty under the circumstances of the case to constitute a violation of article 6(2) ICCPR.[115] This was based on two grounds: the fact that the 'use of firearms did not produce the death or wounding of any person and that the court could not under the law take these elements into account in imposing sentence'.[116] On remedial measures, it held that the sentence should be commuted and that Zambia has 'an obligation to take appropriate measures to ensure that similar violations do not occur in the future'.[117] As stated in section 3.3 below, the death penalty is not mandatory for murder but is still retained for 'aggravated robbery with a firearm', though with some exceptions. In *Johnson v Ghana*, the Committee found the automatic and mandatory death penalty in the case to constitute a violation of the right to life and contrary to Ghana's obligations under the ICCPR.[118] This was on the basis of lack of judicial discretion in its imposition, the insufficiency of the existing de facto moratorium 'to make a mandatory death sentence consistent with the [ICCPR]' and insufficiency of 'the existence of a right to seek pardon or commutation' in providing 'adequate protection to the right to life'.[119] As regards remedial measures, the Committee held that Ghana has 'an obligation to provide the author with an effective remedy, including the commutation of the author's death sentence' and 'an obligation to avoid similar violations in the future, including by adjusting its legislation to the provisions of the Covenant'.[120]

African states parties to the ICCPR thus have an obligation to do away with the mandatory death penalty. Failing which, they will be in breach of their obligations under article 6 ICCPR.

3.2 African Regional Treaties

Like the Human Rights Committee, the African Commission is of the view that the mandatory death penalty is a violation of the right to life guaranteed in the African Charter. In this regard, it has categorically stated that '[i]n no circumstances shall the imposition of the death penalty be mandatory for an offence'.[121] In its 2019

[114] See s 5 below for further discussion of this prohibition.

[115] *Lubuto v Zambia*, Communication 390/1990, Human Rights Committee (30 June 1994), UN Doc CCPR/C/55/D/390/1990/Rev.1 (1995) para 7.2.

[116] ibid.

[117] ibid, para 9.

[118] *Johnson v Ghana*, Communication 2177/2012, Human Rights Committee (6 May 2014), UN Doc CCPR/C/110/D/2177/2012 (2014) para 7.3.

[119] ibid, paras 7.2 and 7.3.

[120] ibid, para 9.

[121] African Commission, General Comment 3 (n 8) para 24.

resolution, it urged states to abolish the mandatory death penalty on the basis that 'it breaches the right to life and the right to human dignity'.[122]

In its case law, however, the Commission has not seized the opportunity to elaborate further on the question of the mandatory death penalty, considering that there is no substantive elaboration on it as a violation of African Charter rights. In *Egyptian Initiative for Personal Rights* and *Interights v Egypt*, where the complainants argued that the mandatory or automatic death penalty ('imposed by law rather than being applied by a court of law in light of all relevant circumstances') was a violation of the right to life,[123] the African Commission did not explicitly state its substantive view on the issue. It, however, stated in passing that the death penalty in Egypt 'is effectively mandated by law for certain categories of offences' without any room 'for a competent judiciary to evaluate the appropriate penalty, in light of all of the circumstances of the case' and 'with the President empowered to decide not to apply that sentence if he so decides', which is 'at odds with the requirements of right to life, as reflected in international legal practice'.[124] In the previous case of *Amnesty International and Others v Sudan*, where the issue of the mandatory death penalty for murder was mentioned by the complainants,[125] the Commission did not rule specifically on it. However, it did find the execution of the death sentence following an unfair trial to be a violation of the right to life under the African Charter. Notwithstanding, based on the unequivocal statement in its general comment and resolution, it is clear that the mandatory death penalty is prohibited under the African Charter.

The question of the mandatory death penalty in Ghana and its compatibility with human rights, as stated above, was raised before the African Human Rights Court in *Johnson v Ghana* but the case was found to be inadmissible.[126] However, the Court's provisional measures decision did recognize that 'the risk of execution of the death penalty' in the circumstances of the case (that is, the context of the mandatory death penalty, imposed without consideration of relevant circumstances of the offender or offence) 'will jeopardize the enjoyment of the rights guaranteed under Articles 4, 5 and 7 of the [African] Charter, Articles 6(1), 7, 14(1) and 14(5) of the [ICCPR] and Articles 3 and 5 of the [UDHR]'.[127] In *Rajabu and Others v Tanzania*, the Court addressed the question of the mandatory death penalty for murder in Tanzania, provided for in section 197 of the country's Penal Code.[128] It found that the provision 'does not uphold fairness and due process', as it does not

[122] African Commission, Res 416 (n 7) para 4.
[123] *Egyptian Initiative for Personal Rights* and *Interights v Egypt*, Communication 334/06, ACHPR (01 March 2011) para 142.
[124] ibid, para 230.
[125] *Amnesty International and others v Sudan*, Communications 48/90, 50/91, 52/91 and 89/93, (2000) AHRLR 297 (ACHPR 1999) para 11.
[126] *Johnson v Ghana*, Ruling (n 83).
[127] *Johnson v Ghana*, Provisional Measures (n 80), para 17.
[128] *Rajabu and Others v Tanzania*, Application 007/2015, Judgment (28 November 2019) para 97.

allow convicted persons to present mitigating circumstances, hence not permitting judicial discretion in the imposition of the sentence.[129] It further found, taking into consideration the arbitrary nature of the mandatory death penalty, that hanging, as a method of implementation of that penalty, is 'inherently degrading' and 'inevitably encroaches upon dignity in respect of the prohibition of torture and cruel, inhuman and degrading treatment'.[130] Tanzania was thus also in breach of the right to dignity under article 5 of the African Charter.[131] Considering Tanzania's obligation to adopt legislative and other measures to give effect to Charter rights (which in the context of the mandatory death penalty requires it to remove the penalty from its laws following entry into force of the Charter), the Court found a consequential violation of article 1 of the Charter 'in relation to the provision of the mandatory imposition of the death penalty in the Penal Code, and its execution by hanging'.[132] It then ordered Tanzania to, inter alia, abolish mandatory death penalty for murder within a year and 'take all necessary measures for the rehearing of the case on the sentencing of the Applicants through a process that does not allow a mandatory imposition of the death penalty, while upholding the full discretion of the judicial officer'.[133] In addition, the Court granted reparations of four million Tanzanian Shillings for each applicant for the 'moral and psychological suffering' endured, to be paid free of tax and within six months from the date of the judgment.[134] The decision is seen as groundbreaking and affirms that states parties to the African Charter are required, as part of their general obligation under the Charter, to remove the mandatory death penalty from their laws.

3.3 Compliance in Practice

The use of the mandatory death penalty has dwindled significantly not just at the global level but also in Africa.[135] This has been a result of challenges, on human rights grounds, to its application. State practice and jurisprudence in Africa reveal increasing compliance with UN and African regional standards prohibiting the mandatory death penalty. Non-abolitionist African states that have abolished the mandatory death penalty, either generally or for specific offences that previously carried the mandatory death penalty, include Botswana, Kenya, Lesotho, Malawi,

[129] ibid, paras 107–114 and 171(viii). See also paras 92–106.
[130] ibid, para 119.
[131] ibid, paras 120 and 171(ix).
[132] ibid, paras 123–126.
[133] ibid, paras 163, 167, 171(xv–xviii).
[134] ibid, paras 146–150 and 171(xi–xii).
[135] See generally, Andrew Novak, *The Global Decline of the Mandatory Death Penalty: Constitutional Jurisprudence and Legislative Reform in Africa, Asia, and the Caribbean* (Ashgate, 2014); Andrew Novak, 'The Abolition of the Mandatory Death Penalty in Africa: A Comparative Constitutional Analysis' (2012) 22(2) Indiana International and Comparative Law Review 267–295; Anyangwe, 'Emerging African Jurisprudence' (n 9) 2, 20–21.

Swaziland, Zimbabwe, Zambia and Uganda.[136] Its abolition stemmed from constitutional or legislative amendments or constitutional challenges before the courts.

Constitutional amendments have resulted in the abolition of the mandatory death penalty in, for example, Swaziland (with a constitutional provision stating that '[t]he death penalty shall not be mandatory'[137] and in Zimbabwe (constitutional reform abolishing the mandatory death penalty, limiting the imposition of the death penalty to 'murder committed in aggravating circumstances' and subject to judicial discretion on its imposition[138]. Legislative amendments abolishing the mandatory death penalty have occurred in, for example, Zambia (amendment to the country's Penal Code excluding 'murder committed in the course of aggravated robbery with a firearm' where 'the accused person was not armed with a firearm' and 'was not aware that any of the other persons involved in committing the offence was so armed' or 'dissociated himself from the offence immediately on becoming so aware';[139] in Botswana (amendment to the country's Penal Code abolishing the mandatory death penalty for murder and treason where extenuating circumstances exists);[140] in Lesotho (amendment to the country's Penal Code prohibiting the mandatory death penalty for murder where extenuating circumstances exist)[141].

In addition, constitutional challenges in Malawi, Uganda and Kenya have resulted in the abolition of the mandatory death penalty.[142] The Constitutional Court of Uganda in 2005 in *Kigula and 416 Others v Attorney General* declared the mandatory death penalty as unconstitutional, subsequently upheld by the Supreme Court

[136] Novak, 'Abolition of Mandatory Death Penalty' (n 136) 267; Andrew Novak, 'Capital Sentencing Discretion in Southern Africa: A Human Rights Perspective on the Doctrine of Extenuating Circumstances in Death Penalty Cases' (2014) 14(1) AHRLJ 24–42, 33, 35, 39; FIDH, 'Triggers for Abolition of the Death Penalty in Africa: A Southern African Perspective' (2017) 12, <https://www.fidh.org/IMG/pdf/death_penalty_in_africa_703a_eng_25_oct_2017_web_ok_ok.pdf (14 March 2020).

[137] Constitution of the Kingdom of Swaziland Act, 2005, s 15(2).

[138] Constitution of Zimbabwe Amendment (No 20), 2013, art 48(2)(a).

[139] Penal Code Act, Chapter 87 of the Laws of Zambia, ss 201 and 294(2). A 2016 effort to achieve a general prohibition of the death penalty in Zambia was unsuccessful.

[140] See, eg Botswana Penal Code, 1964 (Law No 2 of 1964) (as amended up to Act No 14 of 2005), ss 34 and 35 read with s 40 (on treason) and s 203 (on murder).

[141] Lesotho Penal Code Act, 2010 (Act No 6 of 2012), s 40(3)(c). The mandatory death penalty is also prohibited for sexual offences: where the accused is infected with the Human Immunodeficiency Virus and, at the time of commission of the offence, 'had knowledge or reasonable suspicion of the infection'; where extenuating circumstances exist; or where the individual circumstances of the accused or lawful intimate relations between the victim and the accused dictates otherwise (Lesotho Sexual Offences Act No 3 of 2003, s 32(a)(vii) read with s 31(1); African Commission on Human and Peoples' Rights, Lesotho: Combined Second to Eighth Periodic Report under the African Charter on Human and Peoples' Rights and Initial Report under the Protocol to the African Charter the Rights of Women in Africa (2018) para 34.

[142] The cases have been discussed in detail in Novak, *Global Decline* (n 136) 99–123; Novak, 'Abolition of Mandatory Death Penalty' (n 136) 279–293; Novak, 'Judicial dialogue' (n 10) 12–18; Mwiza Jo Nkhata, 'Bidding Farewell to Mandatory Capital Punishment: *Francis Kafantayeni and Others v Attorney General*' (2007) 1 MLJ 103–112; Chenwi, 'Downfall of Mandatory Death Penalty' (n 57).

of Uganda in 2009.[143] The mandatory death penalty was unconstitutional on the basis that it deprived the trial court of the opportunity to consider mitigating factors and exercise sentencing discretion, and thus a violation of, inter alia, the right to a fair trial. Full implementation of the decision is still a challenge, as by 2019, 'not all death row prisoners have been granted hearings in mitigation of their death sentence more than a decade since the Supreme Court abolished the mandatory imposition of death sentences'.[144] The High Court of Malawi in 2007 in *Kafantayeni v Attorney General* held that the mandatory death penalty was unconstitutional, as the lack of opportunity to consider mitigating factors and an avenue for the defendant to appeal the conviction and sentence results in its imposition constituting a violation the rights to life, fair trial and not to be subjected to cruel and inhuman punishment, and the right of access to courts, respectively.[145] The Supreme Court of Appeal of Malawi in 2008 in *Jacob v Republic* confirmed the *Kafantayeni* decision with approval.[146] The Supreme Court of Appeal of Kenya in *Muruatetu* and *Mwangi v Republic* found the mandatory death penalty for murder under section 204 of the country's Penal Code to be unconstitutional and thus invalid, because it violated the rights to a fair trial, equality and freedom from discrimination, human dignity and access as well as the principle of the rule of law.[147] The Kenya decision was welcomed by the Working Group on Death Penalty as a 'historic ruling' that 'sends a very strong signal to the effect that there is need for Kenya to consider the legal abolition of the death penalty'.[148] In March 2018, as a step towards implementing the decision, a 13-member task force was appointed 'to review the legislative framework on the death penalty and other matters and set up a framework to deal with rehearing of sentencing of persons on death row'.[149] Influenced by the *Muruatetu* decision, the Court of Appeal of Kenya on 22 March 2018 declared the mandatory death penalty for robbery with violence to be unconstitutional.[150] Constitutional challenges to the mandatory death penalty have, however, not been successful in every instance raised. In Ghana, for example, the mandatory death penalty was found by the Supreme Court of Ghana to be constitutional,[151] resulting in the mandatory sentence being challenged before the Human Rights Committee and African Court as stated above in sections 3.1 and 3.2, respectively.

[143] *Kigula and 416 Others v Attorney General*, Constitutional Petition 6 of 2003 [2005] UGCC 8, (2005) *African Human Rights Law Report* 197 (UGCC 2005); *Attorney General v Kigula and 417 Others*, Constitutional Appeal 03 of 2006 [2009] UGSC 6, [2009] 2 EALR 1.

[144] Amnesty International, 'Death Sentences and Executions 2018' (n 2) 45.

[145] *Kafantayeni v Attorney General*, Constitutional Case 12 of 2005 [2007] MWHC 1, (2007) 46/3 International Legal Materials 566–571.

[146] *Jacob v Republic*, Criminal Appeal 16 of 2006.

[147] Petition 15 and 16 of 2015 (consolidated), Judgment of 14 December 2017, [2017] eKLR.

[148] African Union, '62nd Ordinary Session of African Commission' (n 64) para 20.

[149] Amnesty International, 'Death Sentences and Executions 2018' (n 2) 42.

[150] *Meja* (alias Uncle 'P') *v Republic*, Criminal Appeal No 98 of 2015 [2018] eKLR. See also, *Kittiny v Republic* Civil Appeal No 56 of 2013 (unreported).

[151] See *Johnson v The Republic* [2011] 2 SCGLR 601.

Despite the positive developments relating to the decline of the mandatory death penalty, concerns have been raised over some state's continuous retention of it. As an example, the Human Rights Committee was concerned that Sudan retains the mandatory death penalty for various crimes, including adultery, apostasy and armed robbery resulting in death, drug trafficking and murder.[152] In 2017 and 2018, mandatory death sentences were imposed in Ghana and Nigeria, despite their inconsistency with human rights.[153] The Human Rights Committee has raised concern over the imposition of the mandatory death penalty in both countries, requesting them to revise their domestic law so as to ensure compliance with the ICCPR and eliminate the mandatory death penalty.[154]

4 Prohibition of the Death Penalty for Certain Offenders

4.1 UN Treaties

There is a general prohibition of the death penalty in UN treaties with respect to certain categories of offenders. Article 6(5) of the ICCPR provides that the death sentence 'shall not be imposed for crimes committed by persons below eighteen years of age'. Likewise, article 37 of the Convention on the Rights of the Child[155] (CRC) prohibits the death penalty for persons below 18 years of age. The prohibition of the death penalty for children is a rule of customary international law, not subject to reservations;[156] and seen to have developed into a *jus cogens* norm.[157] The prohibition implies that children 'can never face the death penalty for that offence, regardless of their age at the time of sentencing or at the time foreseen for carrying out the sentence'.[158] In the absence of 'reliable and conclusive proof' regarding the age of the person at the time of the commission of the offence, states have to afford the person the benefit of the doubt and thus are prohibited from imposing the death penalty.[159] Fifty-four African states have ratified the CRC,

[152] Human Rights Committee, CO: Sudan, CCPR/C/SDN/CO/5 (n 71) para 29.

[153] Amnesty International, 'Death Sentences and Executions 2017' (n 2) 8; Amnesty International, 'Death Sentences and Executions 2018' (n 2) 12.

[154] Human Rights Committee, CO: Ghana, CCPR/C/GHA/CO/1 (n 49) para 20; Human Rights Committee, Concluding Observations on Nigeria in the Absence of its Second Periodic Report, UN Doc CCPR/C/NGA/CO/2 (2019) paras 24–25.

[155] Adopted 20 November 1989, entered into force on 2 September 1990, UN Doc A/44/49 (1989).

[156] Human Rights Committee, General Comment 24: Issues Relating to Reservations Made upon Ratification or Accession to the Covenant or the Optional Protocols thereto, or in Relation to Declarations under Art 41 of the Covenant, UN Doc CCPR/C/21/Rev.1/Add.6 (1994) para 8.

[157] The Inter-American Commission on Human Rights has also noted that international law has developed so as to prohibit as a *jus cogens* norm the execution of persons who were under 18 years of age at the time of their crimes (*Graham v United States*, Case 11.193, Report No 97/03 (2003); *Domingues v United States*, Case 12.285, Report No 62/02 (2001); *Thomas v United States*, Case 12.240, Report No 100/03 (2003); *Beazley v United States*, Case 12.412, Report No 101/03 (2003))

[158] Human Rights Committee, General Comment 36 (n 21) para 48.

[159] ibid, para 48.

thus bound by the above prohibition, irrespective of the status of the death penalty within their jurisdiction.

In addition to children, article 6(5) ICCPR prohibits the carrying out of the death penalty on pregnant women. In elaborating on article 6(5), the Human Rights Committee has held that states parties have an obligation to refrain from executing '*parents* to very young or dependent children'.[160] By using the terminology 'parent' and not 'women' or 'mothers', the Committee, arguably, also extends the prohibition to men with very young or dependent children. In addition, though the Convention on the Elimination of All Forms of Discrimination against Women[161] (CEDAW) is silent on the death penalty, the Committee on the Elimination of Discrimination against Women has, with reference to the UN General Assembly's call for states to establish a moratorium on executions with a view to abolish the death penalty, called on states parties to repeal laws that result in 'discriminatory application of the death penalty to women'.[162] The 52 African states that have ratified CEDAW should heed this call.

Further still, the death penalty is prohibited for persons with disabilities, limited culpability and diminished capacity. In this regard, the Human Rights Committee has held that 'States parties must refrain from imposing the death penalty on individuals who face special barriers in defending themselves on an equal basis with others, such as persons whose serious psycho-social and intellectual disabilities impeded their effective defense, and on persons that have limited moral culpability'.[163] States parties are also required to 'refrain from executing persons that have diminished ability to understand the reasons for their sentence, and persons whose execution would be exceptionally cruel or would lead to exceptionally harsh results for them and their families, such as persons at an advanced age, parents to very young or dependent children, and individuals who have suffered in the past serious human rights violations'.[164]

4.2 African Regional Treaties

Like UN treaties, the death penalty is prohibited for children, pregnant women and mothers of young children and persons with disabilities, among others. In confirming the prohibition of the death penalty 'for crimes committed by children', the African Commission emphasized that 'the burden of proof rests upon the State

[160] ibid, para 49. Emphasis added.

[161] Adopted 18 December 1979, entered into force 3 September 1981, UN Doc. A/34/46 (1979).

[162] Committee on the Elimination of Discrimination against Women, General Recommendation 35 on Gender-Based Violence against Women, Updating General Recommendation 19 (adopted 14 July 2017), UN Doc CEDAW/C/GC/35 (2017) para 29(c)(i).

[163] Human Rights Committee, General Comment 36 (n 21) para 49.

[164] ibid.

to prove the age of the defendant'.[165] Thus, both UN and African regional human rights standards ensure that the burden of proof of age is not placed on the accused person. The African Commission further held that execution of children, irrespective of the circumstances of the trial or offence, 'will always amount to a violation of the right to life'.[166] Likewise, the main African regional treaty on children—the African Charter on the Rights and Welfare of the Child[167] (ACRWC)—prohibits the death penalty for children. Its article 5(3) provides that the '[d]eath sentence shall not be pronounced for crimes committed by children'. Article 5(3) has been seen to be interdependent with the right to birth registration, guaranteed in article 6 ACRWC. The African Committee of Experts on the Rights and Welfare of the Child (ACERWC), giving examples of rights that article 6 interacts with, with article 6 playing a 'significant role' in their realization, held that 'a non-registered child may fail to invoke' article 5(3)'s protection of 'a child found guilty of a crime from a death penalty'.[168]

In addition to children, article 30(1)(e) ACRWC places an obligation on states parties to not impose the death sentence on 'expectant mothers and to mothers of infants and young children who have been accused or found guilty of infringing the penal law'. Forty-eight African states have ratified the ACRWC. The African Commission has also held that execution of pregnant or nursing women as well as older persons or persons with disabilities (psycho-social or intellectual) 'will always amount to a violation of the right to life', irrespective of the offence or circumstances of the trial.[169] The prohibition on carrying out the death sentences on pregnant or nursing mothers is also provided for in article 4(2)(j) of the Protocol to the African Charter on Human and Peoples' Rights on the Rights of Women in Africa.[170] The 40 States parties to the Protocol are obliged to 'take appropriate and effective measures to ... ensure that, in those countries where the death penalty still exists, not to carry out death sentences on pregnant or nursing women'. It is, however, regrettable that the prohibition of the death penalty for older persons and persons with disabilities is not explicitly stated in the main African regional instruments on the rights of these groups.[171]

165 African Commission, General Comment 3 (n 8) para 24.
166 ibid, para 25.
167 Adopted 1 July 1990, entered into force 29 November 1999, OAU Doc CAB/LEG/24.9/49 (1990).
168 African Committee of Experts on the Rights and Welfare of the Child, General Comment on Art 6 of the African Charter on the Rights and Welfare of the Child, ACERWC/GC/02 (2014) para 27.
169 African Commission, General Comment 3 (n 8) para 25.
170 Adopted 1 July 2003, entered into force 25 November 2005, AU Doc CAB/LEG/66.6 (2000).
171 See Protocol to the African Charter on Human and Peoples' Rights on the Rights of Older Persons in Africa (adopted 31 January 2016, not yet in force, with two ratifications and 14 signatories) and Protocol to the African Charter on Human and Peoples' Rights on the Rights of Persons with Disabilities in Africa (adopted 29 January 2018, not yet in force with no ratifications and six signatories).

4.3 Compliance in Practice

While African states have generally complied with the prohibition of the death penalty for children, the issue remains a concern with respect to some African countries. For example, reports indicate that in South Sudan, two in 2017 and at least one in 2018 of those executed were below 18 years of age at the time of the commission of the crime for which they were sentenced to death and executed.[172] Also, those on death row in 2018 in the country included a child.[173] This runs contrary to its obligation under the CRC. In Sudan as well, despite the recent oral assurances' by the government 'that the death penalty was not imposed upon children', this does not seem to be the case when one looks at article 27(2) of the country's Criminal Code.[174] The Human Rights Committee raised concern over the provision in October 2018, as it 'appears to allow for the imposition of the death penalty on children who were under 18 years of age at the time of the offence', in contravention of the ICCPR.[175] The Committee urged Sudan 'to revise' the provision to eliminate this contravention.[176] It should be recalled that reports in 2010 indicated the sentencing in Sudan of four children to death by a special court.[177] This was in contravention of the prohibition of the death penalty for children under the ACRWC, CRC and African Charter, all of which Sudan is a party to. In 2010, the Committee on the Rights of the Child expressed its deep regret over the application of the death penalty for children in Liberia.[178] This was in contravention of its obligations under ICCPR-OP2, CRC, African Charter and ACRWC, which all prohibit the application of the death penalty for children. The Committee thus urged Liberia 'to expedite the revision and amendment of [its] Penal Code in order to abolish the death penalty for children'.[179] In 2019, the Human Rights Committee requested Nigeria to comply with its obligations under the ICCPR in relation to the death penalty based on, inter alia, a concern that 'in some federal states it is still available for offences committed by minors'.[180]

Women have been sentenced to death or executed in some African countries. In 2017, in Egypt, for example, one of the 35 people executed was a woman, and eight of the 402 death sentences passed were imposed on women. In Sierra Leonne

[172] African Union, '62nd Ordinary Session of African Commission (n 64) para 22; Amnesty International, 'Death Sentences and Executions 2018' (n 2) 12.

[173] Amnesty International, 'Death Sentences and Executions 2018' (n 2) 44.

[174] Human Rights Committee, CO: Sudan, CCPR/C/SDN/CO/5 (n 71) para 31.

[175] ibid.

[176] ibid, para 32.

[177] IHRDA Statement on ACERWC-ACmHPR Cooperation and the Sentencing to Death of Minors in Sudan, 16th Ordinary Session of the African Committee of Experts on the Rights and Welfare of the Child (2010), https://www.ihrda.org/2010/11/3104/ (accessed 14 March 2020).

[178] Committee on the Rights of the Child, Concluding Observations on the Combined Second to Fourth Periodic Reports of Liberia, UN Doc CRC/C/LBR/CO/2-4 (2012) para 37.

[179] ibid, para 38.

[180] Human Rights Committee, CO: Nigeria, CCPR/C/NGA/CO/2 (n 154) paras 24–25.

in 2017, two women were among those sentenced to death. In Uganda in 2018, six of those under death sentence were women.[181] It was, however, unclear from the information whether these included women with young children. In South Sudan, those on death row in 2018 included two women, one of them a lactating mother.[182] If the lactating mother is executed, it will contravene South Sudan's domestic and international human rights law obligations.

As regards persons with disabilities, Amnesty International reports on death sentences and executions in Africa in 2015, 2016, 2017 and 2018 did not indicate any persons with disabilities sentenced to death, under sentence of death or executed in African countries (though this happened in some non-African states).

5 Prohibition of the Death Penalty for Certain Offences

5.1 UN Treaties

Article 6(2) of the ICCPR prohibits, for states parties 'which have not abolished the death penalty', its application for offences that are not considered 'the most serious'. A narrow/restrictive approach must be adopted to the interpretation of the provision, with 'the most serious crimes' being limited 'only to crimes of extreme gravity, involving intentional killing'.[183] Crimes not considered the most serious, as stated by the Human Rights Committee, including abduction, adultery, apostasy, armed robbery, attempted murder, corruption and other economic and political crimes, establishing political opposition groups, offending a head of state, drug and sexual offences, homosexuality, and piracy, even though these crimes are of a serious nature.[184] The Committee adds that the death penalty cannot apply in cases of 'limited degree of involvement or of complicity in the commission of even the most serious crimes, such as providing the physical means for the commission of murder'.[185] States parties are therefore obliged to: 'review their criminal laws so as to ensure that the death penalty is not imposed for crimes which do not qualify as the most serious crimes'; and 'revoke death sentences issued for crimes not qualifying as the most serious crimes and pursue the necessary legal procedures to re-sentence those convicted for such crimes'.[186] Failing which, the states would be in 'violation of their obligations under article 6 read alone and in conjunction with article 2, paragraph 2 of the Covenant, as well as of other provisions of the Covenant' such as article 7.[187] Hence, in *Lubuto v Zambia* as stated in section 3.1

[181] Amnesty International, 'Death Sentences and Executions 2018' (n 2) 45.
[182] ibid, 44.
[183] Human Rights Committee, General Comment 36 (n 21) paras 33 and 35.
[184] ibid, paras 35 and 36.
[185] ibid, para 35.
[186] ibid.
[187] ibid, paras 36 and 51.

above, the Committee believed that the crime could not be considered the 'most serious crime' because the use of firearms 'did not produce the death or wounding of any person'.

The prohibition of the death penalty for crimes not considered the most serious is not an absolute prohibition for all ICCPR states parties. It is an absolute prohibition for ICCPR states parties that are also party to ICCPR-OP2, but not the case for those not party to the Protocol. As held by the Human Rights Committee, and 'implicitly recognized' in article 6(2), (4) and (5), 'countries which have not abolished the death penalty and that have not ratified [ICCPR-OP2] are not legally barred under the [ICCPR] from applying the death penalty with regard to the most serious crimes subject to a number of strict conditions'.[188]

It should also be noted that, as stated by the Committee on Enforced Disappearances,[189] the death penalty is excluded as an appropriate sentence for an enforced disappearance in terms of the International Convention for the Protection of All Persons from Enforced Disappearance[190] (CEDAW). Seventeen African states have ratified the CEDAW.

5.2 African Regional Treaties

Similar to the position under the ICCPR, the African Commission in its general comment on the right to life in the African Charter has held that for states that have not yet abolished the death penalty, it must be 'used for only the *most serious crimes* – understood to be *crimes involving intentional killing*'.[191] Previous to its general comment, the African Commission had adopted resolutions calling on states that still retain the death penalty to limit it to the most serious offence.[192]

5.3 Compliance in Practice

Despite the requirement to limit the death penalty to the most serious crimes, not all African states that have not yet abolished it comply with this. For example, in 2018, there were proposals in support of introducing the death penalty for corruption, economic crimes, poaching and sabotage in Kenya, which if adopted would be contrary to its international human rights obligations.[193] In Sudan,

[188] Human Rights Committee, General Comment 36 (n 21) para 16.

[189] Committee on Enforced Disappearances, Concluding Observations on the Report submitted by Burkina Faso under art 29, para 1 of the Convention, UN Doc CED/C/BFA/CO/1 (2016) para 14.

[190] Adopted 20 December 2006, entered into force 23 December 2010, UN Doc A/HRC/1/L.10 (2006).

[191] African Commission, General Comment 3 (n 8) para 24. Emphasis added.

[192] See eg, African Commission, Resolution 42 (n 6) para 2.

[193] Amnesty International, 'Death Sentences and Executions 2018' (n 2) 42.

the death penalty is retained for crimes of adultery, apostasy, espionage, sodomy and undermining the constitutional order provided for in the country's Criminal Code, as well as certain aggravated acts of trafficking that do not meet 'the most serious' threshold, provided for in its Prevention of Human Trafficking Act.[194] The Human Rights Committee has thus urged Sudan to revise its Criminal Code and Prevention of Human Trafficking Act, so as to ensure their compliance with article 6(2) ICCPR, 'and restrict the crimes for which the death penalty may be imposed to the most serious ones, understood to be crimes involving intentional killing'.[195] Recently, the Committee, based on its concern that the death penalty is still imposed in Nigeria for crimes not considered the most serious crimes, recommended that the state revise its Criminal Code 'and restrict the crimes for which the death penalty may be imposed on perpetrators to the most serious crimes'.[196] In Egypt, in 2016, the crimes for which the death penalty was imposed included 'political violence and "terrorism" that did not lead to loss of life' (15 men), murder or robbery linked to murder (at least 11 women), and rape and murder (at least 167 men); in 2017, for 'political violence' (at least 88) and for various crimes, including murder and rape (314 others), and in 2018, for drug-related offences (11).[197] The Working Group on Death Penalty has raised concern over the retention of the death penalty in Egypt, South Sudan and Sudan for drugs-related crimes, holding that it is 'a clear violation of international standards with respect to the death penalty' and, therefore, called on the states to 'immediately take steps to remove these provisions from their statute books'.[198]

6 Conclusion

There is no treaty containing an explicit general prohibition of the death penalty at the UN and African regional levels. Efforts to adopt a regional treaty specific to abolishing the death penalty in Africa have not yet come to fruition. However, existing human rights treaties and standards at both UN and African regional levels place an obligation on states to work towards its abolition, prohibit the mandatory death penalty and prohibit the death penalty for certain offenders and offences. Though not considered in this chapter, application of the death penalty is also prohibited where certain safeguards relation to, inter alia, due process and fair trial rights have not been followed. African states incur obligations in relation to the

194 Human Rights Committee, CO: Sudan, CCPR/C/SDN/CO/5 (n 71) paras 15 and 29.

195 ibid, paras 16 and 30.

196 Human Rights Committee, CO: Nigeria, CCPR/C/NGA/CO/2 (n 154) paras 24–25.

197 Amnesty International, 'Death Sentences and Executions 2016' (n 2) 32; Amnesty International, 'Death Sentences and Executions in 2017' (n 2) 31; Amnesty International, 'Death Sentences and Executions in 2018' (n 2) 12.

198 African Union, '57th Ordinary Session of African Commission' (n 40) para 19.

prohibitions considered in the chapter, which they have complied with to varying degrees. African regional treaties are generally in conformity with UN treaties in terms of the prohibitions, and a significant majority of African states have abandoned the death penalty in law or practice. The recognition of the death penalty's inconsistency with human rights has contributed largely to its decline in Africa. Other contributing factors 'include the fact that in some countries prosecutors got tired of seeking for the ultimate punishment, judges imposed an alternative penalty, especially in cases where the death penalty was provided for less serious crimes and Prison officers who watched over the death row prisoners began to voice the agony and trauma that they faced daily'.[199]

Notwithstanding, the use of the death penalty in some African countries still raises concerns. There are also post-abolition concerns, such as extensive delays in the amendment of laws to remove references to it. Further, while there is a general decline of the mandatory death penalty and general compliance with the prohibition of the death penalty for certain offenders or offences, a few African states have failed to comply with the prohibitions in this regard. Hence, the African Commission and the Working Group on Death Penalty have continuously called upon African states to, in line with international standards, abolish the death penalty or commence the process of its formal abolition, put in place a moratorium on its use, and commute existing death sentences. They have also urged African states to support adopting the draft regional protocol on the abolition of the death penalty in Africa and civil society organizations to promote advocacy and action at national, sub-regional and regional levels towards the abolition of the death penalty.

[199] ibid, para 48.

5

Compliance Beyond Anniversaries

The African Union Convention for the Protection and Assistance of Internally Displaced Persons (Kampala Convention) in Domestic Laws and Policies

Aderomola Adeola

1 Introduction

There is often a pertinent question as to why states developed the African Union (AU) Convention for the Protection and Assistance of Internally Displaced Persons in Africa (Kampala Convention) when a globally accepted standard on internal displacement already existed, the UN Guiding Principles on Internal Displacement 1998 (Guiding Principles).[1] The preamble to the Kampala Convention provides an insight into this question as it often includes the intention of the drafters of a treaty provision. The Kampala Convention is explicit on the fact that states were motivated by the need to close an existing regional gap, notably the absence of a specific law on internal displacement.[2]

There was a sense in which the absence of a regional law on internal displacement seemed to create an imbalance in the attention to the forced displacement crisis in Africa and, specifically, the protection of those displaced within state borders compared to those externally displaced (refugees). Hence, this necessitated the formation of a regional normative response. But there is also the weight of precedence that often the regional response to a significant crisis or issue is the elaboration of a framework that sets a common standard for all 55 AU Member States in the region. This is also evident in the narrative on the formation of the

[1] UN Commission on Human Rights, Addendum, 'Guiding Principles on Internal Displacement' *Report of the Representative of the Secretary-General, Mr Francis M Deng, submitted pursuant to Commission on Human Rights resolution 1997/39*, UN Doc E/CN.4/1998/53/Add.2 (11 February 1998).

[2] In para 13 of the Preamble to the Kampala Convention, states recalled 'the lack of a binding African and international legal and institutional framework specifically, for the prevention of internal displacement and the protection of and assistance to internally displaced persons'. The AU Convention for the Protection and Assistance of Internally Displaced Persons in Africa, adopted at the Special Summit of the African Union Heads of States and Government in Kampala, Uganda (23 October 2009), para 13.

Aderomola Adeola, *Compliance Beyond Anniversaries* In: *Compliance with International Human Rights Law in Africa*. Edited by: Aderomola Adeola, Oxford University Press. © Aderomola Adeola 2022. DOI: 10.1093/oso/9780192856999.003.0005

Kampala Convention. Over the decades, rich historical evidence of this practice has emerged.

When the regional refugee framework developed, it was in response to the crisis of refugee movement in parts of Africa which did not fall squarely within the 1951 UN Refugee Convention given the geographic scope and dateline in the definition of a refugee under the global framework. While a subsequent protocol was adopted in 1967 in response to this gap, there were particular aspects of the refugee problem in Africa that states felt should be included in a specific regional framework.[3] What emerged from this process was an effective complement to the global refugee regime through an infusion of an African flair to the situation, not least in terms of the expanded definition and the ideation of burden sharing. A similar rhetoric also resonates in the Kampala Convention in specific aspects, mainly related to the root causes of internal displacement and actors on the scene of internal displacement.[4] But as with the OAU Refugee Convention to the 1951 UN Refugee Convention and its 1967 Protocol, the Kampala Convention builds on the provisions of the Guiding Principles.

The adoption of the Kampala Convention was met with significant optimism, given its regional coverage, its acceptance by states and the political will that drove the development of the normative framework. Beginning with the decisions of the AU Executive Council in 2004,[5] there was a consensus that the issue of internal displacement was a significant regional concern that had to be addressed.[6] Addressing this crisis required a concerted regional effort, which had to begin with the exposition of a framework on the protection and assistance of IDPs. The AU Executive Council required the AU Commission to 'collaborate with relevant cooperating partners and other stakeholders to ensure that Internally Displaced Persons are provided with an appropriate legal framework to ensure their adequate protection and assistance'.[7] While a crucial starting point in the development of the framework was reflected on existing norms, particularly the Guiding Principles, AU Member States also wanted to reflect the regional context. Indeed, the Kampala Convention defines its path through innovative provisions that significantly reflect the context within which it is formed.

[3] OAU Convention Governing the Specific Aspects of Refugee Problems in Africa (1969).

[4] The recognition of harmful practices as a root cause of internal displacement is notable. Moreover, the Kampala Convention recognizes non-state actors and responds to the evident impact of these actors on the scene of internal displacement in Africa.

[5] See AU Executive Council, Decision on the meeting of experts on the review of OAU/AU treaties, AU Doc EX/CL/95 (V) (25 June to 3 July 2004); AU Executive Council, Decision on the Situation of Refugees, Returnees and Displaced Persons AU Doc EX. CL/108 (V) (25 June to 3 July 2004).

[6] The AU Executive Council emphasized that the 'specific needs of internally displaced persons (IDPs) such as protection and assistance should be addressed through a separate legal instrument'. AU Executive Council, Decision on the meeting of experts on the review of OAU/AU treaties, para 4(i).

[7] AU Executive Council, Decision on the Situation of Refugees, Returnees and Displaced Persons, para 8.

But having been ratified by more than half of AU Member States, a significant question which the emergence of treaties, specifically, the Kampala Convention, brings to the fore is, to what extent has there been compliance by states? In answering this question, this chapter examines the extent to which states have developed laws and policies with significant reference to this instrument. However, in commencing the discussion, it is useful to reflect on the contextual relevance of the Kampala Convention. In the next section, the contextual relevance of the Kampala Convention will be examined with reference to existing frameworks. Following the discussion, this chapter examines the extent of compliance with the Kampala Convention in domestic laws and policies across the continent.

2 Contextual Relevance of the Kampala Convention

As earlier noted, the Kampala Convention emerged from the need to address the regional gap in the protection and assistance of IDPs. While there were norms on human rights and, in fact, legal regimes that mentioned IDPs as a category for protection, there was no comprehensive regional document articulating protection for these persons. Consequently, the need for the development of a regional law on internal displacement was imperative. However, prior to this period, certain normative frameworks in existence were of relevance to the issue of internal displacement, which begs the question as to the contextual significance of a specific regional legal regime on internal displacement.

Put differently, in light of the rich panoply of legal frameworks at the regional level on human rights, was there any significance to the emergence of the Kampala Convention? In answering this question, it is useful to reflect on the distinct contribution of the Kampala Convention with respect to the various instruments. There is little debate as to the pertinence of the Kampala Convention vis-à-vis the regional refugee framework (the 1969 OAU Refugee Convention), given the focus of the latter on persons displaced outside countries of origin. However, it is useful to appreciate the connection between both instruments. The Kampala Convention reinforces this connection in emphasizing the right of IDPs to seek asylum by providing that its provisions 'shall not be interpreted as affecting or undermining the right of internally displaced persons to seek and be granted asylum', referring to relevant frameworks including the 1969 OAU Refugee Convention.[8] Hence, the Kampala Convention makes the point that the rhetoric of protection in situations of internal displacement should not become a strategy for containment. Another evident relationship between both frameworks relates to situations of voluntary repatriation, particularly the protection of displaced persons upon return to the

[8] Kampala Convention, art 20(1).

country of displacement. Evidently, both regimes (on IDPs and refugees) create a continuum of protection that ought to be appreciated in that they close the gap that may be brought on by the absence of protection either for persons displaced within borders or across borders. The distinct contribution of the Kampala Convention resonates in this complementary relationship.

Another pertinent normative framework is the African Charter on Human and Peoples' Rights (African Charter) and, specifically, its provision on the right to freedom of movement and residence within the border of a state.[9] A important question is that given that article 12(1) of the African Charter relates to movements within state borders, including situations of internal displacement, is the Kampala Convention still a relevant regional framework? Prior to the Kampala Convention, there was little, if any, discussion on the right to freedom of movement and residence within state borders within the African context. This was not the case in other regions, particularly the Americas, where jurisprudence has flourished in the last decades linking the right to freedom of movement and residence to situations of forced displacement.[10] For instance, in the case of *Santo Domingo Massacre v Columbia*, the Inter-American Court of Human Rights emphasized that the right to freedom of movement and residence also incorporated the right not to be internally displaced.[11] In the *Case of the 'Mapripán Massacre' v Columbia*, the Inter-American Court emphasized that

> '[t]hrough an evolutive interpretation of Article 22 of the [American] Convention, taking into account the applicable provisions regarding interpretation and in accordance with Article 29.b of the Convention—which forbids a restrictive interpretation of the rights-, this Court deems that Article 22(1) of the Convention protects the right to not be forcefully displaced within a State Party to the Convention.

However, within the African region, much of the discussion on the right to freedom of movement and residence has specifically been within the context of mass expulsion or even restrictions on the right in other composite forms such as the right of entry and exit.[12] However, the substance of this right with respect to movement and residence within state borders did not receive significant attention. By extension, there was little discussion on the relationship of article 12(1) of the African Charter to situations of internal displacement. In the *Centre for Minority Rights*

[9] African Charter on Human and Peoples' Rights (1981) art 12(1).

[10] See A Adeola, *The Internally Displaced Person Under International Law* (Edward Elgar 2020) 79–80.

[11] See the Inter-American Court of Human Rights *Case of the Santo Domingo Massacre v Columbia* (Judgment of 30 November 2012); Inter-American Court of Human Rights *Case of the 'Mapripán Massacre' v Columbia* (Judgment of 15 September 2005).

[12] See *Organisation Mondiale Contre la Torture and Others v Rwanda* (2000) AHRLR 282 (ACHPR 1996); *Mouvement Burkinabé des Droits de l'Homme et des Peuples v Burkina Faso* (2001) AHRLR 51 (ACHPR 2001) paras 46–47; *Ouko v Kenya* (2000) AHRLR 135 (ACHPR 2000), para 31.

Development (Kenya) & Minority Rights Group International (on behalf of Endorois Welfare Council) v Kenya where the African Commission on Human and Peoples' Rights (African Commission) examined the displacement of indigenous communities from their ancestral land, the right to freedom of movement and residence was not elaborated upon to guide the interpretation of this norm in the context of displacement.[13] This was also the case in the *African Commission on Human and Peoples' Rights v Republic of Kenya* (the *Ogiek* case) before the African Court on Human and Peoples' Rights.[14] While it would appear that article 12(1) of the African Charter is explicit, this is not entirely so. For instance, what free movement or residence entails is not definite. Moreover, it is not clear if the right applies to individuals or solely to citizens. This is accentuated by the fact that there are varying interpretations on the right to freedom of movement and residence across African constitutions, linked to nationality and citizenship,[15] which is not the case in article 12(1) of the African Charter.

Evidently, if movement is conceived as citizenship or nationality-centred, this will imply that non-nationals of a state may not be allowed to fully exercise this right. However, in situations of internal displacement, anyone may be affected. And clearly, there have been instances across the continent where non-nationals have been displaced in disaster situations and armed conflict. In states where such right to freedom of movement and residence is linked to nationality and citizenship, the extent to which displaced non-nationals may move freely within areas of the state is not explicit. The pertinence of clarity on the scope of this provision prompted the African Commission to develop a General Comment on article 12(1) of the African Charter. And in providing clarity on movement within the context of internal displacement, the Kampala Convention was integral to defining the scope of the right to freedom of movement and residence for IDPs, given the fact that it is specific law on the issue and provides obvious clarity on aspects of the instrument that is not entirely explicit.[16]

Of the various instruments adopted by the OAU/AU prior to the Kampala Convention, the African Charter on the Rights and Welfare of the Child (African

[13] However, the African Commission examined the displacement of the *Endorois* community referring to art 14 of the African Charter, which provides for the right to property. The shortcoming of the right, however, links back to the question of ownership, particularly where internal displacement also affects persons who do not have property rights. For a discussion on the case, see Communication 276/2003, *Centre for Minority Rights Development (Kenya) & Minority Rights Group International (on behalf of Endorois Welfare Council) v Kenya* (2009) (*Endorois* case). See also A Adeola, *Development-Induced Displacement and Human Rights in Africa: The Kampala Convention* (2021) 55–56.

[14] *African Commission on Human and Peoples' Rights v Republic of Kenya*, Application No 006/2012, Judgment of 26 May 2017).

[15] See, for instance, the Constitution of Algeria (1989), art 44 'Every citizen enjoying all civil and political rights, has the right to choose freely the place of residence and to move about on the national territory.'

[16] See Aderomola Adeola, Frans Viljoen and Trésor Makunya-Muhindo, 'A Commentary on the African Commission's General Comment on the Right to Freedom of Movement and Residence under Article 12(1) of the African Charter' (2020) Journal of African Law (forthcoming).

Children's Charter) is the only instrument that incorporates protection for the internally displaced, specifically children.[17] While this is significant, this provision of the instrument is not explicit. In fact, the African Children's Charter seemed to have mentioned internally displaced children in passing given that it is captured under article 23 titled 'refugee children' and states that the provisions of the article shall 'apply *mutatis mutandis* to internally displaced children'.[18] But what this implies is not clear. However, it is significant that when discussions on internal displacement were only emerging at the global level,[19] the African Children Charter emphasized the need to protect internally displaced children. In understanding the implication of protection, reference to the Kampala Convention is imperative as it is evident in the Kampala Convention that the doctrinal scope of protection and assistance for IDPs is explicit. The argument is similar with respect to internally displaced women, protected under article 11(3) of the 2003 Protocol to the African Charter on Human and Peoples' Rights on the Rights of Women in Africa.[20] The Kampala Convention provides a clear prism to define the substance of protection and assistance for IDPs, specifically, for these different groups, including persons with disabilities and older persons.

But there is a question as to the significance of the Kampala Convention, vis-à-vis the 2006 Protocol on the Protection and Assistance of Internally Displaced Persons (Great Lakes Protocol),[21] which incorporates the Guiding Principles within the Great Lakes Region. Evidently, for states that are part of the Great Lakes Region, the Great Lakes Protocol is a significant reference point. As such, that is less debatable. However, for states that are not part of the Great Lakes Region, the absence of the Kampala Convention would have, counterfactually, meant that there was no applicable regime to them if, within their regional blocs, there were also no specific treaty law. The Guiding Principles will still be relevant, however, it does not invoke binding obligations. But there is also an important question as to what contextual relevance the Kampala Convention has for states in the Great Lakes Region, given the existence of the Great Lakes Protocol. An instance where this question becomes even more significant is with respect to Kenya that—while not having ratified the Kampala Convention—adopted a national framework modelling the Great Lakes Protocol.[22] What added value, for instance, does the Kampala

[17] African Charter on the Rights and Welfare of the Child (1990).

[18] ibid, art 23(4).

[19] For further discussion on the global regime, please see: Cardona-Fox, *Exile Within Borders: A Global Look at Commitment to the International Regime to Protect Internally Displaced Persons* (Brill 2019); Phil Orchard, *Protecting the Internally Displaced: Rhetoric and Reality* (Routledge 2019); Aderomola Adeola, *The Internally Displaced Person in International Law* (Edward Elgar 2020).

[20] Protocol to the African Charter on Human and Peoples' Rights on the Rights of Women in Africa (2003).

[21] Protocol on the Protection and Assistance of Internally Displaced Persons, adopted by the International Conference on the Great Lakes Region (2006).

[22] Kenya: Prevention, Protection and Assistance to Internally Displaced Persons and Affected Communities Act 2012.

Convention hold for the state for which ratification and/or revision of its law is essential? In answering this question, it is useful to reflect on the novel substance of the Kampala Convention.

With respect to the substantive obligations, the Kampala Convention introduces root causes of internal displacement that are contextually relevant to Africa, however, not explicit in the Guiding Principles, due in part to its global nature and the time in which it was created. For instance, harmful practices are an important root cause of internal displacement in Africa,[23] yet not mentioned in the Guiding Principles and the Great Lakes Protocol. Also, climate change is an issue that is not addressed in either instrument but contained in the Kampala Convention.[24] Having specific guidance on the content of these obligations is integral to protecting IDPs. Also, the accountability of non-state actors is explicitly emphasized in the Kampala Convention.[25] However, this is not the case in either the Guiding Principles or the Great Lakes Protocol. While both instruments emphasize the importance of international humanitarian law, which incorporates obligations required of specific armed groups,[26] in the context of non-international armed conflicts, there are no specific provisions concerning other non-state actors such as private military or security companies and multinational companies in the Guiding Principles or the Great Lakes Protocol. The Kampala Convention, on the other hand, emphasizes the need for states to ensure the accountability of these actors in situations of internal displacement. Clearly, this creates an added value to the legal landscape on internal displacement in Africa. Implementation, however, remains to be seen.

3 The Kampala Convention at Domestic Level

Treaty anniversaries often present an opportune moment to reflect on the value of the treaty and, indeed, consider the extent to which it has been significant in the advancement of its objectives. Ahead of 2019, the AU Assembly adopted a resolution declaring 2019 as the Year of Refugees, Returnees and IDPs against the backdrop that 2019 marked the 50th and 10th anniversary of the frameworks on refugee and IDP protection, respectively.[27] This spurred several discussions on IDP protection at various forums, including the:

[23] Kampala Convention, art 4(4)(e).
[24] Kampala Convention, art 5(4).
[25] Kampala Convention, art 3(h) and (i).
[26] See Guiding Principles, para 3; Great Lakes Protocol, art 4(a).
[27] Decision on the 2019 theme of the year, 'The Year of Refugees, Returnees and Internally Displaced Persons: Towards Durable Solutions to Forced Displacement in Africa' AU Assembly/AU/Dec.707 (XXXI) (1–2 July 2018).

- 5th Session of the African Union Humanitarian Architecture: Law and Policy Training Programme (Livingstone Syllabus) (Livingstone, Zambia, 18–21 March 2019);
- Pan-African Parliament Recommendation on the African Union Theme for the Year 2019: The Year of Refugees, Returnees, and Internally Displaced Persons: Pan-African Parliament's Contribution Towards Finding Durable Solutions to Forced Displacement in Africa (Midrand, South Africa, 17 May 2019);
- Declaration and Action Plan of the Third AUC-NANHRI Policy Forum on the State of African National Human Rights Institutions in Africa under the Theme, "National Human Rights Institutions' (NHRI's) Contribution to durable Solutions on Forced Displacements in Africa" (Addis Ababa, Ethiopia, 5–6 September 2019);
- 7th Humanitarian Symposium: Gender Dimension of Forced Displacement in Africa: towards durable solutions (Nairobi, Kenya, 18–20 November 2019);
- Continental Youth Consultation: Youth and Forced Displacement in Africa – Trends, Challenges and Prospects towards Durable Solutions (Kampala, Uganda, 2–3 December 2019);
- Continental Consultative Meeting on Promoting the Ratification, Domestication and Implementation of the African Union Convention for the Protection and Assistance of Internally Displaced Persons in Africa (Kampala, Uganda, 2–3 December 2019);
- CSO Pre-Forum to the AU High-Level Dialogue on Refugees, Returnees and Internally Displaced Persons: Towards Durable Solutions to Forced Displacements in Africa (Kampala, Uganda, 3 December 2019);
- 8th High-Level Dialogue on the AU Theme of the Year 2019: Refugees, Returnees and Internally Displaced Persons towards durable solutions to forced displacement in Africa (Kampala, Uganda, 4–6 December 2019).

At these events, the significance of the Kampala Convention was amplified. However, having been in existence for over a decade, there is a question as to the extent of compliance with the treaty. While the term 'compliance' is polysemic and often linked with other pertinent ideations such as implementation, impact and effectiveness, it broadly relates to the question of outcomes at the national level. The extensive literature on compliance reflects the importance of interrogating this imperative in defining the relevance of a treaty.[28] Ultimately, the test of a legal regime

[28] See generally RO Keohane, 'Compliance with International Commitments: Politics Within a Framework of Law' (1992) 86 Proceedings of the Annual Meeting 176–180; A Chayes and AH Chayes, 'On Compliance' (1993) 47(2) IO 175–205; D Shelton, 'Compliance with International Human Rights Soft Law' (1997) 29 Studies in Transnational Legal Policy 119–144; BA Simmons, 'Compliance with International Agreements' (1998) 1 Annu Rev Polit Sci 75–93; AT Guzman, 'A Compliance-Based Theory of International Law' (2002) 90 Cal L 1823–1887; WC Bradford, 'International Legal Compliance: An Annotated Bibliography' (2004) 30(2) N C J Int'l Law 379–428; A Alkoby, 'Theories of

resonates from the extent to which it advances compliance. And by compliance, what is emphasized is the extent to which there is observable progress or alignment with a specific treaty. The issue of compliance raises questions as to the difference made by the existence of a treaty. This consideration resonates with the Viljoen argument that the 'ultimate test of international human rights law is the extent to which it takes root in national soil'.[29] In considering the extent to which this is the case, this chapter examines the tangible outcomes that emerged at the national level in the furtherance of the Kampala Convention, with specific reference to laws and policies.

Prior to adopting the Kampala Convention, at least six countries had laws or policies on internal displacement, including Angola, Burundi, Liberia, Uganda, Sierra Leone and Sudan. However, some frameworks, such as Sierra Leone and Angola, are mostly concerned with specific issues such as durable solutions, with a significant emphasis on return as a solution. Sudan's IDP policy provides a relevant reference document for the furtherance of IDP issues, reinforcing nine specific frameworks in the furtherance of IDP protection. It further emphasizes the role of a High Committee on IDPs in monitoring implementation. But it is not comprehensive in its provision on internal displacement, particularly with respect to root causes of internal displacement. The frameworks of Liberia and Burundi are interesting in that they focus on IDP rights and establish a platform for consultation on IDP protection, respectively. However, they are also not comprehensive in the furtherance of IDP protection. A further innovative approach by Liberia is the development of an instrument incorporating the Guiding Principles 'as a source of ongoing guidance and reference for the protection, dignity and rights' of IDPs.[30] Obviously, this is significant, however, it seems more like a hortatory. However, of these frameworks, Uganda's policy significantly draws on the Guiding Principles in the exposition on protection and assistance to IDPs.[31] It also does not include the innovations of the Kampala Convention, particularly in terms of root causes such as climate change and harmful practices.

However, the adoption of the Kampala Convention brought significant momentum to the issue of internal displacement, enhancing awareness and inspiring law and policy formations beyond these states. Over the last decade, there has been renewed interest in research on internal displacement, advocacy at various levels of governance and sustained support for the protection and assistance to IDPs across

Compliance with International Law and Challenge of Cultural Difference' (2008) 4(1) JILIR 151–198; CM Ryan, 'Discerning the Compliance Calculus: Why States Comply with International Investment Law' (2009) 38(1) Ge J Int'l & Comp Law 63–96; R Howse and R Teitel, 'Beyond Compliance: Rethinking Why Int'l Law Really Matters' (2010) 1(2) Global Policy 127–136.

[29] Frans Viljoen, *International Human Rights Law in Africa* (OUP 2012) 517.
[30] Liberia: Instrument of Adoption of Guiding Principles on Internally Displaced Persons (2004).
[31] Uganda: The National Policy for Internally Displaced Persons (2004).

Table 5.1 Laws and policies Prior to the Adoption of the Kampala Convention (2009)[a]

S/N	Country	Laws and Policies
1	Angola	Decree Number 1/01: Norms on the Resettlement of Displaced Populations (2001) Decree No 79: Implementation of Norms on the Resettlement of Displaced Populations (2002)
2	Burundi	Protocol for the Creation of a Permanent Framework for Consultation on the Protection of Displaced Persons (2001)
3	Liberia	Declaration of the Rights and Protection of Liberian Internally Displaced Persons (IDPs) (2002) Instrument of Adoption of Guiding Principles on Internally Displaced Persons (2004)
4	Sierra Leone	Resettlement Strategy (2001)
5	Sudan	The National Policy for Internally Displaced Persons (IDPs) (2009)
6	Uganda	The National Policy for Internally Displaced Persons (2004) National Internally Displaced Persons Return, Resettlement and Re-Integration Strategic Plan for Lango and Teso Sub-Regions (2005)

[a] The discussion that informs this table is initially contained in Adeola, *The Internally Displaced Persons Under International Law* (n 19).

various countries. While many of these processes have been led by local Non-governmental Organizations (NGOs), humanitarian actors such as the International Committee of the Red Cross (ICRC) and UN institutions such as the UN Refugee Agency and the International Organization for Migration (IOM), the existence of the Kampala Convention has prompted regional action by the AU Member States, specifically from a law and policy dimension. Over the last decade (2009–2019), the Kampala Convention has been ratified by at least 31 AU Member States and signed by no less than 40 states.[32]

However, only one country has adopted national legislation on internal displacement in this period, which is Niger.[33] While Niger's law draws on the Kampala Convention, it does not extensively include the provisions of the Kampala Convention and, particularly, the creative contents of the Kampala Convention, such as its recognition of harmful practices and climate change as root causes of internal displacement. However, it is notable that the country passed the first law leveraging on the Kampala Convention as a significant source. However, some

[32] List of countries that have signed, ratified/acceded to the African Union Convention for the Protection and Assistance of Internally Displaced Persons in Africa (Kampala Convention) (2020).

[33] Niger: Law No 2018-74 of 10 December 2018, relating to the Protection and Assistance of Internally Displaced Persons (2018).

other countries have adopted draft legislation on the Kampala Convention, such as Liberia, the Democratic Republic of Congo and South Sudan, reflecting these root causes of internal displacement.[34] In 2015, Mali adopted a National Strategy on the Management of Internally Displaced Persons and Returnees for 2015–2017, also premised on the Kampala Convention. Similar initiatives have emerged in the Central African Republic and Ethiopia.[35]

On a policy level, Somalia's normative landscape is significant as there are three policies: one at the federal level and two within the state of Puntland and the region of Banadir.[36] All policies significantly refer to the Kampala Convention and allude to the framework in the exposition of specific elements. For instance, Somalia's federal policy describes unlawful displacement as[37]

> Displacement that contravenes either national law or international law and standards, including forced eviction consistent with the prohibited displacement categories listed in *Article 4(4) of the African Union Convention for the Protection and Assistance of Internally Displaced Persons in Africa (Kampala Convention).* [Emphasis added].

In 2013, Zambia adopted a set of Guidelines for the Compensation and Resettlement of Internally Displaced Persons drawing on the Kampala Convention.[38] A pertinent provision it draws from the Kampala Convention relating to the prevention of internal displacement and, specifically also, the need for states to develop early warning systems.[39] The provision is a replica of article 4(2) of the Kampala Convention, which mandates states to devise early warning systems and disaster risk reduction measures.[40] While not having ratified the Kampala Convention, Kenya's IDP policy interestingly makes reference to the Kampala Convention and, in fact, incorporates root causes of internal displacement in the Kampala Convention.[41] However, the policy document has remained a draft for some years.

[34] Democratic Republic of Congo: Bill Providing Protection and Assistance to Internally Displaced Persons (2014); Liberia: An Act for the Implementation of the African Union Convention for the Protection and Assistance of Internally Displaced Persons in Liberia (2018) (Draft); South Sudan: Protection and Assistance to Internally Displaced Persons Act 2019 (Draft).

[35] Central African Republic: National Plan for the Protection and Assistance of Internally Displaced Persons in Central African Republic (2015) (Draft); Ethiopia: Somali Region Durable Solutions Strategy: 2017-2020: The Durable Solutions Strategy of the Somali Regional Government of Ethiopia (2017); Ethiopia Durable Solutions Initiative (2019).

[36] Somalia: Puntland Policy Guidelines on Displacement (2014); Somalia: National Policy on Refugee-Returnees and Internally Displaced Persons (2019); Somalia: Banadir Regional Administration and Municipality of Mogadishu: Internally Displaced Person and Refugee Returnees Policy (2019).

[37] Somalia: National Policy on Refugee-Returnees and Internally Displaced Persons (2019) 8.

[38] Zambia: Guidelines for the Compensation and Resettlement of Internally Displaced Persons (2013).

[39] ibid, guideline 9.

[40] Kampala Convention, art 4(2).

[41] Kenya: National Policy on the Prevention of Internal Displacement, Protection and Assistance to Internally Displaced Persons (IDPs) in Kenya (Final Draft, 2011).

Nigeria also has an elaborate policy on the Kampala Convention that extensively covers various root causes and groups of persons that may be affected in situations of internal displacement.[42] In line with the Kampala Convention, it also incorporates non-state actors.[43] Although elaborate, the policy, first developed in 2007 and twice revised in 2009 and 2012, remained a draft for over a decade and was only adopted by the Federal Executive Council in 2021.[44] In 2015, Malawi developed a durable solutions framework for the protection of flood-affected persons drawing on the Kampala Convention.[45] Below is a tabular representation of laws and policies following the adoption of the Kampala Convention between 2009 and 2021.

The law and policy terrain reflect progress in the furtherance of the Kampala Convention. Overall, some tangible outcomes reflect positive changes in national orientations towards IDPs. However, in comparison to the number of AU Member States that have ratification, this is still slow-paced. Coupled with the fact that internal displacement is a significant challenge, but very few laws exist, there is a need to amplify action.

4 Building Compliance Beyond Anniversaries

Building compliance requires an understanding of the variables that influence the tangible outcome at the domestic level. From the start, it is important to emphasize that these variables will not always be the same across national territories. Moreover, in some states, more than one variable may exist. But overall, it is useful to understand the context in which a variable will be employed. From existing law and policy frameworks on internal displacement, five variables can be discerned.[46]

4.1 Norm Influencers

First, there is a need for norm influencers in the furtherance of the tangible outcome at the domestic level. This crucial point resonates in the context of norm formation, for instance, in Nigeria, where the emergence of a bill on internal displacement was significantly driven by a former Chairman of the House of Representatives

[42] Nigeria: National Policy on Internal Displacement (2021).
[43] ibid.
[44] 'FEC Approves New Policy on IDPs' *Premium Times* 1 September 2021.
[45] Malawi: Durable Solutions for Internally Displaced Persons (IDPs) and Flood Affected Populations in Malawi (2015).
[46] For further discussions on trigger points from a global context, please see Aderomola Adeola and Phil Orchard, 'The role of IDP Law and Policy in Fostering Responsibility and Accountability of Government' Research Briefing Paper, UNSG High Level Panel on Internal Displacement (August 2020).

Table 5.2 Laws and Policies Following the Adoption of the Kampala Convention (2009–2021)[a]

S/N	Country	Laws and Policies
1	Central African Republic	National Plan for the Protection and Assistance of Internally Displaced Persons in Central African Republic (2015) (Draft)
2	Democratic Republic of Congo	Bill Providing Protection and Assistance to Internally Displaced Persons (29 September 2014) Provincial Strategy for Durable Solution for Internally Displaced Persons in North Kivu (2016)
3	Ethiopia	Somali Region Durable Solutions Strategy: 2017-2020: The Durable Solutions Strategy of the Somali Regional Government of Ethiopia (2017) Ethiopia Durable Solutions Initiative (2019)
4	Kenya	National Policy on the Prevention of Internal Displacement, Protection and Assistance to Internally Displaced Persons (IDPs) in Kenya (Final Draft, 2011)[b] Prevention, Protection and Assistance to Internally Displaced Persons and Affected Communities Act 2012[c]
5	Liberia	An Act for the Implementation of the African Union Convention for the Protection and Assistance of Internally Displaced Persons in Liberia (2018) (Draft)
6	Malawi	Durable Solutions for Internally Displaced Persons (IDPs) and flood affected populations in Malawi (2015)
7	Mali	National Strategy on the Management of Internally Displaced Persons and Returnees (2015-2017) (2015)
8	Niger	Law No. 2018-74 of 10 December 2018, relating to the Protection and Assistance of Internally Displaced Persons (2018)
9	Nigeria	Rights of Internally Displaced Persons (IDPs) Bill (2016) National Policy on Internal Displacement (2021)
10	Somalia	Puntland Policy Guidelines on Displacement (2014) National Policy on Refugee-Returnees and Internally Displaced Persons (2019) Banadir Regional Administration and Municipality of Mogadishu: Internally Displaced Person and Refugee Returnees Policy (2019)
11	South Sudan	Protection and Assistance to Internally Displaced Persons Act 2019 (Draft)
12	Zambia	Guidelines for the Compensation and Resettlement of Internally Displaced Persons (2013)

[a] The discussion that informs this table is initially contained in Adeola, *The Internally Displaced Persons Under International Law* (n 19).

[b] The policy refers to the Kampala Convention.

[c] The legislation does not refer to the Kampala Convention.

Committee on IDPs, Refugees and North East initiatives from 2015–2019.[47] Such norm influencers may be individuals or transnational networks of civil society. The relevance of norm influencers also comes to the fore in the context of Zimbabwe, for instance, where the national human rights commission attempted to develop a national action plan on internal displacement in 2019.[48] What is crucial to understand in using norm influencers is to know which influencers exist and how actions such influencers have triggered in the past. Aside from civil society, influencers may also be the private sector, a specific demography within the state, such as youths or women. This could also be organizations at the supranational level. For instance, in the Economic Community of West African States (ECOWAS) region, the support of ECOWAS to Liberia was crucial in the formation of a draft law and expressed in early drafts of the IDP law.[49] It may be useful to note how these influencers engage with relevant state institutions and at what point their voices gain resonance. Such influencers may also need to be well-equipped with support, particularly from a technical perspective, to understand the issue of internal displacement. And in this regard, specialized support from relevant institutions or agencies is useful.

4.2 International Support

International support may also produce a tangible outcome. In this regard, the formation of normative frameworks in Niger and Ethiopia is noteworthy. For instance, the development of the Somali Region Durable Solutions Strategy (2017-2020) was driven with the support of IOM, while ownership remained with the Somali regional government of Ethiopia. International support may come in various forms, not least financial and technical. But such support must be sustained beyond the period of norm formation. This requires that such support should be infused with sustainability strategies to allow the relevant national-level institutions to drive concrete action. From a law and policy dimension, this is crucial, particularly in contexts where the existence of a specific law on internal displacement at the national level also requires concurrent policy formation within decentralized

[47] Adamu Abuh, 'Nigeria: Representative Seek Domestication of Kampala Convention over IDP's plights' The Guardian (Nigeria) 5 July 2016.

[48] See Zimbabwe Human Rights Commission: Action Plan on Durable Solutions on Internal Displacement in Zimbabwe (2021–2025) (2020) (*Draft*) (On file with author).

[49] The Preamble reads: 'The Economic Community of West African States (ECOWAS) has expressed extreme interest in providing support for the implementation of the African Union Convention and is encouraging member states to ratify and domesticate the Kampala Convention so as to place the issue of IDPs on the national agenda of member states.' See Liberia: An Act for the Implementation of the African Union Convention for the Protection and Assistance of Internally Displaced Persons in Liberia (2018) (Draft).

systems in order to spurn action. But overall, such sustained support is crucial for impact at the ground level, particularly in the IDPs' lived experiences.

4.3 External Spotlight

Another significant variable is the external spotlight on the issue of internal displacement. This influenced the emergence of the normative framework on IDPs in Kenya. Although this was not linked to the Kampala Convention but rather to the Great Lakes Protocol, it is significant to emphasize that the spotlight on the 2007/2008 post-election violence spurred action in the development of a national law on internal displacement.[50] Overall, the role of civil society cannot be overemphasized. Sustaining the momentum created by an external spotlight will require the involvement of an active civic space. One of the pertinent allies in this process is the media. However, it is crucial that the media is engaged early on to build the narrative on protection and assistance of IDPs to ensure that factual details are captured accurately.

4.4 Post-Conflict Reconstruction

Post-conflict reconstruction processes could also serve to foster law and policy formation on IDPs. Examples of this may be found in norms in Angola and Sierra Leone, although these predate the Kampala Convention. Article 3(2)(e) of the Kampala Convention mandate states to '[e]ndeavour to incorporate the relevant principles contained in this Convention into peace negotiations and agreements for the purpose of finding sustainable solutions to the problem of internal displacement'.[51] Such inclusion will ensure that IDP issues are not left out in the process of reconstruction. It is important, however, that a holistic approach to IDP protection is taken during this process. In practice, there is often a tendency to focus on one aspect of a durable solution—return. However, this is just one of the solutions and IDPs may not always integrate locally or be resettled in another part of the state. The ability to make such choices must be significantly grounded in law and policy. It is crucial that the post-conflict reconstruction process serves as a catalyst for the development of a comprehensive law on internal displacement as opposed to the development of legislation on one root cause of internal displacement—conflict. As other root causes may emerge, such as natural disasters, including climate

[50] Norwegian Refugee Council and Internal Displacement Monitoring Centre, *A Review of the Normative Framework in Kenya Relating to the Protection of IDPs in the Context of the Kampala Convention and Other Supranational Frameworks* (2015), 10–11.

[51] Kampala Convention, art 3(2)(e).

change, it is useful to have such a comprehensive framework to avoid legal fragmentation. Hence post-conflict reconstruction processes should serve as a trigger for a conversation on holistic protection, leveraging the Kampala Convention.

4.5 Peer-to-peer Learning

Spaces for peer-to-peer learning are also essential. This was relevant, for instance, to the emergence of the Abuja Action Statement, which emerged from the Regional Protection Dialogue between states in the Lake Chad region.[52] This could be carried out within the sub-regional groupings such as the regional consultations held in 2019 within the ECOWAS and IGAD regions.[53] Alternatively, it could be through regular meetings of the Conference of State Parties to the Kampala Convention (the Conference) established under article 14 of the Kampala Convention. During the first meeting of the Conference held in 2017, countries shared experiences on practices in the furtherance of IDP protection and challenges experienced in IDP protection and assistance. At this meeting, an action plan for the Kampala Convention was also adopted.[54] A benefit of this forum is that it creates the much-needed space for engagement between states on the furtherance of IDP protection and assistance.

5 Conclusion

Over the last decade, the emergence of the Kampala Convention on the regional scene of internal displacement has indeed been notable. Evident progress can be discerned from national contexts, although there is a need for tangible outcomes in reflecting the Kampala Convention within domestic contexts. Understanding the trigger points for action is fundamental to this process, and such triggers will vary across countries. It is relevant to examine what works vis-à-vis other relevant human rights treaties to understand these triggers. But overall, international support must be constant to drive technical capacity and provide resources, particularly in situations where states cannot provide adequately. It is crucial, however,

[52] Abuja Action Statement: Regional Protection Dialogue on the Lake Chad Basin (6–8 June 2016); Abuja Action Statement: Reaffirmation of the Commitments of the Abuja Action Statement and their Implementation – Second Regional Protection Dialogue on the Lake Chad Basin (28–29 January 2019).

[53] *Regional Exchange Series: Comparative Experiences on Preventing, Addressing and Resolving Internal Displacement* – West Africa regional exchange on law and policy to prevent and address internal displacement, Dakar, Senegal (21–22 Mar. 2019); *Regional Exchange Series: Comparative Experiences on Preventing, Addressing and Resolving Internal Displacement*—Experiences in supporting resilience and durable solutions to internal displacement in the IGAD region, Addis Ababa, Ethiopia (7–8 Oct. 2019).

[54] Conference of State Parties, *Harare Plan of Action for the Implementation of the Kampala Convention (2017–2022)* (2017).

that states establish conducive spaces for the furtherance of such support, particularly through consent when such offers are made and the promotion of international cooperation at sub-regional, regional and global levels. Overall, the voices of IDPs must be amplified through deliberate processes geared at ensuring that these persons participate in the formation of laws and policies for their protection and assistance in the development of lasting solutions to the issue of internal displacement in Africa.

6

Legitimacy as a Challenge to Compliance with the Norms on the Protection of Children in Africa

Remember Miamingi

1 Introduction

In 1979, in commemoration of the International Year of the Child declared by the United Nations General Assembly, African leaders within the framework of the Organization of African Unity (OAU) adopted the Declaration on the Rights and Welfare of the Child (the Declaration). The OAU considered the Declaration the first step towards a regional binding instrument on children's rights and welfare in Africa. Therefore, at the Monrovia Summit of 1979, it directed the Secretary-General of the OAU to explore the possibilities of bringing to fruition binding national and regional instruments.[1] In 1990, just a year after the Convention on the Rights of the Child (CRC) came into force, the OAU adopted the African Charter on the Rights and Welfare of the Child (ACRWC). Having participated in the drafting process and ratified CRC in significant numbers, it is intriguing why African countries opted for a regional treaty dealing specifically with children's rights. Scholars have put forward many reasons for the adoption of the ACRWC. Thus, apart from briefly sketching these reasons, the focus of this chapter is on whether, in fact, African countries did achieve the rationale for adopting a regional-specific children's rights instrument.

2 Raison D'Etre for Adopting the African Children's Charter

A number of process-related and substance orientated reasons were put forward by academics and policymakers in Africa as to why it was desirable for Africa to adopt a regional instrument dealing with children's rights.[2] As to the process, it has

[1] http://www.issafrica.org/AF/RegOrg/unity_to_union/pdfs/oau/hog/pHoGAssembly1979.pdf

[2] CILSA 199; Dejo Olowu, 'Protecting Children's Rights in Africa: A Critique of the African Charter on the Rights and Welfare of the Child' (2002) 10 Int J Child Rights 127; Danwood Chirwa, 'The Merits and Demerits of the African Charter on the Rights and Welfare of the Child' (2002) 10 Int J Child

Remember Miamingi, *Legitimacy as a Challenge to Compliance with the Norms on the Protection of Children in Africa*
In: *Compliance with International Human Rights Law in Africa*. Edited by: Aderomola Adeola, Oxford University Press.
 DOI: 10.1093/oso/9780192856999.003.0006

been argued that there was inadequate participation by many African states in the movement leading to and the actual drafting and adoption of the CRC. In addition, as to substance, the CRC was considered to have not adequately included some of the challenges faced by children in Africa. Furthermore, the image of childhood in the CRC was considered as not reflective of an understanding of childhood in Africa and thus, lacking an African cultural fingerprint. Arguably, there was a need for an African children's instrument rooted in the philosophical and cultural heritage of African communities.

Moreover, only four African countries participated meaningfully in the drafting process of the CRC.[3] There was minimal participation by African states in the drafting process. However, an important question to ask is, why was Africa not adequately represented in the negotiating process? This question is pertinent in light of the fact that many more African countries participated in the drafting process of the International Covenant on Civil and Political Right and the International Covenant on Economic, Social and Cultural Rights—both adopted in 1966, just a few years after most states had gained independence. However, there was limited participation in the CRC during the 1980s.[4] It is possible that this was because the subject matter of the CRC was not accorded a high priority, at that time, by African states and that for this reason, they did not take their participation seriously.

Nevertheless, it can be argued that irrespective of this lack of participation by African states, the near-universal ratification of the CRC by African states, with the exception of Somalia and South Sudan, should be indicative of the general acceptance of the image of childhood in the CRC on the continent. But while the CRC is regarded as the most comprehensive treaty on children's rights, there are a number

Rights 157; Lloyd, 'Evolution of the African Charter on the Rights and Welfare of the Child and the African Committee of Experts: Raising the Gauntlet' (2002) 10 179; J Sloth-Nielsen and BD Mezmur, 'A Dutiful Child: The Implications of Article 31 of the African Children's Charter' (2008) 52 J Afr Law 159; Benyam D Memzur, 'The African Children's Charter Versus the UN Convention on the Rights of the Child: a Zero-sum Game?' (2008) 23 Home SA Publiekreg = SA Public Law 1; T Kaime, *The African Charter on the Rights and Welfare of the Child: A Socio-Legal Perspective* (Pretoria University Law Press (PULP) 2009).

[3] Viljoen, 'Supra-National Human Rights Instruments for the Protection of Children in Africa: the Convention on the Rights of the Child and the African Charter on the Rights and Welfare of the Child'; Russell Lawrence Barsh, 'The Draft Convention on the Rights of the Child: A Case of Eurocentricism in Standard-Setting' (1989) 58 24.

[4] Zehra Arat, 'Forging A Global Culture of Human Rights: Origins and Prospects of the International Bill of Rights' (2006) 28 HRQ 416; John P Humphrey, *Human Rights & the United Nations: A Great Adventure* (Transnational Pub Inc 1984); Menno T Kamminga, 'J Morsink, The Universal Declaration of Human Rights: Origins, Drafting, and Intent [Pennsylvania Studies in Human Rights]. University of Pennsylvania Press, Philadelphia [1999]. XIV+ 379 (2000) 68 The Legal History Review 605; Take eg, in drafting the International Bill of Rights, only the following countries from North Africa participated meaningfully, Algeria, Egypt, Libya, Mauritania, Morocco, Somalia, Sudan and Tunisia. See Susan Waltz, 'Universal Human Rights: The Contribution of Muslim States' (2004) 26 HRQ 799 for the extent of the contribution of these African countries.

of issues that the CRC does not cover.[5] Those who drafted the ACRWC held the view that there were African specific challenges facing children in Africa for which the CRC failed to provide. These included apartheid, harmful cultural practices, children affected by armed conflicts, which was thought to be inadequately provided for in the CRC and the challenges facing the girl child, such as early marriage and internal displacement. Therefore, it was argued that there was a need for a regional children's rights framework in Africa to deal with these issues.[6]

However, the most credible justification is the nature and scope of the image or conception of childhood provided for in the CRC. However, the ACRWC does not provide an alternative image of childhood. Even though at the time of drafting the ACRWC, there were differences between the CRC and the ACRWC, these differences were those of standards and not theoretical differences with respect to the conception of childhood. That is why, conceptually, the ACRWC is substantively similar to the CRC. If the case against the CRC is poor participation by African states and lack of autochthony of its norms and standards in Africa, how participatory was and autochthonous is the ACRWC?

2.1 A Critique of the Process and Autochthony Arguments

There are not publicly available and accessible *travaux préparatoires* of the ACRWC. Any historical account of the drafting process of the ACRWC is, therefore, a patchwork of surviving members of the drafting team and scholars. In 1979, African leaders within the framework of the OAU, 'aware of the deep concern of African states about the future of African children as inheritors and keepers of African cultural heritage',[7] adopted the Declaration on the Rights and Welfare of the Child (the Declaration). This marked the first time that African countries at the highest level deliberated, agreed and declared that children in Africa are entitled to human rights, and their welfare is a subject of public policy at all levels. The OAU Declaration advances a number of philosophical and conceptual arguments.

Firstly, as its title suggests, the Declaration advances the arguments that the rights and welfare or well-being of children are not the same. Rights may result in the well-being of children, but they are not the only means of ensuring welfare. Rights are just one of the vehicles needed to secure a child's physical, economic, mental, spiritual, moral or social well-being. Secondly, the drafters of the

[5] Some of the issues included, eg, the girl child, responsibilities and duties of the child, role of extended families, children and armed conflicts, internal displacement, children under apartheid, children of imprisoned mothers.

[6] See generally ANPPCAN, 'The Rights of the Child Selected Proceedings of a Workshop on the Draft Convention on the Rights of the Child: An African Perspective' (1988).

[7] Preamble to the Declaration on the Rights and Welfare of the Child (1979) para no 6 available at: http://www.issafrica.org/AF/RegOrg/unity_to_union/pdfs/oau/hog/pHoGAssembly1979.pdf

Declaration promoted a hybrid approach to contemplating an African framework for children's rights and welfare. The idea postulated through the Declaration seems to be that an African instrument on children must benefit from the best of two worlds—that is, it must incorporate international agreed values, norms and concepts, and at the same time also benefit from the African cultural heritage. Thirdly, the drafters seem to have taken a minimalistic view of culture, as 'African arts, language and culture',[8] and adopted a 'harmful' approach to dealing with culture. Thus, for example, the Declaration states as follows,[9]

> Member States should thoroughly examine cultural legacies and practice that are harmful to normal growth and development of the child such as child marriage and female circumcision and should take legal and educational measures to abolish them.

Finally, the drafters envisaged the centrality of the family in the welfare of the child because the 'welfare of the African Child is inextricably bound up with that of its parents and other members of its family'.[10] This is the first time in the preamble that one of the concepts in the title is singled out, probably for emphasis. Either the drafters envisaged that the welfare component of the Declaration was more a function of the family environment of the child, or they did not conceive that rights could apply within the family environment. This emphasis on the vertical application of the rights of the child, that is, that child's rights are held with respect to the state, is one of the legacies that the ACRWC inherited.

The OAU considered the Declaration the first step in a process towards a regional binding instrument on children's rights and welfare in Africa. Therefore, at the Monrovia Summit of 1979, it directed the Secretary-General of the OAU to explore possibilities of bringing to fruition such a binding national and regional instrument. In the mid-1980s, the African Network for the Prevention and Protection of Children against Abuse and Neglect (ANPPCAN)[11] and United Nations Children's Emergency Fund (UNICEF) convened a meeting in Nairobi to discuss a draft Convention on the Rights of the Child and sought African inputs into that draft. In the course of the deliberations, participants agreed that although the draft CRC was comprehensive, it did not cover context-specific issues peculiar

[8] There are two ways to look at this—one is to consider adding the word culture to the list in para 10 of the Declaration as an intention to adopt a broader view of culture. The difficulty of this is the fact that language and arts are aspects of culture. To have mentioned this specifically would mean the exclusion of aspects not directly listed.

[9] Para 3 of the Declaration. The expression 'such as would imply the possibility of more additions to the list of specific cultural legacies and practices'.

[10] Preamble to the Declaration para 7.

[11] The African Network for the Prevention and Protection Against Child Abuse and Neglect (ANPPCAN) is a Pan African Network that Promotes Child Rights and Child Protection in Africa (http://www.anppcan.org/).

to Africa.[12] The ANPPCAN and the OAU co-hosted a working group of experts to brainstorm and develop an African Charter on the Rights and Welfare of the Child.[13] After a number of meetings of the Working Group, a draft ACRWC was completed and presented to the OAU for adoption. The OAU deliberated on the draft ACRWC and in 1990 adopted it, just over a year after the CRC had entered into force.

However, it is important to emphasize that the drafting process of the ACRWC was non-state-actor-centred. According to available records, seven representatives of government departments participated, while 57 representatives of national and international Non-governmental Organizations (NGOs), nine representatives of African governments and only one participant from the OAU took part in the discussion and drafting process of the ACRWC.[14] Thus, unlike the CRC, even though NGOs played a significant role, the process was primarily government proposed and led, while the ACRWC was civil society led. There is no record of participation by communities in Africa or other important stakeholders, except for the OAU, whose main role was to adopt the draft document presented. Thus, the processes that lead to the adoption of the ACRWC could best be described by adopting the words of Ibhawoh as follows,[15]

> The ACRWC have merely been decreed from above through the OAU, while cultural orientations and attitudes have been expected to confirm by legislative fiat with this new image and understanding of childhood. Culture evolves, however, rather than transforms and the process of evolution is painstakingly gradual and complex.

The result of the participation deficit by key stakeholders in the ACRWC drafting process begs the question as to whether the drafting of the ACRWC was perhaps, a mere transplantation of legal norms and standards.

[12] See generally ANPPCAN, 'The Rights of the Child Selected Proceedings of a Workshop on the Draft Convention on the Rights of the Child: An African Perspective' (1988).

[13] See generally ANPPCAN, 'The Rights of the Child Selected Proceedings of a Workshop on the Draft Convention on the Rights of the Child: An African Perspective' (1988).

[14] See generally ANPPCAN 'The Rights of the Child Selected Proceedings of a Workshop on the Draft Convention on the Rights of the Child: An African Perspective' (1988).

[15] This is the original expression 'In many African nations, human rights have merely been decreed from above through constitutional and other legal provisions, while cultural orientations and attitudes have been expected to conform by legislative fiat with these new human rights standards. Culture evolves however, rather than transforms and the process of evolution is painstakingly gradual and complex' in Bonny Ibhawoh, 'Between Culture and Constitution: Evaluating the Cultural Legitimacy of Human Rights in the African State' (2000) 22 HRQ 838. The 'above' here would refer to the AU that seems to assume cultural legitimacy on behalf of the communities in Africa.

2.2 The African Charter on the Rights and Welfare of the Child as a Transplant of Foreign Norms and Values into Africa

Often, in efforts to establish new legal standards or reform existing ones to meet new challenges at the domestic level, policymakers 'face a choice between two basic means of supplying new laws: indigenous law-making and transplantation of legal rules from other jurisdictions'.[16] Whatever choice policymakers make will have implications for the implementation of the law. Research indicates that how a country and, in this case, a continent receives its 'laws is a much more important determinant of the current effectiveness of its legal institutions than the particular legal family that it adopted'.[17] Legal transferability comes in degrees. The legal norms more 'resistant to transplantation' are those that 'organise constitutional, legislative, administrative or judicial institutions and procedures' and are meant to 'allocate power, rulemaking, decision making, above all policy making powers.'[18] In situations where 'legal borrowings are incompatible with host country's [culture], they are likely to be rejected ... as alien or imposed'.[19] International lawmakers face similar challenges as those faced by policymakers at the domestic level. Therefore, the concept of indigenous law making and transplantation of norms through law making applies with respect to treaty making.

Going the route of indigenous law making might avoid challenges around 'illegitimacy, incompleteness, ineffectiveness and exclusion'[20] of the outcome of the law-making process. Indigenous efforts at law making might also result in the 'accumulation of knowledge' due to 'an incremental and practical process of trial and error' and engagement of a wider constituency in the debate and law-making process. Consequently, such a process and resultant law are more likely to reflect and respond to the state or continent's 'own history, process, and context, constantly evolving and adapting in response to its own challenges internal or external', nourished by 'its own culture, institutions, and nationalist mythology'.[21] It would seem that the drafters of the ACRWC opted out of an indigenous law-making process while opting in favour of transplantation of international norms and standards into Africa.

[16] Peter Grajzl and Valentina Dimitrova-Grajzl, *The Choice in the Lawmaking Process: Legal Transplants vs Indigenous Law* (2009).

[17] Merris Amos, 'Transplanting Human Rights Norms: the Case of the United Kingdom's Human Rights Act' (2013) 35 HRQ 386.

[18] ibid.

[19] John Gillespie, 'Transplanted Company Law: An Ideological and Cultural Analysis of Market-Entey in Vietnam' (2002) 51 Int'l & Comp Law Q 641.

[20] Makau Mutua, 'Standard Setting in Human Rights: Critique and Prognosis' (2007) 29 HRQ.

[21] Abdullahi Ahmed An-Na'im, *African Constitutionalism and the Role of Islam* (University of Pennsylvania Press 2010) 171.

3. How ‘African’ is the African Charter on the Rights and Welfare of the Child?

One of the arguments for the regionalization of international human rights and international human rights laws is that the impact of human rights law depends, as do all laws, on changing local consciousness of rights and relationships.[22] In order for human rights ideas to be effective, they need to be translated into local terms and resonate, favourably, within local contexts of power and meaning. In the fields of human rights, regionalism and regionalization were supposed to narrow the gap between people and the international human rights norms and mechanisms. It is believed that with a shared history, geography and, in some cases, language and religion, as well as a commonality of values, regions will best meet the human rights yearning of their people and the aspirations of the international human rights system.[23]

This desire to bring the benefits of international human rights closer to Africans, as well as temper these benefits with the context-specific realities of the continent, resulted in the adoption of the regional human rights system. Other reasons that motivated the OAU and its legal successor, the AU, to put in place human rights instruments and mechanisms (that should reflect and respond to the specific needs of the continent) included the absence of participation by Africans in determining the concepts and content of the international human rights norms and standards, as well as specific political, economic and cultural needs of Africa.

This human rights system was conceived to perform a two-fold function—first, it should provide the first port of call when something fundamental goes wrong at the country level, and the country has failed to address it adequately and second, it ought to provide a common minimum human rights standard specific for the region.[24] As already mentioned, the regional specificity and context-specific nature of human rights systems are among the virtues of the regional human rights systems.

Context and cultural specificities of regional human rights norms and institutions are critical in the areas of children’s rights and welfare.[25] Even though African cultures tend to share core common values and understanding of childhood, there are significant differences within and among countries in Africa. Two of the drafters of the ACRWC have publicly stated that cultural specificities and the benefits of regionalization drove the desire to adopt a regional instrument on children’s

[22] HJ Steiner, P Alston and R Goodman, *International Human Rights in Context: Law, Politics, Morals: Text and Materials* (OUP 2008) 369.

[23] Christina M Cerna, *Universality of Human Rights and Cultural Diversity: Implementation of Human Rights in Different Socio-Cultural contexts* (1994).

[24] ibid.

[25] Bart Rwezaura, ‘Competing “Images” of Childhood in the Social and Legal Systems of Contemporary Sub-Saharan Africa’ (1998) 12 International Journal of Law, Policy and the Family 253.

rights. Muthoga, one of the drafters of the ACRWC, noted that the motivation to draft the ACRWC 'originated from a desire to address certain peculiarly African problems'.[26] Wako, credited with the preparation of the first draft of the ACRWC, on his part, predicated the African move to adopt the ACRWC on the fact that 'each region, with its unique culture, traditions and history, is best placed to handle and resolve its human rights situation'.[27]

Many scholars and commentators have taken at face value without critically subjecting the ACRWC to a context-specific analysis to ascertain their validity.[28] Most analysis and critique of the ACRWC have been done in comparison to the CRC or the international human rights system. This section will attempt a critique of the ACRWC with reference to the image of childhood in traditional African communities along four main themes, who is a child, the autonomy rights of the child, the best interests of the child and child participation.

3.1 Who is a Child?

Article 2 of the ACRWC provides that 'for the purposes of this Charter, a child means every human being below the age of 18 years'. This 'straight 18' position of the ACRWC is a deviation from the flexible position taken in article 1 of the CRC.[29] By placing the age of majority for all purposes at 18 years, the ACRWC sets a very high and uniform standard of protection for all children in Africa under all circumstances, thereby avoiding one of the criticisms against the CRC. The question that the drafters of the ACRWC did not answer is whether 'below the age of 18' included the unborn child.

The position of those African countries that participated in the drafting process of the CRC, such as Algeria, Morocco and Senegal, was that the CRC should protect life 'from the moment of conception',[30] because 'it was only logical to guarantee the right to life from the moment life began'.[31] This position is in consonance with the views of communities in traditional African societies as well as Islamic customary law and practices and Christian values in Africa.

[26] L Muthoga, *Analysis of the International Instruments for the Protection of the Rights of the Child* (1992) 123.

[27] AS Wako, 'Towards an African Charter on the Rights of the Child'Paper Delivered at a Workshop on the Draft Convention on the Rights of the Child' (1988) Nairobi (9–11 May 1988).

[28] Thoko Kaime, 'The Foundations of Rights in the African Charter on the Rights and Welfare of the Child: A Historical and Philosophical Account' (2009) 3 120.

[29] Art 1 of the Convention on the Rights of the Child provides that a child is any human being below the age of 18 unless the majority is attained earlier under national laws applicable to the child. This provision allows for some margin of flexibility for national authorities to determine the upper limit of childhood.

[30] George Kent and Lawrence Leblanc, 'The Convention on the Rights of the Child: United Nations Lawmaking on Human Rights' (1995) 89 APSR 1076.

[31] ibid.

Therefore, it is possible to anticipate that whenever the ACERWC is seized with an opportunity to expound on the ambit of article 2 of the ACRWC, it might interpret it to include the unborn child. However, it is difficult to understand why such a concept (wherein the African position seems fairly and arguably clear, that life starts upon conception),[32] an African children's instrument should fail to engage with this question directly. This is, even so when African representatives at the drafting process of the CRC tried without fail to include this African specific conception into the CRC. If the purpose of drafting the ACRWC was to provide for the elucidation of African specific values around childhood, at least the beginning of life should have been given due consideration.

3.1.1 Childhood End Point

In addition to the starting point of childhood, another area where article 2 of the ACRWC fails to take cognizance of African cultural values and heritage is in its strict numerical prescription with respect to the endpoint of childhood. The idea that a child turns, by some magic spell, into an adult on attaining 18 is strange to the way African traditional cultural heritage and philosophy of life treat the transition from childhood to adulthood. In African philosophy, how a child transits from childhood to adulthood is a function of demonstrated physical, mental and emotional maturity.[33]

The straight 18 position of the ACRWC has also become a source of legal tension between the ACRWC and the African Youth Charter. For example, the rights and freedoms provided for in the African Youth Charter accrue to 'minors' and 'youth' or young people. The African Youth Charter defines 'minors' 'as young people aged 15 to 17 years, subject to each country's laws' and the 'youth' as 'every person between the ages of 15 and 35 years'.[34] The spirit of flexibility with respect to the conception of young people in Africa, though commendable, is achieved at the cost of housing children together with young people, two different categories with divergent needs. In international law, specific treaties should take precedence over general treaties, and the provisions of treaties that offer more protection should normally prevail over those with less protection.[35] In this case, the two instruments are specific, and the question which ones offer more protection is more of a context-specific question.

[32] Roderick Fulata Zimba, 'Indigenous Conceptions of Childhood Development and Social Realities in Southern Africa' (2002) Between Cultures and Biology: Perspectives on Ontogenetic Development 89.

[33] Rwezaura, 'Competing "Images" of Childhood in the Social and Legal Systems of Contemporary Sub-Saharan Africa'.

[34] See the definition section of the African Youth Charter.

[35] See eg art 41 of the Convention on the Rights of the Child.

The upper age limit serves to clarify the nature of the relationship between the state and the child in question. Therefore, it is an essential tool to ensure protection for vulnerable children. However, vulnerability and immaturity differ from one context to another and among children from one point in time to another. Therefore, using a uniform shield of protection such as age to offer all children protection might not be useful in all cases. For instance, strict age delineation could disempower, rather than protect, certain categories of children, such as the breadwinners of the child-headed households. In such situations, the age requirement could be more effective when flexible and sensitive to context. Allowing these children to engage in income-generating activities could, for example, serve a bigger goal than using age to limit them.

The question that arises is thus if article 2 of the ACRWC does not reflect the African context of childhood, where did it come from? The nearest definition of the child in the ACRWC was the proposal by Finland in the Working Group while discussing draft article 1 of the CRC. This proposal is to the effect that, 'For the purpose of the present Convention, a child means every human being *who has not attained* the age of 18 years.' Maybe the drafters of the ACRWC simply deleted the highlighted phrase and replaced it with *below*, the result being 'for the purposes of this Charter, a child means every human being below the age of 18 years.' In the alternative, if we take the definition in article 1 of the CRC, which states, 'for the purposes of the present Convention, a child means every human being below the age of eighteen years *unless under the law applicable to the child, majority is attained earlier*;' then delete the exception as highlighted, then we will get the definition of the child stated in article 2 of the ACRWC.

The image of childhood articulated in the ACRWC is closer to that proposed by Finland than to the understanding of childhood in traditional African values. In fact, the only mitigating factor introduced into that Western image of childhood, to reflect the diversities of understanding of childhood in the world was precisely what the drafters of the ACRWC simply deleted. So, the child in article 2 of the ACRWC is even more of a Western child than the child anticipated in article 1 of the CRC.

3.2 Autonomy Rights of the Child

The ACRWC confers children with the rights and freedom to think, talk, choose, meet and share, in public and private, whatever they are capable of conceptualizing and communicating. These rights and freedoms are limited only by the ability and willingness of the child, the law, and, in some instances, the reasonable supervision of parents. The following rights epitomize the nature and spirit of the autonomy rights provided for children in Africa under the ACRWC: freedom of expression, freedom of association, freedom of thought, conscience and religion and the protection of privacy.

These four articles of the ACRWC are probably the most radical, potentially empowering and transformative provisions. However, the efficacy of these provisions will depend, at least, on whether they reflect and respond to the way African families, communities and states understand childhood. To simply transplant such rights and freedoms from other contexts without adapting them to local realities is problematic. The way a society sees and treats children is a subset of the way that society sees and treats itself. So, a brief sketch of the broader debate on whether human rights as codified in different instruments are alien to Africa or not is appropriate here.

There is no consensus among scholars writing on Africa as to whether human rights, as codified in international human rights instruments, are indigenous to Africa. Where there seems to be some agreement among scholars across the divide is that human rights, as codified in the international human rights instruments, have their roots in particular thinking, history and circumstances of the West. But within this broad consensus, there are variations of positions. Some believe that even though what is codified in the human rights instruments may have originated from the West, it does not mean that there are no corresponding values that could serve the purpose that human rights serve in the West, in non-western cultures, including Africa. Others hold that 'there is no specifically African concept of human rights'.[36]

In the opinion of some scholars, human rights, regardless of their historical and philosophical origins, should apply universally.[37] This is because the conditions, institutions and structures that gave rise to human rights in Western society are prevalent in different parts of the world, so also will human rights norms apply to these parts of the world, including Africa.[38] Others insist that the presence of externally imposed circumstances, institutions and structures should not be used to justify the application of external values and norms such as human rights to non-western societies.[39]

The debate about the 'Africanness' of human rights has implications for the rights of children in Africa. The rights of children operate within the broader human rights framework. If the nature, scope and identity of the broader human rights framework in Africa are still a subject of scholarly debate, it is reasonable to expect

[36] Rhoda E Howard, 'Cultural Absolutism and the Nostalgia for Community' (1993) 15 Hum Rts Q 315; Rhoda E Howard and Rhoda E Howard-Hassmann, *Human Rights in Commonwealth Africa* (Rowman & Littlefield 1986) 23.

[37] Jack Donnelly, 'Human Rights and Human Dignity: An Analytic Critique of Non-Western Conceptions of Human Rights' (1982) 76 APSR 303; Jack Donnelly, 'The Relative Universality of Human Rights' (2007) 29 HRQ 281; Michael Goodhart, 'Origins and Universality in the Human Rights Debates: Cultural Essentialism and the Challenge of Globalization' (2003) 25 HRQ 935.

[38] Donnelly, 'The Relative Universality of Human Rights'.

[39] G Van Bueren, *The International Law on the Rights of the Child* (Springer Netherlands 1998).

that the nature and scope of children's rights, as a subset of this bigger framework, is also subject to similar debate. Examining the content of the autonomy rights of children, as outlined in the ACRWC, and juxtaposing this with the traditional understanding of childhood, as outlined above, is necessary in order to reveal any possible tension between the human rights conception of childhood and the traditional understanding of childhood in Africa.

The freedoms of expression, association and religion are interrelated. The Committee on the Rights of the Child has treated them as such.[40] In the absence of any practice by the ACERWC to the contrary, the provisions for these rights under the ACRWC are analysed with this understanding in mind. The ACRWC assures every child capable of communicating their views the right to express and disseminate those views freely, subject only to any lawful restrictions. Further, every child is granted the right to free association and peaceful assembly in conformity with the law. The freedom of thought, conscience and religion concretize and reinforce the legal autonomy and individualized agency of the child in the African context.

In the absence of a *travaux préparatoires*[41] and an interpretation of these provisions by the ACERWC, this section uses interpretations of similar provisions at the international level, the practice of the Committee on the Rights of the Child, and academic opinion to analyse these articles and speculate on their possible application and implications in Africa. Thus, the first level of analysis will be upward—using the international framework to interpret these provisions, and the second level will be downward—investigating their application and implications in the traditional African context.

At the international level, freedom of expression, association and assembly was not considered appropriate for children until the CRC, and by implication, the ACRWC incorporated article 19 of the ICCPR and rendered it applicable to children.[42] There were a number of reasons why it was thought that granting these rights to children was not in their best interests. Firstly, it was believed that 'to confer the full range of choice rights on a child is also to confer the burdens and responsibilities of adult legal status, which necessarily removes the protection rights of childhood'.[43] Secondly, granting autonomy and choice rights to children without any clawback clauses and with no lower age limit was thought to be problematic because 'young children . . . seem to have virtually no direct expressive, deliberative or informational interests that are served by freedom of expression'.[44] It would be

[40] Colin M Macleod, 'A Liberal Theory of Freedom of Expression for Children' (2004) 79 Chi-Kent L Rev 55.

[41] With the exception of the selected proceeding report of the Workshops organized during discussions leading to the drafting of the African Charter on the Rights and Welfare of the Child, there is no proceeding report of the actual drafting process publicly available.

[42] Van Bueren, *The International Law on the Rights of the Child.*

[43] Bruce Hafen and Jonathan O Hafen, 'Abandoning Children to Their Autonomy: The United Nations Convention on the Rights of the Child'(1996) 37 HILJ 449.

[44] Macleod, 'A Liberal Theory of Freedom of Expression for Children'.

understandable if autonomy rights granted to children allow the nature and scope of autonomy and choice rights to increase with age. Thirdly, children's autonomy is not a uniform experience that takes place at the same time for all children across time and space. It is rather a 'child-specific element and not merely an aspect of children's general "personhood" because it is gradual, depending upon children's maturity and their evolving capacities'.[45] For these reasons, some scholars before the adoption of the CRC held the view that article 19 of the ICCPR should not be extended to children.

Article 19 of the ICCPR epitomizes the classic freedom of expression as an autonomy right. According to the Human Rights Committee, the freedom of expression includes not only freedom to 'impart information and ideas of all kinds', but also the freedom to 'seek' and 'receive' them 'regardless of frontiers', and in whatever medium, 'either orally, in writing or in print, in the form of art, or through any other media of his choice'.[46]

This should naturally include 'every communicable type of subjective idea and opinion, of value-neutral news and information, of commercial advertising, art works, political commentary regardless of how critical, pornography'.[47] Granting children such enormous verbal and non-verbal expression rights were considered detrimental to children's well-being because it will likely make any effort intended 'to close out undesirable contents, such as pornography or blasphemy'[48] extremely difficult. The drafters of the CRC and the ACRWC thought differently. The fact that this provision was lifted *verbatim* from the ICCPR is probably indicative of the CRC's and ACRWC's vision of children—as autonomous individuals whose rights and freedoms are equal with those of adults.

There are a number of reasons why children are conferred with autonomy rights under the CRC and, by implication, the ACRWC. In the case of children, some scholars hold the view that the freedom of expression cultivates 'deliberative capacities and can stimulate critical reflection on a range of options' and, thus, develops more 'reflective and mature individuals and so benefiting society as a whole'.[49] It protects children's development, fulfilment, participation in society and imparting of information. There seems to be an inverse relationship between the child's right to freedom of expression and parental guidance—the nature and scope of the rights expand as the child matures, while parental ability and freedom to

[45] Eva Brems, 'Children's rights and universality', *Understanding Children's Rights: Collected Papers Presented at the Sixth International Interdisciplinary Course on Children's Rights, Held at the University of Ghent, December 2003*, vol 7 (Ghent University. Children's Rights Centre 2004).

[46] Human Rights Committee, General Comment 10, art 19 (19th session, 1983), Compilation of General Comments and General Recommendations Adopted by Human Rights Treaty Bodies, UN Doc HRI/GEN/1/Rev.1 at 11 (1994).

[47] Manfred Nowak, *UN Covenant on Civil and Political Rights: CCPR Commentary* (NP Engel 1993) 358.

[48] ibid, 341.

[49] Tom Campbell, 'Rationales for Freedom of Communication' (1994); Teoksessa Tom Cambell and Wojciech Sadurski (toim): Freedom of Communication Dartmouth, Aldershot 17

provide appropriate direction and guidance diminish.[50] Thus, 'as children develop cognitive, emotional, and moral capacities, the range of material from which they need to be protected diminishes. Similarly, as children mature, the scope and content of their rights to expression increase'.[51]

That is why freedom of expression is considered a developmental right as well as an autonomy right.[52] The obligation to ensure that children enjoy these developmental rights rests with states. According to the CRC Committee, states parties must 'refrain from interference in the expression of those views, or in access to information, while protecting the right of access to means of communication and public dialogue'.[53]

It would seem that the CRC Committee considers the right to freedom of expression as mainly creating a vertical obligation between the child and the state.[54] The CRC Committee seems to take a very formalistic view of this right and the process of realizing it. According to the CRC Committee, freedom of expression imposes positive and negative obligations. Positively, the state must create structures, mechanisms and proceedings through which children can express their views freely in all matters affecting them and ensure that children's views are given due weight in accordance with their age and maturity.[55] Some scholars have expressed concern with imposing positive obligations on states. The reason for the criticism is that it is 'unrealistic [because of] the financial costs of ensuring that everyone',[56] can exercise these rights. UNICEF holds the view that the scope of the right to freedom of expression is wide enough to include the family environment.[57]

There are few concerns with this casting of the right to freedom of expression in the CRC and the ACRWC. First, on a general note, the concept and content of the right to freedom of expression demonstrate the tension among autonomy, developmental, protection and relational rights. It represents a clash of visions, philosophies and ideologies struggling to colonize and control the childhood space. On the one hand, children need protection from the negative effects of the rights and privileges of the adult world. On the other hand, children need all the rights to live, survive and develop. To strike a balance is always not easy for policymakers because each child is unique and lives in a unique set of circumstances.

Second, the evidence of this tension is demonstrated when the drafters of the CRC and the ACRWC diverted from their trademark of age restrictions to a

50 Macleod, 'A Liberal Theory of Freedom of Expression for Children'.
51 ibid.
52 John Eekelaar, 'The Emergence of Children's Rights' (1986) 6 Oxford J Legal Stud 161.
53 See Committee on the Rights of the Child General Comment No 12: The right of the child to be heard, 1 July 2009, CRC/C/GC/ para 81.
54 Sylvie Langlaude, 'On How to Build a Positive Understanding of the Child's Right to Freedom of Expression' (2010) 10 Hum Rights Law Rev 33.
55 ibid.
56 Eric Barendt, *Freedom of speech* (OUP Oxford 2005) 104.
57 Rachel Hodgkin, Peter Newell and UNICEF, 'Implementation Handbook for the Convention on the Rights of the Child' (1998) 140.

customized and individualized approach to determining maturity or evolving capacities when discussing these rights and freedoms.[58] On the one hand, this should be commendable in the sense that, for once, the drafters of the CRC and the ACRWC acknowledged that it is virtually impossible to capture the diversities within the structural space called childhood through the age-based classification system. However, on the other hand, this concession complicates the situation for children and policymakers. The reliance on capabilities and maturity as the minimum threshold for the exercise of these rights are problematic. The concept of maturity, as used in the CRC, is already 'hopelessly complex and subjective'.[59] This will make going about 'customized findings of maturity',[60] as anticipated within the parameters of the right to freedom of expression, inherently difficult. Firstly, because of the nature of maturity itself, but secondly, because of the non-existing 'reasoned generality - and, hence, the lack of neutrality-in subjective decisions' which might affect the quality of decisions about maturity.[61]

Freedom of association flows naturally and complements the right to freedom of expression. Association is a means as it is an end right. It enables the child to express views, contribute to the debate and form alliances for the purpose of realizing other rights. There is a close link between the component of freedom of association and participation. When discussing participation below, issues around freedom of association will be touched upon again.

The right to freedom of thought, conscience and religion is 'far-reaching and profound'.[62] It confers on an individual 'freedom of thought on all matters'.[63] It is non-derogable 'even in time of public emergence'.[64] The right holder is at liberty to manifest their freedoms 'individually or in community with others and in public or private'.[65] The freedom to manifest is limited only by law enacted to protect public safety, order, health or morals (such morality should not derive exclusively from a

[58] See art 5 of the Convention on the Rights of the Child and art 9(2) of the African Charter on the Rights and Welfare of the Child.

[59] Hafen and Hafen, 'Abandoning Children to Their Autonomy: The United Nations Convention on the Rights of the Child'(1996).

[60] ibid.

[61] ibid.

[62] Human Rights Committee, General Comment 22, art 18 (48th session, 1993). Compilation of General Comments and General Recommendations Adopted by Human Rights Treaty Bodies, UN Doc HRI/GEN/1/Rev 1 at 35 (1994).

[63] Human Rights Committee, General Comment 22, art 18 (48th session, 1993). Compilation of General Comments and General Recommendations Adopted by Human Rights Treaty Bodies, UN Doc HRI/GEN/1/Rev 1 at 35 (1994).

[64] Human Rights Committee, General Comment 22, art 18 (48th session, 1993). Compilation of General Comments and General Recommendations Adopted by Human Rights Treaty Bodies, UN Doc HRI/GEN/1/Rev 1 at 35 (1994).

[65] Human Rights Committee, General Comment 22, art 18 (48th session, 1993). Compilation of General Comments and General Recommendations Adopted by Human Rights Treaty Bodies, UN Doc HRI/GEN/1/Rev 1 at 35 (1994).

single tradition),[66] or the fundamental rights of others. These rights and freedoms enable an individual to hold, develop, refine and, ultimately, change their thoughts, conscience and religion without any form of interference or anyone compelling them 'to reveal his thoughts or adherence to a religion or belief'.[67] The rights and freedoms place on the state a positive and negative obligation to refrain from interfering with the protected rights and take active steps to put in place a favourable environment for the exercise of these rights and freedoms.

The codification of these rights and freedoms in the CRC and ACRWC was done within the spirit of similar provisions in the ICCPR.[68] The implication is that the rights and freedoms apply to children as they would apply to adults. However, the CRC introduces an additional limitation with respect to children not provided for under the ICCPR. This limitation provides for 'direction to the child in the exercise of his or her right in a manner consistent with the evolving capacities of the child'.[69]

The CRC Committee has not adequately clarified the nature, scope and content of 'the rights and duties of parents' and under what circumstances they are 'applicable' to 'provide direction' in the manifestation of these rights and freedoms. It would seem from the text that parental rights and duties are limited to reasonable supervision and guidance with diminishing scope, as the capacities of the child to take reasonable decisions increases.

Therefore, from the analysis so far, it could be argued that the understanding of autonomy rights provided in the CRC and, by implication, the ACRWC is compatible with the neoliberal and individualistic conception of personhood and society. The direct applicability of this view of children's autonomy rights in societies is yet to develop a mature neoliberal and individual-based societal structure and bound to be an uphill task. Traditional communities in Africa are more or less communitarian in their conception of society and worldview and the role of individuals in society.[70] The image of the child whose interests, rights and freedoms must trump societal interest is not common to all societies.

The reason why the ACRWC has been implied from the provisions of the CRC throughout this section is that even though textually the provisions within the ACRWC (with respect to freedom of expression, freedom of association, freedom

[66] Human Rights Committee, General Comment 22, art 18 (48th session, 1993). Compilation of General Comments and General Recommendations Adopted by Human Rights Treaty Bodies, UN Doc HRI/GEN/1/Rev 1 at 35 (1994).

[67] Human Rights Committee, General Comment 22, art 18 (48th session, 1993). Compilation of General Comments and General Recommendations Adopted by Human Rights Treaty Bodies, UN Doc HRI/GEN/1/Rev 1 at 35 (1994).

[68] Kent and Leblanc, 'The Convention on the Rights of the Child: United Nations Lawmaking on Human Rights' 45.

[69] Art 14(2) of the Convention on the Rights of the Child.

[70] John S Mbiti, *African Religions & Philosophy* (Heinemann 1990); Zimba, 'Indigenous Conceptions of Childhood Development and Social Realities in Southern Africa'; Augustine Shutte, 'Philosophy for Africa' (1995); Ifeanyi A Menkiti, 'Person and Community in African Traditional Thought' (1984) 3 African Philosophy: An Introduction 171.

of thought, conscience and religion) are not the same as corresponding provisions in the CRC, substantively these provisions mirror the image and understanding of childhood and liberty rights as anticipated in the CRC. Article 7 confers freedom of expression on a child 'who is capable of communicating his or her own views' and subjects the exercise of this right and freedom to 'such restrictions as are prescribed by laws'. This is not to say that there are no minor differences; for instance, the use of 'capable of communicating' is different from the similar provision in the CRC. This ACRWC version of the corresponding provision in the CRC has been criticized as excluding children who may not be able to communicate their opinion.[71] It is reasonable to presume that capability could be defined here broadly as including both verbal and nonverbal abilities. In addition, capability, as used here, could be seen not only as an objective test but also as a minimum threshold, thus ruling out infants and younger children who may not be able to benefit meaningfully from the expectations of this right and freedom.

In addition, the deference to national law could be interpreted as some level of flexibility, allowing for a margin of appreciation for state parties. However, not qualifying this law with either 'reasonable or acceptable in a democratic society' might mean that this margin is wide enough to include just about any 'law'. The provisions of the ACRWC cannot be interpreted in isolation, though other provisions relating to the best interests of the child might come into play. But the reference to law only might give the impression that childhood in Africa is the sole responsibility of the law. Except for children who stay in the urban centres, most children in Africa live their lives outside the reach of formal law.[72]

Furthermore, the rendition of the freedom of expression in the ACRWC is not clear on the scope of this right and freedom. In other words, who should assure that the child who is capable of communicating his view actually does so? Is it the state only or also the family? It would seem that, like the CRC, the ACRWC was conceived primarily to create a vertical obligation between the child and the state. The ACERWC's Guidelines on Initial State Party Report as well as the draft Guidelines on Periodic State Party Report give credence to the presumption that the ACRWC anticipates the application of rights and freedoms in a formalistic way.[73] In addition, while discussing the right to freedom of expression, the ACERWC, in its concluding observation on Uganda's report, commended the constitutional rights in Uganda that 'allow children to express their points of view, *outside the family boundaries*'.[74]

[71] Ramphal Mxolisi Sillah and Tawanda William Chibanda, 'Assessing the African Charter on the Rights and Welfare of the Child (ACRWC) as a Blueprint Towards the Attainment of Children's Rights in Africa' (2013).

[72] ibid.

[73] See http://acerwc.org/state-reports/ (accessed on 26 October 2013).

[74] The African Committee of Experts on the Rights and Welfare of the Child Concluding Observation to the Republic of Uganda available at: http://acerwc.org/state-reports/ (accessed on 26 October 2013).

Even though there is evidence to suggest that children in traditional communities in Africa expressed themselves in various ways, there is still not sufficient evidence to suggest that they did it as a matter of rights.[75] This provision is, therefore, more a reflection of development within the international human rights system overly driven by neoliberal and individualistic motivation than a reflection of the traditional value system around child upbringing and participation in traditional African communities.

Additionally, the provision of the right to freedom of thought, conscience and religion in the ACRWC is textually and substantively similar to the CRC provision, which in turn, is very similar to the provisions in the ICCPR. However, the ACRWC introduces the element of the best interests of the child as a possible limiting factor in consideration of the nature and scope of the enjoyment of this right and freedom by a child. This is the only place the drafters used, in text, the concept of 'best interests' of the child without the usual qualifications of 'a' paramount or 'the' paramount prefix.[76] It is not clear what the intention of the drafters was, but maybe it might mean that 'best interests' is not the only consideration but one of the considerations. This is similar to the implication of using 'a' to prefix 'best interest' concept in the CRC. It can be argued that by requesting that parents and legal guardians provide 'guidance and direction in the exercise of these rights having regard to the evolving capacities, and best interests of the child', the best interest principle here is just one of the considerations.

There are few concerns with the contextualization of the right to freedom of thought, conscience and religion for children in Africa through the ACRWC. The first concern is that in traditional African communities, religion is a way of life rather than a specific belief or a practice.[77] Thus, the question of choice may not even arise. The relevant question might be that of change of religion, and this would be relevant in communities where there are alternative religious beliefs. The second concern is that the text of the limitation is problematic. The ACRWC anticipates that only 'parents, and where applicable, legal guardians'[78] would play a role in the life of a child. In traditional communities across Africa, there are more actors in the life of a child than anticipated here. In fact, the CRC's provision is more accommodating to traditional family arrangements in Africa than the ACRWC. Article 5 of the CRC reads,[79]

[75] Constantine Ngara, 'African ways of Knowing and Pedagogy Revisited' (2007) 2 JCIE; IN Goduka, 'Indigenous Epistemologies-Ways of Knowing: Affirming a Legacy' (1999) 13 S Afr J High Educ 26; Mark A Runco, 'Creativity as an Extracognitive Phenomenon', *Beyond Knowledge* (Routledge 2004); Chuma Himonga, 'African Customary Law and Children's Rights: Intersections and Domains in a New Era' *Children's Rights in Africa a Legal Perspective* (Routledge 2016); Chuma Himonga, 'The Right of the Child to Participate in Decision Making. A Perspective from Zambia', *Law, Culture, Tradition and Children's Rights in Eastern and Southern Africa* (Dartmouth, 1998).

[76] Chirwa, 'The Merits and Demerits of the African Charter on the Rights and Welfare of the Child'.

[77] Mbiti, *African Religions & Philosophy*

[78] See eg art 9(3) of the African Charter on the Rights and Welfare of the Child.

[79] Art 5 of the Convention on the Rights of the Child.

> States Parties shall respect the responsibilities, rights and duties of *parents or, where applicable, the members of the extended family or community as provided for by local custom, legal guardians or other persons legally responsible for the child*, to provide, in a manner consistent with the evolving capacities of the child, appropriate direction and guidance in the exercise by the child of the rights recognized in the present Convention.

Those who step in to take care of children in many traditional African communities do not necessarily do so in accordance with the law. So, the emphasis on legal guardianship may not reflect adequately the context in which the ACRWC is meant to be implemented. The third concern is that it is difficult to understand the imposition of 'a duty to provide guidance and direction' without a corresponding right or mechanism for enforcing such a duty if, indeed, it is a legal duty. The appropriateness of the language of rights and duties for some of the responsibilities which parents and communities discharge affectionately in the traditional community is debatable. Parents provide guidance and direction to their children not necessarily because it is a duty imposed by law but because it is the right thing to do, and the community expects this from them. They do it because it is thought to be in the best interest of their children, an issue to which this study now turns.

3.3 The Best Interest of the Child

The ACRWC refers, at least four times, to the concept of the 'best interests'. First, as an overarching principle;[80] second, relating to the freedom of thought, conscience and religion;[81] third, with respect to parental responsibilities;[82] and, finally, relating to alternative family care.[83] However, this concept is not defined anywhere in the ACRWC. Nevertheless, there is significant literature on the best interests of the child. Reviewing this body of knowledge will not add any new dimension to this study. What will be attempted here is a textual analysis of article 4 of the ACRWC, which is the main provision in the ACRWC dealing with the best interests of the child as an overarching principle. References will be made to literature on the concept of the best interests of the child at the international level, when necessary.

Children and their interests are at the centre of African philosophy, culture, religion, families and communities. It would be difficult to argue that traditional communities in Africa did not put the interests of the child first. The difficulty, though, is with the use of the adjective 'best' qualifying that interest. What are best for a

[80] Art 4(1) of the African Charter on the Rights and Welfare of the Child.
[81] Art 9(2) of the African Charter on the Rights and Welfare of the Child.
[82] Art 20(a) of the African Charter on the Rights and Welfare of the Child.
[83] Art 25(3) of the African Charter on the Rights and Welfare of the Child.

child are child, family and community-specific first and foremost; it differs and varies across various groups of children, across families and contexts, as well as over time. In addition, this adjective is value-laden. Values are cultural products. All cultures are equal partners in the development of common humanity. It is possible to imagine that some of the interests considered best in one part of the world may not be so in other parts of the world. Therefore, putting children's well-being first is a common aspiration for all cultures; how this is to be done should, as much as possible, be left to each culture to determine. This is probably why the concept of the best interests of the child has not been defined or prescribed in the CRC as well as the ACRWC, even though the practice of the monitoring bodies might sometimes seem to indicate that there is probably a predetermined content to this concept. Article 4 of the ACRWC expects the best interest of the child to be protected 'in all actions' by 'any person or authority'. What is meant by the reference to 'all actions'? What about inactions? Are the actions contemplated here legal or non-legal actions? It is, therefore, useful to examine the nature and scope of these actions that must take the best interests of the child into consideration. The Black's Law Dictionary defines 'action' as,[84]

> [a]n ordinary proceeding in a court of justice, by which one party prosecutes another party for the enforcement or protection of a right, the redress or prevention of a wrong, or the punishment of a public offense.

In this sense, action is synonymous with a lawsuit. If this is what the drafters of the ACRWC intended, then it would mean that the ACRWC guarantees children's best interests only in and through a formal process. Examples of such formal processes could include custody and divorce proceedings, foster care and adoption, medical decisions, dispute settlement or other formal decisions. The emphasis seems to be on law, policies, legislative or administrative remedies or interventions. This state-centred, legally focused and formalistic approach to ascertaining and determining the best interests of the child seems to be the primary emphasis of the CRC Committee. According to the CRC Committee, the best interests' principle 'requires active measures throughout Government, parliament and the judiciary. Every legislative, administrative and judicial body or institution is required to apply the best interest principle by systematically'.[85]

However, taking such a restrictive approach to defining the expression—'all actions' cannot be in the best interests of all children, especially in Africa, where the majority of them will spend their childhood in the rural areas outside the

[84] Black's Law Dictionary 9th edn.

[85] General Comments CRC/GC/2003/5 03/10/2003 General Comment No 5 (2003): General Measures of Implementation of the Convention on the Rights of the Child para 12.

meaningful reach of the state.[86] It is, therefore, possible to understand 'all actions' in a wider and broader sense. The Oxford Dictionary of English defines 'action' as 'the fact or process of doing something, typically to achieve an aim'.[87] In this sense, the best interests of the child should encompass any process that involves children or targets them, for whatever aim, to ensure that the well-being of children is the first aim.

The CRC Committee has, in some instances, employed the concept of the best interests of the child in this sense. For example, the CRC Committee noted as follows, 'All decision-making concerning a child's care, health, education, etc. must take account of the "best interests" principle, *including decisions by parents*,[88] professionals and others responsible for children'.[89] Since the ACRWC refers to 'any person or authority', it is reasonable to presume a wider intention. This is because a 'person' in law is 'any being whom the law regards as capable of rights and duties'.[90] While 'authority', as used in this provision, might mean an entity that 'has the right or permission to act legally on another's behalf'.[91] Therefore, it is legally possible to imagine that the scope of this provision would include the actions of natural and artificial persons when their actions concern children. If this is the intention of the drafters of the ACRWC, it would seem that the nature and scope of the obligation to primarily take cognizance of children's best interests in all actions are wider under the ACRWC than the CRC. The CRC seems to anticipate only the actions 'undertaken by public or private social welfare institutions, courts of law, administrative authorities or legislative bodies'.[92]

Even though, theoretically, the phrasing of the best interest provisions under the ACRWC is plausible, translating such an aspiration into policy and enforcing such policy are fraught with challenges. Maybe the reference in article 4(2) to 'all judicial or administrative proceedings affecting a child' is a reality check on the overly aspirational nature of article 4(1) and, therefore, a necessary narrowing of the scope of the best interests of the child's obligation under article 4 of the ACRWC.

Whatever the interpretation, there are a number of concerns with the concept of the best interests of the child as provided for in the ACRWC. This legalistic approach to the concept of the best interests of the child in the African context is likely to be exclusionary. Many children in Africa live their childhood outside the

[86] UNICEF 'Children in an Urban World' The State of the World's Children 2012 where it is noted that although most children still live in the rural areas, those living in the urban areas mainly live in slums and are not in touch with state services available at http://www.unicef.org/sowc2012/pdfs/SOWC%202012-Main%20Report_EN_13Mar2012.pdf (accessed 26/10/2013).

[87] OUP 2013.

[88] Committee on the Rights of the Child, General Comment No 7, Children's Rights in Juvenile Justice 2005, CRC/C/GC/7/Rev1, para 13). Emphasis added.

[89] Committee on the Rights of the Child, General Comment No 7, Children's Rights in Juvenile Justice 2005, CRC/C/GC/7/Rev1, para 13).

[90] Black's Law Dictionary 9th edn.

[91] Black's Law Dictionary 9th edn.

[92] See art 3(1) of the Convention on the Rights of the Child for an example.

scope of formal law. In addition, the fact that it is so state centric in its approach is also limiting because a number of states in Africa are either weak or at different stages of formation and, thus, even though some might be willing to promote and protect children's best interest, they might simply not be able to. As a result, a significant number of children in Africa might complete their childhood experiences without meaningful contact with the state.

Furthermore, the ACRWC's reference to any 'person or authority' is too wide and, at best, aspirational and, therefore, this is in conflict with its legalistic tendencies. Finally, the ACRWC seems to explicitly anticipate a child's contribution to determining their best interests, mainly in judicial and administrative proceedings, since it provides that a 'child who is capable of communicating his or her own views,' within the context of judicial and administrative proceedings. Children's participation in determining their interests should be allowed for in all actions.

3.4 Children's Participation Rights

For children, participation rights are multifaceted and could 'include a wide range of activities that differ in form and style when children are at different ages'.[93] Langlaude is of the opinion that participation 'of the child in society enables the child to be heard, to be informed about public affairs and to play a role in the life of the country'.[94] The ACRWC mentioned directly the word 'participation' only twice. The first reference is to the participation rights of children with disabilities, and the second to the meaningful participation of NGOs.[95] The ACERWC has not sufficiently engaged with clarifying the conceptual implication of this right within the ACRWC. However, the reference in article 4(2) to 'provide for the views of the child' could be interpreted to give children the rights to participate in the determination of their interests. The reference to 'judicial or administrative proceedings' seems to give the impression that participation, in this context, is expected to happen outside private settings. Such a restrictive rendition arguably is sensitive to the traditional context in Africa.

In traditional African communities, children, as part of the family and community, participate in family and community processes.[96] However, there is insufficient evidence to suggest that such participation is a matter of right. What is evident among many traditional communities in Africa is that the right to participation is

[93] UNICEF, the Participation Rights of Adolescents: A Strategic Approach (2001) 11 a working paper quoted in S Langlaude 'On How to Build a Positive Understanding of the Child's Right to Freedom of Expression' (2010) 10 HRLR 33.

[94] Langlaude, 'On how to Build a Positive Understanding of the Child's Right to Freedom of Expression'.

[95] See arts 13(1) and 14(i) of the African Charter on the Rights and Welfare of the Child.

[96] Himonga, 'African Customary Law and Children's Rights: Intersections and Domains in a New Era'.

determined by the position of the person in the social hierarchy. For instance, the ability of a child to participate in decision making within the family is affected by the social status of the child and the hierarchical position of that child among their siblings. In the context of West Africa, it has been said that 'as long as one's parents are alive a child is always a child' and must come under 'some sphere of parental authority even vicariously'.[97] Such parental authority determines a child's level, method and approach to participation. This is because this authority demands respect in return. According to Pellow, 'respect for one's elders, when carried to extreme, rules out any chance of exercising one's free will'.[98]Thus, conceptualizing child participation, as a matter of rights, within the family setting is bound to be challenging in traditional communities in Africa.

However, article 12(2) of the CRC, which provides that the child 'be heard in any judicial and administrative proceedings', has been the subject of intensive debate. A child's right to participation is the 'most debated and examined aspects'[99] of the CRC. The manner in which article 12 of the CRC deals with what constitutes participation, when participation should be considered a right, how participation should take place, where and why the child should participate all constitute part of the reasons for this debate. According to article 12 of the CRC and article 4(2) of the ACRWC, the right to participate accrues to 'the child' who is 'capable of forming ... views' in the case of the CRC and 'capable of communicating ... views' in the case of the ACRWC.

These provisions could be interpreted to mean, first, that this right accrues to a child on an individual basis and not to a group of children.[100] If so, this could make the right to participation more of a private than a public experience for children. Second, these provisions could be interpreted in a broader manner to support public and collective forms of participation for children.[101]

The first interpretation seems to be faithful to the texts of the CRC, while the second interpretation is more teleological. The drafters of the CRC used different expressions to convey their intentions to individualize rights to children. These included 'a child',[102] 'each child',[103] 'every child'[104] and 'the child'.[105] The first three expressions are mainly used within the context of the CRC to confer rights, while the last expression is mainly used to denote the specific application of the

[97] A Bame Nsamenang, *Human Development in Cultural Context: A Third World Perspective*, 16 (Sage Publications 1992).

[98] Deborah Pellow, *Women in Accra: Options for Autonomy* (Reference Pubns 1977).

[99] Gerison Lansdown, 'The Realisation of Children's Participation Rights: Critical Reflections', *A Handbook of Children and Young People's Participation* (Routledge 2009).

[100] Barry Percy-Smith and Nigel Thomas, *A Handbook of Children and Young People's Participation: Perspectives from Theory and Practice* (Routledge 2009).

[101] Lansdown, 'The Realisation of Children's Participation Rights: Critical Reflections'.

[102] See art 1 of the Convention on the Rights of the Child.

[103] See art 2(1) of the Convention on the Rights of the Child.

[104] See art 6(1) of the Convention on the Rights of the Child.

[105] See art 12(1) of the Convention on the Rights of the Child.

conferred rights.[106] The use of 'the child' in article 12 conforms to this general trend. Therefore, it is reasonable to conclude that within the meaning of article 12, participation is more an individual right of a child than a collective right for children. The child's right to participation is further limited to the expression of 'views' on issues that affect the child only. It is debatable if this right is wide enough to include the involvement of children in different forms of collective social action and whether the views referred to here are on public or private issues.

The challenge with interpreting article 12 of the CRC and, by implication, article 4(2) of the ACRWC as conferring private participatory rights on children is that this provision places a public obligation on states to ensure the realization of this right. At the domestic level, governments are obliged to make this right a legal entitlement, make efforts to systematically provide the child with means that facilitate meaningful participation, raise local awareness and provide well-resourced mechanisms for children to influence public decisions at all levels.[107] The CRC Committee expects that such participation enabling mechanisms should facilitate consultative participation, collaborative participation and child-led participation in the public spheres.[108] Participation right envisages a situation wherein children should be empowered to determine the process as well as the outcome of decision making.

However, participation in the private and public spheres in different cultures provokes 'different concerns and approaches'.[109] Thus, interpreted as sensitivity to the feelings and views of children by families and communities, child participation is an almost less problematic concept in traditional communities in Africa. The teleological interpretation of article 12 and article 4(2) of the ACRWC to include collective rights to participation as a matter of rights is equally not problematic when considered in the context of the vertical relationship between citizens and their governments. On the other hand, it could be difficult to implement horizontally within the family and communal setting in traditional Africa. However, the ACERWC seems to suggest that participation, as provided for in the ACRWC, might be different from such traditional understandings. That is probably why the ACERWC would expect state parties to 'advocacy in families, communities and traditional settings'[110] to ensure that children participate in decision-making.

The CRC Committee holds the view that states have positive obligations to facilitate the participation of children in all actions that affect them, and state parties

[106] Compare eg the usage in art 1 of the Convention on the Rights of the Child. A similar pattern is followed in many articles of the CRC.

[107] Lansdown, 'The Realisation of Children's Participation Rights: Critical Reflections'

[108] ibid

[109] Editorial: 'International Child Research: Promise and Challenge' (1997) 4 Childhood 147.

[110] See Concluding Recommendations by the African Committee of Experts on the Rights and Welfare of The Child (ACERWC) in the Republic of Tanzania Report on The Status of implementation of The African Charter on The Rights and Welfare of The Child available at http://www.acerwc.org/wp-content/uploads/2011/03/ACERWC-Recommendations-Tanzania-initial-English.pdf

are expected to 'continue to assist children when they want to establish organizations with the goal of promoting and protecting their rights'.[111] As a component of this obligation, state parties should provide children with 'information, support and favourable conditions in order to participate appropriately and in a way that enhances their dignity and self-esteem'.[112] Since the 'circle' of participation closest to children, where they impart information and their views, is the family, within the framework of the CRC, children's participation rights are expected to be respected within the family environment as well.

From the above brief analysis, with respect to article 4(2), the ACRWC is more substantively akin to article 12(2) of the CRC than to the African context, which it was supposed to reflect.

4 Cultural Legitimacy as a Challenge to the Implementation of the African Children's Charter

While implementation could be undertaken in spite of norms resistance from significant portion of domestic stakeholders in its technical sense of incorporating human rights norms into domestic laws, compliance, which is a result of a change in beliefs and behaviours, is less likely to happen, voluntarily, in the absence of acceptance of norms. The acceptance of human rights norms by individuals and institutions is pivotal if the norms are to change beliefs and behaviours. Acceptance of human rights norms is less problematic when human rights norms have local equivalents or could easily be approximated to the 'spirit and purport' of local norms and values. Acceptance of human rights norms, therefore, is a critical component of the legitimacy of the norms.

The continued inability of human rights norms and standards to effectively end impunity is forcing international and national policymakers to shift the policy battlefront to issues of implementation of human rights. By implementation is meant the ability to translate and transfer the values and norms embodied in human rights instruments to enhance the quality of life and dignity of every human being.[113] There is a direct correlation between the effectiveness of the methods and mechanisms used to implement human rights norms and values and the acceptance of these norms and values by their beneficiaries.[114]

[111] See eg CRC, Concluding Observations regarding the Dominican Republic, 11 February 2008, CRC/C/ DOM/CO/2 para 34.

[112] UNICEF 'Circles of Participation' The State of the World's Children (2003) 3. Available at http://www.unicef.org/sowc03/contents/pdf/SOWC03-eng.pdf

[113] Christof H Heyns and Frans Viljoen, *The Impact of the United Nations Human Rights Treaties on the Domestic Level* (Martinus Nijhoff Publishers 2002).

[114] Linda Camp Keith, *National Constitutions and Human Rights Protection: Regional Differences and Colonial Influences* (Burlington VT: Ashgate Publishing 2004); Linda Camp Keith and Ayo Ogundele, 'Legal Systems and Constitutionalism in Sub-Saharan Africa: An Empirical Examination of Colonial Influences on Human Rights' (2007) HRQ 1065.

Acceptance is easy to measure at a formal level. The voluntary ratification of a human rights treaty by a state and its willingness and ability to domesticate that treaty should suffice as a good indicator of acceptance of the treaty norms and their implications. Unfortunately, formal acceptance is an insufficient indicator of acceptance. This is so because ratification, as an exercise of state volition, is a multivocal undertaking—it may be genuine, hypocritical and utterly false.[115] Consequently, 'ratification in itself [could] largely [be] a formal, and in some cases an empty, gesture'.[116]

In addition, ratification is state-centred. This is problematic, at least in the African context, because the nature, intention and scope of the state are subjects of academic debate. Some scholars have argued that the states in Africa, as colonial projects, were created 'to be totalitarian, oppressive, and exploitative'.[117] As a result, states are not 'necessarily the most reliable [representatives] of the people whom they govern.'[118] In addition, it has been claimed that in Africa, 'power ... radiates outward from the core political areas and tends to diminish over distance'.[119] As a result, the 'state plays only a limited role in the daily lives of many Africans'.[120]

Furthermore, there are concerns that ratification by weaker and small states may not be genuinely voluntarily. The powerful and richer states use 'a form of coercion by intellectual means [in addition] to the use of "soft power" par excellence',[121] to ensure ratification by small and weaker states. According to An Na'imi, 'it is misleading to assume genuine representation of popular perceptions and attitudes towards human rights in our countries from the formal representation of "our delegates" to international fora'.[122] In other words, 'popular acceptance' by families and communities is crucial to the cost-effective implementation of human rights. Therefore, in the debate of what should constitute commonly agreed standards of human rights and how these should be implemented, the values and voices of local families and communities must not be neglected, dismissed or discounted.

Whatever implementation strategy is adopted, it is important to note that the cultural values, needs, opinions and expectations of the recipient communities are crucial building blocks for or stumbling blocks to implementation. Empirical research, academic admonition and states admissions all bear witness to the powerful

[115] Beth A Simmons, *Mobilizing for Human Rights: International Law in Domestic Politics* (CUP 2009).

[116] Heyns and Viljoen, *The Impact of the United Nations Human Rights Treaties on the Level.*

[117] Makau Mutua, 'Justice Under Siege: The Rule of Law and Judicial Subservience in Kenya' (2001) 23 HRQ 96.

[118] Michael Freeman, 'Human Rights and Real Cultures: Towards a Dialogue on "Asian Values"' (1998) 16 NQHR 25

[119] Jeffrey Herbst, *States and Power in Africa: Comparative Lessons in Authority and Control*, vol 149 (Princeton University Press 2014).

[120] ibid.

[121] Lynda Schaefer Bell and others, *Negotiating Culture and Human Rights* (Columbia University Press 2001).

[122] Abd Allah Ahmad Naim and Abdullahi Ahmed An-Na'im, *Human Rights in Cross-Cultural Perspectives: A Quest for Consensus* (University of Pennsylvania Press 1995).

role that culture plays in the human rights debate, dialogue as well as implementation. The influence of culture gets stronger as human rights norms get closer to the basic unit of society, family and children. Therefore, the implementation of human rights norms that impact the lives of families and children should be sensitive to cultural context. For instance, a study of the implementation of the CRC in three South American countries concluded that the level of implementation was 'conditioned by the interface between understandings of rights and broader questions of politics, cultures and institutions'.[123]

Similarly, in the African context, states, academic institutions and NGOs have identified socio-cultural contexts as posing significant challenges to the effective implementation of children's rights in Africa.[124] Perceptions around how culturally legitimate the provisions of treaties dealing with children's rights are in an African context are at the core of these implementation challenges.[125] A number of state parties to the CRC and, in a few instances, the ACRWC[126] have stated that culture and traditions in their own countries presented the greatest challenge to their efforts to implement children's rights.[127]

The acceptance and effective implementation of the CRC and, by implication, the ACRWC (in the light of the textually, normative and substantive similarities between the two instruments) in Africa have been hampered by its perceived lack of cultural legitimacy.[128] At the level of formal acceptance, some states have significantly minimized the extent of their obligations under the CRC and the ACRWC[129] through reservations, citing religious and cultural factors.[130] Some states in Africa base their willingness to implement article 18 of the CRC, for example, on the condition that it will be interpreted and 'implemented in accordance with the Islamic law'.[131] Or, more generally, to take one example, 'the Government of Djibouti shall not consider itself bound by any provisions or articles that are incompatible with its religion and its traditional values'.[132] It is difficult to imagine which principle or provision of the CRC falls outside this blanket reservation.

[123] Jean Grugel and Enrique Peruzzotti, 'The Domestic Politics of International Human Rights Law: Implementing the Convention on the Rights of the Child in Ecuador, Chile, and Argentina' (2012) 34 HRQ 178.

[124] http://www.odi.org.uk/sites/odi.org.uk/files/odi-assets/publications-opinion-files/6050.pdf.

[125] Kaime, *The African Charter on the Rights and Welfare of the Child: A Socio-Legal Perspective*.

[126] See eg the Initial State Report of the Republic of Senegal to the ACERWC.

[127] Sonia Harris-Short, 'International Human Rights Law: Imperialist, Inept and Ineffective? Cultural Relativism and the UN Convention on the Rights of the Child' (2003) HRQ 130.

[128] ibid.

[129] The Republic of Egypt, Botswana and Sudan, among others, have entered their reservations to the ACRWC.

[130] Harris-Short, 'International Human Rights Law: Imperialist, Inept and Ineffective? Cultural Relativism and the UN Convention on the Rights of the Child'.

[131] See eg the reservation of Algeria to the CRC.

[132] Reservation entered by Djibouti to the CRC and Mauritania entered a similar reservation to the CRC.

State reports to the CRC Committee have also attributed implementation challenges with respect to the CRC to communities with different cultural values and norms. According to the Democratic Republic of Congo,[133]

> Africa is moving towards a form of modernity, which nevertheless retains 'authentic' aspects; these should be taken into account and safeguarded. For this reason, legislation which is too advanced in relation to mental, social, economic and cultural structures is sometimes more dangerous than an outdated legal system.

The Malian delegation advancing the same argument that law is a blunt tool for addressing entrenched cultural values and practices in the context of FGM said that it is 'impossible to legislate against voluntary excision'.[134] Things are made more difficult because of the 'perception among the local population that the general civil and criminal law, as opposed to customary law and practice, enshrines "alien ideas" that have been forcibly imposed on them by more powerful outsiders'.[135] Chad admitted that the 'weight of custom and tradition' has made 'it difficult to implement some provisions' of the CRC.[136] The implementation of the 'foreign' nature of the values codified in the CRC standards,[137]

> [c]omes up against the enormous complexity of the concrete realities of nations, such as inter alia, ethnic particularism and cultural diversities ... these factors ... mean that implementation of the provisions of the Convention is somewhat relative and variable depending on the country.

Because of cultural hurdles to implementing the provisions of the CRC and in the light of the similarities between it and the ACRWC, state parties are forced 'to steer

[133] See the addendum to the Initial Report of the Congo (UN Doc CRC/C/3/Add 57 209) as cited in S Harris-Short, 'International Human Rights Law: Imperialist, Inept and Ineffective? Cultural Relativism and the UN Convention on the Rights of the Child' (2003) 25 HRQ 130.

[134] Summary Record of the 571st Meeting of the Committee on the Rights of the Child: Mali, UN Committee on the Rights of the Child, UN Doc CRC/C/SR.571 (1999) 26 as cited in S Harris-Short, 'International Human Rights Law: Imperialist, Inept and Ineffective? Cultural Relativism and the UN Convention on the Rights of the Child' (2003) 25 HRQ 130.

[135] According to the delegation of the Republic of Uganda, referring to the successes the state has recorded in its efforts to eliminate FGM, see Summary Record of the 409th Meeting: Uganda, UN Committee on the Rights of the Child, UN Doc CRC/C/SR.409 (1997) 55 as cited in S Harris-Short, 'International Human Rights Law: Imperialist, Inept and Ineffective? Cultural Relativism and the UN Convention on the Rights of the Child' (2003) 25 HRQ 130.

[136] See the summary records of the meeting of the Committee on the Rights of the Child in the initial report of the Republic of Chad UN Doc CRC/C/3/Add 50 (1997) 35.

[137] Initial Reports of The Republic of Guinea Addendum: Guinea, UN Committee on the Rights of the Child, UN Doc CRC/ C/3/Add 48, (1996) 164 cited in S Harris-Short, 'International Human Rights Law: Imperialist, Inept and Ineffective? Cultural Relativism and the UN Convention on the Rights of the Child' (2003) 25 HRQ 130.

a course between the desirable and the feasible'.[138] This might be due to the fact that 'the entire Convention was not suited to the realities of African life',[139] or because the state could not 'force its citizens to abide by ideas and principles that were alien to them and there would be no point in adopting laws that could not be enforced';[140] or simply the conceptual difficulties involved in implementing the CRC because,[141]

> [t]raditionally, the law developed in the wake of social changes and changes in the ways of thinking. In the case of the Convention, however, the contrary would appear to be the case in the Sudan, where changes in attitudes and in the organisation of institutions were apparently supposed to follow in the wake of the law.

There is increasing evidence in the different state reports submitted by states in Africa that the challenges they face concerning implementing the provisions of children's rights are partly rooted in the differences in the cultural values and image of childhood in the CRC and by implication in the ACRWC in traditional African communities. In the words of the Democratic Republic of Congo's state report,[142]

> Traditional African culture in general and Congolese culture in particular makes for conformity in behaviour, the notion of collective responsibility and the principle of linear authority – of the father over the son and the elder over the younger. Respect in traditional society is more than a rule for living; it designates each individual's place and role.

What the states seem to be saying through the reporting exercise relevant to this topic is that they are willing to implement their obligations under the CRC, but

[138] Summary Record of the 136th Meeting: Burkina Faso, UN Committee on the Rights of the Child, UN Doc CRC/C/SR.1 36 (1995) 31 as cited in S Harris-Short, 'International Human Rights Law: Imperialist, Inept and Ineffective? Cultural Relativism and the UN Convention on the Rights of the Child' (2003) 25 HRQ 130.

[139] Summary Record of the 420th Meeting: Togo, Committee on the Rights of the Child, UN Doc CRC/C/SR.420, (1997) 46 as cited in S Harris-Short, 'International Human Rights Law: Imperialist, Inept and Ineffective? Cultural Relativism and the UN Convention on the Rights of the Child' (2003) 25 HRQ 130.

[140] Comments from the delegation of the Republic of Benin see Summary Record of the 543rd Meeting: Benin, UN Committee on the Rights of the Child, UN Doc CRC/C/SR.543 (1999) 58 as cited in S Harris-Short, 'International Human Rights Law: Imperialist, Inept and Ineffective? Cultural Relativism and the UN Convention on the Rights of the Child' (2003) 25 HRQ 130.

[141] Summary Record of the 69th Meeting of the Committee on the Rights of the Child: Sudan, UN Doc CRC/ C/SR.69 (Sudan) 40 as cited in S Harris-Short, 'International Human Rights Law: Imperialist, Inept and Ineffective? Cultural Relativism and the UN Convention on the Rights of the Child' (2003) 25 HRQ 130.

[142] Initial Reports of States Parties Due in 1992: Addendum: Democratic Republic of Congo, UN Committee on the Rights of the Child, UN Doc CRC/C/3/Add 57, 50 as cited in S Harris-Short, 'International Human Rights Law: Imperialist, Inept and Ineffective? Cultural Relativism and the UN Convention on the Rights of the Child' (2003) 25 HRQ 130.

effectively unable to do so because 'the weight of tradition were extremely heavy',[143] due to the 'social and cultural backwardness'[144] of their people or generally because their people consider the childrearing values of the CRC to be alien to theirs.

Some scholars have cautioned against this victim-like attitude of states. It has been argued that 'putting the blame on "entrenched cultural practices" for ineffective implementation provides useful excuses for inaction',[145] thereby allowing governments 'to get the benefits of international legitimacy without the "inconvenience" of compliance with human rights standards.'[146] So, such submissions by state parties before human rights treaty bodies should be thoroughly examined for 'dangers of distortion, political manipulation and unfounded appeals to a mythical past'.[147] This is so because some of these states might simply be engaging in 'self-serving opportunistic' efforts to 'invoke conjured traditions to justify economic, social and political repressions'.[148] These critics advise that those who are the victims of the abuse should rather be consulted 'to determine whether those who are subordinated, excluded and or marginalized regard their situation as culturally legitimate'.[149]

These arguments are not without merit. However, conceptually, they are inherently self-defeating. Firstly, to accuse the states of not being the authoritative and authentic representative of the values of their people is to legitimize the perception that these same states actually do not know their people and thus, have no mandate in the first place to negotiate international human rights treaties on their behalf. So, therefore,[150]

> [i]f state elites are not faithfully representing the culturally rooted views, attitudes and opinions of the people whom they govern, the norms enshrined within the UN Convention on the Rights of the Child, despite near-universal ratification, lose their claim to cultural legitimacy.

143 Summary Record of the 89th Meeting: Sudan, UN Committee on the Rights of the Child, UN Doc CRC/C/SR.89 (1994) 18 as cited in S Harris-Short, 'International Human Rights Law: Imperialist, Inept and Ineffective? Cultural Relativism and the UN Convention on the Rights of the Child' (2003) 25 HRQ 130.

144 Summary Record of the 657th Meeting: Central African Republic, UN Committee on the Rights of the Child, UN Doc CRC/C/SR.657 (2000) 46 as cited in S Harris-Short, 'International Human Rights Law: Imperialist, Inept and Ineffective? Cultural relativism and the UN Convention on the Rights of the Child' (2003) 25 HRQ 130.

145 Abdullahi An-Na'im, 'Human Rights and Islamic Identity in France and Uzbekistan: Mediation of the Local and Global' (2000) 22 HRQ 906.

146 Ibid.

147 Harris-Short, 'International Human Rights Law: Imperialist, Inept and Ineffective? Cultural Relativism and the UN Convention on the Rights of the Child'; Adamantia Pollis, 'Towards a New Universalism; Reconstruction and Dialogue' (1998) 16 NQHR 5; Donnelly, 'The Relative Universality of Human Rights'; Howard, 'Cultural Absolutism and the Nostalgia for Community'.

148 Pollis, 'Towards a New Universalism; Reconstruction and Dialogue'.

149 Freeman, 'Human Rights and Real Cultures: Towards a Dialogue on "Asian Values"'

150 Harris-Short, 'International Human Rights Law: Imperialist, Inept and Ineffective? Cultural Relativism and the UN Convention on the Rights of the Child'.

If the policy value of human rights is dependant and determined by its translatability and transferability into lived realities through implementation, and implementation, in turn, relies on formal and cultural acceptability of the human rights norms, it is reasonable to assume that the gap between human rights values and cultural norms of the beneficiaries is a determining factor for effective implementation. Therefore, since there is a conceptual and cultural gap between the image of childhood in the CRC and the understanding of childhood in traditional communities in Africa, its implementation in Africa will continue to be challenging until the CRC either creates an African culture in its image or the CRC is Africanized in its implementation.

Maybe some of the reasons why state parties to the CRC ratified the ACRWC was out of fear that the implementation of the CRC in their countries might be difficult and also because these states perceived the ACRWC to be 'more responsive to traditional African values and concerns'[151] relating to childhood. However, as demonstrated in this work, the ACRWC is but an 'edited' version of the CRC. Its textual, conceptual and substantive similarities are not coincidental; hence, it is reasonable to presume that the implementation of the ACRWC will face the same challenges that its mother treaty, the CRC, is facing in Africa and elsewhere. Since the normative commonality between the ACRWC and the CRC calls into question the autochthony of the former, it is better to regard and treat the relationship between the CRC and the ACRWC simply as an act of legal transplantation.

5 Conclusion

The ACRWC was conceived to address African specific challenges facing children and reflect and respond to African philosophy of childhood and cultural heritage. The ACRWC has addressed these African specific challenges and offers children in Africa a higher threshold of protection. However, textually and substantively, the ACRWC does not adequately reflect and respond to an African understanding of childhood and African cultural heritage. Even if the ACRWC, in its preamble, expresses its intention to be cultural and context-specific, textually and substantively, it is a mere transplant of the CRC. It is even worse that the CRC, whose focus is globally is, in some instances, more flexible and attuned to or aligned with the African cultural context than the ACRWC, whose primary audience are communities in Africa for whom it was ostensibly meant to reflect their cultural norms, practices and aspirations for childhood.

[151] Initial Reports of States Parties Due in 1992: Addendum: Uganda, UN Committee on the Rights of the Child, UN Doc CRC/C/3/Add 40, (1996) 18 cited in S Harris-Short, 'International Human Rights Law: Imperialist, Inept and Ineffective? Cultural Relativism and the UN Convention on the Rights of the Child' (2003) 25 HRQ 130.

Therefore, what the drafters of the ACRWC have denied Africa of, by their decision to transplant the CRC, is Africa's ability to preserve its 'entitlement of historical communities to maintain a local connection with their laws as a legitimate vector of cultural identity'.[152] The possible result of this decision is that the ACRWC, unless interpreted contextually, threatens to deprive the continent of an African conception of childhood that is 'historically, sociologically, economically and politically' African. What the drafters of the ACRWC have achieved, instead, is to expose the ACRWC to the same conceptual and normative defects inherent in the CRC and, consequently, subject the implementation of the ACRWC to the same cultural legitimacy challenges confronting the CRC. The new image of the child and vision of the family and its roles in the upbringing of the child, introduced by the ACRWC, is more deeply rooted in the CRC than the cultural practices and values of its member states.

Since the failure of the ACRWC to promote and portray an African understanding of childhood exposes it to the same accusation of lack of cultural legitimacy that the CRC faces, and suffer from the same defects inherent in the CRC, it is reasonable to ask if there is any value in retaining two duplicative instruments and whether it is efficient to fund two processes to eventually arrive at the same goal. How the ACERWC interprets and applies the provisions of the ACRWC will be relevant in answering this question. The fact that two treaties are similar textually, normatively and substantively does not, in itself, guarantee that the two treaty bodies monitoring such treaties will inherently interpret and apply the provisions of those treaties similarly. Therefore, if the ACERWC interprets the ACRWC through the lenses of an African philosophy of childhood and cultural heritage, the ACRWC will be value-adding. However, if it interprets and applies the provisions of the ACRWC according to the liberal, neoliberal and universalistic approach of the CRC Committee, it will be difficult to justify the usefulness of retaining the ACRWC.

[152] Pierre Legrand, 'On the Unbearable Localness of the Law: Academic Fallacies and Unseasonable Observations' (2002) 10 European Review of Private Law 61.

7
Member States' Compliance with the Recommendations of the African Commission on Human and Peoples' Rights

Lirette Louw

1 Introduction

This chapter is premised on data and analysis, which dates back to 2005 when a study was undertaken to empirically determine Member State compliance with the recommendations of the African Commission on Human and Peoples' Rights (African Commission or Commission).[1] Fast forward to the year 2020, and to quote from the Commission's latest Activity Report, 'the level of compliance by State Parties with the Commission's Decisions ... is relatively low'.[2] It would, therefore, appear that attempting to conduct an update of empirical data on state compliance will not contribute much to the debate on improving state compliance, but what appears to be relevant 15 years later is a discussion on factors that influence state compliance and a realization that there is a renewed effort to improving compliance. The latter is the focus of this chapter.

The African regional human rights system is based on the normative framework provided by the African Charter on Human and Peoples' Rights (African Charter). The African Charter was adopted by the Assembly of Heads of State and Government of the Organization of African Unity (OAU) on 27 June 1981 and

[1] The full results of this study are contained in Lirette Louw 'An Analysis of State Compliance with the Recommendations of the African Commission on Human and Peoples' Rights' (Unpublished Thesis submitted in fulfilment of the requirements of the degree Doctor of Laws (LLD), Centre for Human Rights, Faculty of Law, University of Pretoria, South Africa, 28 January 2005). A discussion on factors that influence state compliance in the African regional human rights system, based on findings contained in the doctoral thesis, was published in 2007; F Viljoen and L Louw 'State Compliance with the Recommendations of the African Commission on Human and Peoples' Rights, 1993-2004' (2007) 101 AJIL 1–34. The bulk of this chapter formed the basis of an unpublished paper delivered in Yamoussoukro, Cote d'Ivoire, in October 2012, during the *Review of 25 Years of the Work of the African Commission on Human and Peoples' Rights in Africa*. An attempt has been made to update those views with the latest developments as reflected in Activity Reports of the Commission, the latest Rules of Procedure as adopted in 2020 and recent seminars held on the topic.

[2] Forty-seventh Activity Report of the African Commission on Human and Peoples' Rights, para 32. The same sentiment is expressed in the 46th and 45th Activity Reports at paras 30 and 36, respectively.

Lirette Louw, *Member States' Compliance with the Recommendations of the African Commission on Human and Peoples' Rights* In: *Compliance with International Human Rights Law in Africa*. Edited by: Aderomola Adeola, Oxford University Press.
 DOI: 10.1093/oso/9780192856999.003.0007

entered into force on 21 October 1986.[3] In terms of the African Charter, the African Commission was established to ensure compliance with the Charter's norms.[4] In fulfilling its protective mandate, the African Commission receives and considers individual complaints alleging violations by state parties of the African Charter.[5] In finding a state party in violation of the African Charter, the African Commission not only lists the articles violated by a state party but also recommends remedial measures to be adopted by the state party concerned.

There is no direct reference in the African Charter authorizing the Commission to issue recommendations upon finding a state party in violation of the provisions of the Charter. The Commission has developed its mandate in a progressive manner by relying on the 'implied powers doctrine' to adopt recommendations upon having found a state party in violation of the Charter.[6] When the Nigerian government questioned the Commission's competence to issue recommendations, in reference to the Commission's findings in Communication 101/93, the Commission stated the following,[7]

> As has been made clear above, Nigeria is bound by the African Charter. The Commission is likewise bound by the Charter, to consider communications fully, carefully, and in good faith. When the Commission concludes that a communication describes a real violation of the Charter's provisions, its duty is to make that clear and indicate what action the government must take to remedy the situation. Naturally the Commission could not make such judgments with regard to states outside its jurisdiction. But in ratifying the African Charter without reservation, Nigeria voluntarily submitted itself to the Commission's authority in this regard.

In 2012, the Commission took exception to the Republic of Botswana's position that it was not bound by the decision of the Commission, as expressed in Communication 313/05—*Kenneth Good v Botswana*, by bringing this refusal to implement its decision to the attention of the Executive Council of the African Union (AU) for appropriate action.[8] It is not, however, clear what action, if any, was taken subsequently.

[3] All member states of the AU, apart from Morocco, have ratified the African Charter.

[4] The African Commission is established under art 30 of the African Charter, and its mandate is set out in art 45. The mandate of the African Commission is twofold; it has to both promote and protect the rights guaranteed in the African Charter.

[5] The Commission developed the practice of considering complaints from individuals, groups of individuals and NGOs according to arts 55–58 of the African Charter.

[6] GJ Naldi, 'Reparations in the Practice of the African Commission on Human and Peoples' Rights' (2001) 14 Leiden J Int Law 169.

[7] *Account of Internal Legislation of Nigeria and the Dispositions of the Charter of African Human and Peoples' Rights*, Second Extraordinary Session, Kampala, 18–19 December 1995, DOC II/ES/ACHPR/4; See also F Viljoen and L Louw, 'The Status of the Findings of the African Commission: From Moral Persuasion to Legal Obligation' (2004) 28 JAL 11.

[8] Combined 32nd and 33rd Activity Report of the Commission, 9, 24.

Three decades down the line, it appears that some states still view the implementation of recommendations on communications as voluntary because the Commission is viewed as a quasi-judicial organ.[9]

The African Commission held its first session in Addis Ababa, Ethiopia, in November 1987. From its third Ordinary Session onwards, it received communications from individuals, groups of individuals and Non-governmental Organizations (NGOs) on behalf of individuals, alleging violations of the African Charter. The Commission published its findings on communications decided under the individual complaints' procedure for the first time in 1994, in an annexure to its Seventh Annual Activity Report.

This chapter sets out to briefly restate the 2005 analysis of Member State compliance with the findings and recommendations issued under the individual complaints system. Given that the African Commission in 2019 records such compliance as 'relatively low', a fresh analysis of empirical data will not in all likelihood impact the discussion of factors that influence compliance. As will be seen below, a study or measurement of state compliance is in no way an exact science, and the arguments put forward here should, therefore, rather be viewed as theories on the level of state compliance, the factors that influence it and how to encourage improved compliance in future.

2 Measurement of State Compliance with the Recommendations of the African Commission

In 1997, ten years after its first Ordinary Session, the Commission through its Chairman stated 'that none of the decisions on individual communications taken by the Commission and adopted by the Assembly had ever been implemented'.[10] In the Eleventh Annual Activity Report, covering the November 1997 Session, the Commission reflected further on the issue of non-compliance with its recommendations. It noted that not only did it affect its credibility, but that it could also probably be to blame for the reduction in the number of communications submitted to it.[11] At the Commission's Twenty-fourth Ordinary Session, in October 1998, the Secretariat distributed a document entitled *Non-compliance*

[9] *Report of the Regional Seminar on the Implementation of Decisions of the African Commission on Human and Peoples' Rights*, 12–15 August 2017, Dakar, Senegal, 6. (Available at: http://www.achpr.org/news/2018/08/d344/; accessed on 30 October 2018). This prompted a recommendation from the Regional Seminar to urge state parties to 'comply with their obligations under art 1 of the African Charter, which extends to implementation of decisions of the Commission, rather than focussing on the non-binding nature of decisions of the Commission' (8).

[10] R Murray, 'Report on the 1997 Sessions of the African Commission on Human and Peoples' Rights—21st and 22nd sessions: 15-25 April and 2-11 November 1997' (1998) 19 Human Rights Law Journal 170.

[11] See s VIII Protective Activities, 11th Annual Activity Report of the African Commission adopted by Decision AHG/DEC 126 (XXXIV) of the OAU AHSG, June 1998.

of State Parties to Adopted Recommendations of the African Commission: A Legal Approach.[12] This document recorded that 'the attitude of state parties ... with the exception of Cameroon has been to generally ignore its recommendations'.[13] Again in 2003, as part of an evaluation of its functioning and 16 years into its existence, the Commission recorded problems of non-compliance by state parties with its recommendations.[14]

The African Commission noted the above concerns with the non-compliance by state parties with its recommendations in the absence of any formal follow-up mechanism to enable it to monitor state compliance. A subsequent empirical study, however, confirmed an overall lack of state compliance with the final decisions and recommendations of the African Commission.[15] The study attempted to gather information on state compliance with all the individual communications decided by the Commission as published from its Seventh Annual Activity Report to its Sixteenth Annual Activity Report.[16] Follow-up was established until the end of 2004, covering a total of 17 years of the Commission's activities.

During the 17 years under review, the Commission issued final decisions on violations of the provisions of the African Charter in a total of 44 individual communications. These communications involved 17 of the 53 states that are party to the African Charter.[17] The study endeavoured to classify state compliance with the

[12] DOC/OS/50b(XXIV) (1998) *reprinted in* Documents of the African Commission on Human and Peoples' Rights (Rachel Murray and Malcolm Evans (eds) 2001) 758.

[13] The reference to Cameroon was made in relation to Communication 39/90 *Annette Pagnoulle (on behalf of Abdoulaye Mazou) v Cameroon.* After serving a five-year sentence and being placed under house arrest, the accused was not reinstated as a magistrate, although others condemned under similar conditions were reinstated. The Commission found Cameroon in violation of arts 6, 7(1)(b) and (d) and 15 of the African Charter. The Commission recommended that the government of Cameroon draw all the necessary legal conclusions to reinstate the victim in his rights. According to Cameroon, Mr Mazou was reinstated in the judiciary and compensation was offered to him, but he declined to accept. (Comments made by the state representative of Cameroon during the delivery of Cameroon's initial state report on 6 May 2002 at the Thirty-first Ordinary Session held in Pretoria, South Africa). It appears that years later Cameroon can still be listed among the few states that do comply with the Commission's recommendations. In 2019, in its Forty-seventh Activity Report, the Commission noted as follows in this regard (at para 33), 'During the reporting period, the Commission wishes to report with commendation that the Government of Cameroon informed the Commission on 29 June 2019, of the implementation of the Decision adopted in Communication 389/10 – *Mbiankeu Genevieve v Cameroon*'.

[14] *Report of the Retreat of Members of the African Commission on Human and Peoples' Rights (ACHPR) facilitated by the Office of the High Commissioner for Human Rights*, Addis-Ababa, Ethiopia, 24–26 September 2003, 4. Available at https://nhri.ohchr.org/EN/Regional/Americas/AfricanDocumentsPage/ACHPR-Retreat-Report-Final.pdf.

[15] See fn 1.

[16] Only communications in respect of which the Commission found a state party in violation of the African Charter, whether its findings were accompanied by recommendations or not, formed part of the study. Those cases where the Commission only ruled on admissibility were not included as obviously the case did not proceed any further. Also, cases where the Commission reported an amicable settlement, were not included. An attempt was initially made to determine the details of these amicable settlements, but without success because no access was granted to the specific files of the Commission, and when approached, the Commissioners could not give details as to what these settlements entailed.

[17] At the time of the study, Morocco was not a member of the AU and South Sudan was not a party to the African Charter.

recommendations of the African Commission in terms of five broad categories, namely, full compliance, partial compliance, non-compliance, situational compliance (classified as partial compliance after a change of government) and 'unclear' cases.[18]

The study found that in only six of the 44 communications (or 14%) of state parties complied fully with the recommendations of the African Commission. State parties clearly did not comply with the Commission's recommendations in 13 cases (or 30% of the total). Cases of partial compliance and situational compliance (where partial or full compliance was only accounted for as a result of the transition from an undemocratic to a stable and democratic government) accounted altogether for 47% of cases, respectively broken down as 14 cases of partial compliance (or 32%) and seven cases of situational compliance (15%). Finally, in four cases (or 9%), insufficient information excluded any finding on state compliance, making them instances of 'unclear' compliance.

It must be stated that the study suffered from a number of limitations in establishing follow-ups to the recommendations of the African Commission.[19] Similarly, subsequently categorizing such implementation efforts were fraught with uncertainties, not to mention that such classification is necessarily subjective rather than objective in nature.

If state compliance with the recommendations of the African Commission is to be measured only in instances of full compliance, then it is apparent that the African Commission was accurate in its assessment to conclude that there has been an overall lack of state compliance. If partial compliance was, however, to be interpreted as a positive sign, as opposed to complete indifference to the African regional human rights system's individual complaints mechanism, then a more optimistic outlook is presented by the above statistical findings.

The above empirical analysis took place in a situation where no data was recorded by the Commission at the time, apart from its own sense of non-compliance with its recommendations, as alluded to above. The Commission has since adopted Rule 112 of its Rules of Procedure in 2010 to allow a process of follow-up to monitor compliance with recommendations as issued in individual communications. However, it was only in its Thirty-Sixth Activity Report, covering the period November 2013 to May 2014, that the Commission indicated that pursuant to Rule 112(8) and (9) of its Rules of Procedure, it will henceforth include in its Activity Reports a section detailing the implementation of the decisions of the

[18] For a detailed discussion on the categorization of these 44 cases and the difficulties experienced in attempting to do so, see Viljoen and Louw (2007) s II.

[19] The following are some of the limitations experienced in the course of the empirical enquiry: communication difficulties with all role players, insufficient records, inability to trace victims and authors of communications, lack of quality and continuity in state representatives attending the Commission's sessions, opposing views about compliance by those involved and a lack of media coverage on the continent.

Commission by the Member States.[20] An analysis of this section in the Activity Reports, covering the period 2014 to 2019, shows that the Commission records the level of compliance as 'relatively low', which seems to be diplomatic speak for an overall lack of compliance.[21] The latter statement flows from the fact that most of the reports stretching from the Thirty-Sixth Activity Report to the Forty-Seventh Activity Report merely notes that the Commission did not receive any information regarding the implementation of its decisions for the reporting period.[22] In at least three instances, the complainants reported ongoing non-implementation to the Commission.[23] Since the adoption of a follow-up mechanism in 2010, full compliance has only been recorded in relation to one state party in 2019, namely Cameroon, to implement the Commission's decision in Communication 389/10.[24] Partial compliance has been recorded in the Thirty-Sixth Activity Report, in relation to Uganda, where the complainant informed the Commission of such, which prompted the Commission to request the state to implement the outstanding part of the decision.[25] In the same Activity Report, in relation to Egypt, the Respondent state indicated efforts made to protect the rights of women, which seems to be partial compliance as the Commission asked for further information as to concrete measures taken.[26] The third and final example of partial compliance is in the Thirty-eighth Activity Report of the Commission, in relation to Kenya, where the Commission reported that it was informed by the state that a Taskforce was established to implement the Commission's decision in Communication 276/03.[27]

The Rules of Procedure have been updated in 2020, and Rule 125 now details the follow-up actions to be undertaken by the Commission in an effort to monitor and encourage compliance. In particular, the Rule has been bolstered by providing a role for national human rights institutions to facilitate the implementation of the Commission's decisions.

3 Comparative Evaluation of State Compliance Under Individual Complaints Mechanisms

Another way of evaluating state compliance with the recommendations of the African Commission could possibly be found in juxtaposing the 2005 study's

20 36th Activity Report, para 27.

21 In its 42nd Activity Report, the Commission did go further by stating that it continues to 'lament the low compliance rate of State Parties with decisions of the Commission, and encourages States to acknowledge receipt of the Commission's correspondence and implement its recommendations'.

22 See, for instance, para 37 of the 45th Activity Report and para 31 of the 46th Activity Report.

23 See, for instance, para 18 of the 40th Activity Report, para 25 of the 41st Activity Report and para 35(a) of the 42nd Activity Report.

24 Para 33 of the 47th Activity Report.

25 At 9, para 25 of the 36th Activity Report.

26 At 10, para 26.

27 38th Activity Report, 9, para 30.

empirical findings, read together with the above-mentioned limited reporting done by the Commission from 2014 to 2019, with the categorization of state compliance in other human rights systems.

Many of the African states that are party to the regional human rights system are also party to the global human rights system established under the International Covenant on Civil and Political Rights (ICCPR) and the individual complaints procedure under the First Optional Protocol to the ICCPR.[28] In contrast to the African system, where very little is known about the implementation of the Commission's recommendations, the Human Rights Committee has an established follow-up mechanism through which it has since 1991 recorded follow-up information on state compliance with its views.[29]

The Human Rights Committee (the Committee) has, from its inception until the end of 2003, which is roughly the same period as the above-mentioned study, finalized 31 individual communications against 13 African states. An evaluation of state compliance with the views of the Committee in these cases similarly revealed a low compliance rate.[30] Overall compliance with its views, not limited to African state parties, has been recorded at approximately 30%.[31] A closer analysis, focusing on the compliance records of the five states found in violation of both the African Charter and the ICCPR during the same period, reveals no difference between the adherence or non-adherence of a state party to either system.[32] In other words, where states are party to both systems, they either consistently implement or ignore the views or recommendations of the human rights body.

[28] The Human Rights Committee (Committee) is the treaty body established under the ICCPR to ensure compliance with treaty norms. Under the Optional Protocol, the Committee is mandated to receive and consider individual communications alleging violations of the rights guaranteed in the ICCPR (art 1).

[29] The Committee adopted follow-up procedures in 1990, and from 1991 onwards, it has followed up on all the views issued where a state party was found in violation of the ICCPR (See M Schmidt, 'Follow-up Mechanisms before UN Human Rights Treaty Bodies and the UN Mechanism Beyond' in AF Bayefsky (ed), *The UN Human Rights Treaty System in the 21st Century* (2000) 233).

[30] Mutua quoted McGoldrick from his 1991 work, noting that 'the ultimate concern of an alleged victim is of course with the observance of the HRC's views in an individual case rather than with the procedural merits of the OP [Optional Protocol] system. It must be frankly admitted that compliance with the HRC's views by state parties has been disappointing' (M Mutua, 'Looking Past the Human Rights Committee: An Argument for De-Marginalising Enforcement' (1998) 4 Buff Hum Rts L Rev 234–235). Schmidt mentioned that in the absence of a follow-up mechanism, individuals 'with increasing frequency' complained to the HRC that state parties 'had failed to take any measures to implement the Committee's views' (M Schmidt, 'Follow-up Mechanisms Before UN human Rights Treaty Bodies and the UN Mechanism Beyond' in AF Bayefsky (ed), *The UN Human Rights Treaty System in the 21st Century* (2000) 234). See further M Nowak, 'The International Covenant on Civil and Political Rights' in R Hanski and M Suksi (eds), *An Introduction to the International Protection of Human Rights – A Textbook* (2000) 97.

[31] See, for instance, the Committee's annual reports for 1995 (A/50/40), para 547 and for 2002 (A/58/40) para 178, where it repeatedly stated that only approximately 30% of the follow-up replies received were satisfactory.

[32] Interpreting the table: C = full compliance; PC = partial compliance; NC = non-compliance

An analysis of state compliance in the African regional human rights system can also draw on the experiences of the Inter-American regional human rights system. This assumption is based on the parallels that can be drawn between the historical, political and legal similarities that form the background against which these regional systems operate today.[33] In 1965, the Inter-American Commission on Human Rights was provided with powers to examine individual petitions.[34] From the provisions of the American Convention on Human Rights, it is clear that the Inter-American Commission expects its decisions with accompanying recommendations to be implemented within stipulated time frames. Indeed, the Inter-American Court of Human Rights has held as follows,[35]

> In accordance with the principle of good faith, embodied in the aforesaid article 31(1) of the Vienna Convention, if a state signs and ratifies an international treaty, especially one concerning human rights, such as the American Convention, it has the obligation to make every effort to comply with the recommendations of a protection organ such as the Inter-American Commission, which is, indeed, one of the principal organs of the Organisation of American States, whose function is "*to promote the observance and defence of human rights*" in the hemisphere.

Country	African Commission	Human Rights Commission
Angola	NC	NC
Cameroon	C, NC	NC, C
Sierra Leone	C	PC
Zaire	NC	NC
Zambia	C, PC, PC	C, C, C, PC, NC

These were the only five countries that overlapped between the two systems. From this tabular overview, it appears that state parties' behaviour does not differ from one system to the other. For a detailed analysis of the specific cases referred to here, see Ch 2 of L Louw 'An analysis of state compliance with the recommendations of the African Commission on Human and Peoples' Rights' (Unpublished Thesis submitted in fulfilment of the requirements of the degree Doctor of Laws (LLD), Centre for Human Rights, Faculty of Law, University of Pretoria, South Africa, 28 January 2005).

33 For an overview of the 'similarities and differences between the Americas and Africa', see D Padilla, 'An African Human Rights Court: Reflections from the Perspective of the Inter-American System' (2002) 2 AHRLJ 186–187.

34 See the Final Act of the Second Special Inter-American Conference. Organization of American States Official Records, OEA/Ser C/I.13, 1965. As reported Basic Documents pertaining to Human Rights in the Inter-American System (2001) 7.

35 The Court continued further by stating that '[a]rticle 33 of the American Convention states that the Inter-American Commission, is as the Court, competent "with respect to matters relating to the fulfilment of the commitments made by the state parties", which means that by ratifying said Convention, states parties engage themselves to apply the recommendations made by the Commission in its reports'. Inter-American Court of Human Rights *Loayza Tamayo* Case, Judgment of 17 September 17 1997, Ser C, No 33, paras 78–82 available at: http://www.corteidh.or.cr/seriecpdf_ing/seriec_33_ing.pdf.

Notwithstanding the measures that form part of the Inter-American Commission's legislative framework or established practice, which aimed to encourage state compliance, various commentators have highlighted the general lack of state compliance with the Commission's recommendations.[36] However, these observations were made in the absence of empirical evidence, as the Inter-American Commission only adopted follow-up measures to verify state compliance with friendly settlement agreements and its recommendations on 1 May 2001 with the adoption of new Rules of Procedure.[37] The Inter-American Commission publishes a table on the status of state compliance as part of its Annual Report. The Commission has indicated that it evaluates 'whether or not compliance with its recommendations is complete and not whether it has been started'.[38] After 11 years of measuring state compliance, the Commission recorded total compliance in 16% of cases, partial compliance in 63% of cases and no compliance in 20%.[39] In 2017, after 14 years of measuring state compliance, the Commission recorded total compliance in 22% of cases, partial compliance in 64% of cases and compliance pending in 14% of cases.[40] Full compliance with the recommendations of the Commission, therefore, remains low and not much different from the 14% full compliance recorded in the African system. But there does appear to be an improvement in state compliance in the Inter-American system if statistics from 2011 are compared to 2017. This could be ascribed to a new way of categorizing state compliance (no compliance versus compliance pending) or as a result of continued efforts to attain better state compliance at a political level.[41]

[36] Grossman wrote that 'compliance with the Commission's reports is, for lack of a better word, uncertain' (Grossman (1998) 190). Other commentators have reported that, for the most part, states did not comply with the recommendations of the Inter-American Commission. See, for instance, Van der Walt and Krsticevic, (2000) 373 and D Cassel, 'Inter-American Human Rights Law: Soft and Hard' in D Shelton (ed), *Commitment and Compliance – The Role of Non-Binding Norms in the International Legal System* (2000) 394. The President of the Inter-American Commission in 2001 observed that the Commission's review of follow-up on the implementation of the Commission's recommendations showed no instances of full compliance and emphasized that member states 'must do everything possible to comply in good faith with the Commission's recommendation' (Address by Juan E Mendez, President of the Inter-American Commission on Human Rights, upon presenting the IACHR Annual Report for 2001 to the Juridical and Political Affairs Committee of the Permanent Council of the OAS. Available at: http://www.internationaljusticeproject.org/ pdfs/Mendez-writing.pdf).

[37] The new Rules of Procedure has been reprinted by the General Secretariat of the OAS in *Basic Documents pertaining to Human Rights in the Inter-American System* (2001) 127. Art 46 of the amended Rules of Procedure provides as follows in relation to Follow-Up Measures: (1) Once the Commission has published a report on a friendly settlement or on the merits in which it has made recommendations, it may adopt the follow-up measures it deems appropriate, such as requesting information from the parties and holding hearings in order to verify compliance with friendly settlement agreements and its recommendations. (2) The Commission shall report on progress in complying with those agreements as it deems appropriate.

[38] 2002 Annual Report of the Inter-American Commission on Human Rights, OEA/Ser L/V/II.117Doc1rev 1, par 108.

[39] 2011 Annual Report of the Inter-American Commission on Human Rights, Ch III, Section D *Status of Compliance with the Recommendations of the IACHR.*

[40] 2017 Annual Report of the Inter-American Commission on Human Rights, Ch III, Section F *Status of Compliance with the Recommendations of the IACHR and Friendly Settlements of the IACHR.*

[41] The 2017 Annual Report (s F, para 80) of the IACHR records as follows in this regard: 'on several occasions OAS General Assembly encouraged member states to follow-up on the recommendations of the IACHR.'

The above overview of state compliance under the United Nations and Inter-American human rights systems shows that an evaluation of state compliance under the African regional human rights system is not comparatively that much worse. In this context, the focus should, therefore, not be on the overall lack of state compliance but rather on factors that influence it in those instances where there was full compliance in order to strengthen the regional human rights system by ensuring greater compliance going forward.

4 Factors that Influence State Compliance

A previous analysis of factors that have influenced state compliance with the recommendations of the African Commission, in the communications wherein there was full compliance, as well as the cases in which there was no compliance, revealed that there are no clear-cut answers, but rather that a combination of factors may actually be at play.[42] Some of these factors, which could explain a general trend towards a lack of state compliance, are permanent features of the African regional human rights system.[43] Factors falling in this category relate to the fact that the African Commission is a quasi-judicial body and, therefore, issues non-binding decisions and recommendations. The fact that the Commission suffers from a legitimacy deficit, not helped by the lack of prominence given to human rights matters at the political level of the AU, has also been noted as part of the permanent features of the system, which negatively impact compliance.[44]

On the other hand, a breakdown of so-called 'variable' factors, which are not permanent features of the system, revealed that the following factors could be discarded as not playing a significant role in influencing state compliance with the recommendations of the African Commission: Maturity of the regional human rights system; length of time it takes to decide on a communication; the level of state involvement; the level of reasoning in decisions on communications; the formulation of detailed remedies; the nature of the right most prominent in the decision; the nature of the obligation imposed on the state; the scale of the human rights violations; the nature of the remedial action required and the presence of international pressure.[45]

Three 'variable' factors were, however, identified as having played a role in influencing state compliance. These factors seem to be representative of the three main schools on theories of state compliance with international law, namely, the realist

42 Viljoen and Louw (2007) s IV.
43 As above.
44 As above.
45 Viljoen and Louw, (2007) see the discussions under ss 4.1(a) to (e); 4.2; 4.2; 4.4(d); 4.5(b) and 4.6.

school,[46] normative school[47] and those authors that subscribe to a hybrid view combining realist and normative theories.[48]

The first relates to whether or not follow-up efforts were undertaken by the African Commission in an effort to ensure state compliance with its recommendations.[49] It was found that in the majority of the case sample where full compliance was recorded, the Commission made some attempt at following up on the steps taken by the relevant state parties to implement its recommendations. The opposite was true in the case sample of non-compliant states. It could, therefore, be deduced that the existence of a follow-up mechanism may lead to increased state compliance. In the past, the Commission has used avenues available to it as part of its broader promotional and protective mandate, such as state reporting or promotional visits, to enquire as to compliance with its decisions under the individual complaints system. These efforts were, however, few and far apart and no formal follow-up system had been adopted as is the case in the United Nations or Inter-American human rights systems discussed above.

In May 2010, during the Forty-seventh Ordinary Session, the African Commission, for the first time, took steps towards formalizing its follow-up efforts by adopting amended Rules of Procedure, which made specific provisions for establishing follow-up to its decisions under Rule 112. As indicated above, the Commission adopted an amended set of Rules of Procedure in 2020, with Rule 125 now outlining the follow-up steps to be taken, including allowing national human rights institutions to monitor or facilitate implementation. A reading of Rule 125 and its predecessor Rule 112 makes it clear that the Commission expects state parties to implement its findings. The adoption of these rules signals another step taken by the African Commission in the progressive interpretation of its mandate in consideration of individual communications. Only time will tell whether state parties took note of this new development in strengthening the Commission's mandate and whether states will actually cooperate in the follow-up efforts of the Commission. Initial indications are that since the Commission adopted the practice of reporting on compliance with its decisions in its Activity Reports, as from 2014, it had recorded one case of blatant refusal to comply,[50] one case of full compliance,[51] three cases of partial compliance[52] and for the majority a lack of feedback from state parties.[53]

[46] See eg OA Hathaway, 'Do Human Rights Treaties Make a Difference?' (2002) 111 Yale Law Journal 1935 and LR Helfer and A Slaughter, 'Toward a Theory of Supranational Adjudication' (1997) 107 YLJ 331–335.

[47] See eg A Chayes and AH Chayes, *The New Sovereignty: Compliance with International Regulatory Agreements* (1995) and TM Franck, 'Legitimacy in the International System' (1988) 82 AJIL 67.

[48] See eg HH Koh 'Why Do Nations Obey International Law?' 106 YLJ (1997) 2599.

[49] Viljoen and Louw (2007) s 4.1(f).

[50] Against Botswana, see fn 8 above.

[51] Cameroon, see fn 24 above.

[52] See fn 25 to 27 above.

[53] See fn 22 above.

In 2017, the Commission organized a *Regional Seminar on Implementation of the Decisions of the Commission* for countries of Central, North and West Africa.[54] As noted above, the Commission has, in the past, in reviewing its work after ten years and then again after 16 years, made attempts at highlighting the lack of compliance by state parties with its recommendations issued under the individual complaints mechanism.[55] It appears as though the Regional Seminar, which took place 30 years into the existence of the Commission, represented an even greater focus on highlighting challenges with the implementation of the decisions of the Commission (which is not limited to recommendations under the individual complaints system) and formulating recommendations to address those identified challenges.[56] The establishment of a follow-up mechanism to monitor state compliance seems to have been embraced by the African Commission and other participants at the Regional Seminar.[57] Commissioner Reine Alapini Gansou, in addressing the Seminar, stated that 'the Commission is committed to improving the situation (regarding implementation of decisions) and is currently working on an implementation database and strategy to be able to systematically monitor compliance and keep updated records, in addition to developing collaborative relations with NHRIs, NGOs and other actors who can assist in collection and publication of information'.[58]

In 2018, a further Regional Seminar was organized for the countries of Southern and East Africa on the implementation of decisions of the Commission. In addressing the Seminar, Prof Frans Viljoen recorded the need for a comprehensive approach to implementation to be adopted, with a dedicated unit within the Commission's Secretariat taking responsibility for monitoring compliance.[59] The latter was subsequently adopted as one of the recommendations to emanate from the meeting.[60] Among other challenges identified in relation to the lack of monitoring mechanisms, the Seminar identified an absence of guidelines to assist the

[54] *Report of the Regional Seminar* fn 9 above.

[55] See the discussion under s 2 above.

[56] *Report of the Regional Seminar* fn 9 above.

[57] As part of the challenges identified by the Regional Seminar in relation to the Commission, it noted specifically the lack of monitoring mechanisms and, in turn, made the following detailed recommendations to address this challenge: 'Include a provision on monitoring of decisions in its Rules of Procedure; Institutionalise a mechanism to monitor the implementation of its recommendations and decisions; Establish an effective and systematic implementation process for implementation of provisional measures adopted by the Commission; Develop a database with up-to-date information on the status of implementation of decisions by State parties; Evaluate every two years, the level of implementation of its decisions; Continuously report on the non-implementation of its decisions to the policy organs, to enable the Executive Council to urge States to comply; Develop Guidelines to assist the various stakeholders in monitoring the implementation of its decisions/recommendations;'. As above at par B(b)(iii), 9.

[58] As above at para 9, 3.

[59] *Report of the Second Regional Seminar on the Implementation of Decisions of the African Commission on Human and Peoples' Rights*, 4–6 September 2018, Zanzibar, Tanzania, 3. (Available at: https://www.achpr.org/news/viewdetail?id=3; accessed on 24 November 2020).

[60] As above, 10.

various stakeholders in monitoring the implementation of the Commission's recommendations.[61] Participants also recommended that the Commission should continuously report on the non-implementation of its decisions to policy organs to enable the Executive Council to urge state parties to comply.[62]

The role of follow-up in ensuring state compliance could also be explained in terms of the normative theory on state compliance. The normative school, as opposed to the realist school, bases its theories on state compliance with international law on the normative framework put in place by the founding treaty.[63] Another group of factors, also closely associated with the founding treaty, relate to the treaty body system put in place by the treaty.[64] In terms of the normative theory, the provision of a formalized system on follow-up, as part of the features of the African Commission, could lead to increased interaction by state parties with the system, which may, in turn, lead to greater compliance.

The second set of 'variable' factors that influence state compliance relate to the state party. These factors could be explained under the realist school of thought on state compliance with international law. The realist school includes theories on structural realism, institutionalism and liberalism, which differ primarily according to Hathaway 'in the types and sources of interests that they claim motivate country decisions'.[65] The realist school holds that states comply with international law not based on the obligations that arise out of the ratification of a treaty but out of self-interest. According to the theory of liberalism, state behaviour in the international sphere is directly informed by a state's domestic system of governance.[66] Therefore, factors that could influence state compliance would also be based on state interest, but in this instance, state interest is determined by its domestic political policies.

Based on the above-mentioned 2005 empirical analysis of state compliance in the African regional human rights system, the system of governance and level of political stability within a state plays a role in as far as a stable, open and free democratic system was found to be more conducive to compliance.[67] Whereas non-compliance with the Commission's recommendations took place in countries affected at the time by high levels of political instability under authoritarian rule. The importance of filing complaints under regional or international human rights systems during periods of instability in a particular government would seem to lie in the fact that these complaints were not lodged in an effort to necessarily receive the

[61] As above, 7.
[62] As above, 10.
[63] Chayes and Chayes (1995) 2.
[64] Refer to the managerial model formulated by the Chayeses according to which states obey international law not out of fear of sanctions but due to their interaction with the system put in place through the normative framework of the founding treaty (Chayes and Chayes (1995) 2).
[65] Hathaway (2002) 1944.
[66] Hathaway (2002) 1953.
[67] Viljoen and Louw (2007) s 4.4(a).

relief asked for but rather to mount international pressure in an effort to oust the non-democratic government of the day.[68]

The Regional Seminar held in 2017 also identified challenges with the implementation of the Commission's decisions concerning state parties and formulated responses to such, but these were not in relation to the system of governance or the level of political stability in place, probably due to the participation of state parties in the formulation of the said challenges and recommendations. The challenges identified by the gathering rather focused on practical problems experienced by states in relation to institutional and financial limitations, a lack of knowledge on the functioning of the Commission[69] and a lack of effective communication between the Commission and state parties.[70] Similar challenges were identified by the second Regional Seminar.[71] Addressing these challenges is important in relation to countries where there is already a system of governance in place to encourage compliance, and the level of political stability is supportive of compliance, but addressing these practical challenges in state parties where the former is lacking, will not have any impact in light of the findings of the empirical analysis of state compliance referred to above.

The second Regional Seminar, held in 2018, also focused on practical aspects of state party involvement to ensure implementation on a national level, with Prof Rachel Murray citing best practices in those states where ministerial engagement, through for instance Inter-Ministerial Committees, resulted in implementation.[72] She further stressed the need for governments to assign the responsibility internally to specific role players to coordinate implementation.[73]

The final set of 'variable' factors found to impact state compliance relate to the role played by civil society, in particular by NGOs[74] who may apply for observer status with the African Commission. In the majority of cases of full compliance with the recommendations of the African Commission, the communications were lodged by NGOs. NGOs also played a significant role in following up on the actions or in-actions of states in instances where state parties had violated the provisions of the African Charter. Going forward, the activist role played by NGOs will be

[68] In 2011, the African Court on Human and Peoples' Rights ordered provisional measures against Libya amidst ongoing conflict in that country, which the Court described as a 'situation of extreme gravity and urgency', which posed 'a risk of irreparable harm to persons who are the subject of the application'. (*African Commission on Human and Peoples' Rights v Great Socialist Peoples' Libyan Arab Jamahiriya*, Application No 004/2011). In light of the role played by factors relating to the state party to compliance, it should be no surprise that the Libyan government did not heed these provisional measures. At the same time, the importance of the Court's ruling as part of ongoing regional pressure for a change in government should not be discarded.

[69] After 30 years of the existence of the Commission, it is unfortunate that a lack of knowledge of its operations can still be highlighted as a challenge to state parties.

[70] *Report of the Regional Seminar* fn 9 above, 5–6 and 8–9.

[71] *Report of the Second Regional Seminar* fn 60 above, 6.

[72] *Report of the Second Regional Seminar* fn 60 above, 3–4.

[73] As above.

[74] Viljoen and Louw (2007) discussion under s 4.5(a).

important in developing the Commission's follow-up efforts under Rule 125 of the Rules of Procedure.[75] It would appear that the role played by NGOs in contributing to state compliance could be explained in terms of both the realist and normative theories on state compliance. In terms of the realist school, factors associated with a democratic political order, such as freedom of association and freedom of expression, could result in NGOs and civil society pressurizing states to comply with their international obligations arising from treaty body findings.[76] The role played by NGOs is, however, also explained by supporters of the normative theory, in as far as it is reasoned that the treaty body framework put in place by the founding treaty is not limited to the treaty body and state parties, but also involves other role players such as NGOs, civil society and the international community. The resultant interaction between these various role players within the treaty framework also influences state compliance.[77]

Apart from the factors that form part of the permanent features of the African Commission and those 'variable' factors discussed above, a final mention must also be made of factors that influence state compliance under the hybrid theory on state compliance with international law. According to this school, factors that influence state compliance are based on the internationalization of the treaty norms in the domestic legal system of a state party.[78] In effect, this translates into an argument that state compliance is influenced by the level of domestic incorporation of a treaty, whether it has been domesticated through the adoption of legislation, whether domestic courts rely on treaty provisions to interpret legal problems domestically, or whether treaty body findings can be enforced or implemented through domestic courts. The latter would require the adoption of enabling legislation by a state party.

Gutto listed the 'weak incorporation of international agreements in the domestic legal system and/or popular political space' as a factor that affects state

[75] The Regional Seminar of 2017 also acknowledged the importance of NGOs in ensuring the implementation of the Commission's recommendations through sustained advocacy and engagement. *Report of the Regional Seminar* fn 9 above, 11. The second Regional Seminar of 2018, similarly, focused on challenges facing NGOs such as limited funding, limited understanding of the work of the Commission and shrinking civic space and thus formulated a number of recommendations concerning the dissemination of information at a national level, organizational capacity and cooperation with the Commission. *Report of the second Regional Seminar* fn 60 above, 8, 12. Mention must also be made of National Human Rights Institutions (NHRI), especially since the 2020 Rules of Procedure now specifically envisages a role to be played in the monitoring and facilitating implementation by these institutions. NHRIs were also identified by both regional seminars as important role players in the national sphere to promote cooperation with the Commission and, ultimately, awareness of the decisions of the Commission. See, for instance, *Report of the second Regional Seminar* fn 60 above, 11–12.

[76] According to Helfer and Slaughter, '[l]iberal democratic governments will be more likely to comply with supranational legal judgments than are other states because international legal obligations mobilise domestic interest groups that in turn pressure the government to comply' (LR Helfer and A Slaughter (1997) 331–335).

[77] Chayes and Chayes (1995) 25.

[78] Koh (1997) 2599, 2655–2656.

compliance with international agreements.[79] In the African system, the African Charter should theoretically have direct force in Francophone and Lusophone countries in line with the monist traditions applied in those countries. According to the monist theory, treaties duly ratified by a state party form part of national law without necessitating any further incorporation through national legislation.[80] In countries following the dualist approach to international law, in Africa, these are mostly the countries with common law traditions, where treaty provisions have to be incorporated into domestic law to have any direct effect before domestic courts.[81] However, such stark delineations of monist and dualist traditions are not applied in practice.

Another factor is whether specific 'enabling legislation' has been adopted by a state party to provide for the domestic implementation of treaty body findings. Schmidt explained that 'enabling laws' are laws 'under which decisions of UN human rights treaty bodies and regional human rights instances are given legal status'.[82] The Committee, in its Annual Report, regularly lists the absence of specific enabling legislation as a 'crucial factor which often stands in the way of monetary compensation to victims of violations of the Covenant, or the granting of other remedies based on the Committee's views'.[83] The Committee furthermore 'urges state parties to consider the adoption of specific enabling legislation and, pending that, to make *ex gratia* payments by way of compensation'.[84]

In general, no such enabling legislation exists in the domestic law of African countries. In Communication 231/99, against Burundi, the Commission

[79] SBO Gutto, 'The Rule of Law, Human and Peoples' Rights and Compliance/Non-Compliance with Regional and International Agreements and Standards by African States' 6, a paper prepared for presentation at the African Forum for Envisioning Africa held in Nairobi, Kenya, 26–29 April 2002. Available at: http://www.worldsummit2002.org/texts/ShadrackGutto2.pdf.

[80] MN Shaw, *International Law* (1986) 98.

[81] JG Starke, *Introduction to International Law* (1984) 68.

[82] Schmidt (2000) 241.

[83] See the *Report of the Human Rights Committee*, Official Records of the General Assembly, 51st Session, Supplement No 40 (A/51/40) para 432. The HRC mentioned that the government of Austria (in its follow-up reply on the views in case no 415/1990) and the government of Senegal (in reference to case no 386/1989) argued that the absence of enabling legislation meant that they could not implement the Committee's views. Padilla, a specialist on the Inter-American human rights system, addressing NGOs during the 32nd ordinary session of the African Commission, mentioned that one of the legal obstacles hindering implementation is the lack of domestic legislation that provides for the implementation of the decisions of treaty bodies. He referred to Law No 288 (1996) of Columbia that specifically provided for implementing decisions in the Inter-American system. Dr Padilla addressed NGOs on the follow-up to the decisions of the African Commission on 16 October 2002 in Banjul, The Gambia (notes on file with author).

[84] *Report of the Human Rights Committee*, Official Records of the General Assembly, 51st Session, Supplement No 40 (A/51/40) para 432. Peru was the first country to enact enabling legislation in 1985 and undertook to cooperate with international and regional human rights treaty bodies and implement their decisions. Schmidt, however, reported that Peru 'rescinded' the enabling legislation under the government of President Alberto Fujimori in 1996 (Schmidt (2000) 241). In 1996, Columbia also adopted enabling legislation to provide for the implementation of the findings of both the UN Human Rights Committee and the Inter-American Commission and Court on Human Rights (See para 433 of the *Report of the Human Rights Committee*, Official Records of the General Assembly, 51st Session, Supplement No 40 (A/51/40)).

recommended that Burundi should 'take appropriate measures to allow the reopening of the file and the reconsideration of the case in conformity with the laws of Burundi and the pertinent provision of the African Charter'.[85] However, due to the fact that Burundi's domestic legislation did not provide for the reopening of criminal cases, the Commission's recommendations could not be implemented.[86]

The African Commission regularly calls on the Member States to domesticate the provisions of the human rights treaties to which it is a party.[87] The Commission should continue these efforts in regard to the adoption of enabling legislation as part of its follow-up efforts under Rule 125 of the Rules of Procedure. The Regional Seminar held in 2017 also specifically recommended that state parties domesticate regional and international treaties that they have ratified and enact the necessary laws to promote the effective implementation of decisions of the Commission without going through the AU political process.[88] The second Regional Seminar of 2018 specifically cited the non-harmonization of national laws in accordance with regional/international law as one of the institutional challenges facing state parties.[89] To this end, the participants recommended that state parties take all necessary measures to implement the Charter through integrating it in their Constitutional and legislative provisions rather than focusing on the non-binding nature of decisions of the Commission.[90]

5 Conclusion

When the empirical study of 2005 was undertaken to measure state compliance with the recommendations of the African Commission, there were no other data or measurement tools available at the time to confirm the overall sense of non-compliance among the Member States. A brief overview of reporting done by the Commission itself, since the adoption of a follow-up mechanism in its 2010 Rules

[85] Communication no 231/99 *Avocats Sans Frontieres (on behalf of Gaetan Bwampamye) v Burundi*, 14th Annual Activity Report, final paragraph.

[86] *l'Association Burundaise pour la Defense des Droits des Prisonniers* (ABDP), an NGO based in Bujumbura, Burundi, reported that it had lobbied for the implementation of the Commission's recommendations. However, in the absence of any domestic legislation to provide for the reopening of criminal cases, its efforts were to no avail. In order to ensure that criminal cases could in future be reopened on the domestic level, following a decision by an international judicial institution or a quasi-supranational institution, ABDP on 3 September 2004 approached the Parliament of Burundi to amend the existing legislation (Interview with ABDP held by Frans Viljoen at the 36th Ordinary Session of the African Commission in Dakar, Senegal).

[87] The Commission makes such calls upon the Member States by means of its Annual Activity Reports. For instance, the 31st Annual Activity Report provides as follows in para 39, 'Further to this, the African Commission is also concerned about the low rate of implementation and domestication of those regional and international human rights instruments that have been ratified by State Parties, as this impedes the realization of human and peoples' rights on the continent'.

[88] *Report of the Regional Seminar* fn 9 above, 8.

[89] *Report of the second Regional Seminar* fn 60 above, 6.

[90] As above, 9.

of Procedure, still shows only one case of full compliance to date and three cases of partial compliance over the last ten years.

However, there should not be despair amongst the observers of this system as a lot has changed since 2005, which seems to set the scene for improved compliance and monitoring of compliance going forward. There is now a follow-up mechanism spelled out in the Rules of Procedure of the Commission, first adopted in 2010 and since improved upon in 2020. The Commission has since 2014 started to report on compliance with its decisions in individual communications, amongst others, in its Activity Reports.[91] These reports are tabled and adopted at the bi-annual sittings of the AU. There are now continent-wide discussions and debates on the need for compliance with the decisions of the Commission, which did not take place when the empirical study was undertaken in 2005. Two regional seminars held in recent years managed to succinctly capture not only the challenges facing the various role players but also resulted in the formulation of clear-cut recommendations to work towards the implementation of the recommendations/decisions of the Commission.

Factors relating to the state party play an important role in influencing state compliance. The continued pursuance of the African Commission's broader promotional and protective mandate is central to ensuring that the principles underlying stable, open, free and democratic governance are embedded in the governance systems of the Member States. Promoting stability and good governance on the continent will ultimately create a system where states will comply with their regional human rights commitments as a result of first committing to the protection of human and peoples' rights within their own territories.[92]

In the meantime, the challenges identified and recommendations formulated at the recent regional seminars should not be allowed to gather dust but be part

[91] As indicated above, both the United Nations Human Rights Committee and the Inter-American Commission on Human Rights include specific tables showing the level of state compliance in their annual reports, making it possible to not only empirically report on the level of compliance, but also track compliance on an ongoing basis. Analysis of how the African Commission currently reports on compliance in its Activity Reports since the adoption of Rule 112 and now Rule 125 of its Rules of Procedure shows that there is still much room for improvement. There will most likely only be proper monitoring if, as is suggested by the second regional seminar above, the Commission appoints a dedicated unit to do this work in its Secretariat. As a start, the Commission could consider attaching a table as an annexure to its Activity Reports listing all communications issued since 1987 and clearly showing the status of compliance for all State Parties.

[92] State compliance with the decisions of the European Commission of Human Rights, before a single Court replaced it, was often described as remarkably good. This led commentators to conclude that 'the success of the European system may be attributed in large part to the fact that there were more "good guys" than "bad guys"'. LF Zwaak, 'The Effects of Final Decisions of the Supervisory Organs Under the European Convention on Human Rights' in AF Bayefsky, (2000) 272. Merrills and Robertson echoed this sentiment by stating that 'the European system was able to function effectively because the governments concerned were willing to co-operate with the Convention organs and genuinely wished to secure the effective exercise of human rights within their territories' (JG Merrills and AH Robertson, *Human Rights in Europe – A Study of the European Convention on Human Rights* (2001) 296).

of a larger debate that involves all stakeholders on the continent to keep the focus on the implementation of the decisions of the Commission. Ultimately, the aim should be for open reporting on state compliance and discussions thereof at the level of the AU, with a General Assembly resolution calling for state compliance and follow-up to the recommendations of the Commission.

8
'Horizontal' Compliance with Decisions of the African Court on Human and Peoples' Rights

Adem K Abebe

1 Introduction

Compliance with decisions and orders of international, continental, sub-regional and other supranational human rights is key to the added value, success, effectiveness and legitimacy of the human rights systems in which they operate. Compliance with decisions of supranational tribunals is also necessary to build their reputation, which, in turn, contributes to their autonomy and independence. While challenges of compliance exist at the domestic level, international tribunals face particularly more complex contexts emanating from their loose connection with the domestic political and judicial institutional set-up.

In the African context, scholars have studied the levels of compliance with decisions of the African Commission on Human and Peoples' Rights (African Commission or the Commission), the African Court on Human and Peoples' Rights (African Court or the Court), the African Committee on the Rights and Welfare of the Child (Committee on the Rights of the Child or the Committee), the ECOWAS Court of Justice and other courts of sub-regional economic communities.[1] These studies have relied on or developed a framework to assess compliance, identified the exact levels of compliance and developed complex explanations on the various factors affecting the level of compliance, from the nature of the remedy ordered to the institutional and political context in the relevant countries.

The existing scholarship mainly focuses on what may be called 'vertical' compliance, where the target of the assessment is the specific country that has violated the African Charter on Human and Peoples' Rights and other relevant human rights instruments. This chapter relies on the experiences of the African Court to

[1] Roger-Claude Liwanga, 'From Commitment to Compliance: Enforceability of Remedial Orders of African Human Rights Bodies' (2015) 41(1) Brook J Int Law 99; Frans Viljoen and Lirette Louw, 'State Compliance with the Recommendations of the African Commission on Human and Peoples' Rights: 1994–2004'(2007) 101 AJIL 5.

Adem K Abebe, *'Horizontal' Compliance with Decisions of the African Court on Human and Peoples' Rights*
In: *Compliance with International Human Rights Law in Africa*. Edited by: Aderomola Adeola, Oxford University Press.
 DOI: 10.1093/oso/9780192856999.003.0008

introduce a novel idea to the discourse of compliance—'horizontal' compliance—in relation to decisions of international tribunals that touch on the validity of legal provisions, beyond the specific remedies to correct the violations of the rights of the applicant, such as release from imprisonment, reparation, reinstatement of the pre-violation situation and moral remedies, such as formal apologies.

While most decisions of international, continental and sub-regional human rights tribunals relate to specific remedies connected to the situation of the applicant, there are also instances where the tribunals rule on the compatibility of the legal framework of the relevant country with human rights standards. As comparable legal frameworks, unlike individual circumstances, can exist in countries other than the respondent state, cases dealing with the validity of such frameworks raise the issue of whether the decisions should have relevance and authority to countries that are not a party to the relevant case. For instance, the African Court has held in a case against Burkina Faso that sentences of imprisonment for defamation cases are incompatible with freedom of expression.[2] As many other African countries, which are parties to the African Charter, provide similar legal provisions, the decision must have some implications for those countries. There is, therefore, an issue of ensuring 'horizontal' compliance, which has largely escaped scholarly attention, certainly in the African context.

Section 2 briefly explains the concepts of vertical and horizontal compliance. Section 3 discusses significant decisions of the African Court involving the compatibility of domestic legal provisions with continental human rights standards, beyond specific cases of violation of the rights of the applicant. Section 4 discusses how this notable jurisprudential approach may necessitate or at least make possible horizontal compliance to enhance the efficacy, impact and visibility of the African Charter and African Court. Section 5 explores how 'horizontal' compliance can help bypass the limited individual and NGOs avenues of access to the African Court. Section six discusses how under the current legal framework, horizontal compliance can be operationalized. Section seven concludes the chapter.

2 Vertical and Horizontal Compliance

Studies of compliance with decisions of supranational human rights entities primarily focus on the extent to which the respondent country, which has been found in violation of the relevant supranational human rights standards, has complied fully, partially or not at all—referred to here as 'vertical' compliance. Related work focuses on why countries choose to subscribe to international human rights standards and the conditions under which they are more or less likely to comply

[2] *Konaté v Burkina Faso*, Application No 004/2013 (African Court 5 December 2014).

with these standards, including when the standards have been enunciated in specific cases.

The focus of studies on compliance in the respondent country is understandable. As a matter of accepted international law, decisions of international tribunals, including human rights tribunals, are binding only on the parties to the case. Specifically, the Protocol to the African Charter on Human and Peoples' Rights Establishing the African Court on Human and Peoples' Rights[3] imposes a duty of compliance and execution of judgments on Member States to the Protocol only 'in any case to which they are parties'.[4]

Moreover, human rights cases in international tribunals generally focus on violations of the rights of the applicants through final judicial or executive decisions. The decisions and individual circumstances cannot, therefore, be exported to other cases in other countries. Essentially, the decisions and remedies granted cannot be delinked from the specific applicant and respondent country. In some cases, such as the European Court on Human Rights, the tribunal must focus on the compatibility of a state decision with fundamental rights and may not be allowed to rule on the legal basis of the decision.[5] Indeed, in cases of repeat applications, resulting from violations rooted in the regular application of a legal framework, the European Court has resorted to 'pilot' judgments where it initiates a voluntary arrangement with the relevant country to reform the source of the violations without actually finding the source of the violation incompatible with the European Human Rights Convention.[6]

The specificity of human rights decisions and remedies generally obtains in Africa as well. At the same time, the African Court, as well as the African Commission[7] and the African Committee on the Rights and Welfare of the Child,[8] have rules on the key issues concerning the compatibility of legal frameworks with continental human rights standards, beyond requested for specific remedies, such as reparation, release from imprisonment, ending of bans on publishing or

[3] Protocol to the African Charter on Human and Peoples' Rights Establishing the African Court on Human and Peoples' Rights (1998).

[4] ibid, art 30.

[5] Alec Stone Sweet, *On the Constitutionalisation of the Convention: The European Court of Human Rights as a Constitutional Court* (2009) Yale Law School Faculty Scholarship Series 71.

[6] Dominik Haider, *The Pilot-Judgment Procedure of the European Court of Human Rights* (Brill 2013).

[7] For instance, the Commission has found the composition of the Judicial Service Commission of Cameroon, headed by the president and where the minister of justice is a key member, incompatible with the requirements of judicial independence—*Kevin Mgwanga Gunme et al v Cameroon*, Communication 266/03 (May 2009).

[8] For instance, the Committee was expected to find a provision of the Malawian Constitution that included a lower age limit for the definition of the child incompatible with the African Charter on the Rights and Welfare of the Child. Subsequently, the Committee agreed to the withdrawal of the case after Malawi undertook to amend the Constitution to correct the legal problem, which was subsequently implemented—Luke Bisani, Malawi MPs Change Law to End Child Marriage, MALAWI24, 15 February 2017, https://malawi24.com/2017/02/15/malawi-mps-change-law-end-child-marriage/ accessed 25 November 2020.

reinstatement of the situation prior to the violation. In cases where the focus is on the compatibility of a legal provision with continental human rights standards, beyond the circumstances of the individual applicant, the decision can have relevance for issues of compliance beyond the respondent state. As legal provisions can more easily be compared across borders and legal systems, decisions involving their validity have a bearing on countries with comparable legal frameworks to the respondent state.

The vertical compliance regime is inadequate to capture the broader implications of decisions invalidating legal provisions. To have a more complete understanding of such decisions, it is helpful also to consider how countries with comparable legal provisions to the one that was found incompatible respond to the judgment. Here is where the concept of horizontal compliance comes in. An assessment of horizontal compliance provides a useful complement to measurements of vertical compliance. It is, therefore, crucial to examine how continental human rights tribunals, particularly the African Court and their partners, have and/or can pursue horizontal compliance.

3 The African Court as a Constitutional Court for Africa and Opportunities for Horizontal Compliance

The African Court is the sole judicial organ at the continental level dealing with human rights issues. Although the African Union (AU) Constitutive Act anticipates the establishment of a Court of Justice, it is yet to be constituted. Moreover, as at August 2021, a Protocol that seeks to merge the African Court and the Court of Justice has only received seven ratifications, eight fewer than the minimum required for the new Court's establishment.[9] Although it started slowly, the Court has issued critical judgments with significant implications. Notably, the Court has asserted its authority not only to assess the compatibility of state judicial and administrative decisions as they relate to the specific applicant, with continental human rights standards, but it has also reviewed the compatibility of legal frameworks, including constitutional provisions. In this regard, the Court has emerged as a unique supranational judicial organ, certainly compared to the European Court, but also in comparison with the Inter-American Court of Human Rights. The lack of reluctance to review the validity of laws has led to its characterization as a '(super)Constitutional Court for Africa', with the authority to review not only laws but also constitutional provisions and amendments.[10]

[9] Protocol on the Statute of the African Court of Justice and Human Rights—available at: https://au.int/en/treaties/protocol-statute-african-court-justice-and-human-rights accessed 24 August 2021.

[10] Adem K Abebe, 'Taming Regressive Constitutional Amendments: The African Court as a Continental (super) Constitutional Court' (2019) 17(1) Int J Const Law 89.

In its first judgment on merits, the African Court found unconstitutional the provision banning independent candidates from local, parliamentary and presidential elections in Tanzania.[11] The case reached the African Court after a number of domestic legal processes. The High Court of Tanzania initially found a legislative ban on independent candidates incompatible with the constitutional right to political participation, specifically the right to stand for elections. The government initially appealed the decision to the Supreme Court of Appeal. But before the appeal was finalized, the government successfully pushed through a constitutional amendment banning independent candidates. This amendment was then challenged in the High Court, which found it unconstitutional, based on an implied hierarchy among the provisions of the Constitution, with fundamental rights sitting on top. The government appealed the decision, and the Supreme Court of Appeal reversed the High Court judgment and ruled that all provisions of the Tanzanian Constitution could be amended as long as the prescribed procedure was followed. The Court also rejected any implied limits on the power of amendment based on the 'basic structure doctrine' well developed in the Indian Supreme Court jurisprudence.

When the case reached the African Court, the Court did not have to face the same dilemmas as the Supreme Court of Tanzania. As a supranational tribunal, the Court considers the legal system of a country as subordinate to the continental framework. It was, therefore, not affected by the constitutional status of the ban. The Court ruled that the ban on independent candidacy violated the individual right to equal protection of the law and the prohibition against discrimination, the right to association, which specifically includes the right not to associate, and the right to political participation guaranteed in the African Charter. The Court also held that Tanzania did not satisfactorily argue that the ban on independent candidacy served a legitimate interest. In any case, the Court found that the absolute ban on independent candidacy was disproportional to any stated aim of fostering national unity and solidarity. The Court ordered Tanzania to review relevant provisions of the Constitution. While the decision is yet to be implemented, draft constitutional provisions developed as part of the constitutional reform process could allow independent candidacy, although the reform process has stalled following the postponement of the constitutional referendum initially planned for 30 April 2015. The case represents the first time a supranational tribunal prohibited bans on independent candidates. In fact, it directly contradicted the conclusions of an earlier decision of the Inter-American Court of Human Rights that a Mexican ban

[11] *Mtikila and Others v Republic of Tanzania*, Application Nos 009/2011 and 011/2011, Judgment of 14 June 2013, available at: http://www.african-court.org/en/images/Cases/Judgment/Judgment%20Application%20009-011-2011%20Rev%20Christopher%20Mtikila%20v.%20Tanzania-1.pdf accessed 24 August 2021.

on independent presidential candidates did not violate relevant guarantees in the American Convention on Human Rights.[12]

In a case against Cote d'Ivoire, the Court was confronted with the question of the compatibility of the Composition of the Independent Electoral Commission with continental standards, notably guarantees of independence and impartiality of election management bodies in the African Charter on Democracy, Elections and Governance and the ECOWAS Protocol on Good Governance and Democracy.[13] The Court ruled that the composition of the Commission with representatives of political parties and office-holders violated the principle of impartiality. It also ruled that the disproportionate representation of the ruling party and the head of executive in the Commission, compared to representatives of opposition groups, violated not only the independence and impartiality of the Commission but also the principle of equality before the law. Côte d'Ivoire reviewed the composition of the Commission in 2019, more than five years after the date of the decision of the Court. While the ruling party and opposition balance is better than the previous arrangement, the revised law retains the system of political representation, found to be incompatible with the principle of impartiality.[14]

In another case involving Burkina Faso, the African Court found that legal provisions providing for sentences of imprisonment for the crime of defamation were incompatible with the African Charter, therefore necessitating non-custodial sentences.[15] Four of the Court's judges added dissenting opinions finding the crime of defamation incompatible with the freedom of expression, thus suggesting that civil suits should replace criminal defamation laws. The Court, therefore, ordered the country to review the relevant criminal laws to remove sentences of imprisonment for defamation cases. In addition, the Court ruled that the requirements to hold a press-card, which can be equated to licensing requirements, to practise journalism were incompatible with the freedom of expression.[16] This was in addition to finding violations of the rights of the specific journalist imprisoned for defamation and granting of an order for compensation.

In 2019, the African Court found that the inclusion of mandatory death penalty sentences in Tanzania in relation to certain crimes, which requires judges to

[12] Case of *Castañeda Gutman v Mexico*, Inter-American Court on Human Rights, Judgment of 6 August 2008.

[13] *Actions Pour la Protection des Droits de L'Homme (APDH) v The Republic of Cote d'Ivoire*, Application No 001/2014, Judgment of 18 November 2016, available at: http://www.african-court.org/en/images/Cases/Judgment/JUDGMENT_APPLICATION%20001%202014%20_%20APDH%20V.%20THE%20REPUBLIC%20OF%20COTE%20DIVOIRE.pdf accessed 24 August 2021.

[14] Pierre Olivier Lobe, 'Cote d'Ivoire's Contested Electoral Commission and Ouattara's Third Term: A Recipe for Political Crisis?', ConstitutionNet, 5 November 2019, http://constitutionnet.org/news/cote-divoires-contested-electoral-commission-and-ouattaras-third-term-recipe-political-crisis accessed 24 August 2021.

[15] *Konaté v Burkina Faso*, n 2 above.

[16] Matt J Duffy, '*Konate v Burkina Faso*: An Analysis of a Landmark Ruling on Criminal Defamation in Africa' (2016) 6(1) J Int'l Media & Ent Law 1, 6.

impose death sentences if the material facts of murder have been proven, was found to be 'automatic and mechanical' and, therefore, incompatible with the right to life, and also principles of fairness, due process and judicial impendence.[17] Tanzania is unlikely to amend its laws in line with the decision of the African Court. A few days before the official delivery of the judgment, the Tanzanian government submitted a letter to the AU withdrawing the declaration allowing individuals and NGOs to submit cases before the Court.[18] Although this declaration applies prospectively and, therefore, does not affect the validity of the judgment, it signals the lack of political will towards implementation. Nevertheless, there is still a possibility that Tanzanian domestic courts may refuse to hand mandatory death sentences in view of the decision of the African Court.

The above decisions are notable in that the African Court not only ruled in favour of the specific applicants but also invalidated the legal provisions that provided the basis for decisions. Crucially, the cases concerned legal provisions that similarly exist in the statute books of other African countries that have ratified the African Charter and are parties to the Protocol establishing the Court. For instance, South Africa bans independent candidates from running for provincial and national legislative elections, although they may run in local elections. Similarly, independent candidates are prohibited from running for elections in Nigeria. Electoral commissions in many Francophone (eg Cote d'Ivoire and Togo) and Lusophone African countries (eg Mozambique) include a significant number of representatives of political parties, which the African Court has found to be incompatible with continental standards of independence and impartiality of election management bodies. Sentences of imprisonment for defamation are also still prevalent across Africa.[19] Finally, mandatory death sentences also exist in the statute books of many African countries.[20] As such, while the Court's interpretations should be considered seriously and are relevant in all cases, they are particularly crucial in cases of decisions on the validity of legal provisions. Interestingly, despite these similarities in legal frameworks, no country requested to intervene as an interested third party. Such interventions are quite common at the European Court level.[21]

[17] *Ally Rajabu and Others v United Republic of Tanzania*, Application No 007/2015, 28 November 2019 https://en.african-court.org/index.php/56-pending-cases-details/873-app-no-007-2015-ally-rajabu-and-others-v-united-republic-of-tanzania-details accessed 24 August 2021.

[18] 'Alarm as Tanzania Blocks Cases from African Rights Court' Al Jazeera, 4 December 2019 https://www.aljazeera.com/news/2019/12/alarm-tanzania-blocks-cases-african-rights-court-191204162424981.html accessed 24 August 2021. This makes Tanzania the second country to withdraw the art 34(1) declaration, following Rwanda, which withdrew the declaration in 2016.

[19] Pen International 'Resolution on Criminal Defamation in Africa', available at https://pen-international.org/app/uploads/RESOLUTION-ON-CRIMINAL-DEFAMATION-IN-AFRICA.pdf accessed 25 November 2020.

[20] Andrew Novak, 'The Abolition of the Mandatory Death Penalty in Africa: A Comparative Constitutional Analysis' (2012) 22 Ind Int'l & Comp L Rev 267.

[21] Nicole Bürli, *Third-Party Intervention Before the European Court of Human Rights* (2017, Intersentia) ch 3.

Accordingly, in addition to the issue of compliance of the specific respondent state with the decision of the African Court, as required in the Protocol establishing the Court, these decisions invalidating legal provisions (whether constitutional statutory or even executive decrees and customary laws) raise the issue of horizontal compliance by other Member States to the African Charter with similar or comparable legal frameworks. A resort to horizontal compliance in these cases would avoid the submission of similar cases to the African Court, with limited possibility, if any, for a variant decision. Considering the long time it takes to decide each case, the Court and key stakeholders should preferably engage in initiatives to pursue horizontal compliance. This requires the Court to identify the relevant countries with similar or comparable legal provisions and craft modalities of engagement.

4 Horizontal Compliance as a Means to Bypass Challenges of Access to the Court

One of the major challenges, decried by scholars and practitioners alike, to the effectiveness of the African Court is the limited access of individuals and NGOs to the Court.[22] The Protocol establishing the Court allows only the African Commission, a state party which is an applicant or a respondent in a case before the African Commission, a state party whose citizen is a victim of human rights violations and 'African Intergovernmental Organizations' to submit cases to the Court.[23] The accessibility of the Court to individuals and NGOs with observer status before the African Commission is subject to a special declaration to that effect.[24] As of May 2020, ten of the 30 countries (four withdrew) had made the necessary declaration allowing individuals and NGOs with observer status before the Commission access to the Court.[25]

Because of the limited access to the Court, cases before the Court have almost exclusively been against the countries that made the article 34(6) declaration. Individuals and NGOs submitted 235 of the 238 cases presented to the Court as of January 2020, since it formally started operations in November 2006.[26] The African Commission submitted the remaining three cases to the Court—the only cases (two against Libya and one against Kenya) involve countries that have not made

[22] Anthony Jones, 'Form over Substance: The African Court's Restrictive Approach to NGO Standing in the SERAP Advisory Opinion' (2017) 17 African Human Rights Law Journal 320.

[23] Art 5.

[24] Art 34(6).

[25] The countries are Benin, Burkina Faso, Côte d'Ivoire, Tanzania, The Gambia, Ghana, Mali, Malawi, Rwanda and Tunisia. Rwanda (2016), Tanzania (2019), Ivory Coast (2020) and Benin (2020) have withdrawn the declaration allowing individual and NGO access.

[26] Dates on the number of cases submitted to the Court is available here: https://www.african-court.org/en/index.php/cases accessed 24 August 2021.

an article 34(6) declaration. Individual and NGO access can, therefore, be said to be the only demand engine of the continental human rights adjudication mechanism. Hopes and suggestions for the African Commission to fill in as proxy access to the Court for the lack of individual and NGO access have not significantly materialized.

Access to the Court is similarly limited in relation to its advisory jurisdiction.[27] Accordingly, only Member States of the AU (and not just Member States to the Court Protocol), the AU, any of its organs and 'any African organisation recognised' by the AU may seek advisory opinions on the interpretation of the African Charter or other relevant human rights instruments. The Court has ruled that NGOs with observer status before the African Commission may not submit requests for an advisory opinion.[28]

The standing rules of the Court have proved very restrictive. In nearly a decade and a half of existence, the Court has only finalized 62 cases and referred four cases to the African Commission, while 172 cases are pending. About 40% of the finalized cases are against the host country, Tanzania, which may partly explain the withdrawal of the declaration allowing individual and NGO access.[29] The total number of cases before the Court can, therefore, be expected to significantly plummet following Tanzania's withdrawal.

In cases that involve the compatibility of domestic legal provisions with relevant continental and other human rights standards, a resort to horizontal compliance initiatives can partly substitute for the limited access to the Court. The process would allow the Court to be a proactive judicial actor rather than merely acting at the trigger of mere trickles of direct applications. While such an active engagement could take the Court out of traditional judicial functions of adjudication, it may be justifiable by the limited access. Crucially, the Court's horizontal compliance initiative would rely on direct voluntary and informal engagement and complementary procedures to expand its reach and impact. While the absence of a formal legal duty on non-party states to a case, the dialogic feature of the negotiated approaches that horizontal compliance necessitates could prove more effective in advancing continental human rights standards.

It may be argued that efforts towards horizontal compliance may raise issues of independence of the Court if an actual case is submitted against another country. Nevertheless, the Court's initiative should not be seen as determining the legal validity of the relevant legal provisions. Instead, it constitutes a nudge to consider the relevant laws based on the interpretations, reasoning and outcomes of comparable cases before the Court. The Court can also be expected to maintain its

[27] Art 4 of the Protocol Establishing the Court.

[28] Jones (n 22).

[29] Amnesty International, 'Tanzania: Withdrawal of Individual Rights to African Court will Deepen Repression' 2 December 2019, https://www.amnesty.org/en/latest/news/2019/12/tanzania-withdrawal-of-individual-rights-to-african-court-will-deepen-repression/ accessed 24 August 2021.

independence and consider all the unique contextual factors in each state while determining the validity of similar or comparable legal provisions.

Having argued that the Court should engage in horizontal compliance initiatives, the following section outlines some possibilities in working towards horizontal compliance.

5 Avenues for Enhancing Horizontal Compliance

As noted above, the Protocol establishing the Court only anticipates mechanisms of execution of judgments of the Court in relation to the state that is a party to the specific case—referred to as vertical compliance in this chapter. There is no express provision dealing with the possibility of engaging in efforts to ensure compliance by countries other than the respondent state. In practice, there is no record of the African Court engaging in efforts to identify countries with comparable legal provisions as the laws it has invalidated and engage them based on the outcomes of the relevant case. Nevertheless, there are several potential avenues that the Court could take advantage of to expand the horizon of the impact of its decisions involving the compatibility of legal provisions with continental standards.

The first possibility lies in the process of admitting third party interveners and *amicus curiae*[30] in proceedings before the Court. The Protocol establishing the Court allows states parties with interest in a case to submit a request to the Court to join proceedings in contentious cases.[31] While the provision does not define the effect of the decision on such third-party interveners, the provision on the execution of judgments refers to the duty of member states to comply with decisions 'to which they are parties'.[32] It is, therefore, not clear whether the ultimate decision will be binding on third-party interveners. The Rules of Procedure of the Court do not anticipate or deal with the issue of the impact of judgments on third-party interveners.[33]

In practice, third-party interventions are rare, if they happen at all, in contentious cases before the Court. This partly manifests the low level of awareness of states parties and, crucially, the relevance that states parties attach to the proceedings and jurisprudence of the Court. The only major instance where states

[30] For the *amicus curiae* procedure before the African Court, see Frans Viljoen and Adem Abebe, '*Amicus Curiae* Participation before Regional Human Rights Bodies in Africa' (2014) 58 JAL 22–44.

[31] Protocol to the African Charter on Human and Peoples' Rights Establishing the African Court on Human and Peoples' Rights (n 1), art 5(2).

[32] Protocol to the African Charter on Human and Peoples' Rights Establishing the African Court on Human and Peoples' Rights (n 1), art 30.

[33] See Rule 53 of the Rules of Procedure of the African Court http://en.african-court.org/images/Protocol-Host%20Agrtmt/Final_Rules_of_Court_for_Publication_after_Harmonization_-_Final__English_7_sept_1_.pdf. accessed 24 August 2021.

submitted interventions was in relation to requests for advisory opinions.[34] The absence of interventions in contentious cases is despite the fact that the Rules of Procedure of the African Court require the Registrar to invite states parties other than the respondent state to intervene in the proceedings.[35] In cases involving the compatibility of legal provisions with continental human rights standards, the Registrar should engage in preliminary research to identify those other Member States which have similar or comparable laws and specifically indicate the issues before the Court and invite them to submit their views, in view of the issues in the pending case, in lieu of or in addition to the general invitations to all Member States. Countries are more likely to engage the Court upon invitation and submit interventions when they realize that the determination directly affects their legal framework.

Such third-party interventions from relevant countries are likely to enrich the deliberations before the Court. The intervention would also allow the states parties to influence the outcome of the judgment that would affect them. Crucially, the interventions would allow the states parties to take note of the outcome of the case and consider measures to adjust their legal framework in line with the interpretations and outcome, even though it is arguably not binding on them. In addition to these benefits, frequent third-party interventions would raise the profile and popularity of the Court as a prominent continental judicial forum. While countries may be reluctant to respond to a general invitation to consider joining pending cases, they are more likely to be interested in cases that involve legal provisions in their respective countries.

The Court may also engage relevant countries with legal standards comparable to those found incompatible with relevant continental human rights standards after the finalization of the decision, whether or not the relevant state intervened in the case. Under the Protocol Establishing the Court,[36] the Court is required to transmit its judgments to all Member States of the AU. In cases where the judgment relates to the validity of a legal provision, before transmitting the judgments, the Court should conduct preliminary research to identify which countries have

[34] For instance, in the advisory opinion on whether the African Committee on the Rights and Welfare of the Child has the standing to submit requests for an advisory opinion and contentious cases, the Court Registrar transmitted the request to the Member States and Kenya, Senegal and Gabon submitted its opinions. See 'In the Matter of: Request for Advisory Opinion by the African Committee of Experts on the Rights and Welfare of the Child on the Standing of the African Committee of Experts on the Rights and Welfare of the Child before the African Court on Human and Peoples' Rights' Request no 002/2013 https://www.african-court.org/en/images/Cases/Advisory%20Opinion/Advisory%20Opinions/Advisory%20Opinion%20no%20%20002-2013.pdf. accessed 24 August 2021.

[35] Rule 35(4)(b), Rules Procedure of the African Court (n 27).

[36] Art 29(1) of the Protocol to the African Charter on Human and Peoples' Rights Establishing the African Court on Human and Peoples' Rights (n 3). See, however, Rule 64 of the Court's Rule of Procedure which only refers to the notification of judgments to the states parties and does not replicate the duty of the Court to transmit the decision to all Member States of the AU. While there is a generic duty to notify 'any person or institution concerned of the judgment', this does not seem to refer to other states parties.

similar or comparable legal provisions and specifically note this connection while transmitting the judgment to the Member States. This process would allow the states to realize not only the delivery of a judgment but also how it affects them.

The principal organ in charge of monitoring compliance with decisions of the African Court is the AU Executive Council, the second-highest organ of the Union composed of representatives of all Member States. Although both the Protocol Establishing the Court and the Court's Rules of Procedure refer to follow up with the specific respondent state, there is nothing that precludes the Court from providing an addendum detailing how the specific decision relating to the validity of a law affects other Member States with a view also to ensure horizontal compliance. As the AU Executive Council has representatives from all Member States of the AU, such an addendum would allow the Council to proactively use the representatives as mediums to note the implications of the decision to their relevant country and follow up on the decision.

Under the Rules of Procedure of the Court,[37] the Court is also required to inform the AU Commission, the most active implementation entity, of all its decisions. In cases where the decision is amenable to horizontal compliance because it relates to the validity of a legal provision, the Court should include a brief addendum indicating a list of the countries with comparable legal provisions. This would allow the AU Commission, particularly its Department of Political Affairs and the Constitutionalism and Rule of Law Unit, to take account of the judgment and its implications as part of their various engagements with the relevant states.

The African Court is also required to submit annual reports to the Assembly of Heads of States and Governments.[38] As part of the Report, the Court must specifically indicate where a respondent state has not complied with its judgment. In cases that can be subject to horizontal compliance, in addition to specific reports on the level of compliance of the respondent state, the Court should attach the research addendum indicating the countries for which the judgment has implications because of the existence of legal provisions comparable with those found to be incompatible with continental human rights standards.

The Court's promotional visits could also provide useful entry points to present and discuss the outcome of its decisions with relevant legislative, executive, judicial and civil society actors. Such visits and engagements can trigger interest in and/or generate momentum for those stakeholders, notably NGOs, advocating for legal reform.

In addition to the visits, the Court could also take advantage of its other engagements to work towards horizontal (and vertical compliance). For instance, the Court organizes the African Judicial Dialogue, which brings together every two years, the highest judges from many African countries, as well as other

[37] Rule 64(1).

[38] Art 31, Protocol Establishing the Court, and Rule 11(1)(f) of the Rules of the Court.

stakeholders. The event provides a great opportunity for the Court to engage the judges and stakeholders from relevant countries to discuss relevant decisions with a view to creating awareness and understanding, as well as to brainstorm ways of ensuring horizontal compliances.

As the Court can only engage in a limited number of promotional visits or other activities, and usually to countries that have either not ratified the Protocol establishing the Court or made a declaration allowing individual and NGO access to the Court, it must identify other lines of communication to reach out to relevant countries. In particular, the Court may collaborate with the African Commission to ensure that the Commission brings relevant decisions of the Court concerning the validity of legal provisions to the attention of all countries, particularly those whose periodic state report is under consideration. The Commission already uses the state reporting system to follow up on compliance with its recommendations, although this tends to occur only in relation to the respondent state.[39] In collaboration with the Court, an adaptation of this practice could enable the Commission to inquire with the relevant states regarding their awareness about the Court's decisions and how that may affect their legal framework. For this purpose, the Court would have to identify the relevant states, follow up when their reports are due and communicate with the Commission.

The state reporting procedure may not provide enough opportunities for ensuring horizontal compliance. As the Commission often engages in several other activities, including promotional visits, the Court should seek to convince the Commission to mainstream the idea of horizontal compliance in all its activities, including promotional visits, work involving special rapporteurs and working groups. A systematic look at how the various engagements of the African Commission can support the work of the Court and enhance the impact of its decisions through horizontal compliance is critical to advance our understanding of the concept. Although the Rules of Procedure of the Court do not anticipate the possibility of working together on horizontal compliance,[40] such collaboration between the Court and the Commission is anticipated and compatible with the official role of the African Court to complement the protective mandate of the Commission.[41]

Beyond the above platforms, which are in one way or another connected with procedures anticipated in the Protocol Establishing the Court and the Rules of the Court, the Court could also collaborate with the African Peer Review Mechanism

[39] Frans Viljoen, 'State Compliance with the Recommendations of the African Commission on Human and Peoples' Rights' (2015)—available at https://lawexplores.com/state-compliance-with-the-recommendations-of-the-african-commission-on-human-and-peoples-rights/ accessed 24 August 2021.

[40] See Rule 29 of the Rules Procedure of the African Court (n 28).

[41] Art 2 of the Protocol to the African Charter on Human and Peoples' Rights Establishing the African Court on Human and Peoples' Rights (n 1).

(APRM), the Africa Governance Architecture (AGA) and the Pan-African Parliament to pursue horizontal compliance. As such, in cases where a country under review in the APRM process happens to have comparable legal provisions incompatible with continental standards, the Court should bring this to the APRM's attention for inquiries in the relevant thematic cluster. The Court should pursue similar initiatives with AGA, the entity charged with receiving and reviewing reports under the African Charter on Democracy, Elections and Governance.[42] The Pan African Parliament has parliamentarians from across Africa. It, therefore, provides an additional avenue to follow up on compliance, both vertical and horizontal.

Overall, the current legal framework contains no hindrances to the Court in pursuing horizontal compliance. The Court can also explore other avenues which have not been anticipated in the relevant legal frameworks, even for vertical compliance. Such a comprehensive strategy is compatible with the broader objectives of the AGA framework to systematically integrate and establish a productive loop among all the key institutions engaged in protecting and promoting democratic governance, fundamental rights and constitutionalism—issues central to African shared values.

6 Conclusion

In conclusion, the pursuance of horizontal compliance would allow the Court to radiate its key decisions involving the validity of legal provisions beyond the specific respondent state. Horizontal compliance would necessitate the enhancement of the research capabilities of the Court to identify countries with comparable legal provisions to that challenged in a pending case to allow it to specifically target those states to intervene as third parties, engage them post-decision and work with partner institutions at critical moments in their work. Horizontal compliance would also require an adaptation of the Court's functions from merely serving as a reactive to a proactive protector of continental human rights standards.

While this new function may be seen as crossing the blurry boundaries of the Court's protective mandate towards a promotional mandate, this would not constitute an undue expansion of the Court's reach as it will be limited to instances where the decision involves the validity of legal provisions, which is true in a small minority of cases. The potential expansion of the popularity, legitimacy and impact of the Court's decisions justifies an investment in a systematic strategy towards horizontal compliance, even if needed only in a few cases. Moreover, as horizontal compliance would be directly connected with decisions of the Court, it would

[42] African Charter on Democracy, Elections and Governance (2007).

not entail a wholesale duplication or substitution of the promotional work of the African Commission.

Finally, while this chapter has focused on the possibilities and potential relevance of horizontal compliance with relevant decisions of the Court, the ideas outlined here are applicable to the African Commission, Committee on the Rights of the Child, as well as sub-regional tribunals as long as they issue decisions involving the compatibility of legal provisions with continental/regional standards, beyond the specific circumstances of the applicant. Indeed, as briefly noted, the African Commission and the Committee have issued decisions amendable to horizontal compliance.

9

Enforcing Compliance with the Judgments of the African Court on Human and Peoples' Rights

Prospects and Challenges

*Tarisai Mutangi**

1 Introduction

In the African regional human rights system, as in the global system, the focus has increasingly moved away from standard setting to implementation and enforcement of international human rights standards.[1] Along with the 'humanization' of international law came greater concern for the 'victim',[2] and the realization that remedies should ultimately have an actual, practical effect on an individual's life situation. A critical test for the success of the African Court on Human and Peoples' Rights (African Human Rights Court or African Court) will, therefore, be the extent to which state parties enforce and comply with its remedial orders, particularly those affecting individual complainants. Compliance with the orders of the African Human Rights Court will be a test of the commitment of state parties to the African Charter on Human and Peoples' Rights (African Charter)[3] and the Protocol to the African Charter on the Rights of Women in Africa (African Women's Protocol)[4] regarding the protection of human rights on the continent.

Established under the Protocol to the African Charter on Human and Peoples' Rights on the Establishment of the African Court on Human and Peoples' Rights

* Tarisai Mutangi completed the degree LLD at the Centre for Human Rights, University of Pretoria, on the topic An examination of compliance by states with judgments of the African Court on Human and Peoples' Rights: Prospects and Challenges (on file with the authors and the OR Tambo Law Library, University of Pretoria) website http://repository.up.ac.za/upspace/handle/2263/1152. This article is a summarized reworking of Tarisai Mutangi's doctoral thesis, completed under Frans Viljoen's supervision.

[1] For a relatively recent example, see Interights Bulletin (2010), devoted to 'Increasing the Impact of Human Rights Litigation: Implementation of Judgments and Decisions'.

[2] Theodor Meron, *The Humanization of International Law* (Martinus Nijhoff Publishers 2006).

[3] African Charter on Human and Peoples' Rights, 27 June 1981, 21 ILM 58 (1982) (African Charter).

[4] Protocol to the African Charter on Human and Peoples' Rights on the Rights of Women in Africa, 11 July 2003 (African Women's Protocol).

Tarisai Mutangi, *Enforcing Compliance with the Judgments of the African Court on Human and Peoples' Rights*
In: *Compliance with International Human Rights Law in Africa*. Edited by: Aderomola Adeola, Oxford University Press.
 DOI: 10.1093/oso/9780192856999.003.0009

(African Human Rights Court Protocol or Court Protocol),[5] which entered into force in 2004,[6] the African Court decided on several cases since the election of the first complement of 11 judges in 2006.[7] As of September 2019, the number of cases filed before the Court stood at 238, while 172 are pending. Of these cases, individuals filed 223, civil society organizations filed 12 and the African Commission filed three (3). Finalized cases stood at 62, and four (4) were transferred to the African Commission.[8]

In its first judgment, the Court found that it lacked jurisdiction to entertain the submitted matter.[9] The issue of enforcement of the Court's judgments (or, more precisely, its remedial orders) only arose from the second case before the Court, when the Court ordered precautionary measures against Libya.[10] So far, the Court has heard a number of cases on the merits in every session.[11] The general view is that African states are not fully complying with decisions to which they are parties. In the Annual Activity Report of the African Court on Human and Peoples' Rights (2018 Activity Report),[12] the African Court cited the following as challenges,[13]

> The above positive developments notwithstanding, the Court continues to face a number of challenges, which may compromise the successes recorded thus far and threaten its effectiveness. These *challenges include*, but are not limited to, the

[5] Protocol to the African Charter on Human and Peoples' Rights on the Establishment of the African Court on Human and Peoples' Rights (African Human Rights Court Protocol or Court Protocol). On 10 June 1998, the OAU adopted the Protocol establishing the African Human Rights Court as a complement to the protective mandate of the African Commission on Human and Peoples' Rights (African Commission).

[6] After ratification by the requisite number of 15 states, the Protocol entered into force on 25 January 2004. For a list of state parties to the Protocol, see the AU Website, <http://au.int/en/sites/default/files/achpr.pdf>.

[7] After some delay, in January 2006, the AU Assembly of Heads of State and Government (AU Assembly) elected the first 11 Judges of the African Human Rights Court, and subsequently re-elected a number and replaced some of the Judges. The Court created a Registry and established its seat in Arusha, Tanzania. At the time of writing, 11 more cases are pending before this Court. On the Court, generally see Frans Viljoen, *International Human Rights Law in Africa* (1st edn) (OUP 2007) 418–475 (Viljoen).

[8] Available at: https://www.african-court.org/en/index.php/cases/2016-10-17-16-18-21.

[9] *Yogogombaye v Senegal*, Application 1/2008, 15 December 2009. Cases may only be submitted directly against state parties if the particular state has made a declaration under art 34(6) of the Court Protocol. Yogogombaye submitted his case directly against Senegal, but Senegal had not made the requisite declaration.

[10] *African Commission on Human and Peoples' Rights v Great Socialist People's Libyan Arab Jamahiriya*, Application 4/2011, Order for Provisional Measures, 25 March 2011.

[11] A total of 15 advisory opinions have been filed before the African Court to date. The number of cases heard on the merits is growing, which include the very early cases such as *Femi Falana v The African Union*, Application No 001/2011; *Urban Mukandawire v Malawi*, Application No 003/2011; *The Beneficiaries of Late Abdoulaye NIKIEMA aka Ablassés, Ernest Zongo, Blaise Ilboudo, Norbert Zongo and the Burkinabe Movement for Human and Peoples' Rights v Burkina Faso*, Application No 013/2011. The rest of the cases in the ealry days were disposed of at the admissibility stage as the African Court ruled that it had no competence to hear the cases because the Respondent States had not lodged the Declaration accepting the competence of individuals to submit cases directly to the Court.

[12] Activity Report of the African Court on Human and Peoples' Rights (AFCHPR) Executive Council 34th Ordinary Session 7–8 February 2019 Addis Ababa, Ethiopia, EX CL/1126(XXXIV) (2018 Activity Report).

[13] ibid, 45.

> level of ratification of the Protocol, the slow rate of deposit of the declaration allowing individuals and NGOs direct access to the Court, lack of awareness of the Court, *non-compliance with Court decisions* and inadequate resources. (My emphasis)

This means a worrying trend is already developing, for instance, in the consolidated applications of *Tanganyika Law Society and the Legal and Human Rights Centre—Rev. Christopher R. Mtikila v United Republic of Tanzania* (Mtikila),[14] the applicants filed a matter claiming that the respondent had, through certain amendments to its Constitution, violated its citizens' right of freedom of association, the right to participate in public/governmental affairs and the right against discrimination by prohibiting independent candidates from contesting presidential, parliamentary and local government elections. In its findings, the Court ordered Tanzania to publish the judgment on the official government website and effect necessary amendments to the law to ensure it recognizes the participation of independent candidates. The government has so far not taken the constitutional, legislative and other measures to remedy the violations found, as ordered by the Court, although it published the judgment on its website but not the summary prepared by the Court for this purpose.

In other instances, the respondent states such as Rwanda and Tanzania publicly declared their desire not to comply with the judgment of the Court. Inevitably, the two states ended up withdrawing the competence of individuals and Non-governmental Organizations (NGOs) to file cases directly before the Court. A case in point is *Ingabire Victoire Umuhoza v Rwanda*,[15] in which the African Court found several violations of various treaties by the Respondent State and ordered the Respondent State to take all necessary measures to restore the rights of the Applicant and submit to the Court a report on the measures taken within six (6) months. However, during the presentation of the 2017 Activity Report of the Court before the Executive Council in January 2018, the Respondent State reiterated its decision of not cooperating with the Court although there are reports that the Applicant was released from prison on a presidential pardon, the government has not submitted any formal report to Court.[16] Perhaps more telling are cases against Tanzania in which the Respondent State indicated that it would not comply with the judgment of the Court.[17]

[14] Application Nos 009 and 011/2011, African Court on Human and Peoples' Rights, Judgment on Merits (14 June 2013).

[15] Application No 3/2014, African Court on Human and Peoples' Rights, Judgment on Merits (24/11/2017).

[16] 2018 Activity Report (n 12).

[17] ibid. This attitude perhaps culminated in Tanzania's withdrawal of the Declaration that allows individuals and NGOs to file cases before the African Court. However, whatever the reason, public declarations of non-compliance with court decisions undermine the legitimacy and integrity of the Court. Tanzania being the host of the Seat of the Court, needs to lead by example and conduct itself in a manner that promotes the objects and purposes of the Court.

However, in other scenarios, respondent states applied for interpretation of judgment as opposed to complying with it. The effect of that is to prolong the time to implement the decision of the African Court, thereby delaying the remedy on victims of violation. Application for interpretation of decision has so far been witnessed in at least two cases. In the first case, namely, *Actions Pour la Protection des Droits de L'Homme v Côte d'Ivoire*,[18] the Court ruled that the Respondent State violated its obligation to establish an independent and impartial electoral body. Also, it violated its obligation to protect the right of citizens to participate freely in the management of the public affairs of their country. Consequently, the Court ordered the Respondent State to amend Law No 2014-335 of 18 June 2014 on the Independent Electoral Commission to make it compliant with the state's international law obligations. The other case was the *Alex Thomas v Tanzania*.[19] After finding a violation of the right to a fair trial, the Court ordered the state to take all 'necessary measures, within a reasonable time to remedy the violation found, specifically, precluding the reopening of the defence case and the retrial of the Applicant, and to inform the Court, within six (6) months from the date of the judgment, of measures taken'. The Respondent State wanted the interpretation of several terms and phrases used in the Court's order. In spite of receiving the interpreted judgment, the Respondent State has not done anything to implement the decision of the Court, begging the question as to the necessity of requesting interpretation.

As to the dearth of cases generally, this may be ascribed to the African Commission on Human and Peoples' Rights (African Commission or Commission) and potential litigants rather than the Court itself. Referral of cases by the African Commission to the Court is, at least at this stage, the most likely way in which cases would reach the African Court.[20] For some time, in the absence of Rules of Procedure regulating the conditions under which 'communications' (cases) may be referred to the Court, the Commission has been inclined not to proceed with referrals.[21] With the adoption of final Rules of Procedure, harmonized

[18] Application No 001/2014, African Court on Human and Peoples' Rights, Judgment on Merits (18/11/2016).

[19] Application No 005/2013, African Court on Human and Peoples' Rights, Judgment on Merits (4/07/2019).

[20] Some cases could have been referred to the Court on this basis, eg *Centre for Minority Rights Development (Kenya) and Minority Rights Group International on behalf of the Endorois Welfare Council v Kenya*, Communication 276/2003, decided 4 February 2010.

[21] Obviously, the failure of states to ratify the Court Protocol also contributes to the dearth of cases being referred. Some of the states most often found in violation by the African Commission, such as Eritrea, Sudan and Zimbabwe, have not become party to the Court Protocol. A further complicating factor is the temporal jurisdiction of the Court, which removes from the Court's competence cases in which the African Commission's finding relates to events that occurred before the entry into force of the Protocol in general, or for a particular state—unless a case is made out of a continuing violation. However, the irony is that there has not been any noticeable increase of applications against the few states that lodged the Declaration.

with those of the Court, in 2010,[22] this obstacle has been removed, and a steady flow of cases may be expected.[23] Under these Rules, 'communications' may be referred to the Court if the Respondent State had been found in violation by the Commission and does not implement the Commission's remedial 'recommendation' within the prescribed period—provided that the state has ratified or acceded to the Court Protocol.[24] Cases may also be submitted directly to the Court, bypassing the Commission, against those states that made an optional declaration to that effect—provided that domestic remedies have been exhausted.[25] While it is correct that only a few states have made such a declaration,[26] it is also true that no case has yet been submitted against many of those states. The Commission may refer a case to the Court *at any stage* of the proceedings,[27] that is, without determining admissibility or deciding on the merits, as in the *Libya* case.

This chapter builds on the seminal contribution of Frans Viljoen and Lirette Louw,[28] in which state compliance with the Commission's 'recommendations' was analysed.[29] In the present contribution, the legal basis and possible modalities of enforcement of the Court's orders are under scrutiny. There is a logic in the shift of focus in this contribution away from the Commission to the Court, as all unimplemented Commission findings are in the future likely to end up before the Court: either a state complies with the recommendatory (and thus non-binding) finding of the Commission, or the matter is referred to the Court for its binding decision. To a large extent, questions about compliance with the Commission's recommendations, therefore, become questions about the enforcement of the Court's remedial orders.

This contribution poses the following four questions: (1) Are state parties to the African Human Rights Court Protocol under a legal obligation to enforce the Court's judgments domestically? (2) If so, what form could and should domestic

22 African Commission's Rules of Procedure adopted May 2010 and entered into force 18 August 2010; Court's Interim Rules of Court [Herein Rules of Procedure].

23 The African Commission has since made its first referral to the Court following human rights issues that arose from the unrest in Libya. At the insistence of the African Commission, the Court issued provisional measures calling upon Libya to desist from and to ensure no other actor violates human and peoples' rights amidst ongoing civil war in that country.

24 Rule 118(1) of the Rules of Procedure.

25 Rule 43(6) of the Rules of Procedure, supra note 22.

26 As of May 2020, ten states (4 later withdrawing) had made the declaration under article 34(6) of the Court Protocol: Burkina Faso, Ghana, Malawi, Mali, Tanzania (withdrew), Ivory Coast (withdrew), Rwanda (withdrew), Benin (withdrew) and Tunisia. Following a promotional visit by the Court in 2019, the government of Zimbabwe made a public undertaking to ratify the Court Protocol and lodge the Art 34(6) Declaration.

27 Rule 118(4) of the Rules of Procedure, 'at any stage of the examination of a communication'.

28 Frans Viljoen and Lirette Louw, 'State Compliance with the Recommendations of the African Commission on Human and Peoples' Rights, 1994–2004' (2007) 101 AJIL 1.

29 See also, on this subject, Obiora Chinedu Okafor, 'The African Human Rights System: Activist Forces and International Institutions' (2007) and 'Open Society Justice Initiative, From Judgment to Justice: Implementing International and Regional Human Rights Decisions' (Not Dated) 93–115 [hereinafter Judgment to Justice].

enforcement of the Court's orders take, with specific reference to the role of the three branches of government? (3) What role may national human rights institutions, of which at least 23 have been established in African states, play in domestic enforcement? (4) What is the residual role of the African Court, as a supranational institution, in the *domestic enforcement* of its own orders? In answering these questions, reliance is placed on the comparative experience of and scholarly reflections on the two major regional human rights courts, the European Court of Human Rights and the Inter-American Commission and Court of Human Rights.

The term 'enforcement' with reference to orders is used here as denoting not just implementation in a general sense, but the actual and effective domestic rendering of (or giving effect to) a remedy in line with a judgment of an international court. It envisages the adoption of specific measures designed to redress the harm caused by the violation of human rights as confirmed in the judgment of an international court such as the African Human Rights Court. The 'radiating' and or 'orientation' effect of judgments of the African Court, serving as a source of domestic constitutional interpretation, is thus not captured here.

We should also clarify what this contribution is *not* about: It investigates the enforcement of the Court's orders in the domestic arena and not at the regional level. Its main concern is what states—and not courts—should do to enhance domestic enforcement. According to the Court Protocol, state parties undertake to comply with the Court's judgments.[30] However, this Protocol neither contains any direct reference to the domestic process nor provides any guidance regarding the way in which judgments are to be enforced at the national level. What the Protocol does, instead, is to focus on the intergovernmental dimension of enforcement within the African Union (AU) structures. To the African supranational domain of monitoring, compliance should be added to the African Peer Review Mechanism (APRM), developed under the aegis of the New Partnership for Africa's Development (NEPAD).[31] Most state parties to the Court Protocol have also signed the APRM Memorandum of Understanding (MOU).[32] Although compliance with the decisions of the African Human Rights Court is not mentioned specifically as part of the APRM standards, this aspect is by necessary implication part of the supervision of participating states' support for and upholding of the African Charter, provided for in the APRM standards.

Still, although the main focus of this contribution is not the institutional mechanisms at the regional level, domestic enforcement cannot be isolated completely

[30] Art 30 of the Court Protocol.

[31] See eg Magnus Killander, 'The African Peer Review Mechanism and Human Rights: The First Reviews and the Way Forward' (2008) 30 Hum Rts Quarterly 41–75.

[32] Of the 30 state parties to the Court Protocol, 6 (Burundi, Comoros, The Gambia, Libya, Niger and Tunisia) have not signed up the APRM. Thus, at least 20 states have accepted both the Court Protocol and the APRM. Thirteen of the 37 states accepting the APRM have not accepted the Court's jurisdiction (Angola, Cape Verde, Djibouti, Egypt, Equatorial Guinea, Ethiopia, Liberia, Namibia, Sao Tome e Principe, Sierra Leone, Sudan and Zambia).

from efforts within the regional institutions to ensure compliance. One of the possibilities open to victims or litigants who come up against a wall of intransigence at the domestic level is to approach the regional human rights court to obtain a compliance order, akin to the contempt of court proceedings at the national level. To this limited extent, we also deal with the role of the African Court in the enforcement of its orders against the background of the established and emerging practice of the other two main regional human rights courts mentioned above.

This contribution also does *not* deal with the African Court of Justice and Human Rights (Merged Court).[33] Some confusion exists about the merging of the African Human Rights Court and AU Court of Justice into the African Court of Justice and Human Rights.[34] Although a process is irrevocably underway to establish the African Court of Justice and Human Rights,[35] at the moment—and for the foreseeable short-term future—only the African Human Rights Court is and will be in existence. In any event, as far as the issues under consideration in this chapter are concerned, there is no fundamental difference in the legal framework establishing the two courts. Possibilities raised and conclusions reached here should also apply to the future African Court of Justice and Human Rights.

2 Link Between International Remedies and Domestic Enforcement

Before investigating the obligations of states to give effect to the reparation orders of the African Human Rights Court, and discussing the role of governments, NHRIs and the Court itself in this process, this part of the chapter establishes the link between the extent of precision, as well as the nature and scope of remedies ordered by international courts, on the one hand, and domestic enforcement, on the other.

2.1 Specificity of Remedial Order

Remedial orders may be formulated with varying degrees of specificity, ranging from open-ended declarations of incompatibility to detailed instructions. International courts are likely to issue more open-ended remedies than domestic

[33] Established by the Protocol on the Statute of the African Court of Justice and Human Rights [Herein Merged Court Protocol], adopted on 1 July 2008.

[34] The AU Court of Justice provided for under art 5(1)(d) of the AU Constitutive Act, will not be established, despite the fact that the Protocol establishing this Court entered into force on 11 February 2009, after 15 states had become part to the Protocol of the Court of Justice of the AU.

[35] The Merged Court Protocol will preside over the transition from the African Human Rights Court to this new judicial institution, 12 months after entering into force. By 31 May 2020, only eight states have become party to the Merged Court Protocol.

courts given their relative remoteness and questionable democratic legitimacy, allowing states some flexibility in forging a specific course of action attuned to their particular circumstances.[36] However, overly vague international remedial orders may complicate national implementation, including assessing and monitoring implementation. Remedial orders formulated in specific terms spell out unequivocally which enforcement measures the state agents are required to take, what remedial expectation the complainants may have and provide a clear yardstick to measure state action and thus improve accountability. The clearer and more precise a remedy by an international court, the less likely it is that a dispute about its domestic enforcement would arise in practice. Even if parties may return to the international tribunal to obtain more clarity,[37] such a course of action is costly and time-consuming and should be avoided if possible.

The extent of remedial specificity depends on a number of factors, including the state obligation involved, the scope of the remedy and the anticipated political resistance to the remedy. Generally, when a state has been found in violation of its obligation to 'respect' rights and freedoms, the remedy would tend to be specific, while the obligation to 'fulfil' may tend to be open-ended. For example, an appropriate remedy following a finding of a violation of a detainee's right not to be tortured may be an order for release and compensation, while the violation of the right to education may lead to a more complex remedial order. An order aiming to remedy an individual's situation may be framed with specificity, while a reformatory remedy speaking to structural or systemic problems, for example, is likely to be less detailed and prescriptive, allowing a measure of flexibility to states, in this instance, to national parliamentary debates and processes. The more politically contentious a finding, the greater the likelihood of an open-ended remedy.

These observations do not imply that enforcement is dependent on specificity[38] or that the specificity of remedial orders is the only factor that may enhance enforcement. Specificity in remedies is neither a necessary nor a sufficient condition for effective enforcement. The main contention is that specificity enables the assessment or supervision of enforcement. However, specificity may fly in the face of principles of subsidiarity and complementarity, which emphasizes that states are best positioned to work out how exactly treaty provisions—and the judgments of international courts interpreting these treaties—should be given effect in domestic law.

36 Giving states the first option to adopt remedial measures following a finding of a violation of the European Convention has been consistently one of the hallmarks of the European human rights system through the Committee of Ministers, which monitors the implementation of court decisions. Only after the Committee of Ministers assesses the measures so adopted and finds them insufficient would specific measures be suggested to add to what that state had already adopted.

37 As is allowed before the European Court, under new art 46 (3).

38 See eg the cases mentioned in Judgment to Justice, supra note 29, 101, in which states complied with findings of the African Commission in the absence of detailed recommendations.

The African Human Rights Court's remedial mandate to make 'appropriate orders to remedy the violation' neither necessarily invites precision nor precludes it. The fact that explicit mention is made of two remedial possibilities, 'fair compensation' and 'reparation', does not guarantee any degree of specificity. The formulation of 'fair compensation' leaves the Court with two options: It may either use the term 'fair compensation', as such, in its order or determine the exact amount that fairness would, in a particular case, dictate. The first option would leave it to national courts (or administrators) to determine the exact amount, thereby inviting uncertainty and the potential of protracted tugs of war of financial considerations determinations. Although this more open-ended approach has been followed by the African Commission,[39] the African Court seems to have taken a mixed approach between the specific and open-ended approach to remedies. For instance, in the majority of cases, the remedies have been specific, while in others not as specific, thereby triggering some state parties to invoke the interpretation of judgment procedure.[40] The Inter-American Court is such a torchbearer in terms of the specific approach to remedies. For instance, that Court quantifies what it decides to be the appropriate amount in compensation and orders the concerned state to pay under the Court's supervision.[41]

2.2 Nature and Scope of Remedial Order

To a great extent, the nature and scope of the Court's remedy—and the concomitant political cost—are the best guides to both the most suitable method and the likelihood of domestic enforcement. A remedy to pay compensation to one person may, for example, be perceived as less invasive of state sovereignty, compared to an order to undertake an investigation into thousands of allegations of ill-treatment or to amend a country's constitution.

Article 27 of the Court Protocol allows much leeway to the Court, leaving it at liberty to adopt any form of remedy imaginable as long as it can substantiate its appropriateness. In applying this provision, the least invasive remedial order is likely to be a declaratory judgment, for example, if the Court merely declares or announces in its finding that the African Charter had been violated. Departing from

[39] See eg Article *19 v Eritrea*, 2007 AHRLR 73 (ACHPR 2007), operative paragraph, in which the African Commission recommends that the government 'takes appropriate measures to ensure payment of compensation' and *Bissangou v Republic of Congo*, 2006 AHRLR 80 (ACHPR 2006), operative paragraph, in which the government is 'requested' to pay an amount previously fixed by the national courts, as well as compensation 'for the loss suffered by the complainant, the amount of which shall be determined in accordance with Congolese legislation'.

[40] See the cases filed against Ivory Coast and Tanzania (18 and 19 above).

[41] For a general discussion on the practice and basis of this Inter-American Court to supervise compliance by states with its decisions, see the case of *Baena-Ricardo and others v Panama Inter-American Court of Human Rights* (Competence) Judgment of 2 November 2003. Series C No 104 Available at: <http://www.corteidh.or.cr/casos.cfm>. (Accessed on 14 October 2021).

a position of deference towards the offending state, such a remedy arguably leaves too much discretion to the state.

The Court Protocol refers to one specific example of a potential remedial order, namely 'the payment of fair compensation'.[42] This formulation may have been inspired by the fact that 'fair compensation' is the remedy mandated—and consequently, most frequently ordered—by the European Court.[43] Also, the Inter-American Court routinely orders monetary compensation. In an analysis of the state compliance record with the Inter-American Court's orders, it was observed that states are much more likely to comply with the remedial orders of an economic nature.[44] In that system, a distinction may be drawn between 'monetary economic compensation' (payment of a sum of money) and 'non-monetary economic compensation' (provision of access to services or goods such as scholarships or land).[45]

Some remedies invite action by the executive (including the administrative authorities). The required remedy may, for example, require the payment of an exact amount in compensation, symbolic reparations such as the renaming of a street name, the release of a detained person, the introduction of training programmes for public officials, the exhumation of bodily remains, the initiation of an investigation, or the setting up of a domestic institution.[46] In this regard, enforcement will differ and become more complex, following a sliding scale of the political contentiousness of the required action, and depending on whether individual, case-specific measures or structural or institutional changes are required. Clearly, the more politically contentious, structural and far-reaching the required measures are, the more difficult enforcement is likely to be. In the Inter-American system, including in respect of the Inter-American Court, symbolic reparations have, for example, resulted in high rates of compliance, while investigation of human rights violations and punishment of perpetrators, as well as orders aimed at protecting witnesses and victims, have mostly not been complied with.[47]

Other remedies are best addressed through legal reform, mostly by way of legislative intervention. For example, a finding that legislation violates the state's international law obligation may result in a remedy that either explicitly or by implication requires legislative amendment or the enactment of new legislation.[48]

[42] Art 27(1) of the Court Protocol.

[43] See Art 41 of the European Convention.

[44] Fernando Basch and others, 'The Effectiveness of the Inter-American System of Human Rights Protection; A Quantitative Approach to its Functioning and Compliance with its Decisions' (2010) 12 Sur International Journal on Human Rights 9.

[45] See Basch and others supra note 44, at 12–13.

[46] For example, in *Assanidze v Georgia*, Application No 71503/01 (Judgment of 8 April 2004), the European Court ordered the release of a person in detention despite having been acquitted by the highest court of the land.

[47] See Basch and others supra note 44, at 15, 19, 21.

[48] For example, in *Avocats sans Frontières (on behalf of Bwampamye) v Burundi* (2000) AHRLR 48 (ACHPR 2000), the African Commission recommended to Burundi that a possibility of reopening closed criminal proceedings that had violated the African Charter in a manner that insinuated change of national law to give a judge judicial discretion in appointing free counsel. In a more direct order for

Some other remedies may require judicial intervention, especially if there is no political will to take administrative measures or legislate. One such avenue for possible judicial intervention by way of judicial activism is the reopening of national proceedings in criminal proceedings. This possibility is most likely to emanate from an unfair criminal trial and will also be linked to the specifics of the remedial order.

3 Basis of State Obligation to Enforce Orders Domestically

In view of the fact that responsibility under international law is derived from states' consensus to be bound, it follows that any form of liability in respect of states is derived from the provisions of the treaties they ratify or customary international law. It is argued here that this principle also applies to liability in respect of enforcing remedial orders of the African Human Rights Court. In fact, actual and effective domestic enforcement should be based on a legal obligation on the part of the state. The more clearly enforcement is grounded as a legal obligation, the more likely the process of enforcement is to be legitimate and free from political manipulation. In my view, state parties to the Court Protocol are legally obliged to enforce the Court's orders. With regards to the concept of the nature of the obligation of states to comply with judgments of a court, the relevant general principles of law include *pacta sunt servanda*, the obligation to repair and the right to an effective remedy, the scope of *effet utile* and state responsibility.[49] The extent to which enforcement under the African Court may be based on these general principles of law is considered below.

3.1 Pacta Sunt Servanda Principle

The clearest basis of such a state obligation lies in the treaty law of the African Charter and the Court Protocol. As parties to these treaties, states are, based on the principle of *pacta sunt servanda*, under an obligation to uphold the terms of their consent in good faith. Reading the African Charter and Protocol together, it is incontrovertible that states parties to both these treaties are under a legal obligation to ensure effective domestic enforcement of the Court's orders. Such a reading of the Charter and Protocol is both purposive and in line with the obligation of

the adoption of national law, the European Court ordered reopening of proceedings against complainants in *Goktepe v Belgique* European Court of Human Rights Judgment of 2 June 2005. This and other judgments requiring the adoption of similar remedial measures resulted in Belgium adopting a law that provided for the reopening of closed proceedings in December 2007.

49 Baena-Ricardo Judgment, supra note 41, paras 61–67.

states to adopt a *bona fide* interpretation of treaties.[50] The obligation of compliance with the African Charter requires state parties to adopt legislative and 'other measures' to ensure that the Charter rights are given domestic effect.[51] One of the 'other measures' for a state that accepted the competence of the Court under the Court Protocol is to 'give effect' to the Court's decisions. In this sense, the obligation of 'giving effect' may be equated with the enforcement of the Court's remedial orders. On ratifying the Protocol, states clearly assume the obligation to comply with judgments in cases 'to which they are parties' and guarantee their 'execution',[52] among others by enforcing the Court's orders within their national legal systems.

The principle of *pacta sunt servanda* has its origin in article 27 of the Vienna Convention on the Law of Treaties.[53] It stresses the requirement that states ought to execute their international legal obligations in good faith. Of relevance in this regard is the Inter-American Court's judgment in the *Baena-Ricardo* case,[54] in which Panama challenged the competence of the Inter-American Court to monitor compliance by Panama with its final judgment. The Court found that, based on the *pact sunt servanda*, Panama was precluded from relying on its domestic law to avoid obligations arising from the Court's order for reparations.[55] It then would follow that allowing Panama to rely on its municipal law would have exposed the bad faith. Furthermore, it would have buttressed the perception that international law obligations arising from these treaties could be evaded with absolute impunity.

While states may not take issue with this obligation, in principle, they may quibble about the exact content of the measures that qualify as good faith enforcement. Paulson, writing on compliance by states with judgments of the International Court of Justice (ICJ), suggests that 'reasonable performance in good faith of any binding obligation' is the pivotal principle guiding compliance with international judgments.[56] The author explains 'performance in good faith' as tantamount to executing a final judgment in such a way as to deliberately avoid 'superficial implementation or otherwise circumventing it'.[57] It follows that 'good faith' is manifest through conduct free from malice and evasiveness in adopting effective remedial measures. In respect of the remedial order, a state meets its good faith obligations when it approaches the remedial process with the intention to enforce the court order, thereby eradicating, as far as possible, all the adverse consequences suffered by the individual due to the violation.

50 In line with art 1 of the Vienna Convention on the Law of Treaties (1969).

51 Art 1 of the African Charter.

52 Art 30 of the Court Protocol, supra note 5.

53 Vienna Convention on the Law of Treaties, adopted in 1969 and came into force on 27 January 1980.

54 Baena-Ricardo and others Judgement, supra note 41.

55 See also art 27 of the Vienna Convention on the general rule that states cannot invoke municipal law or procedures in order to escape responsibility at the international level.

56 Colter Paulson, 'Compliance with Final Judgments of the ICJ since 1987' 98 AJIL (2004) 435–436.

57 Paulson, supra note 56, 436.

A further issue that may arise regarding the obligation relates to the requirement to comply with and guarantee judgments in cases to which a state is a party. A strict reading of the Protocol's wording suggests that a remedial order in a case against a particular state only binds the state in those proceedings. The position seems to be similar even if the same cause of action existed in respect of other states parties to the African Charter. For instance, if a number of states have similarly worded national legislation ousting the jurisdiction of courts to hear petitions against the incumbent government, but a judgment was issued in respect of only one of them, enforcement is, as a matter of law, required in the Respondent State alone.

The evolution of the European human rights system indicates the emergence of a more nuanced approach. As a matter of strict law, state parties to the European Convention have undertaken to 'abide by the final judgments' of the European Human Rights Court 'in any case to which they are parties'.[58] However, European scholars such as Ress have expounded on the concept of the 'orientation effect' of judgments.[59] The argument is that although other states that were not parties to a particular proceeding are not bound by the judicial finding of the European Court rendered therein; they are expected to align their own laws, conduct or national administrative procedures in tandem with the interpretation of the treaty as handed down by the Court in proceedings to which they were not parties. This is what is often referred to as the 'orientation effect' of judgments.[60] This expectation is founded in the collective responsibility of states to protect human rights in the Council of Europe. Whenever invoked, collective responsibility appeals to all parties to the European Convention to identify themselves as the key players in promoting and protecting human rights in Europe, thereby taking deliberate actions in good faith, combining efforts to redress the violation of the Convention and guarantee non-repetition. In other words, states that were not a party to certain proceedings will not fold their hands and wait to align their actions only after a similar proceeding is invoked specifically against them. They need to take preemptive and corrective action once a judgment has been handed down against one of the Member States by the judicial body in question.

3.2 Obligation to Repair

The obligation to repair is a derivative of the responsibility of states to take measures in order to redress a breach of an international legal obligation. The Inter-American Court held in the course of its reasoning in the *Baena-Ricardo* case that

[58] Art 46(1) of the European Convention..

[59] George Ress 'The Effect of Decisions and Judgments of the European Court of Human Rights in the Domestic Legal Order' (2005) 40 Texas Int'l L J 359.

[60] George Ress, supra note 59, generally.

provisions in international treaties, such as article 63 of the American Convention, providing for judicial powers to make orders such as reparations for the breach of treaty obligations,[61] constitute proof of the existence of the obligation to repair.[62] A violation of an international norm immediately invokes the obligation to redress without the need for further formalities to confirm this obligation. As a result, the Inter-American Court has interpreted article 63 of the American Convention as granting it 'a wide margin of judicial discretion to determine the measures' to repair all the consequences of the violation.[63]

The same conclusion might be arrived at with respect to the Court Protocol. By providing that the Court 'shall make appropriate orders to remedy the violation' following a finding of violation against a state party,[64] the Court Protocol confers a wide-ranging remedial competence upon the African Court. Consistent with the Inter-American Court jurisprudence, the quoted provision provides a 'wide margin of judicial discretion' to determine orders properly suited to redress the situation, thereby repairing the injury suffered.

The duty to repair or make reparation was clearly stated in the *Chorzow Factory* case, where the ICJ held that reparation must, as far as possible, 'wipe-out all the consequences of the illegal act and re-establish the situation which would, in all probability, have existed if that act had not been committed'.[65] This statement has two elements that are of paramount importance to the current discussion. First, it confirms the validity of our earlier contention that reparations automatically follows every breach of an international law obligation. It is not in dispute that international human rights instruments such as the African Charter confer rights on individuals and peoples much as they impose international law obligations on state parties who ratify them. Second, reparations are meant to 'wipe-out all consequences of the illegal act and re-establish the situation', which would have been obtained had it not been for the breach. The ICJ stated the principle that states found in violation have a duty to repair the violation by affording a remedy that restores the victim to the original position. In literal language, this means repairing the situation, hence the basis for the duty to repair being argued here. The clearest demonstration of repairing the situation is through the domestic enforcement of an international judicial order that clearly spells out the damage suffered and the nature of remedies required to re-establish the original situation. On this basis, states have a clear duty to enforce international orders by adopting measures that repair the situation of the victim. The state's obligation to repair is linked to the

[61] Baena-Ricardo Judgment, supra note 41, paras 61–64. Art 63(1) of the American Convention requires that the Inter-American Court must rule that the 'consequences of the measure or situation that constituted the breach of such right or freedom be remedied'.
[62] Baena-Ricardo Judgment, supra note 41, para 65.
[63] Baena-Ricardo Judgment, supra note 41.
[64] Art 27(1) of the Court Protocol, supra note 5.
[65] *Germany v Poland* 1928 PCIJ Ser A No 17.

individual victim's right to a remedy. A supplementary basis for a legal obligation to enforce the judgments of the African Court at the national level may be derived from the necessary implications of the 'right to a remedy'. Although a right to an effective remedy is not mentioned explicitly in the African Charter, it may be deduced from the obligation to take 'measures' to give effect to the Charter and from the right of everyone to have their cause heard.[66] To these bases may be added the explicit competence of the Court to order remedies as already mentioned above. The only effective way the remedial order can be made effective is if it is in fact enforced, thus ensuring that the Court's order is complied with where it matters most—the domestic legal order of the state concerned.

I have already argued that the domestic level is where the practical effect of a remedy is felt. If performed in good faith, that is, with the intention to redress the harm suffered by wiping-out adverse consequences effectively, the focus of the state's remedial measures should be at the national level where compensation is paid, detainees are released from places of detention, education and health facilities are provided for the benefit of victims within the territory of the state party. A remedy that is provided in the wrong place would have been improperly rendered. The international plane or sphere is a fictitious world that has no practical significance unless states implement in the domestic order the terms of the concessions arrived at in international forums. Although acknowledged at the international level as satisfying international obligations, effective remedial measures are directed and implemented at the national level. Thus, the obligation to give an effective remedy for a violation of rights escapes illusion by requiring states to act at the national level where the measures are required.

3.3 Effet Utile Principle

Expounded on by the ICJ in the *Corfu Channel* case, the *effet utile* principle, though closely linked to the sanction against relying on national law to avert international responsibility, looks further than just the nature of normative treaty obligations.[67] It is concerned with the 'practical effect' of, for instance, an obligation to pay reparations; hence, it takes into account procedural issues linked to the process of complying with an international legal obligation. To that end, it is insufficient for a court to confirm violations of a treaty obligation and dissociate itself from the compliance process without satisfying itself that the 'practical effect' of the remedy will be achieved.

[66] Art 7 of the African Charter. See also Godfrey Musila, 'The Right to an Effective Remedy Under the African Charter' (2006) 6 Afr Hum Rts L J 1, where the author argues that this right could be easily read in the African Charter.

[67] Baena-Ricardo Judgment, supra note 41, para 67.

It is argued here that the practical effect of every violation of rights is felt by the victim at the domestic level, where violations often take place, resulting in the international responsibility of the state concerned. With similar force, the practical effect of remedial measures so adopted to wipe out adverse consequences of the act and restore the victim to the original position is equally felt by the victim at the national level where the harm occurred. To that end, the practical effect will only be experienced when the state concerned embarks on the process of adopting measures to repair the harm suffered and re-establish the desired position by enforcing the international decision at the national level. Guaranteeing execution of judgments in tandem with the undertaking of states in article 30 of the Court Protocol means that states are obliged to enforce these decisions at the national level. The same conclusion is arrived at when one considers the general obligations of states to 'give effect' to the treaty in question almost always at the national level.

3.4 State Responsibility

The position set out in the Court Protocol and Charter is a reflection of the Draft Articles on State Responsibility (the Draft Articles).[68] According to these Draft Articles, which arguably set out the customary international law position on the topic to which its title refers, states are under an obligation to make full reparation for and guarantee non-repetition of any internationally wrongful act.[69] Given that a treaty violation could constitute such a wrongful act, a violation of the African Charter would give rise to this obligation. As the Court Protocol prescribes that the precise format of this obligation is to be determined by the African Court, states are equally under an obligation to comply with the Court's remedial order.

The Draft Articles prepared by the International Law Commission (ILC) seek to establish the 'basic principle underlying the articles as a whole' in that article 1 states that any 'internationally wrongful act' attracts the 'international responsibility' of that state. Article 2 identifies the primary elements of an internationally wrongful act as that 'attributable to a state under international law' and amounting to a 'breach of international law' in the result. The international law obligation could be owed to individual states (bilateral) or the international community as a whole (multilateral). This distinction was enunciated in the *Barcelona Traction* case,[70] where the ICJ held that those obligations owed to the international community as a whole are obligations *erga omnes* and, therefore, owed to all states. Among them are 'rules concerning the basic rights of the human person.'[71] The 'act' of a

[68] [Hereinafter Draft Articles]. Available at: *untreaty.un.org/ilc/texts/instruments/english/.../9_6_2001.pdf (Accessed on 14 October 2011).*

[69] Art 30 of the Court Protocol.

[70] *Barcelona Traction (Belgium v Spain)* [1970] ICJ Rep 3.

[71] *Barcelona Traction* Judgment, supra note 70, para 34.

state could have been committed by an organ of the state[72] or by a person under the control of a state.[73] Article 12 reiterates a commonly held view that the nature or origin of an international obligation is irrelevant as long as it has been established that a state has breached such a rule.

As regards the effects of a wrongful act, article 30, together with certain provisions that follow it, provide for two fundamental principles in international litigation, namely, the duty to make 'full reparation' and the guarantee of 'non-repetition' of the violation of the international obligation in question. Article 33 goes on to set out the scope of the international obligations falling under the ambit of the Draft Articles. In terms of that provision, the obligation could be owed to 'another state, to several states, or to the international community as a whole'. Article 33(2) envisages that rights might accrue to 'any person or entity other than a state'. Accordingly, individuals are firmly recognized as bearers of rights under state responsibility.

More germane to the current study is the nature of reparation envisaged in Chapter II of the Draft Articles. This part provides that reparations might take the form of restitution,[74] compensation,[75] satisfaction[76] and accrual of interest on the unpaid judgment debt.[77] Chapter III of the Draft Articles engages a plethora of issues related to gross and systemic violation of obligations and the procedure for the vindication of rights by the injured state, including due process principles such as cause of action and available defences.

Furthermore, in the *Baena-Ricardo* case, the Inter-American Court put it beyond doubt that the principles of state responsibility are not only applicable to conventional public international law but also international human rights law. It was held that it is incumbent on the Court to determine the liability of the state. Once the responsibility of the state has been established, remedial measures ought to follow, subject to monitoring by the Court to ensure that the violation has been corrected and guarantees for non-repetition have been deployed.[78]

Having established that the principles of state responsibility apply to the human rights discourse, it goes without saying that once it is established in the form of a judicial order that a state has breached its international obligation in respect of duties it owes individuals in the African Charter, state responsibility applies automatically in terms of which the state in question should pay reparations and guarantee non-repetition. In other parts of this chapter, I have argued that violations of human rights do not occur in the abstract but at the national level where victims

[72] Art 4 of the Draft Articles, supra note 68.
[73] Art 5 of the Draft Articles.
[74] Art 35 of the Draft Articles.
[75] Art 36 of the Draft Articles.
[76] Art 47 of the Draft Articles.
[77] Art 38 of the Draft Articles.
[78] Baena-Ricardo Judgment, supra note 41, para 72.

are located. Furthermore, any guarantees of non-repetition of violations are given at that level. Consequently, it is the duty of states to correct the breach of international law obligations (human rights law) and guarantee non-recurrence of the violation at the national level, which is the theatre upon which the effects of international litigation becomes a reality.

4 The Role of the Executive, Judiciary and Legislature in Domestic Enforcement of Remedial Orders

In fulfilment of this obligation, state parties to the Court Protocol must, in accordance with their respective constitutional arrangements, adopt measures to ensure the domestic implementation of and compliance with the procedures connected to and decisions of the African Court. The nature of the processes required for this purpose varies from country to country and could require action by the executive, the judiciary, legislature, or a combined response of two or three branches of government. In other words, all the branches of government are expected, depending on the nature of measures required, to contribute to the enforcement of judgments in question. In tandem with the 'black-box theory',[79] it does not matter to international compliance supervisory institutions which branch of government has executed the order, as long as appropriate measures have been adopted.

Where the requisite political will is present, the matter may be settled briskly by some form of administrative intervention by the executive. In the absence of such political willingness, or if executive action is inadequate, enforcement must come through a relatively activist judiciary or human rights-minded parliament. When the executive effectively dominates the legislature, the dividing line between the two branches of government authority may be blurred. The assumption here is that the legislature has some degree of autonomy in embarking and implementing a legislative programme. It is well appreciated that in some cases, parliamentary businesses may be sabotaged by party interests. Or in some cases, the violation of human rights confirmed in a judgment would adversely affect the popularity of the ruling political party represented in parliament should there be too much publicity of its enforcement. Political will should be addressed prior to or as part of the implementation of these proposed interventions.

[79] This theory provides that international law supervisory institutions do not concern themselves with determining which government depart has complied with international law obligations as long as compliance has been registered. See generally, Ward Ferdinandusse, 'Out of the Black-Box? The International Obligation of State Organs' (2003-2004) 29 Brook Jnl Int'l L 45.

4.1 Executive

As is the case with international law, generally, the premise of this political enforcement process seems to be that the mobilization of shame will embarrass recalcitrant states into compliance. One consequence would be that political leaders (members of the executive) would take administrative measures to give effect to decisions by international courts in general and the African Court, specifically. Cynicism about this happening may be countered by pointing out that by far the majority of state parties to the Court Protocol have embraced the rhetoric of human rights and would as far as possible try to avoid criticism of their human rights record. There are institutional incentives. Should a state be persistently non-compliant, for example, by ignoring an African Union Assembly of Heads of State and Government (AU Assembly) decision to comply, the AU Assembly may impose sanctions or other measures of a 'political and economic nature'.[80] The political dimension of enforcement brings thus into play the role of political organs of the international arrangement under whose aegis the treaty body functions, such as the AU Assembly or Executive Council. At the national level, the political role of the national executive, whose political decision (or will) may bring about domestic enforcement without anything further, is obviously also of great importance. Domestic 'legal' enforcement of these findings depends on the appropriate judicial or quasi-judicial procedures within state parties.

Should a state abide fully by its obligations under the Court Protocol, it would give complete domestic effect to the Court's orders, as required by the Court Protocol. Ideally, then, enforcement would flow from acceptance and action taken by the respondent state's executive or legislature. Obviously, what will be required is the political will to do so. Such resolve at the highest political level still has to be implemented, as a practical matter, within the administrative structures or legislature of the state.

As far as implementation by means of the administrative structures is concerned, two main possibilities exist. On the one hand, existing administrative structures may be used to ensure effective enforcement. Such possibilities include the relevant government department or ministry responsible for implementing international human rights law obligations of the state.[81] Alternatively, a new administrative body may be established to fulfil this function, such as an inter-ministerial committee to review decisions by the African Court and other international courts. A number of states, especially in Latin America, have adopted legislation to regulate the domestic effect of the findings of international human rights bodies.[82] One

[80] Art 23(2) of the AU Constitutive Act.

[81] For example, when compensation is in issue, the ministry of finance will most likely be involved.

[82] See Centre for Justice and International Law (CEJIL), 'Implementación de las Decisiones del Sistema Interamericano de Derechos Humanos. Jurisprudencia, Normativa y Experiencias Nacionales (Implementation of the Decisions of the Inter-American Human Rights System. Jurisprudence, Regulations, and National Experiences)' (2007) 268–271.

such state is Colombia. To ensure compensation to victims arising from findings of international human rights bodies, in this case, the Inter-American Commission and the UN Human Rights Committee, Colombia adopted Law 288 of 1996.[83] The Law prescribes an administrative process, according to which a special Committee of Ministers, composed of the Ministers of the Interior, Foreign Relations, Justice and Defence, must 'review' final findings of these bodies in terms of which the government is obliged to compensate a successful victim/litigant. If this special executive Committee issues a 'favourable view', a conciliation hearing is held between the government and the victims. If a voluntary agreement is reached through conciliation, an official memorandum containing the agreement is presented to an ordinary administrative tribunal with competence over the substantive issue involved. Once the administrative tribunal approves the agreement, the 'resulting administrative decision is enforceable under Colombian law like any other'. If the Committee of Ministers does not issue a 'favourable view', or if the parties fail to reach a voluntary agreement following a 'favourable view', the parties may appear before the ordinary competent administrative tribunal for a judicial determination of compensation. This Law represents a hybrid of administrative and legislative steps to ensure domestic enforcement of international human rights findings.

In Europe, legislation adopted by Ukraine to facilitate the implementation of the European Court judgments provides a further example of direction given to the executive on domestic implementation, even if this law has not been fully implemented.[84] In addition to providing for the immediate dissemination of the judgment, the legislation also requires the 'Government Agent' to submit a formal proposal ('motion') to the executive on how to implement general measures in response to the judgment within a month of it becoming final.[85] After this has been considered, the country's Prime Minister must designate and provide instructions to 'central executive bodies' in charge of domestic execution.[86]

As part of its 'administrative' response, a state may also decide to establish a Victims' Fund to facilitate the payment of compensation. Although they hold a special position of independence within the state machinery and are quasi-judicial rather than purely administrative bodies, national human rights institutions may also be involved in the domestic process of monitoring and reviewing international decisions.[87]

[83] Christof Heyns and Frans Viljoen, 'The Impact of United Nations Treaty Bodies at the Domestic Level' (2002) 188 and Judgment to Justice, supra note 20, 87–88.

[84] Law No 3477-IV of 23 February 2006. See Philip Leach and others 'Responding to Systemic Human Rights Violations an Analysis of "Pilot Judgments" of the European Court of Human Rights and Their Impact at the National Level' (2010) 149 [hereinafter Pilot Judgments].

[85] Art 14 of the 2006 Law, Pilot Judgments, supra note 84, 149.

[86] Pilot Judgments, supra note 84, 149.

[87] See part V of this paper, below.

4.2 Judiciary

If the trend among African states not to fully implement findings of the African Commission[88] is mirrored in respect of the future judgments of the African Court, it may be futile to rely on the executive or legislative measures to ensure domestic enforcement. Executive action depends on political will and leadership, which is mostly not forthcoming, and parliaments in African states are often dominated by the same party controlling the executive. This lack of faith in the executive and legislature invites greater reliance on and recourse to the judiciary to interpret existing legislation creatively in order to give domestic effect to the Court's orders. Two existing legal principles that may through judicial interpretation and activism become vehicles to translate the African Court's remedial orders into domestic entitlements are: adjusting the existing domestic, international private law procedures for the enforcement of 'foreign judgments'; and the reopening of national criminal proceedings on the basis of 'new facts' (in this case, the African Court's judgment). These two procedural possibilities are now explored more closely.

4.2.1 Creative Adjustment of the Procedure for the Execution of Foreign Judgments

The Court's required remedy may take the form of compensation in the form of a monetary order for damages. Compensation is mentioned as a specific example of what would constitute an 'appropriate' remedial order,[89] although it certainly is not the only order the Court can make.

Although the African Court Protocol does not prescribe a method of domestic enforcement of the Court's monetary orders, a number of instruments relating to sub-regional courts in Africa give clearer indications, stipulating that the existing rules of *civil procedure* should be followed to enforce monetary orders domestically.[90] In respect of SADC, the legal text went as far as explicitly stating that '[t]he

88 Viljoen and Louw, supra note 28, generally.

89 Art 27(1) of the Court Protocol.

90 See eg the COMESA Treaty of 1993, which established the COMESA Court of Justice. Under art 40 (Execution of Judgment), the Treaty provides as follows: 'The execution of a judgment of the Court which imposes a pecuniary obligation on a person shall be governed by the rules of civil procedure in force in the Member State in which execution is to take place. The order for execution shall be appended to the judgment of the Court which shall require only the verification of the authenticity of the judgment by the Registrar whereupon, the party in whose favour execution is to take place, may proceed to execution in accordance with the rules of civil procedure in force in that Member State'. The EAC Treaty of 1999 contains a similar provision in art 44 (Execution of Judgments): 'The execution of a judgment of the Court which imposes a pecuniary obligation on a person shall be governed by the rules of civil procedure in force in the Partner State in which execution is to take place. The order for execution shall be appended to the judgment of the Court which shall require only the verification of the authenticity of the judgment by the Registrar whereupon, the party in whose favour execution is to take place, may proceed to execute the judgment'. Under the Revised ECOWAS Treaty of 1993, a Community Court of Justice has been established. A Protocol setting up the Court was adopted in 1991, entered into force only in 1996 and amended in 2005. The relevant parts of the revised Treaty provide: Art 24(2) (Method of implementation of judgment of the Court): 'Execution of any decision of the Court shall be in the form of a writ of execution, which shall be submitted by the Registrar of the Court to the relevant

law and rules of civil procedure *for the registration and enforcement of foreign judgments* in force in the territory of the State in which the judgment is to be enforced shall govern enforcement'.[91] I propose that the African Court should build on these sub-regional examples and experiences. These frameworks not only recognize the importance of domestic enforcement of the decisions of Courts of the Regional Economic Communities (RECs) but also provide specific mechanisms for such enforcement. The extent to which these provisions may serve as useful analogies to the African Court may be contested on the basis that the REC Courts are mainly concerned with economic integration and inter-state relations. Such misgivings are, however, refuted by the fact that some RECs have an explicit mandate to deal with human rights matters (in the case of the ECOWAS Court) and the implied human rights mandate of the other Courts,[92] and by the competence of individuals to approach these Courts.

Both civil and common law systems in African states allow for the domestic recognition and enforcement of judgments by 'foreign courts'.[93] In the civil law system, this is through an *exequatur* (a declaration by a domestic court allowing for the execution of a foreign judgment).[94] In the common law tradition, legislation usually provides for such a possibility.[95] In both legal traditions, the requirements are that the 'foreign' judgment must be a final decision by a 'foreign court'; the foreign court must have had the jurisdictional competence to decide the matter; the judgment must have been obtained free of fraud; the judgment must be consistent with natural justice; the judgment or order must be of a monetary nature, and the judgment must be consistent with public policy.[96]

member state for execution according to the rules of civil procedure of that member state'. Art 24(4): 'All member states shall determine the competent national authority for the purpose of receipt and processing of the execution and notify the Court accordingly.'

[91] The former SADC Protocol on Tribunal and the Rules of Procedure thereof [hereinafter SADC Tribunal Rules], adopted in 2000 and amended in 2002, art 32 (Enforcement and Execution) (emphasis added). For an illustration of case law where a judgement of the SADC Tribunal was sought to be registered and enforced in a SADC Member State pursuant to art 32, see *Gramara (Pvt) and Another v Government of Zimbabwe and Others* Zimbabwe High Court Judgment of 29 January 2010 [hereinafter *Gramara* case]. Available at: <http://www.saflii.org.za>. However, this provision may have been repealed following the review of the SADC Tribunal.

[92] *Mike Campbell (Pvt) Ltd and Others v Zimbabwe SADC* (T) Case No 2/2007 [hereinafter *Campbell* case]. The SADC Tribunal rendered this controversial judgement of all time in this sub-regional bloc where it ruled that it has jurisdiction to deal with human rights matters. Among other reasons, it is believed that the review process through which this Tribunal is going was necessitated by its radical interpretation of its competence on the basis of the prevailing legal framework. Two outcomes are foreseeable at the end of the review process. Either SADC member states might adopt legislation that clearly empowers the Tribunal to deal with human rights cases or divests the Tribunal of such competence.

[93] Examples of this practice will be fully discussed in subsequent parts of this work.

[94] The exequatur-procedure.

[95] These possibilities include the Foreign Judgments (Reciprocal Enforcement) Act (in Nigeria), the use of the Foreign Civil Judgments Act (in South Africa), and the Civil Procedure Code and Reciprocal Enforcement of Foreign Judgments Act (in Tanzania).

[96] See generally, Christian Schulze, 'On Jurisdiction and Recognition of Foreign Money Judgments' (2005) 17, *Zweni v Minister of Law and Order* 1993 (1) SA 523 (A), *Steinberg v Cosmopolitan National Bank of Chicago* (4) SA 564 (RA), *Abouloff v Oppenheimer and Co* (1883) 10 QBD 295.

Most of these requirements are of a technical nature and should not present obstacles to the domestic enforcement of the African Court's reparations orders. However, four of these issues are likely to arise as potential obstacles to effective domestic enforcement of monetary judgments of the African Court.

First, generally speaking, the judgment has to be that of a 'foreign court'. The question, therefore, arises whether the African Court could be viewed as a 'foreign court'. On the one hand, if a rigid distinction is drawn between 'international' and 'foreign' courts, the African Court may arguably not qualify as a 'foreign' court. In this reasoning, a 'foreign' court is the court of another specific country, while an 'international' court is established under some form of intergovernmental arrangement. On the other hand, it may be pointed out that the laws of at least some common law countries do not define 'foreign court' restrictively, leaving the door open for the inclusion of international courts such as the African Court within this term.[97] Given this flexibility, there seems to be no principled reason why the concept of 'foreign court' has to be understood narrowly, as the court of another country, rather than expansively, as any court different from ('foreign to') the domestic courts—including an international (supranational) court.

Second, the procedure has been put in place exclusively to allow the enforcement of monetary orders. The monetary amount has to be clearly determined so as to allow enforcement without resolving further disputes about the appropriate amount. If a 'foreign court' orders an exact amount of compensation or damage to be paid, such an order is enforceable. While domestic courts are likely to order exact amounts, international courts such as the African Court may—following the practice of other regional human rights courts and quasi-judicial bodies[98]—order 'fair' compensation or defer to national courts to determine the exact amount. Although I argue against deferring the calculation of compensation to national courts, the African Court may adopt this approach. However, I argue that remitting cases to national courts for purposes of quantifying fair compensation has two consequences.

On the one hand, the consequences are favourable when an international court defers the determination of fair compensation to a national court, in that the decision of the latter becomes the ultimate order, which will be as good as an original order by a domestic court. The advantage of such a scenario is that assuming the executive obeys court orders, the hurdles of attempting to enforce a foreign

[97] S 3(2)(b) of the Civil Matters (Mutual Assistance) Act [Ch 8:02] is generously worded to cover international judicial and quasi-judicial institutions. It defines an 'international tribunal as follows: 'any court or tribunal, which, in pursuance of an international agreement or any resolution of the General Assembly of the United Nations exercises any jurisdiction or performs any function of a judicial nature or by way of arbitration, conciliation or inquiry; is appointed, whether permanently or temporarily, for the purpose of exercising any jurisdiction or performing any such function'.

[98] Normatively, Art 30 of the Court Protocol empowers the African Court to determine the appropriate remedy, including an order for payment of fair compensation. So does Art 63(1) of the Inter-American Convention.

judgment would be permanently avoided, given that the order will be a domestic order. Furthermore, in terms of achieving the objective of reparations, a national court might be better placed to fully understand the extent of the injuries suffered by the victim due to violations and quantify adequate compensation. This is because the national court is situated within the society where the practical effects of both violation and remedies are experienced.

Deferring the determination of fair compensation to national courts could gradually develop a working relationship between national and international courts, in terms of which the former would eventually favourably receive international jurisprudence in the domestic legal order. The system may develop into one akin to the referral procedure under the European Community law practice, where national courts refer cases in the form of questions to the European Court of Justice (ECJ) for its observation on the issues. The ECJ decision then becomes the final word at the national level so that there is consistency and uniformity in the application of Community law in what some scholars consider as the 'consitutionalisation' of the treaty system.[99] If that objective is attained, it will be obvious that the decisions of national courts would be enforced as if they were national orders, yet, in fact, the determination was arrived at by an international court in the course of the referral procedure. The same would apply where the African Court shifts the onus to national courts to determine fair compensation even when the international court decided on the responsibility of the state.

On the other hand, as much as it is desirable to domesticate an international judgment by deferring quantification of compensation to national courts, such a course subjects the complainants to the very national judicial and political machinery which did not afford them an effective remedy, thus requiring them to approach a secondary mechanism for protection in the form of the African Court. The complainants may well be reluctant to approach the same national institutions that earlier failed to vindicate their rights.

A further complicating factor, especially (but not exclusively) in respect of an international court such as the African Court with a wide remedial competence, is that the Court's order may contain both monetary and non-monetary elements. The Court may, for example, order the release of an illegally-detained person and order that he or she be compensated for the harm suffered.[100] The obvious solution in such a situation is to apply the principle of severance available under the

[99] Alec Stone Sweet and Thomas L Brunnel, 'Constructing a Supranational Constitution: Dispute Resolution and Governance in the European Community' (1998) 92 Am Pol Sci Rev 63–81, where the authors conduct a general discussion on how the evolution of decisions of the European Court of Justice have the effect of making treaty law have the final say in disputes over trade matters before national courts.

[100] See eg the *Assanidze* case, supra note, 46. In that case, the complainant, who had been prosecuted but acquitted of a crime, remained in the custody of national authorities hence prompting the European Court to order for both the release of the complainant and payment of compensation for unlawful detention.

foreign judgments enforcement procedure.[101] If this approach is followed, one part of the remedial order (and, therefore, one part of the 'judgment') will be enforced according to the 'enforcement of foreign judgments' procedure, while the enforcement of the other part of the remedial order will depend on an alternative procedure, or may not be possible at all. Although this duality may have to be accepted as an imperfect possibility, it renders the enforcement of court orders very complex and, consequently, also costly. However, the dichotomy of monetary/other remedies need not be taken for granted. The question to be posed is whether the field of application of the 'foreign judgment' procedure can be reinterpreted to extend beyond monetary orders. The following fundamental question may be asked: Why do legal systems limit the domestic enforcement of 'foreign' judgments to monetary orders? One answer may be that such an order is precise enough to allow for immediate enforcement. If this is the reason, there should be no material difference between a monetary order in the form of a fixed amount and an order for a specific act by the Respondent State, such as lifting a ban on a political party.

Even if the first two obstacles are overcome, a third potential obstacle to the enforcement of the African Court's orders under the foreign judgments procedure is that the Court's judgments may be resisted with claims that they are contrary to public policy. As an 'unruly horse', public policy can take a judge to a destination never contemplated by them or any other persons.[102] In *Re Beard*, it was held that public policy is seemingly a 'variable thing' that fluctuates 'with the circumstances of the time'.[103] Furthermore, in *Re Jacob Morris (deceased)*, an Australian court held that that the phrase 'appears to mean the ideas which for the time being prevail in a community as to the conditions necessary to ensure its welfare; so that anything is treated as against public policy if it is generally regarded as injurious to the public interest'.[104] In that case, the court concluded that 'public policy is determined by the circumstances of a given society at a particular historic juncture of the development of that society'.[105] I emphasize here the public policy factor because this aspect was successfully invoked in a Zimbabwean case in which a party sought to enforce a regional international human rights-related judgment in the domestic

[101] For a discussion on severance, see generally JCH Morris and others *The Conflict of Laws* (2000). Taking the example of the *Assanidze* case, supra note 46, the European Court found a violation of a number of provisions of the European Convention and ordered, among other things, payment of compensation and release of the complainant from detention. Applying severance would mean that the complainant would have to forego the non-monetary element of the remedy if he had pursued enforcement through the foreign judgement procedure. It would follow that the non-monetary aspect of the remedy (release from custody) would have to be pursued or enforced by way of a different procedure which does not require that the judgement be sound in money.

[102] This famous phrase came out of the mouth of Judge Burrough in the *Richardson* case where he held that 'Public policy . . . is an unruly horse and when you get astride of it, you never know where it will carry you'.

[103] Re Beard [1908] 1 Ch. 383, at 342.

[104] Re Jacob Morris [1943] NSWSR 352.

[105] Supra.

legal order. In the *Gramara* case,[106] the applicants sought to register for enforcement an order of the SADC Tribunal rendered in the *Campbell* case.[107] In the *Campbell* case, the Tribunal held that the land reform programme in Zimbabwe was conducted in a racially discriminatory manner, among other violations of the SADC Community law.[108] When called upon to recognize and register the regional decision for purposes of enforcement in Zimbabwe pursuant to Article 32 of the SADC Tribunal Rules,[109] the Harare High Court of Zimbabwe held that enforcing such a decision in Zimbabwe would be inconsistent with public policy given that the Constitution of Zimbabwe provided for such a programme, and the Supreme Court of Zimbabwe had already ruled to endorse the constitutionality and lawfulness of the land reform programme.[110] The Court further reasoned that the land reform programme was well supported by the majority of Zimbabweans and that it would be costly to the state to reverse what had been achieved by this programme, hence enforcing a decision that sought to reverse the gains of the land reform programme would be inconsistent with the public policy in Zimbabwe.[111]

The Zimbabwean Court's finding shows that public policy is one of the most convenient grounds on which national courts may eschew the recognition and enforcement of international judgments. This approach completely disregards the international law obligations of the state concerned and accordingly runs affront to the good faith principle as espoused in article 27 of the VCLT, namely, that a state cannot rely on its national law to avoid international responsibility.[112]

The mere fact that a party attempted to seek enforcement of an international human rights or human rights-related judgment by utilizing the foreign judgments enforcement procedure is quite encouraging. It fully supports my proposition that there is a need for creative adjustment of the foreign judgments enforcement procedure in order to resort to the judiciary for enforcement of judgments of the African Court where the executive and the legislature are indifferent. If this proposition had no merit, the Zimbabwe High Court ought to have dismissed the petition to seek enforcement of an international judgment for lack of legal basis in national law.[113]

[106] *Gramara* case, supra note 91.

[107] *Campbell* case, supra note 92.

[108] *Campbell* case, supra note 92, para 61.

[109] Art 32 of the SADC Tribunal Rules provides that enforcement of decisions of the SADC Tribunal in the territories of SADC Member States shall be in terms of the law and procedure for enforcement of foreign judgments. This explains why applicants in the *Gramara* case sought to register the *Campbell* decision in Zimbabwe, a SADC Member State.

[110] Put Supreme Court case here; not heeding the warning cited in *Olsen v Standaloft*, by Fieldsend CJ (as then he was) of the Supreme Court of Zimbabwe, quoting with approval Lord Atkin's observation in *Fender v St John-Mildmay* that public policy should 'only be invoked in clear cases in which the harm to the public is substantially incontestable, and does not depend upon the idiosyncratic inference of a few judicial minds' (*Fender v St John-Mildmay* [1938] AC 1, 12).

[111] *Gramara* case, supra note 91, page 18.

[112] Vienna Convention, supra note, 50.

[113] The case of *Louis Karel Fick and Others v Zimbabwe* High Court of South Africa Case No 77881/2009 (Order of 25 January 2010) (Available at: <http://www.saflii.org.za>) [hereinafter *Fick* case] best

A fourth obstacle to the application of the foreign judgments procedure to the African Court's orders may be that the enforcement of judgments from one country in another country may depend on reciprocity, while human rights obligations (as embodied in judgments of the African Court) are binding *erga omnes*.[114] Reciprocity is a product of designation where one state, by virtue of legislation, designates another state in respect of which the 'judgments' by its national courts would be enforced through the foreign judgments procedure, in anticipation that decisions of the designating state would also be enforced in that state.[115] Although a state might be designated by another for purposes of reciprocity, the decisions subject to registration for enforcement are still required to meet the general criteria for the recognition and enforcement of foreign judgments. My concern here is that states might decide to stick to enforcing foreign judgments on the basis of reciprocity. The repercussions of such an approach need to be addressed, especially in view of the fact that the majority of Southern and Eastern African countries pursue the designation approach.[116]

Where reciprocity is followed to the letter, a state will only concern itself with judgments from designated states' national courts. Now that there is no foreign but regional court in the form of the African Court, it is inconceivable as to how reciprocity would play out. This Court is by no means a national court but a regional court established under the auspices of a supranational political establishment—the AU. I observe here that designation is usually by means of legislation. I encourage victims to utilize common law or the *executur* procedure for civil law states, in which the majority of legal principles relating to the enforcement of foreign judgments are provided.

The broadening of the traditional scope of the 'foreign judgment' procedure depends on judicial activism. Depending on how explicitly national legislation limits the procedure to monetary orders, various degrees of judicial activism may

depicts a situation where an international monetary judgement could be successfully enforced by utilizing the foreign judgments procedure. In that case, some parties from the SADC Tribunal successfully enforced the order in the Campbell decision against Zimbabwe in a South African national court. At the time of writing this article, Zimbabwe Government property in South Africa had been attached in execution of that judgment. The South African Government will be in a fix in dealing with the state of affairs as it has an interest in the execution of the Campbell decision considering that some South African nationals lost land by way of acquisition by the Zimbabwe Government. However, as a beacon of hope for democratic rule in Southern Africa, South Africa may deliberately decide not to interfere with the execution process in order to preserve that reputation.

114 *Barcelona Traction* case, supra note 70.

115 Christian Schulze, supra note 96, generally. Designation refers to a practice where a state, by way of legislation, enumerates names of fellow states in respect of which it (designating state) would recognize judgments rendered by national courts of those states (designated states) which appear on the designating list, whether or not designated states would, in turn, recognize judgments from national courts of the designating state.

116 Christian Schulze, supra note 96, generally. The author makes an inventory of legislation from Southern and Eastern African states on enforcement of foreign judgments.

be required. Judicial activism is, for example, very unlikely to expand the interpretation of the procedure if it is clearly limited to monetary orders. However, if the formulation is more open-ended, there may be more space for progressive and expansive interpretation. Current laws that may be interpreted creatively include those dealing with the recognition of foreign judgments and those dealing with the review of final judgments. Although this seems possible, in many countries, it seems unlikely to succeed. Given the constraints and limitations of existing law, relatively far-reaching interpretations preceded by a profound re-orientation of the judiciary would be required.

4.2.2 Court's Judgement as Basis for Reopening of National Proceedings

Another opportunity for the judiciary to take centre stage involves the reopening of national *res judicata* proceedings that led to international litigation before the African Court upon this Court making a finding that the national decision is inconsistent with the state's international law obligations. In my view, international law is violated as long as the national decision remains in force in that state. As a remedy, I suggest that states provide for the possibility of reviewing national decisions whenever an international court finds them inconsistent with international human rights standards subscribed to by the state in question.

I further argue that there is no better way to enforce the international judgment finding national decisions to be inconsistent with the African Charter than reviewing the national decision in view of making it consistent. The majority of such national decisions are criminal decisions in which due process was not followed. The appropriate approach would be to afford the victim a retrial in proceedings where all judicial guarantees are secured.

The main obstacle to a smooth implementation of this recommendation in Africa is the operation of the *res judicata* principle.[117] Where it is applicable, the *res judicata* principle insulates all final national decisions from any form of revision. Adherence to this principle was one of the reasons for the slow percolation of regional human rights standards into the legal orders of the Member States in Europe. In the course of its work, the Committee of Ministers of the Council of Europe (CoM) realized that, in some cases, restitution was only achievable where national decisions were reopened and the victims are given another opportunity to be heard. The CoM accordingly adopted *Recommendation No R (2002) 2 of the Committee of Ministers to member states on the re-examination or re-opening of*

[117] *Bafokeng Tribe v Impala Platinum Ltd and Others* 1999 (1) SA 517 (BH); Lord Simon of Glaisdale expounded on the nature and rationale of *res judicata* in Ampthill Peerage [1977] AC 547, at 575-576 as follows: 'Important though the issues may be, how extensive so ever the evidence, whatever the eagerness for further fray; society says: "We have provided courts in which your rival contentions have been heard. We have provided a code of law by which they have been adjudged. Since judges are fallible human beings, we have provided appellate courts which do their own fallible best to correct error. But in the end you must accept what has been decided. Enough is enough". And the law says: "res judicata", the matter is adjudged'.

certain cases at domestic level following judgments of the European Court of Human Rights,[118] urging member states to provide for the possibility of reopening national proceedings upon satisfying a number of conditions. Of prominence among the requirements are that the victim should continue to suffer from the adverse effects of the impugned national decision at the time of requesting for reopening,[119] and that reopening should be the last resort to achieve *restitutio in integrum*.[120] This Recommendation has resulted in many Council of Europe (CoE) Member States enacting legislation to provide for the possibility of reopening national decisions following jurisprudence from the European Court.[121]

I submit here that a decision of the African Court should be deemed to be an exception to the application of *res judicata* within the national jurisdiction. All acceptable exceptions to *res judicata* derive from the fact that had these factors been known at the time of national proceedings, the court that made the decision would have arrived at a different conclusion.[122] Most commonly, where 'new facts' or evidence have been discovered after a decision has already been taken, such a decision is appropriate for reopening.[123] The existence of doubt over the correctness of the decision in view of the new facts or evidence is the catalyst for reopening the impugned national decision. A judgment of the African Court, I submit, arguably has the same effect on a final national decision as would 'new facts' or new evidence. The argument unfolds as follows: Had the national court known that its decision would be inconsistent with the state's international law obligations arising from ratified international human rights instruments, it would not have arrived at the conclusion that it did. The presumption of lawfulness provides that the national court would not have decided against a lawful judgment of the African Court.[124] In any event, article 27 of the Vienna Convention provides that execution of duties in good faith entails refraining from relying on national law to eschew international state responsibility. In the absence of legislation allowing for the reopening of national proceedings following a judgment by an international tribunal to this effect,

[118] [Hereinafter Recommendation No R (2002) available in 'Applying and Supervising the ECHR: Guaranteeing the Effectiveness of the European Convention on Human Rights: Collected Texts', Council of Europe Publishing (Undated), 52.

[119] Recommendation No 2 (2002), supra, para I(i).

[120] Recommendation No 2 (2002), supra note, 118, preamble.

[121] One good example of states that enacted legislation to provide for a possibility for reopening national proceedings following an adverse ruling by the European Court on those national proceedings is Belgium..

[122] For a general discussion on *res judicata*, see *Karsche v Uganda Transport Co Ltd* (1967) EA 774. Other reputed judicial pronouncements include *Stiftung v Rayner and Keeler Ltd* (1966) 2 All ER 536, *GR Mandavia v Rattan Singh* (1965) EA 118, *New Brunswick Railway Co v British and French Trust Corporation Ltd* (1938) 4 All E R 74.

[123] See eg in the context of ad hoc international criminal tribunals, Art 25 of the ICTR Statute, Art 89 of the Rules of Procedure of the International Criminal Tribunal for the former Yugoslavia (ICTY) and also Art 84 of the ICC Statute.

[124] This presumption stems from the cannons of statutory interpretation to the effect that legislation made by a national parliament is presumed legal and lawful as there is a presumption that parliament cannot legislate for that which is unlawful.

the ingenuity of litigants and the activist and progressive interpretation of judges would be the only basis for following such an approach.

The existence of legislation providing for reopening national proceedings following unfavourable decisions of the African Court would place the matter on a much firmer footing. In Africa, Burundi is the only state that adopted legislation providing for mandatory review of national decisions upon receiving an adverse jurisprudence in respect of national proceedings from judicial or quasi-judicial bodies established by treaties ratified by Burundi.[125] Article 47 of the law of Burundi empowers the Supreme Court of that country to review or revise any decision rendered by any national court in criminal proceedings where an international judicial or quasi-judicial body has ruled that such national decisions are inconsistent with Burundi's international law obligations.[126] Such a piece of legislation puts to rest any debate as to whether or not a state party to the African Charter bears any obligation to enforce judgments of the African Court at the national level. It provides for a national implementation framework that gives effect to an already acknowledged supranational obligation.

4.3 Legislature

There are two main avenues along which national legislatures may become part of domestic enforcement processes; in respect of its legislative competence or in relation to its oversight function. These two functions are now further explored. My contention is that, ideally, national legislation should be adopted to facilitate the domestic enforcement of all international human rights-related decisions. By putting in place an established procedure, other branches of government become legally bound to effectively and efficiently discharge their obligations to enforce judgments of the African Court at the national level.

4.3.1 Domestication of the Substantive Provisions of the African Charter

Domestication of a treaty is the process of domestic legal reform aimed at bringing the laws and practices of each state party into conformity with its international obligations under that treaty. In so far as it provides for substantive rights, the provisions of the African Charter need to be 'given effect' domestically.[127] Legislation domesticating the African Charter may play the role of re-routing at least some

[125] Art 47(7) of the Amendment of arts 47 and 48 of Bill No 1/2003 regulating the court proposed by the Honourable depute Laurent Gahungu.

[126] It must be pointed out that although at a draft level, the national legislature had suggested for the reopening of both civil and criminal proceedings, the final law only applies to national criminal proceedings. On a more or less similar footing, art 12 of the Constitution of Cape Verde provides for the direct domestic application of international judgments. It is not clear whether the effect of such decisions would be to reopen contradictory national decisions in force in that state at that point in time.

[127] Art 1 of the African Charter.

potential disputes about enforcement to the domestic sphere. In fact, if full domestication of the substance of the African Charter would have been achieved in theory and practice, a conflict between national and supranational law—and the potential problem of domesticating the African Court's orders—will be minimized. Clearly, there is no concomitant need to domesticate those parts of the Charter dealing with the composition, mandate and functioning of the African Commission.

4.3.2 Giving Domestic Effect to the Enforcement Provisions of the African Court Protocol

As the African Court Protocol essentially deals with the way in which the Charter rights may be invoked and applied at the supranational level by the African Court, there logically is no express imperative to domesticate the Court Protocol in its entirety. Indeed, most issues at the core of the Protocol, such as the competence to submit a case, the jurisdiction of the Court and relationship between the Court and the African Commission, have no bearing on the national legal system. In order to serve a meaningful purpose, national legislation purporting to domesticate the Protocol should entail something different than the mere adoption of the Protocol, as it stands, into national law. What is required in such legislation is some precision in national legislation about how the Court's orders are to be given domestic effect and how judgment holders may approach domestic courts to ensure compliance. Therefore, a national law domesticating the Protocol has to go beyond the provisions of the Protocol by providing for mechanisms of domestic enforcement—aspects on which the Protocol is silent. By not stipulating the mechanisms for domestic implementation of the Court's orders, the Protocol leaves a legal void, which specific legislative interventions need to address.

The legislature may adopt two broad courses of action. The first is the adoption of comprehensive legislation to establish a permanent process and institutional framework to ensure domestic enforcement of the Court's orders. Such legislation should contain an unequivocal legal recognition of the state's obligation to give domestic effect to the Court's remedial orders to be most effective and establish a permanent comprehensive procedure, including an institutional mechanism, to oversee the compliance process. In this way, the legislation may place on a firm footing and formalize ad hoc enforcement action by the executive. It is desirable that such legislation extends to all forms of remedial orders and not restrict itself to orders for monetary compensation.

The second course of action open to the legislature is to adopt ad hoc legislation to create circumscribed procedures to domesticate some specific remedial orders. Instead of adopting comprehensive legislation, which sets up a permanent procedure covering all future cases, the legislature may enact one or more specific laws of more limited scope or amend existing legislation aimed at facilitating enforcement of remedial orders, such as legislating on the foreign judgments enforcement procedure or reopening of finalized national proceedings.

Under existing legislation in many African states, monetary orders of 'foreign courts' are given domestic effect pursuant to the foreign judgments enforcement procedure. To make it suitable for enforcement of orders by the African Court, amending the law would be required to clarify that the African Court qualifies as a 'foreign court'. The amendment should also allow domestic effect to orders other than those of a monetary nature to give such legislation wider application. Because the amendments to existing laws may be so fundamental, as it seems to be in the case of recognizing the Court's decisions as 'foreign judgments', it may be a preferable option to adopt a new piece of legislation to regulate this specific matter. Such legislation would deal decisively with all issues of concern with the current state of the law I have raised in the earlier discussions. The result will be a clear checklist of requirements that need to be satisfied if a judgment of the African Human Rights Court will be successfully enforced through that procedure. A different, though related approach is that the legislature adopts an open-ended list of detailed remedial orders allowing for domestic enforcement.

A new law may also be adopted to create a new possibility, containing both administrative and judicial elements, as in Colombian law discussed above. The essence of such a new law would serve two purposes, namely, to establish a clear and accessible domestic procedure for the enforcement of the decisions of the African Court and deal with specificities of each remedial measure in terms of adopting measures to implement it fully.

Specific legislation may also provide for the reopening of domestic proceedings. Such legislation in state parties to the African Court Protocol may be inspired by experience of the CoE Member States and by a lone African precedent, that of Burundi.

I have already discussed that the European experience has had resounding results in respect of reopening of national proceedings as a result of the adoption of the *Recommendation No R (2000) 2 of the Committee of Ministers to member states on the re-examination or reopening of certain cases at domestic level following judgments of the European Court of Human Rights* (herein Recommendation) at the supranational level, which influenced to a great deal the adoption of legislation by individual CoE Member States.[128] This experience may lead one to conclude that uniformity and speed in adopting enforcement measures are achieved when the legislative process takes a top-to-bottom approach, as was the case with the Recommendation. This is because when guidelines are adopted at that level, they are adopted by the same states that are expected to convert the guidelines into reality by adopting implementing legislation at home. While at the supranational

[128] Recommendation No R (2000) 2 of the Committee of Ministers to member states on the re-examination or reopening of certain cases at domestic level following judgments of the European Court of Human Rights (Adopted by the Committee of Ministers on 19 January 2000 at the 694th Meeting of the Ministers' Deputies). Available at: https://search.coe.int/cm/Pages/result_details.aspx?ObjectID=09000016805e2f06.

level adoption stage, such an enforcement mechanism would have already been labelled as a common interest among members in the promotion and protection of human rights in the regional bloc.

In contrast, Africa's dearth of experience in this area is spearheaded by Burundi, which did not wait for a common position on reopening instructions by the AU Executive Council. Burundi's national parliament adopted a law that facilitates the reopening of national proceedings inconsistent with the jurisprudence of international judicial and or quasi-judicial bodies created by treaties ratified by that state.[129] This state of affairs leaves us with a clear example of how national legislatures could decisively contribute to the domestic enforcement of international judgments. While it is not the legislature itself enforcing the judgments, by virtue of this law, it has untied the hands of the judiciary to competently deal with requests for reopening of national proceedings on a case-to-case basis.

4.3.3 Ad Hoc Legislative Measures in Response to the Court's Specific Remedial Orders

The African Court may require a national legislature to repeal a law that is inconsistent with the African Charter. Legislative measures in response to the Court's remedial orders may take the form of a new law or amendments to existing legislation. By addressing non-repetition of the violation, legislative measures go beyond satisfying the individual concerned.

State practice in the CoE provides a rich yet varied record of enactment of new legislation or amendments in response to findings of the European Human Rights Court. A good example is the introduction of a national law regarding the reopening of national proceedings by Belgium. In *Goktepe v Belgium*,[130] the Court found that the incorrect formulation of a question to the jury during a criminal trial amounted to a violation of article 6(1) of the European Convention.[131] The judgment having become final, the Secretariat of the CoM was of the view that due to the gravity of the offence, and in tandem with the developing jurisprudence of the CoM and in particular Recommendation No R (2000) 2, reopening of national proceedings was the only effective measure in the circumstances. It should be borne in mind that the European Court on the same date rendered judgment in the case of *Claes v Belgium*, which called for a similar course of action on the part

[129] See Burundian law on reopening national proceedings in supra note 125.

[130] *Goktepe v Belgique* European Court of Human Rights Judgment of 2 June 2005.

[131] In that case, the applicants (then accused persons) were charged and tried for armed robbery, during which one person died. On 27 November 1998, the Eastern Flanders Court sentenced them to 30 years imprisonment. During the proceedings, the domestic court incorrectly assumed that 'possible aggravating circumstances' applied to all the applicants (then accused persons) jointly and not to individual accused persons. The court accordingly formulated the question of aggravation to the jury as if it applied uniformly to all applicants. This resulted in the conviction of all accused persons. They were sentenced to 30 years imprisonment. The applicant in the *Goktepe* case before the European Court challenged the approach of the domestic court on aggravation as violating. He was successful.

of the state.[132] With these two cases in mind, in December 2005, the Secretariat of the CoM contacted the Belgian authorities advising them that some applicants had indicated that they desired to have their cases reopened in view of the finding of the European Court.[133] In other words, the Secretariat communicated to the government its view that effective execution entailed the reopening of national proceedings. The Belgian authorities replied to the Secretariat, stating that the possibility of reopening did not exist due to the absence of legislation or other regulation in the Belgian legal system.[134] However, a draft bill was subsequently adopted; the required law was eventually adopted in March 2007 and entered into force in December 2007.[135] A similar precedent also exists in respect of the African Commission's recommendation in respect of Burundi and subsequent legislative action in that state.

4.3.4 Parliamentary Oversight

Parliaments, or members of parliaments, may also engage with and improve prospects of domestic compliance with international decisions in the exercise of its oversight function. This could be achieved on an ad hoc basis by raising the issue of domestic enforcement during parliamentary question time or on a more consistent basis by establishing a parliamentary oversight committee or expanding an existing committee's mandate to monitor domestic compliance. One such committee is the United Kingdom's (UK) Parliamentary Joint Select Committee on Human Rights, established in 2001 after the UK had passed the Human Rights Act.[136] This Committee is mandated to enter into correspondence with the relevant ministries about the domestic enforcement of the European Court's decisions

[132] *Claes v Belgium* European Court of Human Rights Judgment of 2 June 2005. In this case, the applicants, who had stood trial, convicted and sentenced on the basis of a law that did not apply to them, alleged that their trial and conviction had violated art 6 of the European Convention. They argued that art 103 of the Belgian Constitution provided for the prosecution of ministerial post holders before the *Cour de cassation*. Yet, in their case, two of the applicants were not ministerial post holders. The European Court accordingly held that their right to a fair trial had been violated by being charged and tried on the basis of a law that did not apply to them.

[133] See the Report on the 997DH meeting of the Ministers' Deputies (05 June 2007 10:00–06 June 2007 18:00) available at: https://wcd.coe.int/wcd/ViewDoc.jsp?id=1126649&Site=DG4&BackColorInternet=B9BDEE&BackColorIntranet=FFCD4F&BackColorLogged=FFC679 (accessed on 16 October 2021).

[134] See the summary of the execution of judgments according to Member States of the CoE available at:< http://www.coe.int>.

[135] The bill, unfortunately, coincided with the dissolution of parliament before it was enacted into law, hence it lapsed. During the 976th Meeting of the CoM held in October 2006, the Belgian delegation announced that a new draft law had been adopted on 21 June 2006. On 14 December 2006, the Senate passed the draft law and referred it to the House of Representatives, who passed the law on 15 March 2007 and sent it for royal assent, after which it would come into force on the 7th month of publication in the *Moniteur Belge*. The Belgian delegation announced to the CoM during the 997th Meeting that the law on reopening of national proceedings finally came into force on 1 December 2007 (by Tarisai Mutangi, who attended this DH Meeting at the CoE in Strasbourg, France from 3–5 June 2008).

[136] This Committee is made up of Members of Parliament from both Houses, namely, the House of Commons and the House of Lords.

against the UK.[137] The Committee then publishes its analysis of state implementation in the form of successive reports.[138] The Secretary of Justice is then required to explain areas of concern in the execution process.[139] It may also assess proposed legislation for compatibility with the European Convention.[140]

Any parliamentary committee mandated to oversee the state's compliance with international law could be mandated (or could wrestle a mandate for itself) to follow up on the implementation of judgments against that state in order to ensure effective execution that meets international standards of compliance. By monitoring execution, I suggest that a committee makes an inventory of all judgments against that state and trace, by using all means necessary, the extent to which such judgments have been implemented. Committees yield competence to summon anyone to appear before it, including ministers, litigants, human rights commissioners, administrative staff and so forth. Summoning such key persons is critical as it does not only aid the committee's ability to appreciate the extent of implementation but also integral issues such as the effectiveness of implementation and challenges faced by the government in terms of complying. This will enable parliament to intervene in certain situations falling within their competence, such as proposing an increase in the national budget vote to cater to identified challenges inherent in the implementation process.

4.3.5 Pre-legislative Intervention

Pre-legislative intervention is mostly known as bill scrutiny.[141] It occurs where a parliamentary committee on legal affairs and human rights (in countries where it exists) subject legislative proposals to analysis backed up by public consultations with interested stakeholders in order to test consistency with human rights at the national and international levels. The rationale behind holding preferably extensive public consultations is that most parliamentarians are not technocrats in areas in respect of which they legislate, including human rights. In such processes, the yardstick would be the constitution and international human rights instruments ratified by the state concerned in the context of jurisprudence produced by relevant supervisory institutions such as treaty bodies and or courts. Thereafter, the national parliament is advised on whether the legislative proposal should be

137 See eg Judgment to Justice, supra note 29, 55.

138 The latest report of this Committee is available at: http://www.parliament.uk/business/committees/committees-a-z/joint-select/human-rights-committee/publications/. (Accessed on 16 October 2021).

139 See eg the 13th Report published in 2004 https://old.parliament.uk/business/committees/committees-a-z/joint-select/human-rights-committee/publications/?__cf_chl_captcha_tk__=pmd_Ubv_NP_Io1ihnS6Utn_Pu8RxpQlQHykdjsnZwgVfwBc-1634536604-0-gqNtZGzNAzujcnBszQf9 (Accessed on 18 October 2021).

140 See Judgment to Justice, supra note 29, 55.

141 Jennifer Smookler, 'Making a Difference? The Effectiveness of Pre-Legislative Scrutiny' (2006) 59 Parliamentary Affairs J 522. The author assesses the impact of pre-legislative scrutiny on the quality of the final piece of legislation ultimately enacted following pre-legislative intervention.

adopted as proposed or subject to certain changes based on the outcome of the stakeholders' consultations. 'Bill scrutiny' procedure is well-established in most Commonwealth countries such as Canada, New Zealand, the UK, South Africa and Zimbabwe (presently not a member of the Commonwealth).[142]

In respect of remedial orders by the African Court, bill scrutiny may come into play when parliaments consider the judgments of the African Court in previous cases against the particular state or other states in the process of assessing draft legislation before parliament.

5 Role of National Human Rights Institutions in Domestic Enforcement

By 31 December 2016, at least 25 national human rights institutions (NHRIs) existed in Africa. Togo first took the initiative in 1987, followed by Benin and Cameroon in 1989 and 1990.[143] This West African trio sparked a trend that spread across the African continent with the emergence of the multiparty democracies in the early 1990s. The North Africans (Maghreb) states followed, with Morocco, Tunisia and Algeria inaugurating NHRIs between 1990 and 1992.[144] Southern and Eastern African countries joined in the mid-1990s when South Africa and Chad established NHRIs in 1994. Most other African states did so between 1996 and 1997.[145] Notwithstanding the progress achieved by establishing these NHRIs, most for political reasons, such as assuaging a government's human rights record, particularly in the eyes of the international community.[146]

However, NHRIs have been recognized as important role players in the African regional human rights system. In fact, the African Charter already calls on states to 'allow' the 'establishment and improvement of appropriate national institutions entrusted with the promotion and protection of the rights and freedoms guaranteed by the present Charter'.[147] NHRIs may apply for and are accorded 'special observer' ('affiliate') status with the Commission.[148] The resolution affirms the

142 For a comparison of the English, Canadian and New Zealand models, see generally, JL Hiebert, Parliament and the Human Rights Act, 'Can the JCHR Help Facilitate a Culture of Rights?' (2006) 4 Int'l J of Con Law 1. In Zimbabwe, for instance, there is a committee known as the Parliamentary Legal Committee composed of legally qualified members, whose role is to advise parliament on the human rights implications of a public bill with respect to the bill of rights (Constitution of Zimbabwe (1980), s 80).

143 See Human Rights Watch, *Protectors or Pretenders: Government Human Rights Commissions in Africa* (2001) 31–35. Available: at <http://books.google.co.za/books>. [herein Human Rights Watch].

144 Human Rights Watch, supra, 36.

145 Human Rights Watch, supra note 143, 46. Countries that fall within this category are Uganda, Kenya, Malawi, Ghana, Senegal, Zambia, Liberia, Sierra Leone and Nigeria.

146 Human Rights Watch supra note 143, 46 gave examples of Morocco, Algeria, Tunisia, Cameroon and Sudan in this regard.

147 Art 35 of the African Charter.

148 In 1998, the African Commission adopted the *Resolution on the granting of observer status to National Human Rights Institutions in Africa,* Resolution ACHPR/Res 31 (XXIV) 98, adopted during

African Commission's conviction that NHRIs 'are as essential partners in the implementation of the Charter at the national level'.[149] NHRIs are specifically tasked to assist the African Commission in promoting the African Charter at the national level, and annual reports of such collaboration should be submitted to the African Commission.[150] Almost three decades later, the AU endowed NHRIs with a rare competence to bring cases, not before the African Court, but the future African Court of Justice.[151]

The discussion below considers the potential role of NHRIs in monitoring domestic enforcement of judgments of the African Court. Situated between the government and civil society, NHRIs may be viewed as objective third parties and are thus better placed to identify inconsistencies in legislation and recommend law reform to bring the law, practice and procedures in line with the state's international human rights obligations. However, the lack of objectivity and independence of NHRIs in many African states raises serious concerns about their suitability to play this role.

5.1 Monitoring Domestic Enforcement of Judgments is Integral to the Protective Mandate of NHRIs

No NHRI is explicitly mandated to monitor judgments of the African Court. This competence should, therefore, derive from the NHRI's existing mandate. One source from which to derive this mandate is the competence of some NHRIs to monitor compliance by states with their international law obligations, in general. For example, the Uganda Human Rights Commission has the constitutional responsibility 'to monitor the Government's compliance with international treaty obligations on human rights'.[152] In my view, monitoring enforcement of decisions by an international court is part of monitoring international treaty obligations.

Other sources from which to derive a monitoring mandate in respect of the African Court's judgments are the mandates of NHRIs to monitor domestic human rights and undertake research. The process of enforcing judgments from international courts should not be viewed in isolation from the implementation

the 24th Ordinary Session of the African Commission on Human and Peoples' Rights, 22–31 October 1998, Banjul, The Gambia.

[149] ibid, Preamble..

[150] Resolution ACHPR/Res 31 (XXIV) 98, paras 4(c) and (d). See also In the *Mauritius Plan of Action*, the African Commission envisaged the role played by NHRIs, as including 'providing the Commission with information on human rights violations and by assisting the victims of such violations'.

[151] Art 30(e) of the Statute of the African Court of Justice vests in the 'African National Human Rights Institutions' the competence to bring cases in alleging violation of the African or any other relevant international human rights instruments ratified by the state(s) concerned.

[152] Constitution of Uganda (1995), art 52(1)(h).

of national courts' judgments, which arguably is part of any NHRI's mandate to promote and protect rights domestically. Enforcement of judgments is a constitutive element of human rights protection because such a process affords relief to the victim of human rights violations. NHRIs thus have a role in the process of monitoring compliance with these judgments, even if their mandates make no specific mention of monitoring either domestic or international judgments. On this basis, most NHRIs do not need to have their constitutive statutes amended in order to be able to participate in the monitoring of enforcement. Monitoring enforcement of judgments also falls squarely within the existing competence of most NHRIs to conduct research.

5.2 Reporting on Measures Taken to Enforce Judgments

International supervisory institutions mainly depend on the information supplied by other sources to assess the adequacy or suitability of remedial measures adopted by the state parties concerned following the rendering of a judgment. These institutions are interested in obtaining as much information as possible relating to progress with the execution of judgments at the national level. Comparative experience has shown that states are the key providers of information on measures taken to enforce judgments of the European Court,[153] while in the Inter-American system, the testimony of the state is corroborated or rebutted by the information supplied by the applicants or their legal representatives, as well as the Inter-American Commission, especially in cases the latter has referred to the Inter-American Court.[154] In both cases, the file on monitoring enforcement is only

[153] This is clear from the procedure utilized by the Committee of Ministers during DH Meetings. In such meetings, when a final judgement of the European Court is on the agenda for discussion, the Secretariat of the Committee of Ministers gives a summary of the Committee of Ministers' involvement so far. If the judgement is being considered for the first time, then it will be just a summary of the historical background to the case, violations established and the finding of the European Court, as well as the opinion of the Department of Execution of Judgments Directorate for Human Rights) regarding the measures to be adopted by the state concerned in order to implement that judgement fully. During any subsequent DH Meeting, often the very next one, the state will be given a platform to demonstrate to the Committee of Ministers what measures it has taken to implement the judgement against it. This is why these authors believe that the state is the main source of information, taking into account that the victim is usually not in attendance at these meetings. The victim might have contacted the Department of Execution of Judgments with some information on the stage of implementation of the judgement, but this is difficult to prove. Furthermore, the Department of Execution of Judgements is required to maintain dialogue with national authorities in order to monitor the implementation process. Again, the main source of information on implementation is the state concerned. However, in practice, the Committee of Ministers Secretariat and, more so, the Department of Execution of Judgments is free to use any other information in tracking adoption of remedial measures and use such insight to either challenge the state on the adequacy of the measure so far adopted or recommending to the Committee of Ministers that the measures adopted are sufficient to implement the judgement of the European Court effectively.

[154] Though largely undocumented, pursuant to the Inter-American Court's approach to supervising compliance with its judgments, the basis of which was fully discussed in the Baena-Ricardo Judgment, supra note 41, this Court holds compliance hearings to assess the extent and effectiveness of measures adopted to comply with a particular judgement. These are post-judgement activities. Now they

closed once evidence is produced supporting the view that sufficient (individual and general) measures have been adopted and that more action is necessary to execute the judgment.

In the African system, the AU Executive Council will ultimately have to be satisfied that the state concerned has adopted sufficient measures to fully execute the judgment of the African Court. Whether the state is the exclusive source of information on this issue or whether complainants and other civil society organizations are also allowed to provide evidence, the role of NHRIs will remain pronounced. As a genuinely 'state' body, its midway position between the government and civil society makes it an important potential source of accurate and unbiased information about enforcement. NHRIs should be actively involved in requiring governments to advise them on measures adopted to fulfil a judgment. NHRIs are the right candidates to provide this critical information because they are as close as possible to societies and communities in which violations take place. Where the competence to demand information from the government is lacking, NHRIs could carry out their investigations into individual and general measures adopted during domestic enforcement of judgments against it. Thereafter, NHRIs could advise the African Court on the nature of measures so adopted and their suitability in extinguishing as much as possible all negative consequences of a violation, especially its non-repetition. Such information could also be shared with political supervisory institutions such as the Executive Council, the Specialised Technical Committee on Justice and Legal Affairs or a Working Group under the Permanent Representative Council.[155]

5.3 Identifying Systemic Problems in National Law

Most important is the identification of the manner in which the structural defects could be eliminated from the legal framework, decision-making or existing practices. The competence of NHRIs, where they exist, to engage governments on human rights matters is almost universal. If any of them lacks such competence, the effectiveness of their intervention is fatally curtailed. NHRIs need to engage governments and discuss ways in which violations could be terminated.

are referred to as 'hearings', implying that the Court sits to hear from someone on the progress of compliance/execution. Although the Court might give preference to the state concerned to appraise it on progress made, with equal measure, it also hears (in the same proceedings) from the victim or his or her legal representative on the measures so far taken to comply in order to corroborate the state's position. In cases where the Inter-American Commission referred the case to the Court, the Court also hears from it on the same matter. On this basis, the authors believe that this system provides diverse sources of information on the stage of compliance to the supervisory body.

[155] See art 5 of the AU Constitutive Act. It provides for the various organs of the AU and their respective competences in the subsequent part of this provision.

More critically, they should give insight into how violations could be avoided by identifying and eradicating law or administrative procedures that are potentially inconsistent with human rights norms. That would conclude the responsibility of NHRIs in respect of dealing with systemic problems in municipal laws. In the European human rights system, the discussion on systemic problems in national law leading to violations, which, in turn, resulted in a multiplicity of supranational litigation, is connected to the Pilot Judgment Procedure (PJP).[156] A systemic or structural problem in a legal system refers to causes of violation or rights ranging from statutory provisions to the absence thereof and practices established in a system, but inimical to international human rights norms. Once a systemic problem is identified in a judgment, an NHRI concerned could ensure, during domestic execution, that the problem is uprooted by way of the choice of means to give effect to the judgment. Unless an NHRI appreciates the root of the violation that resulted in litigation, it may not adequately advise the executive on the sufficiency of measures adopted to implement a judgment. NHRIs could assist the African Human Rights Court by identifying systemic or structural problems at the national level leading to individuals resorting to supranational litigation for protection. African NHRIs should assist in the identification of systemic or structural problems at the national level, which have the potential of not only leading to the influx of cloned petitions before the African Human Rights Court but in order to avert the massive, systemic and serious violation of human rights until such a time that an international supervisory institution has identified the structural problem.

The Paris Principles provide that it is the responsibility of NHRIs to 'promote and ensure the harmonisation of national legislation, regulations and practices with the international human rights instruments' ratified by the state concerned. A good example of an NHRI with competence along these lines is the

[156] The PJP was developed in the European human rights system to deal with systemic problems that have led to repetitive violations of the European Convention because the problem is rooted either in administrative practice, national laws or any other national mechanism. Stakeholders in the European human rights system discovered that such problems have led to an unnecessary multiplicity of applications on the same subject matter, before the European Court, thereby clogging the Court system. In particular, the Committee of Ministers adopted Resolution Res (2004) 3 on *Judgments Revealing an Underlying Systemic Problem* Res (2004), 24 May 2004. In this Resolution, it invited the European Court to 'identify in its judgment what it considers to be an underlying systemic problem and the source so as to assist states in finding the appropriate solution'. In order to rid the system of such cases, the PJP was introduced whereby once the European Court discovers a systemic problem in a case, it would consider the case fully paying attention to the systemic problem. Once the problem is identified, the Court renders a judgement with advice on how to rid the national legal system of that problem. The Court would then impose a moratorium on the consideration of any other pending cases based on allegations of violations resulting from the same systemic problem until the judgement in the first case (Pilot judgment) has been fully executed by removing the systemic problem. Once this is done, all the remaining cases are considered at the same time, and no more applications would be received by the Court as the source of violation would have been eliminated. The European Court rendered its first Pilot Judgment in the case of *Broniowski v Poland* Grand Chamber Judgment of 22 June 2004.

South African Human Rights Commission (SAHRC). In line with this competence, the SAHRC established a unit known as the *Parliamentary Unit and Treaty Monitoring*.[157] This unit runs an insightful programme called the *Parliamentary Liaison and Legislation and Treaty Body Monitoring*. One of the objectives of this programme, germane to the current discussion, is to 'conduct research, develop reports and follow up on recommendations from treaty bodies'. Furthermore, it 'liaises with government and civil society concerning South Africa's international treaty obligations'. With regards to the identification of systemic problems through analysis of national law for consistence with international instruments, the SAHRC's programme envisages intervention 'providing input on proposed legislation that impacts on human rights, nationally and provincially'.[158] Admittedly, any study with a view to reforming existing law is a prerogative of a law reform institution in a given state. Even so, intervention at the stage of law creation is a critical responsibility of institutions such as NHRIs. In many places, legislatures hold public hearings in order to gather public opinion and concerns regarding the implications of laws before their adoption. NHRIs usually take advantage of these forums to make their input to the extent that the proposed legislation has implications on human rights, especially the possibility of creating institutionalised violations of rights.

5.4 Advising on Measures to be Adopted in Enforcing a Judgment

NHRIs could advise states on the suitability of remedial measures sought to be adopted by a state in compliance with an international judgment. Situated in societies where the actual execution of judgments should take place and familiar with the range of domestic remedial possibilities, NHRIs are well-positioned to appreciate the nature of violations taking place in those communities and advise the government as to what measures should be adopted in order to remedy the breach of international law. This potential role would come into play, particularly in cases where the Court's remedial order is vague and leaves a great measure of discretion to the state. When the remedy is specific and detailed, NHRIs will play a lesser role in assisting the state to adopt suitable measures that fully comply with the judgment. This role is closely linked to the competence of some NHRIs to ensure that their governments fulfil their international human rights obligations.

[157] Information available at: <http://www.sahrc.org.za/sahrc_cms/publish/cat_index_75.shtml>.
[158] Information available at: <http://www.sahrc.org.za/sahrc_cms/publish/cat_index_75.shtml>.

5.5 Advising States on the Orientation effect of International Judgments

Based on their familiarity with national legal frameworks, NHRIs present themselves as strategically positioned to advise states on the 'orientation effect' of the jurisprudence of the African Court in respect of the national legal framework and assist in bringing a country's legal framework in conformity with the standards of the African Charter without necessarily being a party to the proceedings. Although states are obliged, under regional human rights law, to enforce only the decisions against them, the jurisprudence of regional human rights courts elaborates upon the standards applicable to the region as a whole. Accordingly, the regional court is expected to have influence in the legal orders of the Member States through what is known as the 'orientation effect'.[159] This means that the rest of the Member States constituting parties to a regional human rights bloc in question have to align their behaviour to the norms enunciated by the supranational tribunal even in cases in which they are not parties. For example, assuming the African Court found that customary practices such as honour killings and female genital mutilation are inconsistent with the African Charter, in respect of one state, all states parties to the Court Protocol in which such practices are present should follow suit by putting in place measures to eradicate such practices.

Which entity would be best suited to advise a state on the measures it should take under these circumstances? In Europe, the office of the CoE Commissioner for Human Rights, together with the Venice Commission, are tasked with assisting states to bring national laws in line with the standards embodied in the European Convention.[160] Member States involved in that process submit draft legislation to these institutions, which, in turn, provide opinions based on the prevailing jurisprudence on the issues sought to be addressed by the draft legislation. This facility is also open to those states that decide to adopt general measures in the form of law reform to fully comply with the judgment of the Court following an adverse finding by the European Court.

Unfortunately, no institutions equivalent to the Venice Commission or the CoE Commissioner for Human Rights exists in the African system. States rely entirely on the guidelines in the judgments, supranational compliance supervisory institutions or advice of their own parliamentary committees on how to harmonize national law with international human rights standards. By virtue of its expertise as

[159] Ress, supra note 59, 374. See also E Klein 'Should the Bonding Effect of the Judgments of the European Court of Human Rights be Extended?' in R Ryssdal (ed), *Protecting Human Rights: The European Perspective* (2000) 705, at 710.

[160] The Venice Commission is an inter-governmental organization composed of CoE Member States and non-CoE states. It assists states with regards to constitution-making, elections and referendums, establishment or restructuring of constitutional courts, among other things. For detailed information on this institution, see: <http://www.venice.coe.int>.

a national human rights body, an NHRI would research the implications of the African Court's jurisprudence for the legal system of its state. After such in-depth studies have been carried out, NHRIs would be in a position to advise states on how they should align their behaviour, practice, laws, regulations or administrative procedures that are inconsistent with the jurisprudence of the judicial body. By so advising states, NHRIs would have, in fact, helped to enforce a judgment well beyond the territorial boundaries of the state, which was a party to the proceedings.

6 Role of Regional Courts in Supporting Domestic Enforcement of Orders

The judgment of a regional human rights court triggers but does not constitute domestic enforcement. The regional court does not enforce an order domestically, but through its involvement in the post-judgment process, it may increase the pressure on the state to ensure effective enforcement. Its role can thus be regarded as supportive of domestic enforcement. This aspect of a regional court's role is here referred to as 'residual', as it remains even after the court has given its final judgment on the merits and has made its remedial order (or 'order on reparations').[161] Subsequent to rendering its judgment and remedial order, such a court may play a role in the enforcement of its own orders. In such an event, there is greater judicialization of enforcement, akin to contempt of court orders at the national level. The court also has a role in linking its compliance work back into the political process by regularly reporting compliance to the political oversight bodies.

Under the African Court Protocol, the prescribed mechanism is as follows,[162] Ultimate responsibility to oversee compliance by states with judgments of the Court lies with the AU Assembly. In practice, the AU Executive Council (previously, the OAU 'Executive Council') will have to ensure that this task is fulfilled. The Court notifies the Executive Council of its decisions, and the Council then has to monitor the domestic execution of these decisions. No details of the monitoring means are provided. For its part, the Court is specifically required to report to the AU Assembly on the status of state compliance with Court judgments.[163] This important requirement suggests that the Court itself should—at least to some extent—be involved in the process of monitoring or following-up of its judgments.

Reliance is now placed on the well-established and emerging practices in the other two regional human rights courts, the European Court and Inter-American Court, to explore possible ways the African Court may support efforts at the domestic level to ensure the enforcement of its judgments. In particular, we consider

[161] Term used in Inter-American system. See art 63 of the American Convention.
[162] Arts 29 and 31 of the Court Protocol.
[163] Art 31 of the Court Protocol.

the possibility of the Court including in its judgment a time frame within which states have to report on domestic enforcement, clarifying its own reparations order, monitoring enforcement by establishing levels of enforcement on the basis of scrutinized information about state compliance, allowing complainants to approach it in cases of non-compliance by a Respondent State and issuing specific compliance orders subsequent to its reparation order in respect of non-compliant states.

6.1 European Court

In recent years, the European Court has taken two important initiatives to enhance its role in the domestic enforcement of its judgments in territories of Member States, the 'Pilot Judgments Procedure' (PJP) and the reforms introduced by Protocol 14 to the European Convention.

6.1.1 The 'Pilot Judgment Procedure'

Increasingly faced with cases revealing systemic problems, giving rise to repetitive cases, and governments' failure to address these problems in the measures taken in response to the Court's judgments, the CoM invited the European Court to 'identify in its judgment what it considers to be an underlying systemic problem and the source so as to assist states in finding the appropriate solution.'[164] Where a structural problem was established, the European Court would proceed to deal with one application, and the remaining applications arising from the same facts would be stayed until the root causes of the problem are dealt with. This new approach came to be known as the 'Pilot Judgment Procedure' (PJP). The idea behind it is to identify a structural problem in a policy or national legal system, which, if allowed to persist, would lead to further violation of the European Convention, and that also means a multiplicity of similar cases before an already overburdened European Court.[165]

Through the PJP, the European Court became involved in the supervision of compliance. *Broniowski v Poland* was the first case in which the European Court used the PJP.[166] After assuring the state that it retains the prerogative to choose the means of executing the judgment, the Court, '[w]ith a view to assisting the respondent State in fulfilling its obligations under Article 46', indicated to the state a range of detailed measures that it could take 'in order to put an end to the systemic situation identified in the present case'.[167] In the operative part of the order,

[164] Committee of Ministers Resolution Res (2004) 3 on *Judgments Revealing an Underlying Systemic Problem* Res (2004), 24 May 2004, para 10.

[165] *Broniowski v Poland* Grand Chamber Judgment of 22 June 2004, para 190.

[166] *Broniowski* Judgment, supra.

[167] *Broniowski* Judgment, supra note 165 paras 188–194.

the Court required the parties to report to it within six months in respect of any conciliatory settlement terms they might reach.[168] Meanwhile, in order to make a decision only after assessing the effectiveness of the measures agreed upon by the parties, the Court postponed determination of pecuniary just satisfaction by deeming itself as 'not ready for decision'.[169] I, therefore, argue here that by deferring the determination of the pecuniary just satisfaction pending its own assessment of the suitability of the settlement terms between the parties, it is clear that the European Court charted an era of participating and overseeing the enforcement of its own judgments under the PJP.

6.1.2 Implications of Protocol No. 14

Protocol No 14 to the European Convention amending the control system of the Convention, adopted on 13 May 2004, aims to improve the control system of the European human rights system so as to ease the crippling 'workload' of the European Court and CoM.[170] After the amendments, the situation is now as follows: If there is a dispute about the execution of a judgment, the CoM may request the European Court to interpret this judgment and provide greater clarity in order to resolve the dispute.[171] Again, at the request of the CoM,[172] the European Court must decide whether an apparent refusal by a state party to execute a judgment amounts to a violation of the state's obligation to 'abide by' the Court's final judgments.[173] Although the final competence to decide on appropriate measures to ensure that states provide domestic enforcement remains political and is exercised by the CoM, the European Court has been drawn into the monitoring of domestic execution, and it has the final role of determining the adequacy of measures adopted to execute court judgments.

[168] *Broniowski* Judgment, supra note 165 para 200(5)(b).

[169] *Broniowski* Judgment, supra note 165 para 200(5). See also *Xenides-Arestis v Turkey* European Court of Human Rights, Judgment of 22 December 2005, para 50. In this case, the European Court ordered the state to make remedial procedures available within three months and redress the violation in another three months. Furthermore, the Court ordered the state to provide feedback on the progress in respect of these measures. This procedure is more or less what obtains in the supervision process, whether by a political or judicial institution. Crucial in the supervision process is the recognition by the state concerned that it is obliged to adopt remedial measures and provide feedback to the supervisory body on measures it has taken to implement the decision.

[170] Preamble to Protocol to the European Convention (No 14), para 5.

[171] Art 46(3) of the European Convention, 'If the Committee of Ministers considers that the supervision of the execution of a final judgment is hindered by a problem of interpretation of the judgment, it may refer the matter to the Court for a ruling on the question of interpretation. A referral decision shall require a majority vote of two thirds of the representatives entitled to sit on the Committee'.

[172] Art 46(4) of the European Convention, 'If the Committee of Ministers considers that the supervision of the execution of a final judgment is hindered by a problem of interpretation of the judgment, it may refer the matter to the Court for a ruling on the question of interpretation. A referral decision shall require a majority vote of two thirds of the representatives entitled to sit on the Committee'.

[173] Art 46(1) of the European Convention, '1. The High Contracting Parties undertake to abide by the final judgment of the Court in any case to which they are parties'.

6.2 Inter-American Court

Under the Inter-American human rights system, respondent states are required to comply with judgments 'in any case to which they are parties'.[174] In preparing its annual activity reports for consideration by the General Assembly of the Organization of American States (GAOAS), the Inter-American Court is required to report on cases of non-compliance with its final judgments.[175] However, perhaps due to the void in political engagement with domestic enforcement, the Inter-American Court has increasingly become involved in 'monitoring compliance' with its decisions to the extent that it devised a practice widely known as the 'written procedure'.[176] The applicable procedure is as follows: upon rendering a final judgment finding a state in violation of rights protected under the OAS human rights framework, the Court inserts a paragraph in the operative part of the judgment advising the state concerned that the Court will monitor the execution of that particular judgment and will only close the file when satisfied with the measures taken to implement the order.[177] The Court also stipulates a time frame within which the state has to report steps taken to comply with the judgment. This monitoring is achieved by periodic review of the information tendered by the state on the measures it has taken, as well as the observations and information provided by the victim, victim's legal representative and the Inter-American Commission.[178]

This practice has, in 2010, been formalized in the Court's Rules of Procedure.[179] The process of monitoring reports is now placed on a firm footing, starting with a written procedure, and ending in a compliance order, with the possibility of a compliance hearing.[180] Initially, compliance monitoring takes the form of a written procedure; as in the past, the state has to submit a written compliance report, after which the victims or their legal representatives, and then the Commission, make observations.[181] If the Court 'deems it appropriate, it may order that a compliance

[174] Art 68 of the American Convention.

[175] Art 65 of the American Convention. This provision is similar to Art 31 of the African Court Protocol, with the exception that the phrase 'making any pertinent recommendations' has been omitted from the African text.

[176] Baena-Ricardo Judgment, supra note 41.

[177] See eg *Saramaka People v Suriname*, Inter-American Court of Human Rights, *Preliminary Objections, Merits, Reparations, and Costs*, Judgment of November 28, 2007, Series C No 172. Operative para 15, 'The Court shall monitor full compliance with this Judgment, in exercise of its attributes and in compliance with its obligations under the American Convention, and shall close this case once the State has complied fully with its terms. The State shall, within one year as from the date of notification of the present Judgment, provide the Court with a report on the measures adopted to comply with it'.

[178] Baena-Ricardo Judgment, supra note 41, generally.

[179] Rules of Procedure of the Inter-American Court for Human Rights, November 2009, entered into force 1 January 2010, at <http://www.cotreidh.or.cr/reglamento_eng.cfm>. [Hereinafter Inter-American Court Rules].

[180] See as an example of application of this new Inter-American Court Rules in the *Saramaka People v Suriname*. Monitoring Compliance with Judgments. Order of the President of the Inter-American Court of Human Rights of 20 April 2010.

[181] Rule 69(1) of the Inter-American Court Rules, 'The procedure for monitoring compliance with the judgments and other decisions of the Court shall be carried out by means of the submission of

hearing be held'.[182] On the basis of either the written proceedings or the evidence presented at the oral hearing, the Court 'determines the state of compliance' and issues a compliance order.[183] If satisfied with the information tendered, the Court closes the file. If not, it keeps on rendering periodic decisions addressing specific aspects of the remedial order still in need of effective implementation. Depending on the extent of persistent disregard of the Court's advice on the nature of measures to be adopted, the Court also engages the political compliance supervisory mechanisms referred to above.[184] In other words, the Court would make a 'non-compliance report' to GAOAS, which in practice adopts decisions and resolutions from time to time upon receiving annual reports from the Inter-American Court in terms of article 56 of the American Convention.

7 Conclusion

A case has been made for the effective enforcement of judgments of the African Court at the national level. Numerous possibilities were elaborated on inspired by practices in comparative regional human rights systems such as the European and Inter-American human rights systems.

A two-tier enforcement monitoring framework has been identified. The first tier is at the international level, where the executive in the form of the AU Assembly and the African Court itself is endowed with the responsibility to monitor compliance with judgments. While the AU Assembly role is rooted in the African Court Protocol, the Court's role is largely based on judicial activism at that level following the path charted by the Inter-American Court and, to some extent, the European Court. The Court has a further role of rendering specific and clear orders as an incentive to facilitating enforcement. Rumbled and vague orders would draw indifference from states leading to minimal or non-compliance with such orders.

The second tier lies at the national level. I argue that a number of distinct functionaries may operate in cohorts resulting in improved compliance with international human rights judgments. In order to make such participation less complex and problematic, the roles of these functionaries in monitoring compliance ought to naturally flow from their traditional competences. Accordingly,

reports by the State and observations to those reports by the victims or their legal representatives. The Commission shall present observations to the State's reports and to the observations of the victims or their representatives'.

182 Rule 69(3) of the Inter-American Court Rules.
183 Rule 69(4) of the Inter-American Court Rules.
184 See Part V on the discussion on the political establishment in the Organization of American States (OAS) regarding supervision of compliance with judgments of the Inter-American Court.

the executive simply has to develop a culture of creating an environment, legal or otherwise, of facilitating enforcement of judgments. It should ensure that a law specifically addressing the implementation of judgments is enacted. This law should cater for all grey areas identified, such as permitting the reopening of national proceedings, orienting the foreign judgments procedure to international human rights judgments and developing a clear practice of enforcing judgments of the African Court.

On its part, the legislature ought to be readily available to take the executive to task by organizing itself into a committee that exclusively monitors compliance by the state with judgments of the African Court. The legislature also must allow for bill scrutiny to ensure that all new law is consistent with international human rights obligations of the state and consistent with judgments against that state and general jurisprudence of the African Court.

The judiciary, as often, is expected to do much more than any other player. The national courts should be sufficiently innovative to the extent of accepting international judgments as foreign judgments for purposes of enforcement, notwithstanding the absence of a clear law permitting them to do so.

Even in the absence of legislation to that effect, national courts are expected to allow, whenever approached by litigants, the reopening of both criminal and civil national decisions inconsistent with a state's international human rights obligations. I have argued that the persistence of such decisions is a state of continuous violation of international human rights law, a status quo that could best be addressed by reopening those decisions.

On their part, NHRIs, owing to their unique form, face a number of possibilities to contribute to the enforcement of African Court decisions. In the first place, they advise governments on how to effectively implement decisions in a way that eradicates systemic problems embedded in national legal systems. That approach not only sees decisions with a bearing on systemic problems being enforced but also results in an emphasis on guaranteeing non-repetition of violation once the systemic problem is resolved.

The provision of current and accurate information regarding the measures taken by the state concerned to implement a decision is one of the most important pieces of information required by supervisory bodies to ensure effectiveness in monitoring compliance. The research component of the mandate of most NHRIs places them in a position to provide such information to supervisory bodies, backed up with their own assessment of the adequacy of the preferred measures since NHRIs are found in settings where violations and remedies should occur.

Overall, it is anticipated that the mechanisms proposed in this chapter be appreciated to work in conjunction with each other as opposed to exclusivity. Monitoring of compliance is a process of pooling efforts as opposed to observing a hierarchy of mechanisms. The international character of a monitoring mechanism does not earn it prominence over the national. It is the effectiveness of a mechanism that earns it preference over others depending on a number of factors such as the nature of the order, the state against which an order has been rendered, the subject matter of the remedy given, among other things.

Index

For the benefit of digital users, indexed terms that span two pages (e.g., 52–53) may, on occasion, appear on only one of those pages.

Tables are indicated by *t* following the page number